C1993

Lovers of Deceit

MIKE GALLAGHER

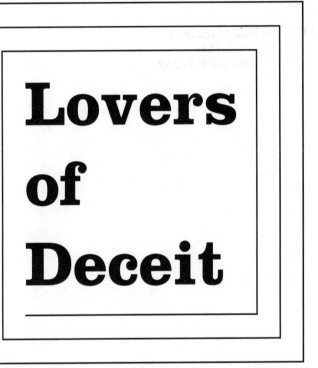

Lovers of Deceit

Carolyn Warmus and the "Fatal Attraction" Murder

DOUBLEDAY

New York London Toronto Sydney Auckland

PUBLISHED BY DOUBLEDAY
a division of Bantam Doubleday Dell Publishing Group, Inc.
1540 Broadway, New York, New York 10036

DOUBLEDAY and the portrayal of an anchor
with a dolphin are trademarks of Doubleday,
a division of Bantam Doubleday Dell
Publishing Group, Inc.

Book design by Paul Randall Mize

Library of Congress Cataloging-in-Publication Data

Gallagher, Mike.
Lovers of deceit: Carolyn Warmus and the "Fatal Attraction" Murder
Mike Gallagher.—1st ed.
    p. cm.
1. Warmus, Carolyn. 2. Murderers—United States—Biography.
3. Women murderers—United States—Biography. I. Title.
HV6248.W43G35   1993
364.1′523′09747277—dc20   92-40725
CIP

ISBN 0-385-41684-9

10 9 8 7 6 5 4 3 2 1

To Lynne for all the love, laughter, and support.
You've made the journey possible, the road less rocky
and the moments so very special;

and

In memory of Lou Silvestre, one of the good guys.

Lovers of Deceit

1

THE FIRST THOUGHT that came to Paul Solomon when he awoke from a fitful night of sleep was that it was Sunday. And like every other Sunday for the past several years that meant no school to teach, no wired-up kids to deal with, nothing to do but relax.

He didn't have to get out of bed and pull up the drawn shades to know that the cold, wintry night had painted his windows with a January frost. Paul grabbed the white down-filled comforter closer to his chin as he shook off the last remnants of sleep.

Turning over, he placed his arm around the sleeping figure next to him, listening to his wife's slow, rhythmic breathing. Watching her face, Paul remembered telling a fellow teacher just the other day he was proud that Betty Jeanne had been able to keep her good looks through the years, especially since she was getting set to hit the old forty-one mark in April. He was forty-one and thought he looked a hell of a lot younger than that.

Yeah, Betty Jeanne had held together pretty well, he'd said, compared to some of her friends, who reminded him of those old 1920s pictures of immigrant women just getting off the boat at Ellis Island: sagging, wrinkled, and plump.

Betty Jeanne opened her eyes as Paul gently caressed her arm, both of them enjoying the warmth of the bed, the quiet, peaceful morning, and each other. She turned toward him and smiled when he pulled her closer, brushing his lips against hers, gently cupping his hand around her breast. It had been a long time since she and Paul had made love.

She returned his kiss and gently tugged the cotton straps of her night-gown off her shoulders.

Paul's thoughts trailed off as he gave his wife one last kiss, got out of bed, put on his robe, and headed toward the front door. He would have yelled good morning to Kristan, but she had left Friday night to go on a ski trip to New Hampshire with a friend from school.

He opened the front door, shivering as he was met by a blast of cold, frosty air. It was already noon, but the day promised to remain frigid. He picked up the newspaper before scurrying back inside.

Paul felt a little queasy as he walked into the kitchen. He was still getting over a bout with the flu that had hit him the day before. He'd almost had to beg off going to the bar mitzvah for David Orloff, the son of their good friends, Jay and Bonnie. He and Betty Jeanne had gone, and although he felt miserable this morning, they had had a wonderful time.

Putting the newspaper down, Paul glanced into the living room. Kristan usually slept in on Sundays, but sometimes she'd get up early and keep him company. He missed having her around and looked forward to her getting back from the ski trip. The place seemed kind of empty without her.

Although he sometimes found their home a bit small, Paul liked it. Even though the complex was called Scarsdale Ridge Apartments, it had been converted into condominiums during the skyrocketing real-estate market that had exploded during the past few years. He and Betty Jeanne had scraped together just enough money in 1987 to put a small down payment on the place.

Although finances were tight, anything was better than continuing to pay rent for their too-small apartment on the upper floor of a two-story house on Harrison Avenue in Harrison. Betty Jeanne had made the new place homey with all her nicknacks, including the dried flower arrangements scattered about and the framed family photographs of which she was so proud.

Paul liked being able to say he lived in the Scarsdale Ridge Apartments. Although they were actually located on South Central Avenue in Greenburgh, most people didn't know that. What most people thought of when they heard the name Scarsdale was money, social status, and more money.

The condo was a pretty good deal for other reasons. It took only a few minutes to drive into White Plains, Scarsdale, or Yonkers. In fact, his job as a sixth-grade teacher at Scarsdale's Greenville School in the posh

Edgemont School District was only a five-minute drive away. He found some parents of his students a bit uppity and really into the flash-and-cash showboating that fit many outsiders' stereotype of the area's social elite, but overall many were down-to-earth, hard-working people like himself. Just a lot richer.

Betty Jeanne also liked the location: a twenty-minute drive through White Plains, or an even shorter run on the Hutchinson River Parkway to the door of the Continental Credit Corporation where she worked as an account executive. And everything from Saks to Bloomie's was only minutes away.

But the best thing of all about living in Scarsdale Ridge Apartments, Paul would say, was that Kristan got to enjoy all the benefits of a first-rate, high-priced school system without her parents being saddled with a Scarsdale mortgage. Not that they were poor by any stretch of the imagination. Just comfortable.

There was never a thought about moving any time soon. Kristan was enjoying her status as a promising basketball player for the girl's varsity team at Edgemont's Greenville High School. The pretty brunette was popular, intelligent, and had an outgoing personality that her parents, friends, and teachers found delightful.

Paul liked having his daughter in the school district where he taught. He also liked his job as coach of the girl's junior varsity basketball team at Kristan's school. She was a point guard and a damn good one. Good enough to make varsity in her first year. He would often see her practicing at the other end of the gym when his team was working out. Their mutual love of the game kept them close. They often shared a ride home after practice, and she would tell him about her classes, the other teachers, and the usual gossip and problems confronting her and every other fifteen-year-old schoolgirl.

Paul put on the coffee and began making himself and Betty Jeanne mushroom omelets, some home fries, and toast and then sat at the kitchen table to read the newspaper. He knew his wife would drag herself from bed once the meal was ready.

He scanned the front page. The usual mix of world tension, local corruption, and a traffic accident or two. January, 15, 1989, was turning into another typical Sunday. He turned to the sports section.

Hunger forced Betty Jeanne from her warm bed, and she headed for the shower. She looked forward to doing what she often did on a lazy, wintry Sunday: have a quick breakfast, finish up some work she had brought home, and then curl up on the couch with a good book.

She could lose herself for hours in her reading. Her favorites were intriguing love stories sprinkled with torrid affairs, calculated deception, and happy endings. She enjoyed all the delicious twists and turns some of these romantic novels took. Paul and Kristan often teased her unmercifully about reading "that trash," as they liked to call her collection, but she didn't care.

Quiet and self-contained, Betty Jeanne rarely traveled the forty-five minutes into Manhattan to enjoy a day of shopping or even a night of dinner and dancing with her husband. She most enjoyed the time she was at work. It was a challenge she was good at and she seldom wanted to take time off for vacations with Paul and Kristan.

A year or two before, Paul had persuaded her to become registrar for the Edgemont Recreation Program, which he headed. That had improved her social life some and had gotten Paul off her back about doing more things with him and Kristan. But when she was home she liked the time to herself, to catch up on one of her romance books or just to vegetate in front of the TV set. It suited her just fine.

The day slowly drifted by with Betty Jeanne stretched out on the sofa, lounging comfortably. She was quite the fashion plate today. An old, extra-large purple T-shirt with a picture of a golden tiger standing in front of some mountains and a pair of light gray sweat pants bearing the Edgemont logo and the number 41 made up her ensemble as she devoured her latest love story. Paul sat on the love seat kitty-corner from her and alternated between reading his newspaper and watching television.

The quiet of the day was interrupted at 1:37 P.M. with the ringing of the telephone in the den. A while back, Paul had gotten the phone company to give him separate numbers for the den and kitchen phones because of a problem they had been having with someone calling at all hours of the day and night and then hanging up when they said hello.

The den number they gave out to just about everyone. The kitchen phone they kept a private line whose number family members and a few very close friends could have. Paul jumped up to answer it and was delighted to find Carolyn Warmus on the other end. Glancing from the den into the living room, he saw that his wife was paying no attention, so he quietly shut the door and kept his voice low.

Just the sound of Carolyn's voice was enough to excite him. They had met in September 1987 when Carolyn was the new elementary computer instructor for Greenville School. When it came Paul's turn to be introduced, he was immediately taken by her soft, blond hair, wide mouth, expressive doe-like eyes, and tremendously beautiful body. She dressed in expensive and stylish clothes that were nevertheless appropriate for her job as a teacher.

From the first time they met, Paul was strongly attracted to her and turned on the old Paulie charm. He felt a warm, sexual stirring when she began to respond to his subtle flirting. It hadn't taken long, only a couple of months, for them to start meeting at little out-of-the-way restaurants, and eventually, at motels and hotels and occasionally at her Manhattan apartment for hours of unbridled sex.

At twenty-three, Carolyn possessed what Paul yearned for the most: youth, beauty, and a sexual appetite that kept them continually hot for each other. Carolyn was always willing to try new things, whether it was making out in a car in a crowded parking lot or just experimenting with different positions. Their relationship had continued even though Carolyn had left her job in the Edgemont district in June 1988 and was now working in the exclusive Pleasantville school system.

A year and four months after they met, Paul knew it was the great sex that kept him coming back for more. Besides, Paul liked what he considered the dashing figure he cut with Carolyn in public. He fancied himself resembling Al Pacino, the actor in his role as Frank Serpico, the handsome, bearded, straight-arrow New York City cop. Paul liked the way he looked in a beard. In fact, he liked the way he looked period. He thought his Lebanese and English heritage provided him a kind of suave, European look that most women found attractive. When he grew the beard, Carolyn said it made him look even sexier. Betty Jeanne seemed to like it, too, although she never really said much about it anymore.

Sometimes Paul would sit and think about how different Betty Jeanne and Carolyn were, both in their looks and in their personalities. Carolyn was blond, voluptuous, and really enjoyed good sex—especially performing the oral sex he liked so well. She was one of the most outgoing women he had ever known, always ready to have a good time.

Carolyn's clingy nature would sometimes get on his nerves, but usually her often arduous attempts to get them together boosted his ego up a few notches, especially when things weren't going well with Betty Jeanne. Paul didn't even mind too much that in her high heels Carolyn was a couple of inches taller than him. He was sometimes a little self-conscious about his five-foot, eight-inch frame, but he knew that it brought out the mothering instinct in some women, and that was sometimes the only edge he needed to get to know them a lot better.

In comparison, he thought, Betty Jeanne had lost a lot of her sexual spark since 1970 when they were married in Nyack. Actually, he couldn't recall her ever being that interested in sex. Still, she was an attractive woman, with shoulder-length brown hair and deep brown eyes that could flash with excitement when something really interested her.

Their life had settled into what he suspected was the routine for most middle-aged couples after almost nineteen years of marriage. Some time ago they had drifted into what he'd told his closest friends was a marriage of convenience, even though he and Betty Jeanne had never really discussed the issue at any length.

Paul suspected that his wife knew of his affairs, but she never brought up the subject. He knew the unspoken agreement was that his relationships must never cause her embarrassment, and they never had. Paul once suspected Betty Jeanne was having an affair as well, but he knew better than to ask. They had talked a few times over the years about getting a divorce, but nothing much had come of it. Now he had his life and she had hers, but they shared the common goals of raising Kristan and growing old together.

When Carolyn first met Paul she did what came naturally to her. She flirted. Nothing too obvious, just giving him the right kind of shy smile, giggling at his jokes, and touching his arm a couple of times ever so gently. She could see he liked the attention. Sizing him up, Carolyn thought he was fairly good looking and had a terrific sense of humor, and his being so short made him just unbelievably adorable and cuddly. More importantly, he seemed to be responding to her flirtations.

When they were introduced, Carolyn noticed Paul imperceptibly turning his left hand away from her, shielding the gold band wrapped around his finger. She tried to suppress a smile.

She'd been through all this before and what Paul had no way of knowing was that it didn't matter to her in the least. In fact, it was kind of a turn-on and added a lot more spice to the game. Besides, she told herself, with her face and body, not to mention her personality, a man would have to be out of his mind not to fall for her charms. It had always been that way and this time would be no different.

Betty Jeanne didn't pay much attention to Paul's telephone conversation. He was always getting calls from someone. Even if she knew the caller was Carolyn, Betty Jeanne wouldn't have said anything. Carolyn was a good friend of her husband, had been for almost a year and a half.

Paul had many friends, both men and women, with whom he spoke regularly.

Carolyn, for instance, had come to their house for dinner on a few occasions and had even taken Kristan shopping and skiing once or twice. While Betty Jeanne knew Carolyn had a crush on Paul—Betty Jeanne had even told her good friend Diane Pillersdorf about it—he had repeatedly denied being involved with Carolyn. While Betty Jeanne didn't particularly like the woman being in their home, the telephone calls didn't bother her as much.

Betty Jeanne's sister, Joyce Green, had once told her she thought Carolyn's interest in Kristan was a little strange, but after thinking about it, Betty Jeanne decided it was all right. If there was anyone Carolyn Warmus was after, it was Paul, not Kristan. That being the case, she knew Carolyn would take good care of their daughter, no matter what. That's why she had finally agreed the year before—after much pressure from Kristan and Paul—to let Kristan go skiing with Carolyn up at Mount Snow in Vermont.

Betty Jeanne stretched out on the sofa. She rubbed her tired eyes and set her book on the coffee table. Between doing the bills and catching up on some schoolwork, Paul had turned the television on and was watching *Empire of the Sun*. Thumbing through the *TV Guide* earlier, he had found that one of his favorite flicks would be on a little bit later: *The Sands of Iwo Jima*. She forgot about the phone call and picked up the remote control to turn up the volume.

Carolyn started out the conversation on a light note, asking Paul about Kristan's basketball games, how she was doing, and when could she come to watch her play. "I'd really love to see her in a game," Carolyn said, anxious for any opportunity to get some kind of commitment to see him.

Paul said he'd arrange it. He also told her that Kristan was away on a ski trip and that he and Betty Jeanne just planned to hang around home for the day. The conversation turned to his friend's bar mitzvah party and how the flu bug had really knocked him for a loop. Carolyn frowned. The bar mitzvah was another of the excuses that had kept Paul from seeing her the night before.

Carolyn steered the conversation toward one of her favorite topics, herself. She told Paul she was still a little upset that they had not been able to go out or see each other for her birthday, which had been exactly a week ago. Paul apologized for the umpteenth time, and again explained that family commitments sometimes took priority over what he really wanted to do, which was to see her. Carolyn pouted for a few more minutes and then pressed him for a time when they could celebrate her twenty-fifth birthday in style.

"I'll tell you what," Paul finally reassured her. "As soon as I'm able, I'll take you to the Chart House Restaurant for a belated birthday present to make up for not seeing you last Sunday." He knew that Carolyn would enjoy going out to the expensive Dobbs Ferry eatery.

"But, remember, it won't be until after the basketball season," he warned her. "I'm just too busy right now."

The conversation turned toward school. Carolyn asked about some of the teachers she remembered from her days at Greenville and told Paul she was enjoying her new job.

When they finished, Paul paused. "Would you like to see me tonight?" he whispered, careful not to speak too loudly. He was warming to the idea of seeing Carolyn.

"Really?" Carolyn asked, sounding surprised. She had intended to ask him the same question, but had steeled herself to expect his usual negative response. "Sure, I'd love to."

Paul smiled. He liked the fact that Carolyn seemed so dependent on him and that she always seemed willing to respond to his every beck and call. Although she was invariably upset when he had to turn her down or cancel a date, she seemed to get over it quickly, although she wasn't above holding it over his head in a usually fruitless effort to make him feel guilty.

"You just have to understand, honey, that there are going to be other times when I can't get away to see you even though I want to," Paul told her.

Carolyn, happy for the chance to see Paul that evening, cheerfully told him she understood, although she told herself that if Paul really loved her and wanted her as much as he said he did he'd leave his wife for her. But at least for this moment, she'd take seeing him on his terms. Anyway, you never know what's going to happen, she thought. She suddenly remembered his complaining about having the flu.

"Are you sure you're feeling okay enough to see me?" she asked, hopeful that her reminder wouldn't cause him once again to bow out of a date.

"No, but I really want to see you. How about the usual place?"

Carolyn thought for a moment. "The Holiday Inn?"

"Yeah, is that okay, about seven-thirty?"

"Sure," Carolyn responded. "I can't wait to see you. Thanks. Bye."

Paul hung up the phone and immediately began thinking of an excuse that would get him out of the house with the minimal amount of aggravation.

In the past, before he severely bruised his shoulder playing basketball the previous summer, he was a member of the Sunday night Mix & Match League down at the Brunswick Yonkers Bowl on South Central Avenue in Yonkers. He'd used that excuse to get out of the house before. In fact, he often had Carolyn meet him there so they could go out afterward. His friends had often seen them leaving together. No one thought much about it, or if they did, no one ever said anything to him.

Betty Jeanne never came with him, preferring to stay at home and catch up on her reading or her work. Normally she wouldn't kick up too much of a fuss if he told her he was going bowling.

But Paul guessed that Betty Jeanne wasn't going to be too happy with his leaving that night, especially after he'd just finished telling her how lousy he felt.

He guessed right.

"You complain all day yesterday and today about feeling sick and now you want to go out. I don't understand you. It's cold and miserable out. Why don't you just stay inside tonight. You can go out bowling next week," she said.

Paul didn't feel like arguing. "I always go bowling on Sunday nights. I'm going. Some fresh air will probably do me some good." He sat down and buried his nose in his paper, effectively cutting off further argument.

At 3 P.M., Kristan called collect from a roadside pay phone to let them know she was okay.

"It's beautiful up here, but Kathy and I had a fight so I can't wait to come home," she told her father, who listened with feigned interest to the details of his daughter's problems. Fifteen minutes later, Paul handed the phone to his wife.

"Hi, honey, is everything all right?" Betty Jeanne asked, as she reached into the bowl of popcorn she had been munching while watching television.

"Yeah, everything's fine," Kristan responded, knowing her mother wasn't really interested in her problems.

Ignoring the exasperated sound in her daughter's voice, Betty Jeanne yawned loudly into the receiver. "I'm just feeling so tired today. I hope I don't catch whatever it is your father has."

The traffic behind the phone booth she was calling from, coupled with her mother's half-garbled voice as she chewed her popcorn, prompted Kristan to end the conversation quickly. "I'll see you tomorrow," she said, hanging up. The next day was Martin Luther King Day so she did not have to be back to school until Tuesday.

Shortly after 5:30 P.M., Paul picked up the phone and called Marshall Tilden, one of his best friends and a great golfing buddy. The two had become real pals since meeting several years before while they were jointly supervising one of Edgemont's many sporting programs. Tilden's two sons, Marshall Jr. and Craig, were the center of their father's life, and Paul had coached them in various sports. Since Kristan was Marshall Jr.'s age and they were in the same grade, the two fathers felt this made them kindred spirits.

"Just wanted to make sure you and the boys are still going to the Knicks game tomorrow," Paul asked, remembering Marshall had mentioned at the bar mitzvah party the night before that one of his sons wasn't feeling too well.

"I'm looking forward to it," Tilden said, enthusiastically. "Either Josette or I will get back to you later to let you know how Marshall's feeling."

Paul hung up the phone and walked into the bedroom to press the pair of black slacks he wanted to wear that night. Finishing that chore, he showered and put on the pants and an old rust-colored sweatshirt and looked around for his car keys. After putting on his warm, black-and-white winter coat and grabbing his bowling bag from the closet, he peeked into the living room. Seeing that Betty Jeanne appeared to be getting over her annoyance at his leaving, he bent down and kissed her good-bye.

"Try to be home early, okay?" she asked, as he turned to leave. Seconds later her attention was once more locked on the television as the American soldiers began pounding the hell out of the Japanese bunkered on Iwo Jima.

Paul checked the battery charger he had running on his car, a 1983 Toyota Celica. Damn battery was always going dead, he said to himself, as he slid into Betty Jeanne's 1988 blue Dodge Colt and drove away. He glanced at his watch. It was 6:30 P.M.

Betty Jeanne didn't let her husband's obstinacy bother her for long. If he wanted to end up in bed for a week because he was dumb enough to go out on a cold night when he wasn't feeling well, so be it. Once again she stretched her arms, stood up, and went to the kitchen. Out of habit more than anything else, she poured herself a bowl of cereal with milk, and brought the snack back to the couch. Paul and Kristan had often kidded her about eating cereal in the middle of the afternoon, but she liked it. She settled back down and continued watching the movie.

At 6:51 P.M., Betty Jeanne was roused from her comfortable couch when the telephone rang. She went to the kitchen and picked up the receiver off the wall telephone. She was pleased to hear Josette Tilden's voice. After chitchatting about their day for a few minutes, Josette told her Marshall was too sick to go with his father and Paul to the Knicks game the next day. "Do you think Paul will mind if I ask Diane Pillersdorf if their son Andrew can take his place? I don't want the ticket to go to waste."

Betty Jeanne quickly agreed it was a good idea. "Paul's not here right now. He went bowling and probably won't be back until late. He's had the flu this weekend, but you know him, won't listen to anybody and just had to go out in the cold. But I'm sure he won't mind taking Andrew."

Telling her friend she would check with the Pillersdorfs and call her right back, Josette hung up and Betty Jeanne slouched back on the couch.

At 7:09 P.M., the phone rang again and Betty Jeanne once more made her way to the kitchen.

"It's me again," Josette said quickly. "Everything's all set. Diane said Andrew would love to go, so if Paul can pick him up at their home it would be great." The short conversation ended with promises to see each other soon.

Linda Viana, a New York Telephone Company operator, was enjoying a busy but generally easy Sunday evening in her Peekskill office. Between answering information calls, she was letting her mind drift to her part-time job as a sergeant in the New York Army National Guard at Camp Smith. She really liked the lifestyle, camaraderie, and duties as a reserve soldier, and it was a nice change from her normally sedate routine as an operator.

A beeping sound at 7:15 P.M. snapped her out of her daydream and she pushed the blinking button to take the call.

Viana barely got out the words "New York Telephone. Miss Viana, may I help you," when she realized there was screaming, yelling, and crying coming from the other end of the phone.

"Hello, this is the operator. What's wrong? Hello?" Viana asked.

". . . is trying to kill me," the voice at the other end screamed, and a second later the telephone line went dead. Try as she might, Viana couldn't make out whether the screaming woman had shouted "he" or "she" was trying to kill her.

Viana knew the telephone company's procedures for handling emergency calls like this one fairly well. She realized that Westchester County did not have an E911 system, like New York City, so that when a person dialed 911 anywhere in the county, it was automatically routed to an operator. For this particular call, she had been the lucky—or unlucky—operator to receive it. Without the E911 system, there was no tape recording being made of the call and it would be up to her to remember everything that was said so she could later put it in a report, called a "ticket procedure," for her supervisor, Deborah Webber.

After the phone line went dead, Viana glanced to her right and saw the computer flashing the telephone number from which the call had originated. Quickly, she dialed the number, but no one answered.

Viana didn't know whether the emergency call she had received was a teen-age prank or the real thing. But company policy dictated she take no chances. The first three digits of the telephone number told her the call had come from Scarsdale, so Viana called the Scarsdale Police Department to alert them to a possible emergency situation. Dispatcher Richard Vizzini took the call.

VIZZINI: "Scarsdale police."
VIANA: "Yes. Hello."
VIZZINI: "Yeah."
VIANA: "This is the operator. I'm getting an emergency."
VIZZINI: "Okay."
Pause.
VIZZINI: "Scarsdale police."
VIANA: "Yes, this is the operator. I just had a customer dial 911 and there was just a lot of screaming in the background and I tried to ring them back, but they didn't pick up. Do you want the number?"
VIZZINI: "They're from Scarsdale?"
VIANA: "723 number."
VIZZINI: "Okay."

After writing down the telephone number Viana had given him, Vizzini pulled out the department's *Cole's Directory*, a book that cross-references telephone numbers with street addresses.

After a few minutes of flipping through the book, he matched the emergency number with an address at Sentry Place. The only problem was that the address was in neighboring Greenburgh and fell into the Greenburgh Police Department's jurisdiction, not his.

The dispatcher quickly called his Greenburgh counterpart. Marlene Farrell was working dispatch at the Greenburgh police station that night.

FARRELL: "Greenburgh Police Department. May I help you?"

VIZZINI: "Yeah, this is Scarsdale. The operator tried to give us a phone call, and the people hung up and they were screaming and crying and yelling. . . ."

FARRELL: "Did you get an address?"

VIZZINI: "Yeah, we looked it up in the reverse directory, Sentry Place, that's S-E-N-T-R-Y Place. The name is Berman."

FARRELL: "S-E-N-T-R-Y?"

VIZZINI: "Right. I believe it's off Central Avenue."

FARRELL: "The name is Berman?"

VIZZINI: "B-E-R-M-A-N. . . ."

FARRELL: "What is it, a dispute?"

VIZZINI: "I have no idea, I never got the call. The operator tried to give it to us."

FARRELL: "Okay."

VIZZINI: "They dialed 911."

FARRELL: "All right. We'll send someone."

VIZZINI: "Right. Okay."

The entire conversation took less than a minute. It took Greenburgh police another twenty seconds to dispatch a patrol car to Sentry Place.

Patrolman Donald Singer, Jr., the son of the chief of police, arrived there within minutes and found the address belonged to an apartment building. The surrounding block was lined with various businesses, from grocery stores to video parlors.

Neither seeing nor hearing any disturbance outside, Singer walked into the apartment house and roused the building manager, who said he hadn't heard anything unusual, certainly no fighting from his tenants.

"Yeah, Officer. We got a couple named Berman here, but I don't think they're even home. Feel free to check it out," the man said, anxious to get back to the easy chair where he'd been napping.

Finding no problem in the building—no one answered at the Berman apartment—Singer walked outside and strolled along the front of the stores on Sentry Place, peering in the darkened windows for any sign of trouble. Twenty minutes later, he radioed headquarters and told the dispatcher he could find nothing wrong. The dispatcher noted the time of the call and cleared Singer to continue patrol.

What neither Singer nor the Scarsdale and Greenburgh police dispatchers knew at that moment was that the phone number they received from the operator had actually been reassigned only weeks before to the residence of Paul and Betty Jeanne Solomon.

Viana knew she could have taken a few extra minutes to get the telephone computers to kick out the most current address for the number she gave to the Scarsdale police dispatcher. But that wasn't part of the telephone company's procedure. Besides, if the police really wanted that information they could call her back and request it. They never did. Viana began to fill out a written report of the incident for her boss.

The traffic on South Central Avenue was light, even for a Sunday night, Paul noticed as he drove toward the Yonkers bowling alley. Ten minutes from his front door, he made a right turn into the nearly empty parking lot and easily found an open slot near the building. He got out of his car, and pulled the collar of his coat tightly around his neck to ward off the whipping wind. He purposely left his bowling ball in the trunk.

Walking through the double-glass doors and past the cashier's counter on his right, Paul scanned the fifty-two lanes until he spotted several of his friends lacing up their shoes, picking out their balls, and shooting a few practice frames on lane 36. Unbuttoning his coat, he sauntered over.

"How you guys doing?" he asked of no one in particular.

Hope Rosenthal glanced up. "Hi, Paul. You gonna bowl tonight?"

"No, just stopped by to say hello," he said, plopping down on one of the white plastic chairs with the blue seats that formed a ring around the two lanes his friends had been assigned that evening.

Walter and Doris Sekinski walked up behind Paul. Putting his hand on Paul's shoulder, Walter gave an easy squeeze. "Hey, guy. You bowling?" he asked, as his wife walked over to the scoring table and sat down next to Hope. Paul hadn't bowled much that fall or winter, so no one was surprised he wasn't playing that night.

"No. I can't stay very long." Paul had known the Sekinskis for years and liked them both. Turning around, he saw Laura Bertuch looking bored, leaning against the counter.

"Hi, Laura. What's new?" Paul asked, walking over to the pretty brunette. They exchanged small talk for a few minutes until a group of bowlers anxious to rent their red, gray, and black bowling shoes surrounded the counter. Paul turned and stood in the aisle way above the lanes, watching his friends.

About forty minutes later, Laura saw Paul walking toward the door. It puzzled her that he was leaving so soon, but she was busy trying to keep score, and he was quickly forgotten.

Paul revved up the car's engine and took a right out of the bowling alley parking lot. He headed south on Central Avenue and then hung a right on Tuckahoe Road. Several blocks later, he rounded a curve in the road and braked when he saw the Holiday Inn sign. He turned right and then a sharp left and drove up the winding roadway that led to the restaurant and his date with Carolyn Warmus. The trip from the bowling alley took less than seven minutes, and by this time Paul could almost drive it with his eyes closed.

The Treetops Restaurant at the Holiday Inn in Yonkers served good food and reasonably priced drinks, and the waitresses were always pleasant. It was his and Carolyn's favorite rendezvous place, although their reasons for liking it had more to do with privacy and proximity to both his home and the bowling alley than with the French continental cuisine. There was hardly one chance in a million that they'd ever be seen here by a nosy neighbor or colleague or anyone else who might think twice about the couple's motives for dining and drinking together in a hotel.

Paul drove the Dodge into the well-lit parking lot and once again emerged into the frosty night. It was 7:25 P.M. and he knew from experience that Carolyn would not have arrived before him. He thought for a moment of waiting for her outside but quickly discarded the thought. More often than not she would show up for a date long after the scheduled time, giggling about the traffic or a phone call she couldn't hang up on. It was too cold tonight to trust that she'd show up on time.

Walking inside and grabbing a seat at the bar, Paul waited only a few seconds before the pudgy bartender came over. Ignoring her smiled hello, he ordered a vodka Collins. Maria Contri pulled out her bill book and put the drink on his tab. She had started at 5 P.M. and the bar was pretty slow. She looked forward to 8 P.M. when the usual crowd showed up. The conversation was friendlier and the tips bigger.

"Someone will be joining me soon," Paul called after her, looking toward the doorway. Contri smiled and said she'd bring him his drink right away. He watched as she walked away. The required black suit, gray vest, and a starched white shirt with black tie covering the waitress's ample figure always seemed to lend a touch of elegance to the dinners he and Carolyn shared there.

Carolyn strode into the bar at 7:45, her tight navy-blue slacks and revealing blouse catching the eyes of more than one hotel tippler. She sat down and touched Paul's hand, telling him she was glad he had made time to see her, even when he wasn't feeling well. Contri, noticing Carolyn's entrance, finished taking another order before interrupting the pair. The woman looked like a champagne drinker, Contri thought to herself as she wrote Carolyn's request on her pad.

Carolyn looked around the plush restaurant. Like Paul, she enjoyed these secret trysts here. The decor matched Carolyn's tastes. Five crystal-beaded chandeliers were dimmed romantically, muting somewhat the colorful, ornate carpeting. Light cranberry tablecloths were adorned with glass-stemmed candle holders, covered with an etched shade. The modern, blue-padded chairs with brass-colored, curved arms and legs, were matched nicely with the also-modern blue and white wallpaper.

Along the far wall hung four perfectly balanced rows of gold plates. During one of their first dinners there, Carolyn had walked over to them for a closer look and noticed that each plate had "Treetops Restaurant" inscribed in script around the top. The inner circle of each plate contained a person's name, presumably a longtime patron, she guessed. On the left side of the plates hung an Ansel Adams black and white print of a barren tree in winter, centered in a light blue border.

At the opposite end of the wall were three scenic photo prints of a sand dune, mountains, and fallen leaves floating upon a gentle, shimmering lake that Carolyn especially liked.

The restaurant itself was actually divided into two tiers, bordered along three sides with brass bannisters. Behind them ran a window wall that overlooked a tree-laden hillside. Carolyn particularly liked the two strategically placed, four-sided mirrors that ran from ceiling to floor. During dinner she would often steal a quick glance at them to check her makeup and hair.

After a couple of rounds of drinks, Paul and Carolyn moved to a table and ordered dinner. Twenty minutes later he began devouring his plate of oysters and watched as Carolyn's meal was brought over. He kidded her about her eclectic tastes: hamburgers and fries washed down by expensive Brut champagne. She smiled at his joke and began eating.

For the next two and a half hours the lovers entered into a deep, hushed conversation, oblivious to the world around them. Several times Carolyn reached across the table with her right hand, smiling when Paul's left met hers.

At one point during the evening, pursuing the conversation about their relationship, Carolyn smiled sweetly at Paul and asked him what he would do if he was no longer married to Betty Jeanne. Paul smiled back, saying he couldn't see himself getting remarried any time soon. It was not an answer Carolyn liked, but she let it pass.

Two hours later, Contri watched as the couple paid their bill and headed for the parking lot. She picked up her tip and soon forgot them as other patrons waved her down. Contri stole a look at her watch; only another half hour. It was 10:30 P.M. and the restaurant closed at 11.

Paul walked with Carolyn along the uphill driveway that ran in front of the restaurant and hotel, past several cars parked on either side. She led him to her almost new, 1988 red Hyundai, parked in a lot overlooking the hotel and beyond reach of the fluorescent lights peppering the paved area. Carolyn unlocked her door, reached over, and pulled the passenger handle, allowing Paul to slide in next to her. She turned the engine over, pumping the gas pedal in an attempt to warm up the heater more quickly.

Once the toasty air chased the chill from their bones, Carolyn and Paul leaned toward each other, a slow, sensual kiss turning into an impassioned embrace, his hand reaching under her coat and feeling her full breasts and hard nipples through her thin blouse. She gently placed her hand along his thigh, moving it in rhythmic strokes until she reached the bulge pressing hard against his tight pants. He unbuttoned her blouse, pulling it aside, and began a slow descent with his tongue, tasting the perfume along her neck until his lips rested between her soft breasts. He pulled her bra carefully upward, exposing her nipples to his darting tongue until he began sucking her as softly as a nursing child.

For forty-five minutes the couple kissed, touched, and caressed one another until Carolyn finally whispered in his ear. "Please, Paul. Can I? Will you let me?"

Paul knew what she meant and nodded his approval, kissing her as she undid his belt and unbuttoned his pants. She watched with delight as he pushed his slacks further down his hips. He quivered slightly as she lowered her head and ran her moist tongue slowly between his legs and suddenly took him into her mouth until seconds later, he came in an explosion of desire. Going down on Paul in the Holiday Inn parking lot with the chance of being seen by passersby only heightened the crackling sexual tension between them. Their lust quenched for the moment, the exhausted couple rebuttoned their clothes and shared several parting kisses, both promising they'd get together again soon.

Paul opened the car door and stepped out, looking back to say he would call her and to be careful driving home. He slammed the door shut and walked to the Dodge Colt, got in, and drove through the parking lot, pulling in behind her at the exit. Warmus turned right on Tuckahoe Road and watched in her rearview mirror until Paul made a left-hand turn onto the same road as he headed toward South Central Avenue and home.

Only a few minutes later, Paul pulled into a slot in front of his building, jumped out of the car, and peered at his watch under the dim lights of the parking lot as he walked up the open wooden staircase to his third-floor condo. It was 11:40 P.M. and he hoped Betty Jeanne would be asleep. He slid his key into the lock, trying to be quiet as he entered and closed the door silently behind him. He began taking off his coat as he walked down the hallway.

He was surprised to hear the television set playing loudly in the living room. Usually Betty Jeanne was fast asleep by this time. He hoped she wouldn't start in on him for being so late.

Walking into the kitchen, Paul didn't notice the telephone receiver lying on the floor, the unhooked phone cord next to it. In a millisecond, by the light of the TV, he caught sight of the unmoving figure lying between the end of one sofa and the wall.

"Honey, wake up," he called, as he threw his coat on the nearby rocking chair.

Betty Jeanne had often complained about back trouble and once or twice he had found her asleep on the floor in front of the TV. He reached for the remote control that was on the sofa nearest her and pushed the button to turn down the volume. It was on so loud he wondered how his wife could sleep through it.

He walked over to the prone figure to shake her awake and in that moment a searing bolt of fear shot through him. She was face down and unmoving, but some instinct deep within his mind told him something was terribly wrong. He bent down and turned her over, her sightless eyes now staring at the ceiling. The coagulating pool of blood under

Betty Jeanne and the feel of the still-wet clothing dripping into his hands almost caused him to retch.

His first shocking thought was that she had fallen and suffered some traumatic internal injury. He placed his ear to her chest, but heard and felt no movement. In a panic he ran to the kitchen phone and found it on the floor. He picked it up and tried to dial for help before noticing the unhooked cord. Now in a state of extreme panic, he fumbled with the cord, wasting precious seconds unsuccessfully trying to reinsert it. Finally he threw it down and sprinted for the phone in the den.

Richard Vizzini, the young part-time dispatcher, stared down at the ringing phone. He was looking forward to ending his shift at the Scarsdale Police Department and had only a few minutes to go. The call meant he'd be there a while longer. "Scarsdale Police Department. May I help you?" he asked.

"It's my wife. I think she's dead. I need help. My name is Paul Solomon. . . . My wife needs help. She's not moving. She's covered with blood. Hurry. Please hurry!"

Trying to calm the agitated caller, Vizzini took down the information and quickly realized the address was in Greenburgh's jurisdiction. He dialed their number.

Solomon went back to his wife, unaware that he was going into shock. He reached down and touched her stiffened arms, held up before her as if she were warding off a blow. He got up and ran out the front door, frantically looking off the balcony for the help that seemed to be taking forever to arrive. Shaking uncontrollably, he walked over and began pounding on his neighbor's door.

Fazlur Rahman, a fifty-year-old engineer, was half asleep when he heard the yells. He looked at the clock radio on the night stand. 11:44 P.M. He climbed out of bed, telling his wife, Nargis, to stay put. As he passed his sons' room, he yelled for Zubair and Junaid to stay in bed. He then went to the front door, cautiously peeked through the security hole, and recognized Paul Solomon.

When Rahman and his family moved into the complex in 1988, Betty Jeanne had come over and welcomed them with an invitation to dinner. That was when they had first met Paul and Kristan. After their first get-together, Fazlur and Nargis didn't really socialize with the Solomons very often, but greeted each other in passing as they came and went from their apartments.

Fazlur opened the door and Paul practically fell through, a shaken, panic-stricken man babbling something about his wife. When Fazlur finally understood what Paul was attempting to explain, he told his neighbor to wait while he went to put on a robe. There was no way in hell he was going to walk over and look at the horrible scene Paul had just described. He watched as Paul raced back out to the balcony to await the police, the bloodstained hands of his neighbor etched in his mind.

2

A FIFTY-TON, GRAYISH-WHITE humpback whale with an immense, slashing tail broke the ocean's ice-blue surface, soaring in a slow-motion arc until its massive weight slammed the behemoth back to its watery kingdom.

Don Singer sat in his family room, nestled in his favorite easy chair with his feet propped up, staring at his color television set, marveling at the beauty and grace of the oversized mammal. He loved watching nature shows, and tonight's special on the world's whales had kept him entranced for the past two hours.

Unlike most of his brethren, he didn't particularly like cop shows. Being Greenburgh's police chief and a twenty-nine year veteran had brought more than its share of harrowing car chases, shootouts, and grisly murders, including more solved and unsolved mysteries than Agatha Christie could ever have hoped to pen. Animals were predictable, he often said. They always followed the laws of nature, while the only thing certain about man was that he could be counted on to find new ways to break the laws of society.

His years on the force, along with his stint as provost marshal for New York's Army National Guard and head of its Criminal Investigations Directorate (CID), hadn't made him cynical, only more practical. Somewhere in his spare time—even his boss, Greenburgh supervisor, Tony Veteran, couldn't figure out how—Singer had earned his law degree, passed his bar exams with flying colors, and taken on some real estate and other civil cases that had no connection with Greenburgh.

His reputation among other Westchester County police chiefs and cops was unmatched. The best his detractors could come up with was that Singer wouldn't join the local police chiefs associations, always saying he was too busy. That wasn't completely true, he would tell his close associates. He just felt that most of the chiefs spent too much time patting themselves on the back and kissing each other's asses and never really accomplished anything. He liked being his own man and running his department. He was proud of the respect he had earned from his peers.

Outside of his police and Army National Guard duties—he had reached the rank of lieutenant colonel—Singer most enjoyed the time he spent flying his four-seater Piper Arrow with his sons and being with his wife, Anne. Only his family took precedence over his job as police chief.

Life with his beautiful, Irish-born, Catholic wife never failed to keep him supplied with humorous stories for his staff. Often those stories would involve himself, or more accurately, his looks. His large ears, sticking out from close-cropped, salt-and-pepper hair, were often the target of good-natured ribbing around home and the department.

One of the few times Singer wouldn't crack a smile was when his own or his department's integrity was questioned. No matter whom the complaint was against, he always took it personally. It didn't happen often, but when a problem arose he was quick to determine the facts and, if necessary, defend his men to the hilt.

The two things he wouldn't stand for were insubordination and shoddy work. His men didn't always agree with his orders, but he always commanded their respect.

Singer's laughing brown eyes, weathered complexion, and self-deprecating sense of humor might lull an adversary into a false sense of security. But his razor-sharp mind and his ability to quote chapter and verse of state penal laws and precedent-setting court decisions would, more often than not, reduce the unwary antagonist to a stammering, apologetic convert or confessor.

Singer enjoyed an easy, bantering relationship with his two captains, Maurice "Butch" Geary and William McDonald, and he loved a good argument with anyone who happened to walk into his office. One of his favorite tongue-in-cheek sayings was, "Even when I'm wrong, I'm right, because I'm the chief."

When the screen credits began to roll at midnight, marking the end of the televised documentary, Singer dragged himself from his chair and headed for bed. The ringing phone stopped him short of the stairs and brought him into the kitchen.

"Chief, it's Sullivan. We've got a homicide at the Scarsdale Ridge Apartments. Forty-year-old female. Her husband says he came home from bowling and found her on the living-room floor with multiple gunshot wounds. Lind and Constantino are on their way now."

Although Singer liked Lieutenant Cornelius "Neil" Sullivan, he found him a little too stoic and unbending at times. At thirty-seven, Sullivan was made head of the detective's division and the good-looking, silver-haired officer wasted no time in putting his brand on the unit.

Things had gotten a little lackadaisical under the former division commander, in his opinion, and he quickly made it clear to his detectives that they would have to shoulder heavier workloads and follow the rules more closely if they expected to work for him.

A tough kid from the Bronx, Sullivan had endured a rough childhood. After both his parents were killed in an automobile accident, he was raised by a strict but loving grandfather. Beneath the rock-hard exterior that he refused to let anyone penetrate, burned a savage desire to put his unhappy past behind him.

While once he would have let his fists speak for him, Sullivan now relieved the tension of his job with hard-fought, and sometimes extremely physical basketball games at the local YMCA.

Detective Sergeant Thomas Lind and Detective Richard Constantino were a good pair to have on the case, Singer noted. Lind was slow, easygoing, but thorough. Constantino was young, inexperienced, but energetic and enthusiastic.

Lind, at forty-three, was nearing the end of his police career and had already mentioned to some of his pals that he might be retiring the following year. He had a security job lined up with a major Manhattan jewelry company, and it was beginning to look more attractive to him.

Between the salary they were offering and his Greenburgh pension, he could do okay for himself. At six foot one, with straight brown hair combed to the side, glasses, and a pronounced pot belly pushing against his starched shirts, Lind knew he and his young partner were as different as night and day.

Constantino was new to the detective ranks, but extremely hungry for that first big case. Short, with a roundish build and a black moustache, Constantino was good-naturedly called "the little general," a moniker quickly slapped on him not only for his looks but for his habit of strutting around the squad room and taking charge of any case he was assigned. Singer would make him lead detective in the Solomon case, his first lead on a homicide, and he would become determined to find the killer.

Singer asked Sullivan a few more questions about the case and then hung up.

Seconds later, he picked up the phone and dialed the number of a good friend and one of the nation's most respected criminologists. Peter R. De Forest, who lived in nearby Hartsdale, was a quiet, low-key individual widely admired for his skills at crime analysis.

He had worked on—and helped solve—several major cases across the country, and the fact that the public never recognized his name was due mainly to his desire to keep it that way. State and federal agencies often clamored for his services, but Singer knew a call for help wouldn't be ignored.

He had met De Forest in 1973 while attending classes at John Jay College in Manhattan where De Forest taught criminology. Their mutual interests in police work, crime scenes, and the law gave them something in common to banter or bicker about over coffee, and they had stayed friends over the years.

When he heard the soft-spoken voice on the other end of the line, Singer apologized for waking his friend. "Peter, we just had a homicide over on Central Avenue and it may be one we could use your help on," the chief said.

He then repeated the sketchy information Sullivan had given him and asked if De Forest would be willing to go to the crime scene as an unofficial analyst the following day. "It's one of those cases where it was probably the husband, but you never know. I'd feel better if you could take a look at it."

De Forest immediately agreed, happy to do a favor for his old friend and student. He wrote down the address and hung up. Although he realized the body would be removed by the time he got there, he still expected to find the usual blood and gore associated with his line of work.

Having placed all the wheels in motion, Singer went to bed. Monday was going to be a long day. He had already made plans to fly to Syracuse in the morning with his police lieutenant, Andy Kelleher, on a state Army National Guard investigation.

Kelleher, also a captain in the Guard and Singer's right-hand man in the CID, had made the plane and hotel reservations and was picking him up at 7 A.M. For a moment, Singer thought about cancelling the trip. Sullivan, he knew, could handle the murder investigation and would keep him posted on any developments.

He checked his beeper to make sure the battery was working and then climbed into bed and turned out the light, careful not to wake his wife.

When Lind arrived at the Solomons' apartment, he found the door open and men from crime analysis strolling about. Greenburgh Patrolman Michael Cotter, the first officer on the scene, stood outside the doorway to keep unwanted visitors away and to protect the integrity of the crime scene.

Lind strode in and watched as the forensic experts collected blood samples and spent bullet casings and photographed the entire layout, concentrating particularly on the bloody heap that had once been, from what he could tell, an attractive woman.

Lind had seen more than his fair share of bodies during his time on the force, and while he kept the cool, composed look on his face that was expected of a veteran cop, his stomach churned as it always did when he caught his first look at a fresh corpse, riddled with bullets and soaked in blood.

He glanced away and surveyed the room. The furniture was remarkably undisturbed considering the life-and-death struggle that had taken place here only hours before. The Sunday paper was folded neatly on the coffee table, partially covering a couple of magazines. A book—one of those romantic trash novels where everyone was always jumping beds and each other, he sniffed—rested on the far end of the table with a plastic marker poking out the top.

The propped up pillows at one end of the cream-colored sofa and a half-eaten bowl of cereal next to the book told Lind someone had been spending most of their day relaxing in the living room, pretty much the same thing he'd been doing before he received the call from Sullivan.

Across from the sofa stood the television and stereo system, and when he walked into the kitchen and glanced down the hallway, he noticed expensive video-recording equipment sitting on a table by the front door.

One of the cops taking notes pointed out to him some marks on a screen door leading from the living room onto a small, wooden balcony, but Lind quickly discarded the notion that a burglar had entered there and possibly whacked Betty Jeanne Solomon when she surprised him.

The usual prizes a burglar would snatch were all in place, including a wad of bills totaling $300 on the living-room coffee table.

Besides, a thin layer of dust around some of the stereo components and the four, round indentations in the carpet beneath the television legs convinced him nothing had even been touched. No, what appeared to have happened here, Lind thought, was that Betty Jeanne Solomon had let someone into her home, or someone with a key had let himself in, and the deadly confrontation began almost immediately.

Unable to put it off any longer, Lind walked over to the body and slowly bent down to examine it more closely, careful not to interfere with the crime analysis cops only a couple of feet away who were busy dusting off the fine, grayish powder they had sprayed on the coffee table in an attempt to bring out any latent fingerprints.

The blood made it difficult to tell, but he could make out the picture of a tiger and some mountains on the front of her T-shirt, and what appeared to be four small, ragged holes piercing the cloth. The once-gray sweat pants were now almost entirely soaked with blood. He found two more holes around the victim's left knee and calf. He gently tried to lift an arm and felt the telltale stiffness of rigor mortis.

For a second Lind considered the possibility that the slaying was a professional hit, but while he wasn't ruling anything out, he personally didn't think that was the case. A pro would have grabbed his victim in the hallway the second the door was opened and not given her the chance to run back inside. A pro would have wrapped his hand around her mouth and put the gun to the back of her head and blown her away immediately. If he got a little blood on him, hell, he would probably have a change of clothes in his car.

Another clue that went against the hit-man theory was the telephone. From the looks of the telephone receiver on the floor, someone—and not likely the killer—had tried to use the phone, possibly to call for help, and had dropped it when the bullets started flying. No hit man worth his salt would let a victim get anywhere near a phone.

But the capper against this being a paid hit was the location of the bullet wounds scattered on Betty Jeanne Solomon's body. Not many hit men would fire away at a moving target and risk only wounding their quarry in the leg. Too many things could go wrong, like the victim screaming and alerting the neighbors. He'd wait for the forensics report, but he was willing to bet a case of Michelob he was right.

Lind stood up and walked over to examine the wall phone in the kitchen.

Why in hell would anyone carefully unplug the wall jack? If the victim had made it to the phone and dialed a number, wouldn't it make more sense for the killer to yank the receiver out of her hands and push the receiver button down to disconnect it, or at the very least to rip the phone cord out of the wall?

One of the first things they'd have to do was find out what calls had been made from this number. There'd been more than one case solved because a phone trail had led to the door of a killer.

Walking from the living room through the dining area and down a short hallway, Lind peered through one of the doors. It didn't take a trained detective, only a father, to know this was the bedroom of a teen-age girl.

Stuffed animals, dolls, and other memorabilia of childhood were mixed with teen posters and discarded bras strewn across the rose-colored bedspread. There was nothing beyond the normal disarray to indicate a struggle had taken place in here.

Lind noticed a framed photograph resting on a dresser. Picking it up, he saw it was a girls' basketball team posing in the usual way. He stared at all the faces and wondered which player was about to have her life shattered.

Taking a right out of the door, Lind walked back down the hallway and turned left through the kitchen until he came to another hallway. Walking through an open door, the detective found himself in a small walkway that led to what he assumed was another bedroom.

The door on his right led into a bathroom and a quick peek revealed nothing out of the ordinary. The door straight ahead yielded the master bedroom. It was about seventeen feet by twelve feet, twice the size of the young girl's room. Once again Lind quickly ruled out the possibility that the killer and victim had run in here and fought.

Satisfied he hadn't missed anything of significance, Lind returned to the living room.

Once again his eyes drifted back to the body. No matter how hard he tried not to, he asked himself the same questions he always asked about a murder victim: What did she say to her killer? What was she thinking during her last, agony-filled minutes on earth and at the exact second she knew she was facing death? These and other morbid thoughts filled his head as he left the stifling room, stepped over the telephone, and walked toward the condo across the hall where a uniformed officer standing guard told him the husband was being questioned by Sullivan.

Lind stopped when he saw Constantino coming up the stairs. Pointing to the door he had just exited, Lind said, "She's in there. I'm going to question the husband now. If you need anything or have any questions, I'll be over here with Sullivan in this other apartment. Come on over as soon as you can."

The young detective grunted his response and walked through the door, pulling a note pad from his back pocket. He didn't really need to examine anything that closely. The crime scene photographs, ballistics, and medical examiner's autopsy report would tell him just about everything he'd need to know.

What he was there to do now was get a feel for the place, to look for the small, almost unnoticeable nuances that would never find their way into any report. More than once over his relatively short but successful career, it was just those tiny bits of evidence that had helped him provide prosecutors with the last piece of an investigative puzzle, more often than not resulting in an arrest and conviction.

Constantino was proud of his accomplishments. He loved nothing better than to go to a crime scene and get a firsthand look at a victim and the surroundings. It wasn't that he got any rush from seeing a mutilated corpse, and he didn't relish the role of professional voyeur like some detectives he knew. He just liked to pit his knowledge and experience against the criminal mind. It was like a high-stakes chess match with a killer making every move to conceal his identity and him trying to strip his unknown adversary's defenses until he could positively identify the murderer.

The phone and the grotesque appearance of the victim with her arms locked out in front of her told him that Betty Jeanne Solomon had made a desperate attempt at staying alive. Examining the body, he noticed what appeared to be a small scuff mark on the back of the victim's T-shirt. To him, it looked to be part of a footprint. If that were true, it indicated to him that the killer's intention was to ensure the death of his prey.

The person who had pulled the trigger in this room was probably filled with anger and hatred. This woman was not the victim of a frightened burglar who had freaked out when he was caught in the act. No, this woman was a target, he was sure. This was overkill.

Constantino began his careful perusal of the condo, every few minutes stopping to scribble another note. No one asked him any questions, and he made it a point to stay out of everyone's way. He'd return the next day to conduct his own search for any ballistic evidence that might have gone unnoticed; tonight was only the start of what could be a long investigation.

About forty-five minutes later, he finished his note taking and walked across the hall to find Lind and the lieutenant.

Before he even entered the Rahmans' apartment, Lind knew from experience what he'd see: the hunched-over frame of the distraught husband, head in his hands, and either crying or staring blankly at the floor and muttering undying love for his wife. He was very close.

Sullivan was sitting next to Solomon, already beginning the questioning. Solomon perched on the edge of the Rahmans' floral sofa, wringing his hands and glancing up only when Sullivan asked him a question. He had the glassy eyes of someone who was either in shock or very scared.

Lind knew two things as he walked over to the shaken man. Eight out of ten times, when a married woman was murdered in her own home, it was the husband who had pulled the trigger or plunged the knife into her heart, usually in the white-hot heat of an argument.

Second, the best time to question a potential suspect was within minutes of the crime, while the horror of the act was just beginning to seep into his soul and the unpleasant consequences started to become tangible fears.

Lind listened from a distance to Sullivan's conversation with the man. After a few minutes, notebook in hand, he sidled up next to the pair to hear the rest of Solomon's story.

The first thing he noticed were the small splotches of blood on Solomon's sweatshirt and pant leg. The detectives had learned—much to their disbelief and anger—that Patrolman Cotter had been stupid enough to allow their suspect to wash the blood off his hands in the Rahmans' bathroom before they arrived.

"I came home from bowling at about 11:40 P.M. and just found her like that," Solomon said, his voice cracking repeatedly. "I don't know who could have done this. What'll I tell Kristan?"

Lind stopped writing and put up his hand, effectively halting Solomon's response. "Let's take this slow and from the beginning. First tell me what you did today, when you last saw your wife, and where you'd been up until the time you found her."

Solomon took a deep breath and repeated the day's activities in detail to the scribbling detective. When he got to the part about arriving at the bowling alley, Solomon's eyes darted around the room, his voice quavering slightly.

"I just went to the Brunswick lanes in Yonkers, just down the road, and I've been there all night," he said. "I go bowling every Sunday and there are friends of mine who'll tell you I was there. When I finished, I came home and found Betty." He broke down, unable to speak through his sobs.

Fazlur, his wife and two sons, stood off to the side, helplessly watching their tormented neighbor struggle with the officers' questions.

"Who could have done such a thing?" the Indian-born engineer said to his wife, silently fearing the deadly intruder could still be around, or worse yet, living in the complex.

Later, after being joined by Constantino, the detectives continued to pump Solomon for more details of his night. Something just didn't seem right, they told each other during a break in the questioning.

"I can't put my finger on it, but Solomon's answers to some of our questions just don't ring true," Sullivan told his men.

The trio walked back to the sofa and smiled at him. He glanced up and when their eyes met he looked away nervously. No problem, the detectives thought. They had all night and he wasn't going anywhere.

While the interrogation continued, across the hall the crime analysis officers completed their work. Among the evidence being brought back to the station in sealed glassine packets, were six shell casings and three flattened .25-caliber bullet fragments.

Their notes and diagrams would show that several of the shell casings were found along the right side of the victim's body while another was picked up near the front entrance. Two of the flattened bullet fragments were found near Betty Jeanne Solomon's left knee and arm and another near the door wall. These also were placed in the packets, which were then coded with a black Magic Marker so the detectives could later re-create the murder scene down to the smallest detail.

Among themselves, the cops tried to figure out how one of the shell casings had ended up by the front door. The living room, where it appeared most of the shooting had taken place, was through the kitchen and to the left. If the killer had walked into the condo and fired a shot, Betty Jeanne Solomon would have immediately realized what was happening and run into the other room.

But would the shooter, knowing the victim was aware she was about to be killed, allow her the time to get to the telephone to call for help? Wouldn't more shots have been fired as soon as the front door was opened? They had found what appeared to be six .25-caliber shell casings, but had the killer scooped some up and then unknowingly dropped one on the way out? Even without an autopsy report, it was easy to see that the victim had been shot at least eight, maybe nine times.

The cops knew that the only .25-caliber equipped to fire nine shots was a Beretta automatic. And when that model gun was fired, the shell casings ejected to the right and backwards. Even with this information, no one could come up with a reasonable explanation for how the one shell casing had ended up by the front door.

They knew it was probably one of those forensic mysteries that wouldn't be solved until they caught up with the shooter. The fact that three shell casings had not been recovered didn't bother them as much. Sometimes a cool-headed killer would try to scoop them up before leaving the scene. In the excitement of the moment, it appeared the murderer had missed a few here. Hopefully it wasn't the only mistake the unknown person made.

The detectives stopped their questioning of Solomon only long enough for him to be given a paraffin test, which would help to determine whether or not he had fired a gun that night.

Solomon obliged, holding out both his hands to be swabbed with specially manufactured chemicals. The cotton swabs, which resembled giant Q-Tips, were then sealed and put away for later testing. The test would indicate whether there were any nitrates on his hands that could have come from discharged gunpowder.

No one bothered to tell the detective conducting the test that Solomon had, only a couple of hours before, been allowed to wash his hands to remove his wife's blood.

At 2 A.M., Assistant Westchester County Medical Examiner Darly Jeanty arrived at the scene and looked the corpse over from head to toe. Fifteen minutes later, after completing his initial examination, he carefully bagged Betty Jeanne Solomon's hands to protect whatever evidence might still be on them.

"Hopefully she got close enough to her killer to grab some hair or scratch some skin from the person's face," he told one of his assistants in his clipped Haitian accent. "It will help us tremendously if we ever find her killer."

At 2:15 A.M. he officially pronounced Betty Jeanne Solomon dead.

When he was done, two paramedics knelt on the floor, unzipping the long, black body bag that would be used to carry the body to a cold, metal slab in the coroner's basement at the county's medical complex in Valhalla for an autopsy later that day.

At that very moment, Paul Solomon was agreeing to the detectives' request that he accompany them to headquarters. Several minutes before—and he couldn't figure out why—the detectives had asked him to remove all his clothes and give them to one of the forensic team.

Somewhere in his tired and confused mind, he tried to figure out why they were so busy checking him out, when they should really be out there looking for the killer, but he was too emotionally drained to argue or object to anything. He was wearing a pair of jeans and a sweater as he walked down the steps to a waiting patrol car. He sat in silence during the short drive to the station, where the questioning continued.

How many hours had it been since he found Betty Jeanne? Two, three? He didn't know. His head was still spinning: murder, blood, Kristan, bowling, police. . . . This was a nightmare. For what seemed like the millionth time that night, a cold chill gripped his body and he shivered uncontrollably. More questions.

Shortly before 3 A.M., almost three hours after Solomon telephoned the police to report his wife's murder, he broke.

The unending, repetitive questions and repeated promises that everything he told the detectives would be thoroughly checked out, finally pressured Solomon into confessing that he hadn't told them the whole story. Sullivan, Constantino, and Lind waited patiently for him to continue, knowing that once the dam had burst, it was only a matter of minutes before the real story would come cascading forth.

"I did go to the bowling alley like I told you, only I didn't come right home from there," he said, minute beads of sweat beginning to form on his forehead. "I met someone afterward, at the Treetops Restaurant in Yonkers. I got there about 7:30 P.M."

The rest of Solomon's story came out in a disjointed, embarrassed flow. He told them about his relationship with Carolyn Warmus and the telephone call earlier that day that had prompted the date.

Mopping his brow, Solomon began to turn a sickening shade of pink as he described the after-dinner sex scene in her car. He gave his inquisitors Carolyn's address and phone number, along with that of his own attorney, Gary Pillersdorf.

Lind and Constantino suppressed the urge to smile and gently prodded their now-drained confessor to describe in detail his exact movements from the time he opened the door to leave his home that night until the first police officers arrived on the scene. No matter how many times they asked him to repeat his story after that, Solomon never wavered in his facts.

Visibly relieved now that he had revealed his lie-by-omission to the detectives, Solomon stuck by the rest of the story that he had given the police throughout the night.

Sullivan listened quietly in the background to Solomon's story and decided to make a quick check for himself. He walked back into his office and picked up the telephone, dialing information to obtain Pillersdorf's home phone number. It was now about four-thirty in the morning, and the ringing phone stirred the middle-aged lawyer and his wife from a dead sleep.

"Hello, Mr. Pillersdorf? This is Lieutenant Neil Sullivan from the Greenburgh Police Department. I'm calling about a friend of yours, Paul Solomon. I have a question for you about him and his wife, Betty Jeanne Solomon. How would you describe their marriage?"

Groggy from being awakened at that early hour, and put off by the detective's direct approach, Pillersdorf flippantly responded, "Perfect. I'd say they had a perfect marriage. What's this all about?"

The lawyer's annoyance turned to anger when he heard Sullivan reply, "Well, I guess you don't know your friend too well then, do you?" as the policeman hung up.

Back in the interrogation room, Constantino and Lind believed that the most likely killer, and certainly their prime suspect, was sitting right in front of them.

The usual interrogation techniques had already brought out what they were looking for, a believable motive for Solomon to kill his wife. It was one of the oldest in the book. The middle-aged man, tired of his mundane life and sexless wife, being pressured by his young, sexy plaything and deciding that divorce was too expensive. The motive and opportunity requirements were falling into place.

Within the hour, Lind drove back to the crime scene and pulled Cotter aside. Cotter, the uniform cop responsible for preserving the murder scene since he'd been the first to arrive, was told to make sure the residence was locked shut and sealed with the yellow police tape that warned people not to enter the premises.

Their suspect would have to find another place to sleep for a while. The thought didn't bother Lind. The daughter would be back late that night and Solomon could find a place for them to stay by then.

Constantino arrived back on the scene a short time later and hooked up with Lind to discuss what they had so far. Neither detective was willing to latch on to any one suspect just yet, but Solomon sure looked promising, they both agreed. There was still a long way to go with this case before anyone ever saw the inside of a courtroom or jail cell.

Besides, Carolyn Warmus was going to be picked up and brought to the station for questioning in an hour or two and both detectives were eagerly awaiting her description of the evening with Solomon, especially the erotic dessert she had served him in the parking lot after their dinner. It was a tough job, but somebody had to do it. They laughed quietly so none of the inquisitive neighbors standing outside the front of the building could hear.

Walking down to the parking lot, both men noticed the Solomons' two automobiles being checked by the forensic team. When they were finished, the cars would be towed back to the station garage where a more thorough check would be made the next day.

Pulling out of the complex for the second time that night, Constantino noticed an empty guard shack only a few hundred feet from the steps of Solomon's building. As he drove away, he made a mental note to check on whether anybody had been on duty the night before.

3

THE LOUD, INSISTENT BUZZING brought Carolyn out of a deep sleep. Still drifting between her dream world and reality, she first thought her alarm clock had mistakenly gone off at 5 A.M. She swatted at the on/off switch, but the piercing noise continued. It took her a full minute to realize someone in the first-floor hallway was pushing her buzzer.

Stumbling from bed in her peach-colored, see-through nightie, Carolyn made it to the living room and pushed the talk button on her intercom.

"Yes, who is it?" she asked, a touch of anger appearing in her voice as she began to realize just how early it was and how much sleep the person in the lobby had probably cost her.

"Miss Warmus? This is Detective John Bonaiuto and Detective Robert Whiting from the Greenburgh Police Department. We're here on official police business. May we come up and talk with you?"

The strong, authoritative voice booming from the box slapped away the last of the cobwebs from Carolyn's head. She pushed another button on the box, which released the electronic lock on the glass door four floors below. She hurried into her bedroom and put on her blue silk robe, the one her father had gotten her as gift on his last trip to the Orient, and slid her feet into a pair of worn slippers.

Carolyn walked back into the living room and peered out through the peephole. Unless these guys wore uniforms and badges she wasn't opening that door. This was New York and she wasn't a fool. She waited several minutes until she heard the purr of the elevator stop and the clanking of the doors as they spread apart. A few seconds later came the knock.

"Miss Warmus? It's Detectives Bonaiuto and Whiting."

Carolyn looked through the security device, saw the badge being held up to the peephole, and slowly unlocked her door. The two men stepped cautiously into the apartment, their right hands hovering near the .38-caliber standard issues hanging off their hips underneath their full-length winter coats. Although this was supposed to be a routine pickup for questioning back at the station, it was still a murder case they were investigating and to them everyone was a potential suspect. Experience had taught them that caution was always the best policy.

Before arriving at Warmus's apartment, the two detectives had stopped at Manhattan's 19th Precinct and found the officer in charge. Procedure called for them to ask for a uniformed cop to accompany them. After almost an hour, a desk sergeant told them it would take a while longer for a uniform to show up, and Bonaiuto and Whiting decided to leave. A patrol cop would meet them in front of Warmus's apartment in about fifteen minutes, the sergeant promised.

After driving to the building and waiting twenty minutes for a patrol car to arrive, the two Greenburgh detectives decided to ignore policy and pay Warmus a visit without the backup.

Finding the address on First Avenue hadn't been easy. Manhattan, especially the Upper East Side, isn't noted for having large block address numbers on each building and doorway. And with pitch darkness enveloping the city at 5 A.M., the five-inch-high black numbers on the glass door leading into Carolyn Warmus's apartment building might just as well have been invisible.

Finally locating the building on the west side of First Avenue, between Seventy-eighth and Seventy-ninth streets, Bonaiuto noted that the neighborhood wasn't exactly Fifth Avenue, but not too shabby either. It was an area diverse in its ethnic flavor, made up mainly of young professional whites, blacks, and Hispanics. While a tourist strolling down the avenue might not be overly impressed with the usual string of delis, Chinese restaurants, and video stores, the detectives knew the rent for an apartment here was more than their Greenburgh police salaries would allow. They finally located Carolyn's apartment door between Fador Jewelers and the Bangkok House restaurant.

Once invited inside, Bonaiuto and Whiting wasted no time.

"Miss Warmus, there has been an incident involving a Mr. Paul Solomon late last night and we'd like you to come up to the Greenburgh Police Department to answer a few questions. Do you mind getting dressed and coming with us?" Before she could answer, Whiting told her he had to read her her rights. "It's only routine," he assured her.

Carolyn stared at the two officers from her perch on the end of the sofa. "Is Paul all right? Did anything happen to him?" she asked.

"Mr. Solomon is okay. We just need you to come with us to answer some questions," Whiting replied.

"Is it Kristan? Was she in some kind of accident?"

The cops assured her they were both fine. Carolyn gave an exaggerated sigh of relief.

"There's been a murder, Miss Warmus," Bonaiuto said, watching her reaction to the news. "Betty Jeanne Solomon was killed several hours ago. Did you know Mrs. Solomon?"

"Yes, I knew her," Warmus replied without emotion. "Of course, I don't mind going with you. I'll be ready in a minute."

She stood up and walked up a flight of steps to her bedroom to change. The policemen caught each other's eyes as Carolyn passed by. They found it interesting that she had first asked about everyone in the Solomon family except Betty Jeanne. But it wasn't their job at that moment to figure out whether Carolyn Warmus had anything to do with the murder. As far as they knew, she was just a witness. Bonaiuto knew he would get a chance to question her further back at headquarters. But the job of finding out who the real killer was belonged to Constantino and Lind. They were just the chauffeurs this morning.

As they stood waiting, they looked over the apartment; contemporary furniture, expensive-looking prints, and a collection of African masks hanging on the walls . . . state-of-the-art stereo system. Then Carolyn emerged from the bedroom. She was still wearing her robe, only this time the belt was a little looser and the top had fallen open, giving both men a delightful look at her ample figure. Carolyn caught their eyes as they glanced at her and smiled.

"I'm sorry. I didn't ask you guys if you wanted something to drink. A soda, coffee, or something?"

The detectives thanked her, but said no. They were anxious to get on the road for the forty-five minute drive back to the station.

A knock at the door startled Warmus, who appeared even more surprised when the visitors turned out to be two New York City uniformed cops.

Stepping inside, the patrolmen saw the two detectives standing in the living room. "We were told to come over here to see if you guys were all right," the younger officer said, glancing at Warmus. "Sorry we're so late, but we were on another call when they radioed us."

Bonaiuto shook his head, waving the men outside, concerned they were beginning to frighten Warmus. "No, we're fine. Appreciate you stopping by, but there's no problem." The cops waved back as they walked into the hallway and headed for the elevator.

"Just so you know, Miss Warmus, it's routine procedure to request a uniformed police officer to accompany us whenever we're outside our jurisdiction," Bonaiuto explained, hoping she wouldn't change her mind and refuse to go with them.

Carolyn smiled but said nothing as she went back upstairs to her bedroom. Once more noticing the curvaceous figure of their witness through her partially opened robe, the detectives looked at one another and rolled their eyes.

In the other room, Carolyn quickly put on a tight pair of jeans and a pink pullover sweater. Ten minutes later they were in the patrol car heading north.

Lind and Constantino were tired when they arrived at the station on their way back from the Scarsdale Ridge Apartments for the second time in the last twenty-four hours. They walked into the squad room and filled in their counterparts about Paul Solomon's statements earlier that morning. They snorted when Constantino told them how Solomon had lied about his alibi and finally coughed up his affair and the details of his sexual acrobatics with Warmus not seven hours before.

Constantino knew that Bonaiuto and Whiting were out searching for Warmus at that moment. If they found her, Bonaiuto—considered an excellent interrogator—would get first crack at questioning her.

Constantino took a swig of lukewarm coffee and began to sort out the reports he had just been given on the Betty Jeanne Solomon homicide. He was grumpy that morning; usually was when he had to be up all night. He reached over to the far left corner of his desk and ripped off the old calendar page revealing the big block-lettered date, January 16. What a great way to start off the new year, he grumbled.

Downstairs, several uniformed cops hung around the front desk, laughing about the story of Paul Solomon, Carolyn Warmus, and the blowjob in the Hyundai. Cops were notorious for being sexually explicit in their humor and this case so far had given them some first-rate new material. It had only taken a few minutes for the story to shoot through the department after the first cops returned from the scene.

Several of the cops hoped to catch a look at Warmus. They knew the jokes could only get better if you had a good description of the woman involved. Besides, there wasn't much else happening that early on a Monday morning.

At about 6 A.M., Bonaiuto and Whiting, with Warmus tucked in the back seat, pulled into the police station driveway off Tarrytown Road and drove around the back of the two-story building, which sat high on a hill overlooking the town of Greenburgh.

They got out of the car and entered the back door. Their attractive cargo was led through a musty basement corridor and up two flights of stairs to the detectives' squad room, where she was led to Bonaiuto's desk. He motioned for her to take a seat.

She looked around the large room and noticed a few desks lined against one wall and several more arranged together in the middle. Near the door were what appeared to be some lockers, similar to the ones in the girls' and boys' shower room at the Bedford Road Elementary School where she taught. A few Most Wanted posters were taped to the dirty, white walls.

She noticed the looks from some of the men seated at their desks and quickly realized she was the main attraction for the day. The thought didn't appear to displease her.

Bonaiuto sat down, and after finally finding a pen that worked, began to fill out the top of a DD1 report.

"This is routine and we have to do it with everybody we talk with," Bonaiuto explained, hoping his soft approach would put Warmus at ease.

"I haven't done anything wrong so I don't mind answering your questions," she responded. "Just ask me what you want and I'll try to tell you what I can." She smiled warmly, once more sizing Bonaiuto up and finally deciding she could handle him without too much trouble.

Bonaiuto excused himself when his desk phone rang, and after a few minutes of conversation, he asked Warmus to follow him downstairs to a large conference room.

Assistant District Attorney Kevin Kennedy stood up as the pair walked in. After taking a seat, she smiled at the men and said she didn't object to their using a tape recorder.

For the next several hours, Warmus answered scores of questions, sometimes responding a little too quickly for Bonaiuto's liking. Also, as the questioning continued, she began to ramble and some of her answers became a little disjointed. He got the feeling that the woman in front of him was carefully weighing each of her responses and was trying too hard to paint Paul Solomon as one hell of a nice guy.

Referring to her conversations with Paul Solomon both on the telephone and at dinner the day before, Bonaiuto asked Warmus whether they were of any importance.

"Well, he did mention that, you know, he asked before at the apartment about our future together and he had, but not necessarily involved . . . terms but we will be together, it will be opposite."

"Meaning opposite, what do you mean?" Bonaiuto asked, puzzled.

"Well, in the car he said that it was difficult for him, I mean from what I know he's a very moral, nice person and he feels guilty seeing me or being married and seeing me or whatever it is. I can't speak for him exactly, but he says he feels better about it and to deal with it, you know, he's completely up front with me and honest—as we have been from the start. And he said, you know, that I love my wife, and he does—"

Bonaiuto interrupted. "Did he say he loved his wife?"

"Uh huh."

"Tonight he said that?"

Warmus paused. "Ah, I can't remember, he may have. I don't know if it was just in my mind . . . but ah, you know whether he, you know he would never get, well, I don't know exactly what he said tonight."

Bonaiuto pursued the thought. "I just want to know what he was referring to."

Warmus's voice took on a testiness that caused the detective to look up from his note pad.

"So he wanted me to know that we wouldn't be together, he just couldn't see it in our future. I mean, not that we might not date—we might continue dating and we might be the best of friends—but he said even if he gets divorced he and Kristan . . . even if he gets divorced he can't think he'll ever get married, from what he said tonight."

"Did anything else happen in the car between you?"

Again she hesitated, unsure of what Paul may already have told the nosy detective. "In terms that in fact we were fooling around?"

"Yes, was there any sexual intercourse?" Bonaiuto asked point-blank. The other detectives in the room held their breath, pretending to study something on their desks, but really straining to hear Warmus's response.

"No," she said, with a defiant look on her face.

Bonaiuto decided to press. "Was there any other type of sexual activity?"

Carolyn reddened slightly. "Yes." Not looking particularly uncomfortable, she began to tell the detective about the previous night's activities. She didn't leave out many details. During her story, no one at the table noticed that the tape recorder had stopped.

Although the questioning continued for a couple more hours, Bonaiuto pretty much had what he wanted: Warmus's first statements about where she was during the day of the murder, the telephone call to Solomon, the dinner, and then sex in the car.

Since Warmus told him she was at home all day in her apartment before she left to meet her lover in Yonkers and hadn't talked to anyone besides him, she really didn't have any alibi. But as far as Bonaiuto was concerned, Carolyn Warmus was still just a witness in the case, and his money was still riding on the husband.

Time would now be the detectives' best ally, he knew. Warmus would be questioned again the next day, and at different times after that, to see if her story remained the same.

One of the first lessons taught in the police academy is that over a period of time people won't tell the exact same story twice if they are lying. Nobody's memory is that good. A person telling the truth about something usually keeps to the same story. It becomes indelibly etched in his mind. A liar constantly has to work at remembering everything he or she has said to keep the story straight. For most people it is just too much work and they usually ended up trapping themselves with their lies.

Bonaiuto thanked Warmus for her time and asked her to return the following morning for further questions. Although they needed a written statement from Warmus, he decided it could wait until the next day.

The detective told her that he and Whiting would drive her back home, so Warmus stood up and began buttoning her coat.

During the trip home, she was already thinking about whom she should contact. One person immediately came to mind. Vincent Parco had to be called. He knew about this sort of thing.

Of course her father would have to know, which meant his corporate attorney, Paul Rosenbaum, would probably handle it. She wondered if her father was back from Florida yet with that bimbo of a wife.

Warmus fought back the anger that always shot through her whenever she thought about the painted, money-grubbing bitch that had completely fooled her father into thinking he loved her. It had been about twenty years since Daddy had unceremoniously dumped Mother for that whore of a secretary, falling for her cutesy, high-pitched voice and sequined, slit dresses.

She forced the unpleasant thoughts from her mind, making herself concentrate on the problem at hand. Betty Jeanne's murder would put a whole new slant on her relationship with Paul.

For the entire trip she sat staring out the window in silence.

Constantino and Lind spent most of Monday morning talking with Solomon, who, no matter how hard they pushed, wouldn't waver from his story. They wondered what the bearded schoolteacher would say if he knew that his sex partner from the night before was downstairs at that very minute being questioned so his alibi could be checked.

Tired, confused, and numb, Solomon finally thought to ask the cops if he could call a friend. Constantino and Lind looked at each other with dismay, realizing the friend was probably a lawyer. If so, it was only a matter of time before they would be forced to end their questioning of the man they were certain killed his wife.

As soon as Solomon had spoken with Pillersdorf, his attorney/golf partner/best friend pulled off his pajamas, dressed quickly, and mumbled good-bye to his sleepy wife, Diane.

He drove away from his Scarsdale home still uncertain what type of trouble Paul was in. The early morning telephone call from some Lieutenant Sullivan came back to him as a garbled memory. At the time he received that call he'd decided it was too early to call Paul. Now several hours later, he had some idea what was going on, but he still wasn't certain. The Solomons had been the Pillersdorfs' best friends since the lawyer and his family had moved into Westchester County about five years before. Diane and he did almost everything with Paul and Betty Jeanne, and even their daughters had become best friends.

Pillersdorf felt a cold, creeping sickness stir in the pit of his stomach as he thought back to Paul's rambling phone call and remembered that his friend had said something about Betty Jeanne being dead.

"It can't be," he said out loud, trying to concentrate on his driving. His own sleepiness and Paul's tired, slurred speech had left him wondering what had really happened. Everything seemed so surreal. The blaring horn of a passing car brought him back to the present and made him realize he had forgotten to turn on his headlights. He flicked the switch and sped to the Greenburgh Police Department with a growing dread.

While the detectives might not have been happy to see the lawyer,

Solomon had never seen so welcome a face in all his life. After hearing the frightening details of Betty Jeanne's murder from his friend, Pillersdorf tried to convince him to stop talking with the police.

"No, Gary. I'm telling them everything I know. I don't have anything to hide. If it will help them catch Betty Jeanne's killer I have to help."

Solomon left his lawyer in the first-floor lobby and returned upstairs to the detectives' squad room. Constantino and Lind wasted no time pulling out a sheet of paper and hammering their suspect harder than ever.

"Make it easy on yourself, Paul," Lind began. "We know you did it, and it will go a lot easier on you and your daughter if you just tell us how and why you did it."

Solomon turned red. The anger that he had kept bottled up inside through the night now began to bubble over. "What, how can you say that to me?" he shouted back. "I didn't kill my wife. What are you trying to do to me?"

Pillersdorf, deciding to make another attempt at persuading Solomon to return home with him for some rest before talking further with the cops, bounded up the one flight of stairs and stopped at the doorway to the squad room. The sight of his friend's contorted, pained expression told him what was happening, even if he hadn't heard the detectives' accusations.

"That's enough," Pillersdorf said with authority. "I will not allow you to ask any more questions. Can't you see that he's in shock?"

Grabbing Solomon by the arm and pulling him to his feet, Pillersdorf assured the miffed detectives that his client would talk with them later. "But since he is obviously distraught over what has happened, further questions will just have to wait."

Sullivan made one last try. "Mr. Pillersdorf, it may help your client if he would just give us a signed statement about what he has already discussed with us."

Pillersdorf politely, but sternly, refused the request. Even though he was a civil attorney and had never practiced criminal law in his life, he knew better than to let a client sign anything for the police, especially only hours after such a horrible and shocking experience.

"We definitely want to cooperate with you," Pillersdorf said, looking at Sullivan. "And Paul will answer your questions, but not now. Just so we understand each other, Paul is not to be questioned by anyone without me being present. And he will not answer repetitive questions. He will answer your questions once and only once."

Pillersdorf knew the old police trick of asking and reasking questions in an effort to get a suspect to slip up by changing his story, and he was determined Paul wouldn't be subjected to it. Even an innocent man could make a mistake about a fact of time or his exact whereabouts, and he was convinced Paul had nothing to do with Betty Jeanne's murder.

"Let me ask you one thing, Lieutenant," the lawyer said, once more turning toward Sullivan. "Exactly how was Mrs. Solomon murdered? If she was shot, how many times?"

Sullivan stared back at Pillersdorf. Keeping an even tone, he responded, "I'm sorry, but that information is privileged and can't be disclosed at this time. When we can tell you something, we'll let you know."

Pillersdorf turned and grabbed Paul's arm, hustling him out the door and, knowing the Solomons' condo would have been sealed as a crime scene, he took his almost incoherent friend home with him. Kristan would be back from her ski trip later that day and Pillersdorf decided they would both stay with his family until they could go home.

The thought of Paul having to tell Kristan about her mother brought tears to his eyes, but he blinked them back several times.

The answers to the questions he had asked the police would be revealed soon enough. He knew he could find out how many times Betty Jeanne had been shot by asking the man at the funeral home who would prepare the body. But for now he would just have to be strong for Paul.

Bothered that their suspect had been whisked away, the investigators went back to their desks and reviewed the notes they had made from the statements they were able to pry out of Solomon. Sullivan had also ordered them to keep Solomon under surveillance when they weren't busy following other leads, and later that night they intended to begin.

They had succeeded in obtaining the names of Paul and Betty Jeanne's friends in the Scarsdale Ridge complex, names and telephone numbers of co-workers at their respective jobs, and those of anyone else that Solomon thought might be able to provide him with an alibi for the last day of his wife's life.

The new widower had told the detectives that friends of his, Hope Rosenthal, Laura Bertuch, and Walter and Doris Sekinski, would vouch for his time at the bowling alley. Carolyn Warmus and the staff at the Treetops Restaurant in Yonkers could swear he was there that night.

The detectives knew it would take days, maybe even weeks to speak with everyone involved. There was still the Solomons' and Warmus's phone records to get, ballistic tests to run, and blood samples to cross match. The ball was rolling, but it rolled slowly.

There wasn't any pressure from the chief yet. He had flown to Syracuse that morning and wasn't expected back for a couple days. The tired investigators poured over their notes, waiting for Bonaiuto to finish his session with Warmus.

Neither detective was certain at that point precisely when their victim had been killed.

Several miles away and at that very moment, Dr. Louis Roh, the deputy county medical examiner, was taking a small, razor-sharp scalpel and expertly slicing open the body of Betty Jeanne Solomon. Roh's job was to determine not only the specific cause of death—there wasn't much doubt about that—but also an approximate time of death.

Armed with that information, it would be only a matter of time before the detectives narrowed the list of suspects and their alibis down to a manageable number. Eventually they would pare those down to only one, and that one should be their killer.

Roh was well respected for his precise autopsy reports. His Oriental accent coupled with a great sense of humor made him a favorite of the Greenburgh police. Although Lind and Constantino were in a hurry for the results, Roh didn't like to be rushed. He promised to call them when his report was completed. Exhausted from their twenty-four-hour shift, the detectives headed home at 11 P.M. for some much needed sleep.

Several hundred miles north, in Syracuse, Singer and Kelleher took a break from their National Guard investigation and drove about five miles to the home of Brian Solomon, Paul's thirty-nine-year-old brother.

When the chief had checked in with Sullivan earlier that day, he was updated on developments in the case, including the interrogations of Paul Solomon and Carolyn Warmus. Sullivan had already run down the locations of their relatives, and when Singer learned Solomon's brother lived only a short distance away in North Syracuse, he decided to take a drive and ask him a few questions.

When they arrived at the small, one-story ranch, no one answered the knock on the door. Singer and Kelleher decided to have some dinner, and when they returned Brian and his wife were at home.

Paul had called them about Betty Jeanne's murder, and they both appeared dazed by the news. After twenty minutes of questioning it was clear that the couple would not be able to shed any light on what had happened.

"Wait a minute, Chief, there is something I can show you," Brian said, hurrying from the comfortable living room. In a moment he was back with two Ruger handguns and the permits to go with them.

"These used to be Paul's when he was in the military, but after he got out he turned them in to the sheriff's department up here as the law requires. He never went back to pick them up, and years ago I got Paul to sign them over to me. I've had them ever since. I don't think Paul ever had any guns in his house, what with Kristan and everything."

Singer examined the weapons and permits and finally apologized for the intrusion. As he and Kelleher left, Singer made a mental note to call Sullivan the next day and report the conversation.

A cold, yet sunny Tuesday brought Carolyn Warmus back to the station. She hadn't appreciated the police telephoning her that morning at school and reminding her they wanted to take a written statement. If her supervisors ever got wind of what she was involved with, her career as a fifth-grade computer teacher in the Pleasantville School District would undoubtedly be over.

Turning down Bonaiuto's offer to have her picked up and driven to the station, she drove herself in the same red Hyundai that was the focus of the sex jokes still being bandied about in the basement locker room.

To keep her off-balance, Whiting, a nine-year veteran who'd spent the last three as a detective, was assigned to do the questioning that day. Later, he would compare his notes with Bonaiuto's to check Warmus's story from the day before. It wouldn't be the first time a suspect's facts changed with her inquisitor.

Besides, Bonaiuto had told him that morning that he felt Warmus was holding back and not telling everything she knew. Just a cop's gut instinct, he'd said. Whiting knew his co-worker to be a sharp detective. Bonaiuto's instincts were good enough for him.

Several hours later, Whiting was convinced Bonaiuto had been on target once again. It wasn't anything that Warmus had told him, it was the way she gave her answers.

From the moment she sat down and he flipped on the old black Sony tape recorder, Warmus remained steadfast in her assertion that she knew nothing of the murder. It wasn't that. It was the care with which she seemed to answer some of the questions, and she was thinking three steps ahead to avoid being caught up in some earlier lie. She was sharp, Whiting thought to himself. A very intelligent girl. The word *conniving* also came to mind.

During that day's questioning, Warmus asked Whiting if she could use the telephone. "I have a tutoring session scheduled for six o'clock and I don't think I can make it now even if you were finished asking questions. I'll have to call to cancel."

The detective apologized and moved his telephone nearer the attractive teacher. He got up to get a cup of coffee and give her some privacy.

Later that afternoon, Whiting asked Warmus to say in her own words what she remembered happening on the night of the murder. With the tape recorder running, he also pulled a piece of plain, white paper from a drawer, inserted it in his typewriter, and nodded for her to begin. Twenty minutes later, Whiting finished typing and handed the two sheets of paper to Warmus. "Read this and see if it is an accurate report of what you've told us," he said. Carolyn took the papers and read:

"My name is Carolyn Warmus. I live at 1485 First Avenue, New York, New York, 10021. My date of birth is January 8, 1964. On Sunday, January 15, 1989, at about 3:30 P.M., I called Paul Solomon at his home phone . . . from my home phone, phone number 212-737-7367. I think Paul answered the phone. I didn't know if his wife was home. If she answered the phone I would have known she was home. Paul and I spoke about Kristan playing on the basketball team and when I could come and watch a game. We spoke about the bar mitzvah he had attended the day before and that Kristan had gone away skiing for the weekend. We spoke about my birthday and why we had not gone out for it. We spoke about going to the Chart House for a belated birthday present. Paul said that it couldn't be until after basketball. I said fine. We also spoke about school. The conversation lasted about forty-five minutes. During the conversation I don't recall any background noises coming from the apartment. We ended the conversation with Paul asking if I would like to see him that night. I said, really? Paul then said that please understand, there may be other times I can't get away. I said okay, but are you feeling okay? Paul then said no, but I want to see you. Paul then said, same place. I then said, the Holiday Inn? Paul said yes, about 7:30 P.M. I said thanks and we ended this conversation. I arrived at the Holiday Inn on Tuckahoe Road in Yonkers at 7:30 P.M. I met Paul at the bar. We had a few drinks and spoke about many things. We spoke about Paul's wife. Paul said that she was unhappy about him going bowling. Paul stated that he had stopped at the bowling alley prior to coming here and that he had met Hope, Laura, Tony and I think Tony's relative. I asked him did they think you were stopping by the bowling alley to say hello or did they know that you were meeting me? I usually meet Paul every Sunday night after he bowls. We left the bar at about 10:30 P.M. We went to the parking lot and got into my car. We had sexual activity in my car. I was with Paul in the parking lot until about 11:30 P.M., at which time Paul got into his car and followed me out. I last saw Paul making a left turn onto Tuckahoe Road. While we were in the car Paul stated to me that he wanted me to be happy, we are best friends."

Warmus looked up and told Whiting it was accurate, except she wanted to add one other thing. After the detective placed the second page of the statement back in the typewriter, Warmus dictated: "Paul's wife didn't want him to go out bowling because he had been sick."

Saying she was now satisfied with the statement, Whiting pulled the paper from the machine and signed both sheets. Once again he asked Warmus to read it. When she told him it was an accurate report of what she had said, he handed her a pen and she also signed the bottom of both pages.

Taking the papers from Warmus, Whiting told her, "Look, I know this can be pretty time-consuming and a pain, but we may want to talk with you again sometime, just so you know."

She gave an exaggerated look of exasperation, but said nothing. Whiting thanked her for her time and Warmus once again left the station for the rush-hour ride back home.

Later that evening, Lind and Constantino drove back to the Scarsdale Ridge Apartments and began the tedious task of interviewing residents to see if they had heard or seen anything suspicious on Sunday.

Constantino thought he'd hit pay dirt on his first try. Michael and Rosie Reilly, who lived in the apartment right below the Solomons', hadn't been home the day before. Michael's story was interesting indeed.

"I was half-asleep that night, I'm not sure exactly what time it was, but I heard some banging noise and I remember thinking the woman above me had fallen and died," Reilly said. "I then heard a set of footsteps running down the stairs. I didn't hear anything else and I finally went back to sleep. I never went upstairs to check and I never looked outside to see who it was that was running out that night. I'm sorry. That's all I know."

Jotting down the information, Constantino knew it was important, but also realized that since Reilly hadn't seen who it was running out of the building, it still left them with a mystery to solve.

Meanwhile, directly upstairs, Lind was busy installing a hasp and lock on the Solomons' door to keep out unwanted visitors, including Paul Solomon and his daughter.

Detective Robert Whiting would have known without being told that Josette Tilden was a teacher. She had that quiet, polite manner and, well, she just looked like a teacher. In fact she had taught sixth grade in Yonkers for the past sixteen years.

Seating himself in the living room of her comfortable Scarsdale home, Whiting declined her offer of coffee and pressed ahead. "Mrs. Tilden, we received a call from Gary Pillersdorf yesterday," he said. "He told us you had called him with some information you wanted us to know about the death of Mrs. Solomon. I understand you and the Solomons were very close. Can you tell me please what it is you'd like us to know?"

Whiting recalled the conversation he'd had with Pillersdorf the day before. The lawyer had been positive that Tilden's information would clear his client.

Now looking up, he could see the woman was still emotionally upset over the murder of her friend but had something she wanted to say.

"On Sunday night," she responded, "I called Betty Jeanne twice. We were trying to get our plans together about our husbands going to see a basketball game. I just thought you would want to know that I spoke with her."

Whiting sat up in his chair, realizing that the woman before him could help them at least narrow down the time of death.

"Mrs. Tilden, what time did you call Mrs. Solomon?"

Wrinkling her brow as she thought back to the night she was now trying to forget, Tilden began recounting as best she could the events of that evening to give her a better fix on the time of the phone calls. "I would say I first called her between 7 and 7:15 P.M. and we talked for about fifteen minutes. The second call was approximately 8 P.M. and we only spoke for a few minutes, I'd say five minutes at the most. That's all I really know."

Whiting knew he had to push harder. "Mrs. Tilden, I know this is difficult, but try to remember. During either phone call did you hear anything or anyone in the background, or did she say she was there with someone?"

"No, I don't believe so," came the answer. "I believe she told me Paul was out bowling, but that's about it. Betty Jeanne didn't sound upset or scared or anything while I was talking with her. It was just a normal conversation. I'm sorry. I don't know if I've been any help."

Whiting closed his notebook and smiled. "You've been a big help, Mrs. Tilden. All information is important. We'll be in touch if we come up with any more questions. If you think of something else, please don't hesitate to call."

Walking to his car, Whiting knew he had just received some valuable information that could very well prove or disprove the alibi of their prime suspect. Now that they knew Betty Jeanne Solomon was alive at least as late as 8 P.M. and was first reported dead by her husband at about 11:40 P.M., the window was narrowing.

The next obvious step would be to reexamine everyone's alibi. If Paul Solomon was at the Yonkers restaurant at 7:30 P.M., maybe Pillersdorf was right and he couldn't have shot his wife.

Tilden's calls were a lucky break, he thought, as he headed back to the station.

At the same moment Whiting was completing his interview with Tilden, Detective John Parks was speaking to the victim's mother and father, Robert and Jean Torrey, at their home in Mansfield, Massachusetts, while Sullivan was on the phone with Betty Jeanne's sister, Joyce Green, whom he had finally managed to reach at her residence in Levittown, New York.

The long conversation with the victim's sister provided no help to the tired lieutenant, as Green was unable to think of anyone who might have wanted Betty Jeanne dead.

"About the only other thing I can tell you about Paul is that for the past few months he thought he had cancer, but he finally went to a doctor who told him recently that it was only a case of stress-related colitis."

Sullivan offered his condolences to Green and hung up. He couldn't hold back a chuckle as he thought about his suspect's medical condition.

"I always felt Paul Solomon was a pain in the ass, now I know why," he joked to one of the patrolmen who had walked into his office.

The next day at about three o'clock, Bonaiuto and Whiting walked into the main office of the Bedford Road Elementary School, the same building where Warmus taught. Identifying themselves to the school's principal, they were directed to Carolyn's second-floor classroom.

Sitting at her desk grading papers, the last of her students having just left for the day, Warmus was first surprised and then angered as the two detectives she had silently dubbed Mutt and Jeff strode into the room.

"What is it now?" she asked, trying but not succeeding in keeping the disdain from her voice. "I just gave you guys a signed statement yesterday and here you are again. I don't want my bosses knowing about any of this. I'm sure you realize that it could cost me my job. I'm trying to be cooperative, but you're not making this easy. What do you want now?"

With just the right apologetic tone, Whiting explained that they needed to ask her a few more questions at the station. "Do you mind helping us out? I'm sure you realize how serious this is."

Warmus stared at the men and decided to play along. Flashing a wide smile, the buxom schoolteacher stood up and stretched her arms. "Of course I want to help," she said, pushing her anger below the surface. "But I don't need a ride. I'll drive to the station myself in about an hour. Is that okay?"

Bonaiuto and Whiting both nodded, and after apologizing again, left Warmus alone with her thoughts. Once they were gone, she walked down the hall to the graffiti-filled pay phone.

Warmus arrived at the police station wearing a tight denim miniskirt with a sheer, peach-colored blouse covered by an unzipped ski jacket. When she was escorted to the detectives' squad room, Bonaiuto noted Warmus had changed her clothes. The new outfit was in stark contrast to the long, white, and loose-fitting dress they had seen her in earlier.

Warmus wasted no time in telling Bonaiuto and Whiting she was finished answering questions without her lawyer present.

Realizing the law required him to end the questioning at that point, even though she was not a suspect in the murder, Whiting told Warmus he would be in touch and watched as she sashayed through the room and out the door.

An hour later, his phone rang and a man who identified himself as Paul Rosenbaum told the detective he was a lawyer now representing Miss Warmus and that she should not be questioned unless he was present.

Whiting hung up the phone wondering what had triggered Warmus's abrupt turn around. She had been fairly cooperative up until that point. Maybe she'd just got too tired of the drive to Greenburgh.

Following the two detectives through the doorway on Wednesday afternoon, Pillersdorf both dreaded and felt compelled to see the inside of the home where he and his wife had shared so many pleasant occasions.

He was followed by a grim-looking entourage. Paul had his arm around Kristan, and for a second Pillersdorf wondered why his friend had finally agreed to let her come with them. Paul's friends, Ron Caruso and Jim and Christine Maslak, were there for moral support, but Pillersdorf knew that, like him, they were all pulled by a morbid curiosity.

"I appreciate you guys letting us inside," the lawyer said to Sullivan and Lind as he ducked under the police tape. "We needed to get a dress for Betty Jeanne, and Paul and Kristan have run out of clothes and there's no telling how much longer you plan on keeping this place sealed up."

Sullivan turned and searched Pillersdorf's face for some sign of sarcasm. Finding none, he pointed down a hallway and motioned the group to walk ahead.

Over an hour later, when Paul and Kristan had packed their car with clothes and received permission to take some cash, jewelry, a checkbook, and a briefcase, Pillersdorf asked Sullivan's okay to see the room where the murder had taken place.

"I'd really just like to take a look to satisfy some questions in my own mind," he said. Sullivan shot a glance at Lind, who shrugged his shoulders and nodded at the lawyer. The men walked single file back into the home.

The phone receiver on the floor in the kitchen made Pillersdorf stop and catch his breath. He hesitated taking the next few steps into the living room, for he could already see the taped outline on the bloodstained carpet where his friend's body had fallen.

Forcing himself forward, he instantly realized that the killer must have stood in the very same place while shooting Betty Jeanne. White powder was everywhere, he noted, courtesy of the fingerprint team.

Try as he might, he couldn't keep his eyes from returning to the spot where Betty Jeanne had fallen. He could feel that morning's breakfast starting to churn deep in his stomach. Perspiration began to stain his shirt and he wondered why he was sweating in the ice-cold room.

Without a word, he spun around and walked out the way he had come, not caring about the exchange of smiles between Sullivan and Lind. Betty Jeanne had been his friend, not theirs, and the pain of her death touched him deeply. In that second he hated everything, including Sullivan's and Lind's phony, macho cop bullshit, life's consummate unfairness, but most of all the putrid scum who had stood there and pulled the trigger. Of only one thing was he sure at that moment. It hadn't been Paul.

When the group finally drove out of the parking lot, Sullivan thought for a moment and then asked Lind if he recalled the words Solomon had used to describe Carolyn Warmus when he was interviewed earlier that day at Pillersdorf's home.

"Yeah, I remember him saying she was 'emotional' and 'sometimes crazy.' Why, you make something of that?"

Sullivan shook his head. "No. Just thinking. That's all. Just thinking."

The next several days found Lind and Constantino interviewing dozens of friends, acquaintances, and relatives of the Solomons. A picture began to emerge of Paul and Betty Jeanne Solomon's life, and for the most part, the detectives agreed, it was pretty much the same as that of any other middle-aged couple. Delving deeper into their victim's past, the pair obtained a profile of a woman who began her life as a happy, carefree child.

Born May 6, 1948, Betty Jeanne was the first child of Robert and Jean Torrey. She was a healthy, brown-eyed little girl, who became the center of her parents' universe. The eventual arrival of three more children didn't seem to bother Betty Jeanne, who loved to play house and dress-up with her siblings.

Her early childhood was enhanced by the wonders of the New England seasons: sledding down snow-covered hillsides or swimming in cool, still ponds, taking long autumn walks along tree-lined paths exploding in blazes of color. The bubbly seven-year-old kept her sunny disposition even after her father, a salesman for the Honeywell Corporation, announced in 1955 that he had accepted a job in New York and was moving the family to the small town of Blauvelt, located just west of the Tappan Zee Bridge that was being built at that time.

Life in Blauvelt was one unending performance for Betty Jeanne, who found her creative niche singing joyfully in several elementary school musicals. Her mother would often laugh at her talented daughter, who might overreact to a simple request like setting the table as if she were performing the lead role in Joan of Arc.

When Betty Jeanne graduated from Tappan Zee High School in 1966, and enrolled at the State University of New York in New Paltz, she had already made up her mind to marry her high-school sweetheart, Earl.

That dream ended tragically when Earl was killed in a car accident in the winter of her freshman year. JoAnn Frisina, Betty Jeanne's freshman roommate, remembered the long, cold nights filled with tears as BJ worked through her grief.

It was the following spring that Paul Solomon entered her life. Frisina described him to her friends as a driven individual suffering from what she called the small-man's disease. According to her, he was always trying to compensate for his shortness by pretending to be a big man on campus, and often strutted around in a self-induced state of importance.

Frisina disliked her roommate's new boyfriend and told her so. She felt her friend was just latching on to the first male since Earl who showed an interest, but Betty Jeanne ignored her advice to break up with him.

Paul's influence brought about pronounced changes in Betty Jeanne. Instead of the outgoing college student she had been up to that point, she became more introverted, quiet, and reclusive. He insisted she always wear her glasses, and go without makeup, and keep her skirts below the knees.

Frisina often half-jokingly called Paul a Svengali and came to despise him even more when she learned that he had persuaded Betty Jeanne to join a rival sorority, and then ordered her to stop seeing her friend.

In 1969, Betty Jeanne dropped out of SUNY but kept an apartment in New Paltz to be near her lover. Paul, also tired of the college routine and dreaming of a life of adventure, dropped out a short time later and joined the Air Force. In 1970, in a small ceremony in Nyack, they were married.

Within the year Paul was transferred to Alaska, and he and Betty Jeanne tried to make the best of their new home, even though she longed to be back in New England and didn't hesitate to tell him so on many occasions. In 1973, the same year Paul's four-year enlistment was up, Kristan was born.

Six months later, the family moved into the home of Betty Jeanne's parents while Paul returned to school to complete his teaching degree. A year later he landed a job at Greenville Elementary School in the Edgemont School District in Greenburgh.

Shortly after he was hired, Paul moved his family to Harrison, New York. With exorbitant rent payments hanging over them, Betty Jeanne decided to help out and took a job as a teller with the National Bank of Westchester. A good employee and well liked by her supervisors, she worked her way up to bank officer and finally branch manager before she left in 1984 to accept a higher-paying job at the Continental Credit

Corporation in Harrison. Betty Jeanne's salary allowed the couple to save just enough to make a down payment in 1987 on the Scarsdale Ridge condo.

The marriage had had its problems. In 1979, Betty Jeanne went to visit her mother in Blauvelt for a few days and told her she was thinking of leaving Paul.

"It just isn't working. I make just as much money as he does, but he has to be the big cheese, the one who's always in charge," Betty Jeanne complained angrily.

Jean Torrey held her breath and she asked her daughter whether there was another woman. Betty Jeanne smiled and said, "No." When her mother suggested counseling, the frustrated wife responded, "Paul refuses to go."

Jean told her to think about her decision. "It would really be a shame. Don't do anything rash."

In the end, Betty Jeanne decided to give her marriage another chance, and never again mentioned any problems to her family.

The interviews with Paul and Betty Jeanne's friends and families resulted in a small pile of notebooks that Constantino and Lind kept carefully locked up in their file cabinets. When the tired duo finally found time to sit down together in the squad room, each thought he was going to spring on the other some newly gleaned information that would throw their case into a spin.

Lind broke first. "You're not going to believe this, but I have some friends of Betty Jeanne who swear she was also having an affair."

A look of disappointment spread across Constantino's face. "Hell, I picked up the same thing. Did you get any names?"

Lind slowly shook his head. Both men realized that this new development would mean many more days, if not weeks, of interviews and running down dead-end leads before the other man in Betty Jeanne's life—if in fact there was one—was identified.

Neither detective minded. They'd been through enough cases to realize they had to follow the flow no matter where it led. Maybe Paul Solomon didn't have anything to do with the murder. Maybe it was a jealous lover who had gotten tired of waiting for Betty Jeanne to divorce her husband and shot her in a rage. Maybe Betty Jeanne had threatened to reveal their relationship to his wife and the guy flipped. Anything was possible. They'd have to keep plugging and hope for that one big break. It didn't take long.

Greenburgh police dispatcher Marlene Farrell was leafing through an accident report at the front desk on January 19 when the call came in.

"Greenburgh Police Department, Farrell speaking. May I help you?"

The woman's voice on the other end of the line sounded muffled. "I don't want to give my name, but I just thought you should know that Gary Pillersdorf should be investigated in connection with the murder case of Betty Jeanne Solomon." The distinctive click told her the caller had hung up from a pay phone.

Farrell checked the time on the big clock hanging on the wall behind her. She picked up another phone and dialed Sullivan's extension. When the head of the detectives' division answered, she described the mysterious call.

Sullivan knew all incoming calls were tape recorded and he ordered Constantino to make a copy of the tape. When the recording was later played in the squad room, nobody recognized the voice as that of anyone they had interviewed over the past several days.

Lind guessed it was Pillersdorf's wife, pissed off about the affair. Constantino chuckled and said it was probably Warmus trying to throw them off the track. Lind picked up a pencil and jotted Pillersdorf's name down on the top of a new notebook. Anything's possible, he reminded himself.

Pillersdorf was an average-looking guy who didn't really seem the type to be having an affair with one of his clients, Lind thought, as he watched the fifty-two-year-old lawyer walk into a supermarket.

A quick check of the telephone book had revealed that he lived at an address in Scarsdale, so his income couldn't be too shabby. The chief had warned Lind to be careful what he said or did while keeping Pillersdorf under surveillance and questioning people who knew him. The department didn't need an angry lawyer making trouble for them by claiming harassment, especially one who was representing their prime suspect in a murder case. Lind had been told to play it low key and he willingly obliged.

At another meeting with Solomon on January 23 at Pillersdorf's home, Sullivan, Lind, and Constantino eyed both men suspiciously, wondering if the victim's husband had ever suspected his lawyer of getting it on with his wife.

"Paul, this is an unpleasant question, but it's one I have to ask," Sullivan started out slowly, carefully masking his eagerness. "Did you ever suspect Betty Jeanne of having an affair, and if so, can you name the guy?"

The angry look that crossed their suspect's face softened after a few moments, replaced by one of dejection and embarrassment.

"I never really knew for sure, but there was a time a few years ago when I thought she might have been seeing an old boss of hers when she worked at the National Bank of Westchester. I think his name was Bourne. John Bourne. But I really don't know for sure. That's the only one I can think of."

The three detectives duly recorded the information on their note pads. The trio had all glanced at Pillersdorf to catch his reaction to Sullivan's question, but his face had remained expressionless. Sullivan proceeded with another line of questioning. A short time later they concluded the interview, telling Solomon they would probably be back soon.

Three weeks later, the same group met in Sullivan's cramped office and agreed that the anonymous tip they had received about Pillersdorf was a dead end. Everyone they'd talked to gave glowing reports about him and considered him a happily married family man. It made the anonymous call all the more strange. Singer told Sullivan to let the lawyer know he had been investigated and allow him to hear the tape. Maybe he could solve the mystery for them.

The next day, Pillersdorf arrived at the station in response to a telephone call from Constantino. He assumed the cops wanted to ask him a few questions about his client and he was glad they had gone through him instead of bothering Solomon. When he was shown into the squad room, he sat down and Lind immediately hit a button on the tape recorder sitting on his desk. "We want you to hear something," he said.

Pillersdorf's eyes grew round, and when the female's voice finished, he stared incredulously at the recorder. "Wait a minute. I know that woman," he almost shouted. "She's a lawyer who used to work for me and my partner when we had our law firm in the city. I can't believe she would do this." Constantino caught Lind's quick wink.

Pillersdorf spent the better part of the next half hour explaining to the detectives that the caller was an attorney who had come to work for him and his partner in their small law firm in Manhattan in 1988. She was apparently angry over the fact that he and his partner had decided to close the firm just months after she had left her other job.

Pillersdorf explained that the decision to close the office was financial and that he had decided to open his own practice in Westchester in order to spend more time with his family.

"Another reason why this woman apparently is angry with me is that

I allowed Paul and his daughter Kristan to stay with me and my family after you guys sealed his home," the lawyer said. "She told me she couldn't understand how I could let a man suspected of murder stay in my house with my children. I knew it bothered her, but I never thought she'd do something like this."

"Where were you the evening of January 15?" Constantino asked, assuring Pillersdorf it was a necessary but routine question.

"I was hooked up to a kidney dialysis machine most of the evening," he said, and gave the detectives the name of his doctor and the hospital where the treatment had taken place.

"Can't have a much better alibi than that." Lind laughed, trying to lighten the mood.

Pillersdorf shook his head, more surprised than angry. He once again gave the investigators the female attorney's name and told them he would provide them with her address and phone number once he returned home to check his records.

A visit the next day to the woman's new office confirmed Pillersdorf's story. While appearing embarrassed, she still maintained that it was unconscionable for her former boss to share his home with a suspected killer. Since she had not given a false report, only asking that Pillersdorf be investigated, the detectives knew they couldn't charge her with anything and left after giving her a stern warning to provide her name the next time she called the police.

On the drive back, Lind and Constantino rehashed their case up to that point. They were back to square one, with Solomon still their primary suspect. And even though Pillersdorf wasn't their man, they both believed Betty Jeanne had had a lover. Maybe it was that Bourne guy, maybe not. It would only be a matter of time before they reeled him in.

The surveillance of Solomon would continue, and Carolyn Warmus's background still needed to be checked. Now, there was an interesting piece of work, they both agreed.

"I don't know if I told you, but Whiting talked this morning with a guy named Jerry Schulman," Constantino said. "He's the principal at Greenville School where Solomon teaches and where he met Warmus. Anyway, Schulman says that when Warmus was teaching there most of the other teachers felt uncomfortable around her. He said they pretty much classified her as 'emotionally disturbed' and 'flaky.'"

Carolyn's history was beginning to yield some interesting items. But neither Lind nor Constantino could yet have guessed just how interesting it would become.

4

NOT MANY THINGS surprised Constantino anymore, but the sight of Carolyn Warmus showing up for Betty Jeanne Solomon's memorial service at the Bennett Funeral Home in Eastchester on January 19 made him shake his head in disbelief.

"This bimbo's got a hell of a lot of nerve," he said out loud, watching her parade inside with a small group of women. He had a great view of her entrance from his car which was positioned so he could observe the coming and going of each mourner. He felt kind of ghoulish, but his job was to keep the place under surveillance, and that's what he intended to do.

When the service ended, and he saw Warmus walk out the door without Paul, he figured they were just trying to play it cool. He wondered whether Solomon even knew she was going to be there.

He shrugged his shoulders. It probably didn't show anything more than bad taste. He started his car and pulled out of the parking lot toward the station. If he hurried and wrote up his report, he could still have most of the day to spend with his family. He pressed a little harder on the accelerator.

The copper-colored casket was carefully lifted off the sculptured pillars that resembled the columns of the Parthenon, placed on a cloth-covered metal gurney, and wheeled outside.

The traditional black hearse was parked beneath the flapping canvas covering the loading dock in back of the funeral home. The driver standing nearby took a last drag from a cigarette as he waited to haul his cargo on the twenty-five-minute ride to Scarsdale.

Dressed in his black funeral tux, he watched as the heavy casket was loaded in back, flowers carefully arranged so passing motorists would see them propped against the windows. When the casket was locked into place and the rear door slammed shut, he threw down the still-lit butt and slid behind the wheel. Pulling away, he hoped the traffic on this Friday wouldn't be too heavy. The woman in back had been murdered only six days ago, and he didn't want her to be late to her own funeral. He smiled at the old joke.

The parking lot of The Church of St. James The Less in Scarsdale was practically empty when the hearse pulled in. Ten minutes later with help from some strong altar boys, the casket was sitting inside the beautiful chapel, sunlight dancing through the stained-glass windows overlooking the polished cedar pews. A churchwoman reverently draped a white linen over the casket and walked back to the vestibule to continue preparing for the morning funeral service.

Paul Solomon entered the church a short time later, dressed in a dark blue suit with a crisply starched white shirt, his highly polished black shoes reflecting the light from the overhead chandeliers. On his arm walked Jean Torrey, wearing a black dress, her reddened, swollen eyes hinting at the sleepless, tear-filled night she had just endured with memories of her daughter.

Behind them walked Robert Torrey and Kristan, who wore a loose-fitting black dress and matching black hat, an outfit the police had allowed her and her father to pick up at home only the day before. She had started to feel nauseous while getting dressed, but she shed no tears —she hadn't yet been able to cry since learning of her mother's murder —because she promised herself she would be strong for her father.

They took their seats in the front row of the church and within the next half hour more than 350 people quietly filed in behind them.

Paul looked around and saw a few of his fellow teachers and dozens of his students. He recognized many other faces, but couldn't remember the names of several of Betty Jeanne's co-workers from the credit office. Many of the people seated behind him he didn't know.

His gaze stopped at one young woman, dressed in black, seated in the rear of the church. He caught his breath as he thought he recognized Carolyn, but when his eyes focused more intently on the woman's face he realized it wasn't her.

Carolyn had shown up for services at the funeral home the night before with a group of other teachers and had wrapped her arms around him, giving him a quick kiss, saying how sorry she was.

It had been a terrible moment for him. He couldn't believe she had actually shown up, and he tried to avoid even so much as eye contact with her for the rest of the evening.

All he could do today was pray she wouldn't come to the funeral. He hoped she'd have the common sense to stay away. He just couldn't handle being near her right now.

No one but the police knew the real story of last Sunday night, and he was counting on the secrecy of their investigation. He'd have a hard time facing anyone, especially Betty Jeanne's family, if the truth ever got out. He turned back around and stared at his wife's coffin.

Solomon turned again to face the front of the church. He never saw Sullivan and Constantino sitting in one of the back pews.

During the funeral mass, Betty Jeanne's sister, Joyce Green, stood up and walked to the lectern, her eyes brimming with tears as she told the gathering about the time her sister had helped her through a personal tragedy—the death of her teen-age son in a car accident.

"Seventeen months ago, my sister stood in another church in another town. She spoke words for my son, words that I couldn't say. She was my strength. I will always love her."

Reaching into her pocket, Joyce Green pulled out a wrinkled piece of paper, saying it was a poem she knew her sister would like.

As quiet sobs rose throughout the church, Joyce read: "Try each day to see the flowers, to laugh, to savor all the hours. Never, never be afraid to die for I am waiting for you in the sky." She crumbled the paper in her hand and silently moved toward her seat, stopping for a moment to run her hand along the white cloth adorning her sister's casket.

Kristan gathered herself and made her way to the now-empty lectern. She looked out over the filled pews and smiled. She rambled for a while about memories of her mother.

"I remember at my basketball games that I would always know when Mom would show up because I would hear above the crowd her distinctive clapping. Also my dad and I would always tease her about what she liked to do every Sunday, read trashy novels. We'd always kid her about it, but she would always tease right back. She always made fun of me and Dad for watching horror movies."

Kristan paused, staring at the lectern as if remembering those happier moments in time, and then she raised her eyes to look over those sitting before her. More quietly than before, she said, "Mom didn't know how many friends she had and how many people loved her. It's nice to see you all here," sending a ripple of tears through the crowd.

Kristan stepped back and waited for her father to come forward. Paul Solomon's face was ashen-gray, his voice filled with emotion. He began by saying how much he loved his wife and how he and Kristan would miss her. He recounted their first years together, the struggles and the good times and the most precious moment of all when Kristan was born. He drifted to the evening before her murder.

"I'll never forget the way Betty looked at a party last Saturday, the night before she died," he said. "I think the picture that I'm always going to have of her is the unique spark and radiance she possessed. Last Saturday she attended a party and this radiance was there. The same radiance that attracted me to her twenty-two years ago."

Paul turned and placed his arm around his daughter, as if steadying himself. Father and daughter returned to their seats and when the service ended, they stood in the doorway of the church and accepted condolences.

When the crowd had dispersed and Paul and Kristan had left together to attend the wake at a friend's home, Betty Jeanne's coffin was once again loaded into the hearse and this time driven to the Ferncliff Cemetery on Secor Road in Hartsdale.

Within the hour, two strong caretakers hoisted the coffin onto a cart and wheeled it inside the building to await cremation later that night.

Carolyn was a little disgusted with Paul as she drove through the dirty, crowded streets of Manhattan on this dreary Friday morning. She had tried to be loving and caring in his time of need the night before in the funeral home, but he had practically ignored her the entire night. A wink or a nod would have been nice, but nothing. After all, she had taken the time to be there for him, the least he could do was appreciate it.

She turned on the radio as she sped through the city after a morning of shopping, having taken a sick day from school. Later that afternoon, she was scheduled to meet with her father's attorney, Paul Rosenbaum, who was flying in from Michigan. Daddy had told her to trust him completely and to do as he said, but she was wary of the plan he had come up with.

When he called the other day and told her not to talk with the police anymore she had told the detectives exactly what he wanted her to say.

She was sure her father believed her when they spoke over the phone, and she swore up and down she didn't know what the hell had happened to Paul's wife.

Daddy nearly had a fit when she first told him about the affair, and when she got to the part about the murder, she thought he was going to have a stroke right there on the telephone. But he eventually calmed down like he always did and now her only concern was getting through this polygraph examination that Rosenbaum had set up.

She was against it from the start, but the attorney had convinced her father that they had nothing to worry about since they were paying for it, and if it came out badly, they were the only ones who would know. It sounded good to her when Rosenbaum explained that the results of a polygraph, or lie detector test, were inadmissible as evidence in court.

On the other hand, if the test came out positive, meaning it showed she was telling the truth about having no involvement in the murder, they could parade it before the Greenburgh cops and district attorney's office to get them off her back. She still didn't like the idea, but her father insisted, and that was that.

Carolyn was surprised to find she was sweating as she pulled up in front of her apartment house to wait for Rosenbaum. She prided herself on putting forth a calm, cool demeanor.

Rosenbaum arrived at 2 P.M. and they discussed the polygraph test while they drove the thirty blocks to the test site at West Fifty-seventh Street. On the way, the lawyer reassured her that everything was going to be fine and that she should just relax.

Carolyn shot him a sharp look. It was easy for him to say relax when it was her neck on the line. Besides, what if something went wrong and the test showed she was lying? How would Daddy react to that? Out loud, she told Rosenbaum she could handle this situation, and had almost convinced herself when she pulled over to the curb and turned off the car.

Several calls to New York attorneys had persuaded Rosenbaum to select polygraph examiner Richard O. Arther of Manhattan to conduct Carolyn's test. Arther's reputation in the field of polygraph examinations was excellent and his firm was known for keeping a strict code of confidentiality whenever a result was less than favorable to a client.

For almost two hours after they arrived, Carolyn and Rosenbaum listened to Arther explain the procedure and the questions he intended to ask. He quickly told them that the test sometimes indicated a client was being deceptive when there were reasons other than lying to account for the result.

He explained that the polygraph machine was really an instrument that recorded simultaneous changes in blood pressure, respiration, and pulse rate and that when a person was not answering truthfully, the deception often had an impact on those bodily functions. Monitors placed on different parts of the body would pick up those changes and inked needles would record the reaction on graph paper.

Rosenbaum was politely asked to wait for them in another room while the test was being conducted.

Arther told them that his usual procedure was to obtain independent information about a particular incident, such as a police report, so that he could formulate pertinent questions and thus get better results from an examination. But Rosenbaum's insistence that the test be expedited hadn't allowed him the time to do that.

When he thought Carolyn was comfortable with the process, Arther placed the monitors on her fingers, arm, and temples and began asking his questions.

During the session, the examiner watched as the paper chart scrolled under the sensitive, inked needles, quivering slightly to Carolyn's reactions as he asked each question. He made marks on the chart at various points when the needles jumped decisively.

About an hour later, after completing the session and reviewing the data, Arther met with Rosenbaum and told him that Carolyn appeared to be telling the truth when she said she did not murder Betty Jeanne Solomon, but that she appeared to be deceptive in some of her answers.

He motioned for Rosenbaum to look over his shoulder at the paperwork, pointing out the areas where the needles had swung wildly.

He then pointed to three locations on the chart where there appeared to be very little movement of the needles. The questions asked at those times, he said, were:

"Did you murder Betty Jeanne?"

"No."

"By 2 A.M. last Monday, January 16, 1989, did you then already know that Betty Jeanne had been murdered?"

"No."

"Were you in the Solomon apartment when Betty Jeanne was murdered?"

"No."

Arther told the lawyer that he was fairly convinced Carolyn had told the truth when responding to those questions, but he was troubled by something else.

Unrolling the chart paper, he pointed to a spot where the needles had made wide marks. He explained that it was at that point he had asked Carolyn whether she believed Paul Solomon might have committed the crime. She had answered no.

Rosenbaum was disturbed by the finding, but somewhat relieved that she had appeared to answer truthfully to the three important questions involving herself in connection with the murder. He thanked Arther for his time.

As they drove back to Carolyn's apartment, Rosenbaum explained the test results to her. After the two had dinner, Carolyn called a cab to take the lawyer to La Guardia Airport and his flight home. As he pulled on his overcoat, Rosenbaum tried to reassure her that she had nothing to worry about.

There appeared to be problems of deception with some other questions, and the overall results weren't entirely clear-cut. Tom Warmus would have to know immediately, and he certainly wouldn't be happy.

Then Rosenbaum would have to call the assistant district attorney, Kevin Kennedy, to let him know Carolyn had passed the polygraph. He certainly couldn't send Kennedy the charts; that would probably cause more harm than good. And Kennedy would probably not only insist on seeing them, he'd more than likely want Carolyn to take another polygraph given by one of their own people. That was something Rosenbaum simply couldn't allow to happen.

The following Monday found Constantino waiting anxiously at his desk, thumbing through his earlier reports on the homicide. A secretary from the medical examiner's office had called to say Dr. Roh would be sending over his completed autopsy report on Betty Jeanne Solomon.

While it was virtually certain that one or more of the nine gunshot wounds had killed her, the report might contain additional clues that would help him piece together the puzzle.

Constantino had already come to the conclusion that this murder wasn't going to be solved any time soon and that, unlike a typical "Murder, She Wrote" plot, it was going to take more than deductive reasoning and finger-pointing suspects to clear this one off the books.

The young detective ran his fingers through his jet-black hair and realized for the first time just how excited he was to be the lead detective on this case.

Whenever he picked up the case file he felt an electric current of anticipation run through him. It was him against Solomon and Warmus and Rosenbaum and Pillersdorf and anyone else who stood in his way of finding out just who was involved in snuffing out Betty Jeanne Solomon.

All those boring lessons drilled into his head during academy and homicide seminars would now pay off. It wasn't theoretical anymore. This was the real thing, and he found himself thriving on it.

Somebody had aimed a gun at another human being and purposely taken her life. She was gone, poof. In an instant her whole life and everything she had said or done or would have done was taken away in the flash of a killer's gun.

And the only thing that could stop her killer from walking away untouched was his desire, intelligence, and ability to sift through the clues and find the ones that pointed to the murderer. What greater challenge could there be than this?

He promised himself to stick with this case no matter how long it took and to leave no stone unturned. He didn't really believe in luck. He believed in hard work. He hoped it would be enough.

At 10 A.M. a courier arrived with the autopsy report and Constantino quickly tore open the envelope. He tuned out the noise of the squad room and concentrated on the typewritten pages and diagrams spread out on his desk. First the summation of the various wounds.

"Wound one: Right posterior aspect of the chest, 50 inches above right heel. Small-caliber, copper-coated lead bullet with pellet in nose of bullet.

"Wound two: Right posterior aspect of chest.

"Wound three: Right lower aspect of thoracolumbar region.

"Wound four: Right lateral aspect of shoulder.

"Wound five: Bullet wound of right arm.

"Wound six: Left retroauricular region (superficial bullet wound of the scalp).

"Wound seven: Right medial and superior aspect of posterior chest.

"Wound eight: Left lower extremity, left thigh, slightly above knee joint.

"Wound nine: Left anterior aspect of leg; mid-portion of left leg."

Reading on, Constantino discovered that Roh had found lacerations on the scalp behind the left ear not caused by a bullet.

"Blunt force injuries to her head and shoulder," the report noted, which told the detective someone had walloped Betty Jeanne a couple of times from behind with something pretty heavy. He wondered if the blows were enough to kill her before she was shot.

He flipped to the end of the report and under cause of death he found: "Bullet wounds of head, chest, back and extremities with penetration through lungs, heart and liver."

No, the bullets had killed her, and that told the detective the smashes to her head and shoulder probably happened before she was plugged. What killer is going to shoot the victim to death and then pound her head and shoulder with something? Didn't make a lot of sense.

Constantino pictured the murder scene in his mind and decided that Betty Jeanne got clocked a couple of good ones before the gun came out. She was probably walking away with her back to the killer, not knowing what was coming.

He leafed through the report quickly and then turned back to the beginning to read every word carefully. Roh had found that Betty Jeanne's stomach at the time of her death contained potatoes, light-tannish grains—probably the cereal they found in the bowl on the coffee table—raisins, and tomatoes.

He read a couple more pages and stopped short when he saw the results of the microscopic examination. This is real interesting, he said to himself.

The autopsy revealed traces of sperm in Betty Jeanne's vagina that apparently had been there only a short period of time, possibly only several hours before her death.

Constantino asked himself the obvious questions. Had Paul Solomon had sex with his wife and Carolyn Warmus the same day? That would be a pretty cold thing for a man to do to his wife even if he wasn't getting along with her. Had the killer raped Betty Jeanne and then made her redress, or did he kill her and dress the corpse himself? Did the sperm belong to Betty Jeanne's lover, who they were still trying to identify?

Constantino decided to start his questioning with Paul Solomon.

Going back to the report, he saw that Roh had identified the bullets found in her body and at the scene as .25-caliber. Constantino had no reason to doubt Roh's findings, but he decided to wait for the official ballistics report before telling Sullivan what kind of gun had been used.

A little patience could keep him from looking foolish later on, or even out of hot water with his boss. Everyone was aware of the pressure being brought on the department by Betty Jeanne's family and friends, and the media were pressing the chief for answers they didn't yet have. Not that they would release the type and size gun used as the murder weapon even if they had the information.

Constantino again leafed through the report, this time looking for an estimate of the victim's time of death. Seeing no mention, he pulled out his Rolodex, yanked out the card for the medical examiner's office, and dialed the number. He hoped Dr. Roh hadn't left for the day.

"Hello. This is Dr. Roh. How may I help you?"

Constantino smiled when he heard the familiar accent. "Hi, Doctor. This is Detective Constantino from the Greenburgh police. I just finished reading the autopsy report on Betty Jeanne Solomon and noticed there wasn't any time of death noted. Were you able to come up with an approximate time?"

Roh cleared his throat as he recalled the recently completed autopsy. "My best estimate is that it was probably between 3 P.M. and 6 P.M. I'm basing that on the food in her stomach, the cereal, you know. I don't usually put a specific time of death in the report because there is no scientific way to determine it exactly."

Constantino's furrowed brow was the only outward sign that Roh's time estimate bothered him. If Betty Jeanne Solomon was murdered between 3 P.M. and 6 P.M., Solomon had to be their man. His statements to them were that he didn't leave for the bowling alley until about 6:20 P.M. and that he was home the rest of the day. But if Paul was the killer, surely he had to know what time he shot his wife and wouldn't he have come up with an alibi to cover that time and not incriminate himself like this? It didn't make sense to the tired detective. Paul Solomon may not be able to keep his zipper up, but he wasn't a stupid man. On the other hand, he knew it was sometimes the simplest of mistakes that often tripped people up. Thanking Roh for his time, he hung up the phone.

Several hours later, as he was preparing to leave work, another courier dropped a large, manila envelope on his desk. Tearing the package open, Constantino pulled out a twelve-page typewritten report.

"Good old Joe," he said out loud.

Joseph Reich was head of the county police ballistics unit, and he must have worked overtime to finish his report on the Solomon killing. Constantino leafed through the pages, skipping all the million-dollar scientific words, until he came to the section marked conclusions.

He began carefully sifting through the text and saw that Reich had found the slugs in the home and in the body to be .25-caliber. Chalk up another one for Dr. Roh. The next paragraph caused him to let out a long, slow whistle.

After hours of testing the slugs taken out of Betty Jeanne and those found near her body, and viewing them under a high-powered microscope, Reich had found micro-thin markings that could only mean one thing: the bullets had been fired through a metallic silencer.

Constantino leaned back in his chair, letting the full impact of this new development sink in. The report ended any speculation that this murder had been the result of a robbery gone awry. It also opened up the door to several new possibilities. Silencer killings weren't even common for mob hits these days. Yet Betty Jeanne Solomon had been killed by someone with a silencer-equipped, .25-caliber gun.

A contract hit? With what little information they had so far been able to dig up on Paul and Betty Jeanne Solomon it just didn't make sense.

A professional, contract killing cost big bucks, and the person paying the freight for the hit usually had some way to recoup his or her investment: insurance, inheritance, business takeover, something that made the murder financially rewarding.

In those cases it wasn't too hard to isolate the person who derived the most benefit from the deceased's untimely demise. But in this case there was nothing so far to indicate that Paul Solomon stood to make a lot of money from his wife's death. Constantino and Lind had already checked with the couple's insurance company, and while there was a policy, it didn't pay the kind of money that was normally worth the risk of hiring a hit man.

Constantino sat in his swivel chair for the next hour, puzzling over the new information and forgetting he had told his wife he'd be home in time for dinner.

The next several days didn't bring any better news for the two detectives. Crime analysis had finished their report, and other than the spent bullets and shell casings, they hadn't come up with very much.

The blood samples taken from the murder scene had all matched Betty Jeanne's blood type. Hair samples removed from the floors and furniture belonged to Paul or Kristan or the victim. Questioning the Solomons' neighbors had so far yielded a big, fat zero. Even the information they had gotten from the couple living downstairs, Mike and Rosie Reilly, about some muffled noise that sounded like small bangs and footsteps, didn't really help the detectives to identify the killer.

No other neighbor had reported hearing anything from the Solomons' condo that night. That's what happens when a silencer is used by some slick son of a bitch, Constantino told his partner.

□   □   □   □

January 26 found Constantino and Detective Joe Delio sitting in the office of Mirta Torres, a branch manager for the Lincoln First National Bank, formerly the National Bank of Westchester.

"All I can really tell you officers is that I heard Mrs. Solomon was having an affair with another man who works for us. His name is John Bourne and he's in the Tarrytown branch office. That's only a rumor, but it's been around a long time. I personally have heard it, but I don't really know what, if anything, was going on. I've also heard that Mrs. Solomon had quite a few extramarital affairs with people she worked with, but to tell you the truth, I only really heard Mr. Bourne's name associated with her. I'm sorry. I wish I could be more helpful."

Delio probed a little more.

"Was there anyone who Mrs. Solomon had a problem with, that maybe didn't like her or that she had a run-in with?"

"Mrs. Solomon was very well liked here," Torres said, trying to recall anything that might be helpful to the two detectives.

"Wait a minute. Now that you mention it, there was an incident a couple years back involving Mrs. Solomon. We had an assistant manager at our Valhalla branch who was Mrs. Solomon's subordinate. His name was Brian Boddie and what happened was she caught him embezzling more than $100,000. Eventually he was convicted and spent time in prison. The last I heard of Mr. Boddie he'd been released and was living in LeHigh Acres, Florida. I don't know if he's still there."

Both men wrote down the new information and made a mental note to check on Boddie. They thanked Torres for her time and left.

Four days later, Constantino was at his desk, working feverishly to catch up on the never-ending reports. He wasn't in a very good mood. The January 27 surveillance he and Delio had set up on Warmus from the time she left the Bedford Road Elementary School at 3 P.M. until she arrived back at her Manhattan home had yielded a big, fat zero.

"This will probably lead us nowhere as well, but I want you to conduct another surveillance of our schoolmarm on February 10. Pencil it in, will you?" Constantino said to Lind without looking up.

He grimaced as the phone rang, interrupting his train of thought.

"Detective Constantino. May I help you?"

The male voice on the other end of the line was muffled.

"Don't let the trail of Paul Solomon grow cold. Check every body of water and gas station from his apartment to the bowling alley for the gun. If you don't find it, check Bear Mountain Camp because Paul takes his sixth-grade students there in the summer for a trip and he might have hid the gun there."

Constantino jotted down the information as quickly as he could and then interrupted the caller.

"Let me ask you this, pal. Why do you think Paul Solomon killed his wife?"

The man sounded sure of himself. "He and his wife were the only ones ever to run the Edgemont Recreation Program and they may have done something illegal with the money. Check this out. It will be worth your time."

The phone line went dead. Replacing the receiver, the young detective noted the time of the call.

"Well, it's starting," he yelled over to Lind, who also was busy scribbling out reports. "The whackos are starting to come out of the woodwork with all their great inside tips. Just got another one."

Lind laughed out loud. "Better you than me, pal. Since you took the call, you write up the report."

Constantino sighed and took a fresh form from a stack on the corner of his desk.

On the last day of January, Constantino decided it was time to try and make something happen. All the reports were in with all the usual equivocations so that everybody's ass would be covered should the chief or the captains come looking for scapegoats.

Lind had called Tim Lacy, security officer for the New York Telephone Company, who was still pulling the Solomons' local and long-distance phone records for the day of the murder. It would probably take a couple more weeks, Lacy had said the other day. Both detectives were hopeful that those records would reveal some new clues, but patience was the name of the game now.

Grabbing his blue overcoat off the old-fashioned coatrack, Constantino yelled that he was heading back to the Scarsdale Ridge Apartments to requestion some of the residents in case someone's memory had improved. Or maybe he'd get lucky and find someone they'd missed on January 15 and 16.

The gray, overcast day matched his mood as he left the station. He wasn't holding out any hope of finding an eyewitness, but it was better than sitting on his ass and reading reports for the fiftieth time. He flicked the car fan to high and hoped the heater would kick in before the short ride ended. Five miles later he turned left off of South Central Avenue into the condominium complex.

The week following the murder he had returned several times to the Solomons' apartment with Peter De Forest and Francis Sheehan, two of the most respected crime-scene experts in the country, as far as he was concerned. Their return visits had uncovered a few more bullet fragments and shell casings, which had been buried in the carpet and floor boards. With luck, the additional evidence would help the ballistics guys. All three men had taken so many measurements of the distance between the body and each bullet fragment, shell casing, and piece of furniture that Constantino didn't even want to see a tape measure any time in the foreseeable future. Pulling into an open space, he parked the car in front of Building D and got out, reaching into his back pocket for his shield.

Building D was set about twenty-five yards from the Solomons, but near enough for someone possibly to have heard something that night, he thought wistfully. Looking at the mailboxes, he counted twenty-four units. He walked down five steps to the first two doors and knocked on one. No answer. He walked next door and his luck was the same.

An hour later Constantino hadn't tried every condo, but he returned to his car to read through the notes he had taken so far. William Oakes told him he'd heard loud talking in front of the Solomons' building at about 11:30 P.M. the night of the murder, but he hadn't been able to make out what the commotion was about. The man's timing was probably a little off and the noise was probably the police arriving on the scene, Constantino guessed.

Richard Katz remembered playing with his son in front of the building that afternoon, but didn't recall anything out of the ordinary happening. The only other information of any interest came from neighbor Keith Pedersen, who recalled seeing Paul and Betty Jeanne in the Candlelight Inn in Scarsdale on a few occasions, but not on the day she was shot.

Not a helluva lot of help, the detective thought as he opened the car door once again, shivering as he walked toward the few condos he hadn't yet tried.

Bobbie Flowers was just putting dinner in the oven when she heard the knock and invited Constantino inside.

"Sure, I heard about the murder," the thirty-eight-year-old housewife said. "It's all anybody's talking about around here. It's a shame. I heard the Solomons were separated before they moved in here, but I don't know if that's true or not." Constantino flipped open his notebook and scribbled down the information. He hadn't heard anything about the Solomons being separated at any time, but it was worth checking. Flowers's next statement floored him.

"You know, I believe I heard the gunshots that night," she said, straightening the slipcover on the arm of the sofa.

"You heard gunshots that night, on the fifteenth?" he asked, trying to keep the note of surprise out of his voice.

"Yes, it sounded like several shots coming from the direction of A Building. I'd say it was about 10 P.M. and the shots were slow and deliberate. I didn't go out and check or anything. But they sounded like gunshots to me."

After another ten minutes of questions, Constantino thanked Flowers for her time and got up to leave. He told her he would probably be calling her again and that she should not share this information with anyone other than those she had already told. Promising not to, she opened the door and closed it behind him.

Turning toward the steps, he thrust his hands deep in his coat pockets. The trip hadn't been a total waste. Only one problem, he reminded himself. If ballistic tests showed a silencer had been used in Betty Jeanne's murder, how in the hell could this woman have heard the gunshots when the people living in the same building as the Solomons hadn't heard anything?

Driving back to the office, Constantino allowed himself a smile. This was the damnedest case. The more investigating he did, the more questions popped up. At this rate, he'd have about a zillion suspects with about as many conflicting sets of circumstances before it was all over. Tommy was going to love this new twist, he thought, pulling into the station.

Back at his desk, Constantino scooped up the documents he had strewn about and stuck them back into the police folder. He shoved the package in his desk drawer, making sure to lock it. The murder only happened sixteen days ago, but already it felt like forever. In six hours January would be over and maybe the new month would bring the break they needed.

Like every night for the past two weeks, Constantino was the last one to leave the squad room. He grabbed his coat and flicked off the light switch on his way out.

5

SULLIVAN STOPPED READING the typewritten report and looked at his two sullen-faced detectives slumped in their chairs in front of his desk. He didn't try to hide the disgust in his voice when he slammed the papers down and told the pair it wasn't their fault, it was just something that had happened. The chief of detectives was very angry, but he refused to allow himself to explode.

The source of his anger was a report on the New York Telephone records for the Solomons' phone that Tim Lacy had finally delivered to his office. It hadn't taken Constantino long to discover the 7:15 P.M. call to the nonexistent 911 that presumably Betty Jeanne Solomon had dialed in a frantic effort to stay alive.

It took the young detective only a day to find out that the operator had routed the call to the Scarsdale police, who in turn reported it to their own department. A quick check of Greenburgh's tape-recording files of all incoming calls for January 15 revealed that the Scarsdale dispatcher had passed on a faulty address, which their own dispatcher had radioed to Officer Singer to check out.

Of course young Singer hadn't found anything wrong, Constantino thought miserably. The real emergency was miles away.

After reviewing a copy of the ticket procedure operator Linda Viana had written up detailing the call, Constantino blamed the telephone company for not checking their computers for the proper address. Instead of going on a wild goose chase, the police just might have been able to catch the murderer, or better yet, to prevent the shooting from occurring.

In fact, their records showed there had been a Greenburgh patrol car in the vicinity of the Solomons' apartment at just about the time the screaming telephone call had been made. It was this mistake, and the slim possibility that Betty Jeanne Solomon might have been saved, that cast a pall over the squad room that day.

Sullivan let his anger subside and began to look at the positive side of the report. Another set of phone records, these belonging to Marshall and Josette Tilden of Scarsdale, also revealed another valuable, but no less disturbing clue.

Josette Tilden, one of Betty Jeanne Solomon's best friends and the woman upon whom Pillersdorf hung his best hope of clearing Paul Solomon of the murder, had been mistaken about the time she talked with the victim. Her telephone records showed that on the night of the shooting, she and Betty Jeanne first spoke at 6:51 P.M. and then at 7:09 P.M., not at around 7:15 and 8 P.M., as she had thought when talking to the police.

Sullivan knew it didn't take much arithmetic to figure out that if Tilden spoke with Betty Jeanne at 7:09 P.M., and the emergency call— presumably made by the victim—was placed at 7:15 P.M., Betty Jeanne Solomon's death must have occurred just minutes after they spoke.

What if the killer had arrived while Betty Jeanne was still on the phone, and what if she had told Tilden who had just come in? She hadn't, of course. That was one of the first questions Constantino asked Tilden when he interviewed her.

"But for a couple of lousy breaks this case would have been solved by now," Sullivan said out loud to no one in particular.

The only good thing about all this was that they now had an almost specific time of death, and with that information, everyone's alibis, including that of their prime suspect, Paul Solomon, could be checked.

Dr. Roh's approximation of the time of death was obviously off, but they could deal with that later. Knowing the precise time of death gave them the edge they needed to go back and review where everyone had been at that exact minute on January 15.

Several days later, with the case effectively stalled, Constantino decided to have Carolyn Warmus's home phone records subpoenaed, to find out if she was still keeping in touch with Solomon and also to double-check her story about calling him on the afternoon of the murder.

He drove over to the Westchester County Courthouse in White Plains and took the elevator up to the third floor, where Assistant District Attorney Kevin Kennedy had his office. Although he had joined the prosecutor's staff in 1983 and been bumped up to the D.A.'s investigative division two years later, Kennedy had never been assigned a murder case until now.

At first, Constantino was bothered that his first lead homicide case was being assigned to a novice. He knew from the stories other detectives had told him that an assistant district attorney could make or break a case, and sometimes a cop.

If you got one who was too careful, who made you dot every *I* and cross every *T,* the case could become so bogged down in paperwork and bullshit that it would never be solved. On the other hand, you didn't want a loose cannon who didn't have the foggiest idea of what to do. You'd end up paying for it in court when a good defense lawyer and an unsympathetic judge could cut all your hard work to ribbons.

When Constantino first met Kennedy, he judged him a bit harshly. Balding, with a small tuft of hair sticking out of his now mostly smooth dome, and wearing a pair of thick, black glasses, Kennedy appeared to be one of the bookworm variety, for whom the detective didn't really have much use.

A few hours later, after the pair had poured through the case file, Constantino began to gain new respect for the man. He seemed to know what he was doing and, like Constantino, this was his first big case and he wanted to come out of it with a sweet notch in his belt.

On this sunny day in early February, Kennedy didn't disappoint him. It would take awhile, he said, but there shouldn't be any problem getting Warmus's phone records.

The pressure Constantino and Lind continued to put on people in an effort to discover the identity of Betty Jeanne's mysterious lover finally began paying off.

After numerous interviews with the victim's former friends and co-workers at the National Bank of Westchester and the Continental Credit Corporation, the detectives learned that while no one knew anything for sure, many had their suspicions about Betty Jeanne's having had an affair while working at the bank. When asked individually whom they suspected was involved, they each gave the name of the man that Paul Solomon had suspected.

February 4 was a cold, rainy day and the detectives passed the time talking about vacations in warmer climates as they pulled into the drive-way of the man they now were pretty sure had had an affair with their murder victim.

John J. Bourne opened the door to his home in Peekskill and beck-oned the men inside. He didn't know what the detectives wanted this time—he had spoken with them a couple weeks before, when they were checking Betty Jeanne's employment history—and their phone call the day before asking to see him again made him nervous. It didn't take him long to find out the purpose of their visit.

"Mr. Bourne, we'll get right to the point," Constantino began. "We have reason to believe that you and Betty Jeanne Solomon were having an affair prior to her death. Would you care to tell us about it?"

Bourne kept a straight face and angrily denied the accusation. "I'll tell you again. I knew Betty Jeanne Solomon because we worked to-gether for the same bank. I was introduced to her at one time and I liked her, but the relationship was never anything more than a profes-sional one. I'm sorry if that disappoints you."

Constantino and Lind both realized they weren't going to get any-thing more from the man at that moment. They left him standing in his doorway, watching them pull away.

Back at the station, the detectives briefed their boss on the interview. Sullivan, anxious to see the case progress and tired of all the roadblocks into which his detectives kept running, decided to stop playing games. If, in fact, Bourne was the lover of their victim, he was as much a suspect in her murder as anyone else.

It wasn't only Betty Jeanne Solomon's sex life that was being dissected and examined. It was every cop's belief that Paul Solomon considered himself quite a lady's man and had tasted the forbidden fruit more than once.

Their assumptions were confirmed on February 8.

Patricia Kushman was a married teacher at the poshy Seely Place School in Scarsdale. She and her husband lived simply in their home in New Rochelle, and many of her fellow instructors knew she was a close friend of Paul Solomon. How close, many never guessed.

Constantino and Delio made themselves comfortable in the Kushmans' living room. Both men wondered whether Mrs. Kushman would have been so hospitable if she knew what questions they had come to ask. Delio wasted no time.

"Mrs. Kushman, we've been told that you've often socialized with

Paul Solomon. Can you tell us, if you know, what the relationship was like between him and his wife?"

"What I can tell you is that on many occasions that I, my husband, Laura Wright, and Danny Antawano socialized with them and I never saw that they had any problem with their marriage. Paul was a very easy person to speak to, very giving."

The two men stole a glance at one another, listening to the tone of her voice as she spoke of Solomon. Delio again dove in head first. "Mrs. Kushman, did you ever have an affair with Paul Solomon?"

The teacher took the question in stride, and only her eyes betrayed her discomfort. "Paul and I would see each other outside of work and have drinks together," she answered. "We attempted a physical relationship once, but it was impossible."

Constantino glanced up from his note pad. "Excuse me. What do you mean by impossible?"

Kushman's face took on a deeper shade of red as she hesitated, searching for the right words. "When I say impossible, I mean that Paul was unable physically to make love. Do you understand?"

Both men nodded, the picture in their minds of the middle-aged Lothario disintegrating.

"What do you know about a friend of Paul's, a man named Ron Caruso?" Constantino asked.

Kushman thought for a moment and then answered. "All I know about Ron Caruso is that he and Paul have gone away on vacations together for the past four years and that Ron is currently on sabbatical from the Scarsdale schools."

Delio turned the subject to Warmus. "What about Carolyn Warmus? Did you know her at all?"

Kushman squinted her eyes and let out a sigh of exasperation. "Carolyn Warmus was a flake. Paul had always told me that he and Warmus did not have an affair, but about a week before the murder she was hanging around the Greenville School obviously looking for him."

Twenty minutes later the detectives finished their questioning and thanked Kushman for her honesty. Driving away, the two men burst out laughing as each began to recite his own collection of limp-dick jokes.

Once again back at the station, Constantino briefed Sullivan.

"Okay, okay," the chief of detectives chuckled. "What's on the agenda for tomorrow?"

"I've got an interview set up with Danny Hwang. He's Kristan Solomon's boyfriend and apparently they've been dating since May 1988.

He's a juvenile, so I called his mother. She'll be there when I talk to him. I also have an interview set up with Ron Caruso, Paul's good buddy. I don't really expect much from either of them, but we'll cover all the bases."

Sullivan nodded as he walked away. "Something has to break our way soon," he yelled over his shoulder.

On February 16, Sullivan decided it was time to put the squeeze on Mr. John J. Bourne. He picked up his phone and dialed the man's number.

"Hello, Mr. Bourne? This is Lieutenant Sullivan from the Greenburgh police. I'd like you to come down to headquarters to answer a few questions for us. Yes, I know my detectives have questioned you twice, but I have some things I'd like to ask you myself."

When the reluctant man finally agreed to come in, Sullivan hung up.

"We're going to get to the bottom of this once and for all," he told Constantino.

An hour later and visibly upset, Bourne was ushered into Sullivan's small office, followed by Constantino.

"Mr. Bourne, I'm going to give this to you straight. Based on evidence we've obtained, I believe you are the man who was having an affair with Betty Jeanne Solomon. We are in the middle of a murder investigation and there will be very serious consequences if you decide to lie to us about your involvement with her. This will be the last opportunity for you to tell us the truth before other steps are taken. Do you understand?"

Bourne began to protest, but when he looked into Sullivan's eyes, his face fell. Clearly, there would be no use concealing the truth any longer. "Yes, it's true," he said resignedly. "Betty and I had a sexual relationship from the fall of 1979 to February 1988. She worked in the bank's Valhalla branch while I worked in Rosedale, and we would carry on the relationship in either her bank or mine. After I left the bank in Rosedale, we continued the relationship."

When he paused, Constantino prompted by leaning forward in his chair, staring directly into the embarrassed man's eyes, asking, "Where else would you meet each other?"

"Well, we would often get together at her apartment in Harrison when she and her husband lived there. When they moved to Scarsdale we would often meet there when her husband was gone or out of town."

Sullivan asked the embarrassed man whether he considered the affair casual or serious.

"All I can say is that in 1984, Betty told me she was in love with me. I was married, I still am, although my wife and I separated in 1987. Yeah, part of the reason we separated was because of my feelings for Betty. Anyway, when she told me she was in love with me, she also said she was afraid to tell her husband, Paul, for fear that she would lose her daughter Kristan. After 1984 we started seeing less of each other and I would say we saw each other sporadically after that, about two or three times a year."

Constantino scribbled in his notebook and then asked Bourne when he had last seen Betty Jeanne Solomon.

"It was in February 1988 in her condo in Greenburgh. We met and had sex there. She told me her husband had gone to a Club Med for the weekend with a friend of his named Ron, and her daughter was away on a ski trip. At that time she told me her husband suspected we were having an affair and she told me that I was the only man she was seeing."

"Did she say anything about any problems she was having with her husband?" Sullivan asked.

"All she said that I can remember was that she was annoyed that her husband had just purchased a new motorcycle and she thought the money could have been better spent," he replied.

Asked about his marriage, Bourne replied, "I don't think my wife and I will reconcile. As far as Betty was concerned, I didn't want the relationship to become any more serious after my wife and I split up because I just felt a day-to-day relationship wouldn't work."

Constantino probed deeper. "When you finally stopped seeing Betty Jeanne, were there hard feelings between you? Was there any anger, either by you or her?"

Bourne shook his head. "No, none at all. We never really officially ended the relationship. I just didn't call her and she didn't call me from that February until the day she was killed."

Sullivan asked him where he was on the night of January 15, 1989.

"I really don't remember, to tell you the truth. I can check and get back to you. Right now I just don't remember."

When the questioning ended, Bourne nervously asked the pair whether the information he had given them would ever become public. The detectives assured him that if the affair had no bearing on the homicide case it was unlikely to surface. But they were careful not to make any promises.

When Bourne left the office, Sullivan and Constantino discussed the new information and agreed a background check on Bourne was necessary.

Constantino briefed Lind later that afternoon, and the older detective couldn't suppress a laugh. "What a couple," he said with disgust. "Paul Solomon's out getting blowjobs and bopping a twenty-five-year-old, at the same time his wife is screwing her lover in her marital bed. What the hell are we going to find out next?"

For the next three months the detectives spent their time rechecking the stories of everyone they had interviewed. Still without any promising leads, Constantino and Lind decided the case had hit a dead end. Their occasional surveillances of Solomon had turned up nothing. They had even come up empty on Boddie, the National Bank of Westchester embezzler in Florida. He, like everyone else, seemed to have an airtight alibi for the day of the murder.

Lind knew from experience that once the initial leads in a murder case were exhausted, the long haul was only beginning. The frustrating part for both men was that the Greenburgh Police Department was like any other business; you couldn't keep your limited manpower devoted to a single project for any length of time. The nature of the business was such that almost every day there was a new case with which to deal. Maybe not all as spicy as a good murder, but crimes that had to be solved and disposed of.

The chief was still gently pushing Sullivan to come up with something on the Solomon murder, but like everyone else, he now knew it was going to take time.

Although Constantino still burned with the desire to bring Betty Jeanne Solomon's killer to justice, he reluctantly began working the new batch of assignments. Meanwhile, Solomon remained in a state of limbo, never knowing for sure if the next moment would bring that knock on the door from the police, armed with a pair of handcuffs and an arrest warrant.

The telephone call Pillersdorf received from Sullivan the morning of May 31 filled him with foreboding. The stoic detective had asked to meet with him and Solomon later that afternoon and the tone in his voice sounded ominous. Pillersdorf quickly called Solomon.

Later that afternoon, Solomon sat silently in his lawyer's living room, trying to control his fear and wondering how things could have gotten so bad for him. He glanced across the room at Sullivan and Constantino as the pair jotted down his answers to more of their questions in their damnable note pads.

"Lieutenant, I have a question for you," Pillersdorf interrupted. "Where exactly is the case and are you any closer to solving it than the day it happened?"

Sullivan glanced up and stared straight at Solomon, who was sitting pensively on the edge of the sofa and trying hard to look his interrogator in the eye.

"I can tell you that we are very close to making an arrest in this case," Sullivan responded, noticing his words were having the desired effect as Solomon shot a furtive look toward his attorney.

Finally, the beleaguered teacher decided it was his turn to ask a question.

"I need to know what to do about Carolyn," Solomon blurted out. "Ever since the murder she's been calling me several times a week and she's also trying to contact Kristan. She's even started sending us notes saying she wants to get together. Gary has warned me not to have any contact with her, but she just won't stop. What should I do?"

Displaying not a shred of concern, Sullivan said, "Sooner or later you're going to have to confront her. There's nothing we can do for you about that."

When the day's questioning ended, Pillersdorf showed the detectives to the door and then returned to his visibly shaken friend.

"I have to be honest with you, Paul. I think it's only a matter of time before they arrest you. For some reason Sullivan is convinced that you killed Betty Jeanne and I don't think he's even trying to come up with another suspect. We'll have to make plans in the event they do arrest you."

Solomon's face turned white. Pillersdorf felt a momentary pang of regret for being so direct, but decided it was better to deal with what appeared to be the inevitable and not to pretend everything was fine.

"One thing I will tell you again," the lawyer continued. "Stay away from Carolyn Warmus. Don't talk with her. Don't let her have any contact with Kristan, and for God's sake, don't meet with her. It just gives the police more of a reason to believe you killed your wife because you were in love with someone else."

Solomon nodded in agreement and then lost himself in deep thought while Pillersdorf went to get them a couple of beers.

□ □ □ □

Spring turned to summer, and with it arrived the subpoenaed records from Warmus's home telephone that Constantino had been waiting for so impatiently. The old adage "the wheels of justice turn slowly" was accurate as hell, but it didn't help a cop who was trying his best to solve a murder case before all the witnesses and clues disappeared.

Peering through the list of telephone numbers, Constantino smiled. This woman was a talker, there was no denying that. Loosening his tie, he glanced through the paperwork and pulled out the list for the December '88–January '89 calls. These would be the most important ones to start with, since Warmus might have called her family and friends right before and after the murder, and possibly an accomplice before that.

He picked up a copy of a *Cole's Directory* and began to look up the first number. He knew it would take days to identify them all, but at least he was back in business with something tangible to work on.

The past several weeks had been wasted, as far as he was concerned. The only good thing about it was that the killer might now be starting to feel a little more confident that he or she was going to get away with it. People had a tendency to let their guard down as time went on and sometimes a real stupid suspect would even start bragging about his crime. Human nature being what it was, some people felt they had to tell someone about their perfect crime.

When he finished writing down the name from the directory that matched the first number on Warmus's telephone records, Constantino reached for his can of Diet Coke and swigged down the last swallow. His wife had gotten him to start drinking the stuff when his waistline had started to balloon. He knew he should drop a few pounds, but he wasn't into joining the YMCA and playing hoops like Sullivan, and the farthest he could remember running was from his sofa to the refrigerator during the Super Bowl. He would worry about his weight later. Right now it felt good to be getting back into this case. Mighty good.

A few weeks later the detectives had put together a list of names and addresses of the people Warmus had called during the months before and after the murder. After crossing out family members and her father's attorney, there were still quite a few people left.

One number puzzled them both. It belonged to the office phone of Vincent Parco, an internationally known private eye in Manhattan. By the looks of the phone records, Warmus must have had some kind of close relationship with him. She'd called Parco numerous times, including the day after the murder.

After checking the specific times those calls were made, Constantino realized that she must have dialed Parco only hours after the detectives dropped her off at her apartment following their interrogation. While it might be just a coincidence, the detectives weren't about to let it pass.

Besides, they knew they didn't have a hell of a lot else to go on. Neither one could figure out what a twenty-five-year-old, single woman needed with a private detective, but they were going to find out.

Before talking with Parco, however, they decided to interview the New York Telephone operator who took Betty Jeanne Solomon's emergency call. Perhaps there was something more about that call they could encourage her to remember.

On June 5, Lind and Constantino drove to Camp Smith Military Facility in Peekskill, New York. After flashing their badges at the manned gate, they drove to the main headquarters building and made their way to room 48.

Linda Viana was already seated when the pair arrived. She was a sergeant in the New York State National Guard and was serving the one-weekend-a-month duty that was required of all guardsmen. The meeting lasted only a few minutes.

"Listen, guys, all I can remember is that the woman who called me was screaming with terror and said 'he or she's trying to kill me.' I've stayed up I don't know how many nights trying to recall just exactly whether that woman said 'he' or 'she.' I honestly can't remember. I'm sorry." Viana looked emotionally drained.

Constantino stood up and put his hand on her shoulder. "Don't worry about it," he said in a reassuring voice. "What you remember is what you remember. You've been very helpful with everything. It's okay, we'll find out who did this. You can count on it."

The trip back to the office was made in relative silence, as both men once again silently marveled at the killer's luck.

"This may sound silly," Sullivan said, when they reported in. "Call the NYPD and ask them to give you the name of any psychics they use to help them solve cases. Get someone who has actually done something, not one of those publicity-seeking crystal-ball assholes. And keep this to yourself. I don't want a word of this to leak out, understand?"

Constantino nodded, watching the redness creeping into the lieutenant's cheeks. He hadn't realized until that moment how desperate Sullivan was to solve this case. The pressure from up above must be tremendous, he reasoned. "Sure boss, I'll get right on it."

Walking back to his desk, the young detective wondered for the first time if they would ever bring the real killer to justice. He felt silly making the call, but orders were orders.

"Hello, Sergeant? This is Detective Richard Constantino from Greenburgh. I've got a strange one for you."

One month later, on July 5, both Constantino and Lind had finally cleared their workload enough to delve back into the homicide case. Constantino decided it was time to talk with Vincent Parco, and the private detective's secretary immediately put his call through.

Driving down to Parco's Manhattan office at 210 East Thirty-fifth Street, Constantino shared with his partner the feeling he'd gotten when talking to the private eye.

"I just called to let him know we were going to pay him a visit this morning, and when I got off the phone I felt like I needed a shower. The guy was trying too hard to be helpful, it just got me wondering why."

When they arrived and finally found a parking spot near the building, they got out and walked inside. Taking the stairs to the second floor, Lind flicked open the black leather case holding his badge and held it out for the secretary, telling her to buzz her boss.

Seconds later, a smiling Parco emerged from his office, extending his hand and patting the backs of his two unfamiliar visitors. He motioned for them to follow him down a well-lit hallway to his office. The private eye's heavy cologne caused Constantino to sneeze.

Parco dropped into his expensive leather chair behind a massive, hand-tooled, oak desk and waved for the men to sit in the thickly cushioned chairs facing him. The office was richly decorated, heavy on dark woods and brass, with the requisite framed awards, degrees, and pictures of Parco with various celebrities lining the wall behind him. A glass-paneled door to the detectives' left led to a balcony overlooking a small courtyard.

Constantino unabashedly stared at Parco, trying to gauge the cost of his well-tailored outfit: navy blue, double-breasted suit, crisply starched white shirt, French cuffs fastened with gold cuff links, suspenders, and a heavy silk tie.

The clothes, along with the carefully coiffed hair—or what was left of it—neatly trimmed moustache, and expensive-looking aviator eyeglasses, told Constantino that Parco was a man who fancied himself a player; he liked his money and letting people know that he had it, and he probably considered himself quite a ladies' man.

Looking at the private eye's hands as he folded them underneath his chin, Lind guessed with distaste that he probably had regular manicures.

Parco was used to the jealous behavior of men less worldly than himself. Appearance was everything in his business, and he played the game well, he thought. He hoped this interview would conclude quickly. He was a busy man.

Constantino noticed the disdainful look plastered over Parco's face. He was sure the private detective was thinking about how much money he was losing by their being there, but he looked like he could afford it.

"Mr. Parco, we just wanted to ask you a few questions about a woman named Carolyn Warmus. Can you tell us what, if anything, you know about her?" Lind asked, flipping through his notebook to find a clean page.

The first question, and the courteous tone of the detective's voice, told Parco that this was a friendly meeting. For the first time since he had okayed their visit to his office, he felt relaxed. "Carolyn Warmus is a former client of mine," he said. "She hired my firm to do some work for her. Nothing out of the ordinary. I can tell you between us she was a real ditzy blonde and somewhat schizophrenic. May I ask what she's done or is being investigated for?"

Constantino looked up from his own notebook. "We haven't said she's done anything wrong. We're in the middle of a homicide investigation and her name happened to come up. We learned she was associated with you and just wanted to know what, if anything, you could tell us about her."

For the next twenty minutes, Parco shared with the detectives what he described as his limited information about Carolyn Warmus. He hoped his conversational tone and outward appearance of cooperation would satisfy them.

"She was simply a client of mine," he said again. "Interesting girl. I don't know if I can tell you much more than I already have."

Constantino shot him a withering look of disbelief that seemed to convince him the police knew more than they were saying. Parco decided to tell the story his way. For the next hour he recounted for the detectives his experience with Carolyn Warmus.

On a hot, summer day in June 1987, Carolyn had walked into his office wearing a short, white tennis outfit and carrying a racquet in one hand, her shoulder-length blond, curled hair bouncing along with every step she took. Parco winked at the detectives when he described Warmus's long, tanned legs and voluptuous body.

"It turned out," he said, "she wanted to hire a private detective to follow around this married bartender from New Jersey she'd been dating. Apparently she wanted to make sure this guy was only having an affair with her and nobody else and to see if he was really going to divorce his wife as he had promised her.

"I told her how much it would cost and she didn't bat an eye, so I figured okay, sure," Parco said. "I put one of my men on it, a guy who used to work here named Russo. Jimmy Russo. He has his own private detective business now called ATI, All-Tech Investigations Limited. He and another guy who used to work for me, Gabe Laura, have an office over on West Fifty-second Street. Anyway, that investigation ended in August 1987."

Lind jotted down the information in his notebook. Carolyn apparently had led a more interesting life than the policemen had imagined. Constantino continued his questioning.

"Have you talked with Carolyn recently, say in the last six or seven months?"

Parco picked up an open file on his desk and pretended to study it in an effort to buy himself a few extra seconds. He knew the two cops had found him either because Carolyn had given them his name or because they had checked her phone records. He couldn't afford to lie and trip himself up.

"Yeah, she calls me now and then," he said finally.

Constantino decided to push a little and let Parco know they had something connecting him to Warmus besides her being an old client.

"What about January 16? We have her making a telephone call to you that day. What was she calling you about?"

Parco filed that information away in his memory bank and thought quickly. "Carolyn called me to talk about a lot of things," he began slowly, collecting his thoughts. "She said she was feeling awfully tired because she'd recently been questioned by the police earlier that day or night. She said they wanted to know something about a murder of some fellow teacher's wife. She also said she was at some bowling affair in Yonkers and that she had gotten there at about 6 P.M. That's all I remember of the conversation."

Both Lind and Constantino knew that Warmus's story to Parco differed from what she had told them. Why would she lie to Parco and give him an alibi different from the one she had given them? It was a question they would have to ask her at a later time.

As the detectives stood up and reached out to shake his hand, Parco seemed to think he had handled them well. Walking the men to the lobby, he told them to call if they had more questions.

As they walked out the building's front door into the simmering heat, Constantino looked at his partner. "I was right," he said. "I do need a shower."

On the way back to the station, the detectives agreed that their next step would be to talk once again with Paul Solomon. Maybe he'd have a few more little tidbits of information to share with them. They would have to pay this guy Russo a visit as well.

When Lind called Pillersdorf the next morning to set up the interview, the lawyer was his usual gregarious self, quickly agreeing to the meeting with his client.

The next day, Constantino and Lind arrived back at the place where their odyssey had begun, Solomon's apartment. It had been several months now since they had authorized the yellow police tape to be taken down, allowing Solomon and his daughter back into their home.

Neither detective could understand why Solomon had brought his daughter back here. It had to be emotionally and psychologically devastating for Kristan to live in the place where her mother had been gunned down. Apparently her father didn't think so. The only thing he did when allowed back in was to have the bloodstained carpet replaced.

Everyone to whom they'd mentioned this thought it was strange, but it certainly didn't prove anything, and more importantly, it was Solomon's call to make, not theirs, so what the hell. Maybe he couldn't afford to go anywhere else.

It gave them both an eerie feeling to walk across the very spot where Betty Jeanne's body had been found, but neither one said a word. Pillersdorf stood up to greet them and they all sat down. He was still genuinely surprised that Paul hadn't yet been arrested. When Sullivan had told him last May that an arrest was imminent, he was sure his best friend would soon be behind bars. But for the past month and a half, nothing. Pillersdorf decided to look at the situation in the best possible light. Maybe they had centered their attention on another suspect. Whatever the reason, Paul was still a free man and that was what mattered most.

"This is going to be brief," Lind said, deciding to get out of the place as quickly as possible. He detested Solomon, and his dislike was growing by the second. He hoped Kristan wasn't home. He felt genuinely bad for the young girl.

"We want to know if you're still seeing Carolyn Warmus and if there's anything else you'd like to tell us that maybe you forgot or that you just remembered."

Paul shot a glance at his lawyer. They had been through this before and he knew that Gary would interrupt if something came up that he didn't want Paul to answer. Otherwise, his advice had been to cooperate fully.

"It's like I told you before. I stopped seeing Carolyn sometime in January, around the end of the month," Solomon said, turning a little red as he remembered that the two detectives sitting on his sofa knew all about his escapades in that hotel parking lot.

"I didn't tell her we were through or anything, I just told her that with everything that had happened it was better if we didn't see each other for a while. She's still calling me and leaving notes and presents for me and Kristan, even though I'm not having anything to do with her. We certainly haven't gone out or anything like that."

Lind asked him about the calls, but Solomon replied that the only thing he remembered was her trying to get him to go somewhere so they could talk. "Other than that it was just small talk. Not much else."

Constantino began hitting him with questions about his earlier statements. He didn't want to tick off Solomon or his lawyer so he kept his tone polite, but it wasn't easy.

"Anything you've remembered that you didn't tell us before? Anything come to mind?"

Solomon shook his head slowly, staring at the ceiling in an attitude of thought. "No, I think you have it all."

The detectives stood up to leave, but quickly sat down when Solomon mumbled something about other women. Asked to repeat what he had said, Solomon cleared his throat and said, "I just wanted you guys to know that I've started dating other women. I don't see Carolyn anymore, but I've begun dating again. Just thought you should know."

Constantino silently marveled at the coolness of the man before him. He decided to see if he could pierce Solomon's apparent sangfroid. "Mr. Solomon, I want you to think back to February 1988. We understand on one particular weekend you went with a friend to a Club Med and that Kristan was also away at that time. Do you recall any of that?" Constantino asked.

Solomon shook his head, telling himself he shouldn't be surprised the police had checked him out in so much detail. "Yes, I remember. It's true. We went to a Club Med in the Caribbean. So?"

Constantino decided to prick his suspect and find out just how much he knew about his wife's secrets. The detectives had never shared with Solomon or Pillersdorf what John Bourne had told them.

"Did you ever give any more thought to the possibility that your wife was having an affair? What about that guy whose name you gave us back in January? Bourne. John Bourne. Anything more you can tell us about him?"

Without so much as a flicker of anger or surprise, Solomon calmly eyed his inquisitor and shook his head. "She never told me directly, but I suspected something might be going on. I'm very familiar with Mr. John Bourne, but I can't tell you anything more than what I've already said."

The fact that Solomon never raised his voice, never gave any sign of being upset about suspecting that his wife had been unfaithful, disturbed the detectives.

Constantino decided to probe deeper into the stone that sat before him impersonating a man. "Can you tell me where Kristan was that weekend?"

For the first time, Constantino thought he saw a moment's hesitation in Solomon's eyes, a nervous twitch tugging at the man's mouth. "I believe Kristan was away on a ski trip that weekend," he finally said. "And before you ask, I'll tell you that she was away on that ski trip with Carolyn Warmus. My daughter and Carolyn had become quite close and Betty Jeanne didn't have any problem with letting them go away together."

Constantino broke his eye contact with Solomon, convinced the man had no notion his wife had been playing around that very same weekend. The whole thing was pretty sordid, now that he thought about it. While Paul Solomon was most likely looking for some fresh action at a Club Med, Betty Jeanne was fucking her lover in her marital bed while Kristan was off on a ski weekend with the woman who was fucking and sucking her father on the side. Incredible!

"Can you believe this guy?" Lind asked, as he spun the car out the parking space and maneuvered it down the winding drive. "This whole family is nuttier than a fucking fruitcake. No one's going to believe us when we tell them about that weekend. And to top it off, his wife's not in the ground six months and he's found himself a new squeeze. This guy's too much."

Constantino nodded. He was thinking how torn apart his entire life would be if anything happened to his wife. She was the center of his universe along with his two little girls. If Marie had been murdered he couldn't even imagine the pain he would feel. But here was a guy it had happened to and he was already out looking for some fresh snatch.

"This guy is a sleaze with a capital *S*," he said.

Their ride up the rickety elevator to the third-floor office of Jimmy Russo didn't do much to change Sullivan and Constantino's low opinion of private detectives. The building that housed All-Tech Investigations Limited, was pretty run down, and the neighborhood around West Fifty-second Street didn't rank among the safest.

Ten seconds after meeting Russo, the detectives were convinced he fit every negative stereotype with which a private eye had ever been slapped.

Standing about five feet, nine inches tall, with jet-black hair and a paunch that would make any beer drinker proud, Russo greeted the detectives in a heavy Brooklyn accent. Tucked under his left arm in a brown leather holster hung his 9-millimeter Glock.

Neither man could help comparing Russo's seedy two-desk office with Parco's high-priced setup they had visited a few days before. Russo introduced them to his partner, and Gabe Laura quickly busied himself reading a report, but Sullivan and Constantino knew his ears were tuned in to their conversation.

"Mr. Russo, we're investigating the homicide of a woman named Betty Jeanne Solomon who was killed up in Westchester in January," Constantino said.

Street smart and wary of any cops he didn't know, Russo decided to play the innocent until he got a handle on just what these two Westchester detectives wanted with him. When Constantino finally brought up Carolyn Warmus's name, he smiled and sat back in his chair, pulling a pack of Kools from his shirt pocket and lighting one up to help settle himself down.

"Oh yeah, do I know Carolyn," he said with a snort. "That is one dizzy broad. Good looking and a great body. She's smart, but a little wacky for my taste, you know what I mean?"

Russo enjoyed telling stories, and he knew he had the rapt attention of the two men before him. After Constantino told him Parco had filled them in about his being assigned to do surveillance on Warmus's New Jersey lover, Russo described the incident with relish.

"Vinnie called me into his office one day and there was this really attractive girl all decked out in a white tennis outfit," Russo said. "She wanted to hire us to surveil and take some photographs of this married guy she was seeing to find out if he was popping anyone else on the side and if he was going to divorce his wife for her.

"Vinnie says, 'Hey, I want you to take this young lady with you to-night and she'll show you where the guy lives and works.' Now, I don't usually take any clients with me on an assignment, it's not professional, but Vinnie insisted, so I said what the hell, he's the boss. So I call home to let my live-in girl friend know I won't make it home for dinner and we take my new Lincoln Towne car to go pay a visit to this guy named Matthew Nicolosi. She tells me he lives in Newton, New Jersey, with his wife and kids and that along with a full-time job he works nights as a bartender at a nearby Ramada Inn in Somerset, New Jersey.

"Carolyn first directs me to the guy's house and there's no one home. Then she tells me maybe we can find him at the Sandalwood Lounge, a bar at the Ramada Inn where he works. We drive there and she spots this black Honda CRX sitting outside and tells me that's his car. She gives me a description of the guy and I tell her to stay put and grab my camera and go inside to see if I can snap his picture. Only there's hardly anyone in the place and I would have stuck out like a sore thumb if I started taking the guy's picture. So I go back to the car and tell Carolyn we got to wait until either the bar fills up so I won't be noticed or until he comes out at closing time. She chooses to wait until closing and when the guy walks to his car I snap a couple shots and we're out of there.

"We drive back and I drop her off at her car and I head home. The next day I develop the pictures and give them to Vinnie and forget about them. By this time I figure out what the game is. Carolyn wanted to get some compromising photos of the guy to send to his wife, hoping this would get her to divorce the guy so she could have him. When I gave Vinnie the shots from the bar, I told him none of them were compromising photos and how in the hell was I supposed to get those.

"Vinnie tells me, 'We'll superimpose them if necessary,' and then I went back to my office and forgot about it.

"Two days later I get called up to Vinnie's office again and he tells me to take a camera over to Carolyn's apartment to take some shots of her. Now I wasn't going to get involved in creating false evidence by superimposing any pictures, but I didn't have any problem taking these shots of her, so I went.

"She meets me at the door in a blue, Oriental silk robe and her hair's all done up nice and enough makeup so she looked really good. She walks into a bedroom and I start setting up the camera equipment. A few minutes later she comes out wearing a pink wig. No shit, a pink wig. Then she opens her robe and she's only wearing some lacey, see-through lingerie.

"She asks me, 'Where do you want me to stand?' and man, I couldn't say a word. I mean the body on this broad was incredible. For the next hour I take a roll of color film, thirty-six shots of her in that outfit and a bunch of others. She changed into a red camisole, a black, see-through body stocking, and a blue little teddy something or other. All the time she's laughing and making small talk.

"For a couple of shots she lays out on the couch and cups her hands under her breasts and squeezes them, like something you'd see in *Playboy*. After I was done, she comes up to me and asks me if she excited me. I tell her no and she gets mad.

"Then she says, 'Maybe this will help,' and knees me in the balls. I got my camera stuff and got the hell out of there.

"The next day I developed those pictures and turned them over to Vinnie. I didn't think nothing more about it until a few days later when I went up to Vinnie's office to get something and I see all these photos of Carolyn and Nicolosi spread out all over his desk. Nicolosi's face had been cut out of some of them and appeared to be glued on photos of Carolyn, you know, like somebody was trying to superimpose the photographs. Real amateur job. Anybody would have seen that they were faked.

"I left the office and I never said anything to Vinnie about it. I saw Carolyn several times after that. She became a pretty regular visitor to the office, to see Vinnie, but I never was asked to take her out on any more assignments or to take her picture again. It was fine by me. She'd call and talk with me on the phone every now and then, but that was pretty much it."

Constantino and Sullivan sat speechless, trying hard to write fast enough to fill their notebooks with all of Russo's intriguing story. Their quiet, demure schoolteacher had just been unmasked as a raving sex queen with a strong penchant for married men and exhibitionism. Apparently she wasn't above manufacturing evidence to get what she wanted, either.

Russo watched the stunned looks on the detectives' faces, then leaned back and took a last, satisfying drag from his dying cigarette before tossing it to the floor and stubbing it out with the heel of his black leather boot. "That's about all I can tell you, guys," he said.

After a few more questions, the detectives left, telling Russo they would probably have some more questions for him in the future. The private eye told them he'd be happy to oblige.

Once the detectives were safely on their way down to the street in the creaking elevator, Russo leaned back in his chair and smiled at his partner. He had given the cops a taste of Carolyn and he was sure it had whetted their interest in her. Since they hadn't asked all the right questions, there were other little bits of Carolyn's history and other things he knew about Parco that he hadn't felt obliged to volunteer. Besides, he wanted to learn more about this homicide case. If things panned out, Parco could be in some deep shit and that would suit him just fine.

He flipped his Rolodex around to the name he was looking for and picked up the phone. It would be the first of many calls he would make that afternoon to try and find out what was really going on.

If there was any chance at all that Parco could take a fall as the result of this case, Russo wanted in on the chance to play a role in the king's demise. His dislike for Parco ran deep, and he didn't care who knew it.

He lit a fresh cigarette, put his feet on the desk, and waited for his call to go through.

6

SITTING ON HIS BALCONY in only a worn pair of gym shorts and white athletic socks, Solomon put down the local newspaper and enjoyed the momentary breeze that did little to cool him this sweltering, late-July afternoon. His mind drifted, and for no particular reason he began to think of Carolyn. Long, lovely, sensual Carolyn.

He was planning to play some basketball in the city that day, which would give him a ready-made excuse to be in the neighborhood. There was one burning question he had to ask Carolyn face to face: "Did you kill Betty Jeanne?"

He slid the glass door open and walked to the kitchen, picking up the phone and dialing the number from memory. After several rings he hung up. He decided to try her again once he was in the city.

Several hours later, exhausted from some quick-paced games of hoop, Solomon found himself at the pay phone in the Catch A Rising Star comedy club just a couple of doors down from Carolyn's apartment. He dropped in his coins and was disappointed when her phone went unanswered.

Sitting back at the bar, he began slowly sipping another vodka Collins. He figured he'd give her another try a little later. Twenty minutes passed and, after paying his tab, he decided to walk the fifteen steps to her apartment. He pressed the familiar intercom button and a noisy buzz filled the air, but again no one answered. Dejected, he turned to go.

Warmus looked shocked when she opened the door off the busy street and walked in.

"Hello, Carolyn."

Despite her best intentions, she rushed to him, giving him a kiss and a tight squeeze.

Try as she might, she couldn't seem to play it cool. Not with Paul. Not with him in her arms. The past several months, what with the police interrogations and the separation, had been horrible, but she had endured it all knowing that one day he would come back to her. And now here he was. It had been what seemed like a lifetime and obviously he was just now realizing how much she meant to him. When he asked her to go back to the bar with him, she smiled her reply. Within minutes they were sitting in a booth with drinks in front of them.

When she looked across at her former lover, the same lustful feelings once again took hold of her soul.

"I'm sorry it's been so long," Solomon began clumsily, but he knew he had been forgiven when she entwined her fingers with his and stared into his eyes.

Over several drinks—and an unnoticed comedy show—the pair talked, first about Kristan, Paul's summer, and then what was really on both of their minds, Carolyn's encounter with the police and, finally, the murder itself.

"Carolyn, I'm sorry I even have to ask this, but I have to know. Did you kill Betty Jeanne or have anything to do with her death?"

The words hung in the air for what seemed like an eternity. The explosion from Carolyn that he expected never came. She reached out her hand and touched his.

"Paul, I'm so happy you feel comfortable enough with me to ask me that question. No. No I didn't," she answered softly. "I'd never do anything to hurt you or Kristan."

Solomon heaved a sigh of relief, and the conversation soon turned to how much they had missed one another.

When the show was over and the waitresses began shooing people along so they could set up for the next performance, Carolyn and Paul walked back to her apartment.

"I want you to come up for a minute to see the decorating job I've done," she said. "It's taken me forever, but I've got everything in place like I want and it's fabulous."

When they reached her doorway and entered the apartment, Warmus didn't try and hide her smile as Paul slipped his arms around her and began caressing her back. She opened her mouth as Paul's lips met hers, his tongue slowly moving in and out. She'd always known he'd be back and this time no one stood in the way of their happiness.

It was a steamy, dog day afternoon, August 15, as Lind and Constantino once again made their way to the office of Vincent Parco and Associates Limited. They both recognized the sour-faced receptionist whose job obviously was to guard the inner sanctum.

As Parco walked down the hall into the waiting area, the detectives once again took the opportunity to size him up. Their visit today was what Lind sometimes referred to as a squeeze play. They really had nothing on Parco, at least not much more than their mutual dislike for the pretentious private eye. But return visits to people connected to a case were part of the job. Sometimes a person's story would change or he'd add or leave something out, letting you know he was hiding something.

Their second visit to Parco seemed to be having an effect, Lind noted, as the pompous private detective appeared much less friendly than he had the first time around.

Once more ushered into the plush office, Constantino and Lind took their seats without waiting for an invitation, while the balding, rotund private eye sank into his chair with a grunt.

"Well, what can I do for you gentlemen today?" Parco asked, noting the detectives' casual glances at his expensively tailored attire. He glanced at his watch. 1:30 P.M. He would have to shuffle them out of here fairly quickly if he was to keep to his schedule.

The broad grin left the private eye's round face when he heard the first question. "Mr. Parco, we'd like to know if you have any problem with giving us a written statement regarding the information on Carolyn Warmus you shared with us on our last visit here?"

Parco searched the smiling detective's face but could find no hint of deception. He'd have to comply or else appear to be hiding something.

Why he had ever gotten involved with that crazy bitch Carolyn he would never know. Now he was trapped and he knew it. Telling the detectives about his involvement with Carolyn was one thing. Signing a false police statement meant he could be charged with a misdemeanor.

"Certainly I'll give you a signed statement," he said confidently, smiling back at Constantino. "Anything that will help you boys out."

Both detectives pulled out their notebooks and asked the nervous private eye to repeat his earlier story. "Only this time with as much detail as you can remember," Constantino advised.

Parco hesitated a moment and then, with all the innocence he could muster, asked the detectives, "I know this is a ludicrous question, but am I a suspect or something in your murder investigation?"

"We're going to be asking the questions, please. Can you tell us again how you met Carolyn Warmus?" Constantino responded politely.

Parco silently tried to figure out how much the detectives knew. He picked up a pencil and began nervously tapping it on the top of his desk. He tried to remember exactly what he had told them when they were here before.

After repeating almost verbatim the story he had told the detectives almost a month and half before, Parco paused, as if unsure whether to continue, and then he drew a deep breath. "There's something else I remembered after you gentlemen left the last time that I was meaning to tell you about," he said with conviction. "It may be important, I don't know."

The incident Parco began describing made both detectives sit straight up in their chairs.

"Some time in the fall of 1988 Carolyn asked me about the possibility of starting an investigation into the cause of a crash of one of her father's airplanes. He's some millionaire insurance guy in Michigan and apparently one of his planes crashed for some unknown reason.

"She also told me that her sister Tracey was involved in a hit-and-run accident in Washington, D.C., and that a girl friend of her father's who lived in Detroit or the Washington area could be the person responsible for both incidents. She never told me the woman's name. Apparently Carolyn blamed her for what happened and said this woman was always causing her family trouble. She wanted to know whether I could have someone investigate what happened, but nothing really ever came of it. We consulted about this possible investigation, but I was not formally retained to handle this matter."

Now on a roll, Parco stunned the detectives with another story, his voice taking on a policelike tone.

"I also remember there was one time in 1988 that Carolyn asked me and Ray Melucci, a guy that did some work for me, how she could obtain a gun. She told us she wanted one for protection in the event of a burglary at her apartment. I told her she could apply for a pistol permit, carry, target, or premises, by submitting an application to the New York

City Police Department. I didn't think much about it and she dropped the matter."

Pressed for further details about Warmus's request for a weapon, Parco told them that he couldn't remember precisely when she had made the inquiry. "It didn't seem like that big a deal at the time," he added.

"Any other involvement with Carolyn Warmus that you haven't shared with us?" Constantino asked politely.

Dropping his eyes, Parco paused and then looked straight at the officers. "There is one thing I should tell you. On January 14, I believe that was the day before that woman was murdered, I was supervising a surveillance case involving a client named Seow. I had occasion to speak with Miss Warmus at about 7:30 P.M. that night and she invited me to stop by her place for a drink or she would make me a light meal.

"When I got to her apartment, she said she wanted to see a movie. After looking in the newspaper, we went out and found a movie theater on Eighty-sixth Street, near Lexington Avenue, and we saw *Tequilla Sunrise*. After we got our seats, I took my gun out of the holster and put it in my pocket and then I took the holster off, folded it up, and gave it to her to put in her purse. When we were leaving the movie, she told me she was concerned that my gun was in her pocketbook. I told her that she only had my holster.

"I went home with her at approximately 11, 11:15 P.M. When I entered her apartment, I took off my jacket, put on the shoulder holster, put my gun back in it, and I left to go back home. That's all that happened."

The detectives sat staring at Parco. He had just provided them information about Warmus that she had failed to give them during questioning.

"There's something else, too," he quickly added. "In June I was contacted by Ray Melucci, he's another private detective that I just mentioned. Melucci told me he had been interviewed by Detective Constantino regarding a homicide that occurred in January. Shortly after that I had a conversation with Miss Warmus about the police inquiries. She seemed surprised that anyone would be calling friends or associates of hers regarding something that happened six months earlier.

"It was between that time and the present that I have had a number of conversations with Miss Warmus regarding the homicide matter and other unrelated matters. These conversations were both in person and on the telephone. In reference to the conversations about the homicide,

I had asked her if she was interviewed by the police, and if her attorney flew down from Detroit to represent her. She advised me that he did not fly down, he just called the police and had some discussions with them.

"She also mentioned that to the best of her knowledge the husband, Paul Solomon, was a suspect. At some point in time I had asked her if she had any involvement with Mr. Solomon and she said no. She had on one or two occasions expressed an opinion that the police felt that Mr. Solomon was a suspect because he had some Air Force or Army training with firearms. That's about all I know."

The detectives tried hard to hide their astonishment as they put down their notebooks. Parco had just given them a wealth of information about Carolyn Warmus that she had been unwilling—for whatever reason—to provide. During the next twenty minutes, Constantino—given permission to use Parco's typewriter—typed up a synopsis of the statements the private eye had given them, and then pulled out a pen for Parco to sign it, verifying that it was accurate. With a practiced flourish, Parco penned his name.

"I hope I've been helpful," he said, standing up to let his visitors know the interview session was over as far as he was concerned.

Parco's story had certainly shed some new light on Paul Solomon's paramour. At the very least, the detectives would now start a more intensive background check into Carolyn Warmus. If married men seemed to be her thing, who knew with what or whom else she may have been involved.

Both men had their suspicions about Parco and their promiscuous schoolteacher, but if there'd been anything going on, they'd find out eventually. They would talk again to Parco's former employee, Russo. Something about the way Parco said Russo's name gave Constantino the distinct impression he didn't like the man. Maybe Russo's memory would improve as well.

Having shown his visitors to the door, Parco walked back into his office, slammed the door shut, and reached for his telephone. He dialed Carolyn's number.

On the afternoon of July 27, Solomon pulled his car into one of the empty slots outside the Greenburgh Police Department and hurried up the winding concrete walkway.

He managed to control a shudder as he recalled the nightmarish morning he'd been brought here more than five months before. It now seemed like an eternity, but the horror remained deep within him and he had long ago realized it would stay that way forever.

The desk sergeant called Constantino, who came downstairs and motioned Solomon to follow him. They walked to the evidence room where the officer on duty took the papers Constantino handed him and disappeared. Several minutes later he returned with a bag of clothes and other items the police seized from the Solomon home the night of the slaying.

As he bent over to sign the release form, Solomon couldn't hold back what he'd been thinking for the past several days.

"Listen, Detective. I know you guys have had me picked out as the killer, but I hope by now you know I had nothing to do with Betty Jeanne's death. I just wanted you to know that if there is anything I can do to help, I will."

Constantino nodded, surprised that he found himself almost believing Solomon's words.

"You seeing anyone else now?" he asked, hoping his question sounded sincere.

"I think I told you a while back that I was seeing a woman named Barbara Ballor. I'm still seeing her."

The detective made a mental note of the remark and then took Solomon back to the front door. He watched as the teacher walked to his car, head hung slightly as if still carrying the weight of all that had happened.

Constantino fought back the urge to feel sorry for the guy as he turned to go back to his desk.

7

CAROLYN WAS FURIOUS with Paul Rosenbaum. He couldn't possibly know what she was going through. Not only were the police asking her friends and neighbors questions about her, but more importantly, Paul was again refusing to see her, coming up with every excuse in the book even after that wonderful night in her apartment just a few weeks before.

She knew he had begun seeing Barbara Ballor, a young teacher at the Greenville School. Paul had never even mentioned the woman's name to her, let alone said they were dating. But Carolyn had followed him on a couple of occasions and had seen them together. Once she had found a strange car in one of Paul's parking spaces outside the condo and she'd had Vinnie run the plate number for her. The painful news was that it belonged to Ballor.

The fact that Paul had met Ballor in the exact same set of circumstances as he'd met Carolyn made her mad as hell. On top of everything else, she had learned just the other day that Paul was planning a trip to Puerto Rico in about two weeks, but he said he wanted to spend some time alone.

It had only taken a couple of days for her to call down to the island to confirm where he was staying. Carolyn could just picture Paul and Ballor lying on the San Juan beaches, enjoying romantic dinners under the stars and dancing the evening away.

Worse yet, she thought about Paul making love to that little bitch and the anger once again welled inside her. She would have to find out for sure whether Ballor was going with him or not.

A few of the underhanded private-eye tricks Parco had taught her would come in handy now. Calmer, with her emotions back under control, Carolyn wished she hadn't told Rosenbaum how much she needed to be with Paul and that she was going to kill herself.

Rosenbaum knew he would have to tell Tom Warmus about his daughter's mental state. He was genuinely concerned that Carolyn might try to commit suicide. Being a suspect in the murder of your lover's wife would be enough to send anyone over the edge, he thought.

Tom Warmus's secretary rang him through immediately. The insurance magnate listened to his attorney for several minutes and then hung up. He buzzed his secretary and told her to get his daughter Tracey and his son Tom Jr., on the phone and to make arrangements for them to fly to New York the next day.

He was convinced Carolyn had nothing to do with that murder in New York, but the concern in Rosenbaum's voice told him something was seriously wrong. If the lawyer really thought Carolyn was even remotely serious about killing herself, it would be worth the expense of sending his other children out there to find out what was happening and to calm her down.

His former wife had always accused Warmus of not spending enough time with the children. But his job had been to make the money for the family, and his hard work had paid off. He had built the American Way Insurance Company from a struggling business to a multimillion dollar enterprise. With that success had come the lavish homes, the cars, and planes.

Elizabeth had always wanted just to stay at home in their house in Troy, Michigan. She never wanted to enjoy the good life, as he did. And as his second wife Nancy did.

Nancy had started out as his secretary and then became his lover. Young and beautiful, she was always ready for a good time. The children didn't like her, but the divorce had been a long time ago, in 1972. Carolyn was eight, Tracey was seven, and Tommy was only three. Elizabeth had initially gotten custody of the kids, but her drinking problem and then her decision to leave Michigan had forced him to regain custody through the courts on October 1, 1979. She had remarried that same year, when Carolyn was fifteen.

As for him, he now lived in a million-dollar home in prestigious

Franklin Hills, and he had enough money to do what he wanted and to go wherever he chose. Life had been good to him, but he had earned it.

Out of all the children, Carolyn was the most difficult. An attractive girl, with an intelligent mind, she always seemed to be getting into some kind of trouble. At first, it had seemed to be typical adolescent rebellion, only Carolyn hadn't grown out of it. She had always seemed to be jealous of her younger sister. Tracey was a beautiful child, who had grown into an even more beautiful woman. And even as a kid she was outgoing and popular. Maybe Carolyn felt the need to do something bad just to get her father to notice her.

Rosenbaum was worried about Carolyn. Although he was concerned that she may try and kill herself, it was just as likely that she might try to take her anger out on Paul Solomon.

As far as he could tell, it was Solomon's not wanting to be with her that had set Carolyn off. The longer he sat and thought about it, the more unsettled he became. Finally, he looked through his Rolodex and dialed Gary Pillersdorf. In a strained voice, Rosenbaum wasted no time in explaining the purpose of his call. "Listen, Mr. Pillersdorf, I just got off the phone with Carolyn Warmus. She was very upset and irrational and is talking about committing suicide. I felt I had to call you so you could warn Paul Solomon that I think she might be capable of causing herself or someone else harm.

"She was out here in Michigan a short time ago and had a big falling out with her father. Her family feels she is in need of psychiatric care due to her present state of mind, coupled with her past history of psychiatric problems and related care," he continued.

"One of the reasons I'm calling is to see if you can arrange for Mr. Solomon to allow for Carolyn to have a soft landing from their relationship, you know, maybe leave her some hope, to allow her to ease away from the relationship before she suffers any more damage to her psyche. The family is very concerned she might harm herself."

Both the warning and the tone in the obviously concerned lawyer's voice frightened Pillersdorf. He thanked Rosenbaum for the call. "But I don't know if Paul or I can be of any help because Paul has already told her that the relationship was over, that he didn't want to see her again, and that he wanted to get on with his life."

Rosenbaum caught his breath, knowing the effect that would have had on Carolyn.

Pillersdorf promised he would try to contact Solomon to let him know what was happening. He knew that something had to be terribly wrong for the woman's own attorney to call and warn him. He had repeatedly told Paul to stay away from Warmus, and now he wondered if his friend had heeded his advice.

He immediately dialed Solomon's number, praying that Kristan wasn't home alone and that Paul would answer. Getting no answer, he hung up and dialed the Greenburgh police. He was quickly put through to Sullivan.

Five minutes later Pillersdorf hung up the phone, more secure now that the detectives had agreed to meet him and Paul the next day. He wondered what they would make of Rosenbaum's call.

The uneventful flight from Detroit to New York's La Guardia Airport on August 8 took a little more than two hours. Tom Jr. and Tracey were anxious to see their sister. Daddy had sounded worried when he told them Carolyn was having problems and asked them to go spend some time with her to see if she was all right.

Carolyn had indeed sounded upset when they phoned to say they were flying in. Normally they wouldn't have bothered their sister once she said she wanted to be left alone, but their father had been insistent.

Carolyn buzzed her brother and sister into the building and waited until she heard the knock before opening her door. Without a hello, she spun on her heel and threw herself on the couch, folding her arms across her chest. Ten minutes later she was screaming at the top of her lungs as Tom Jr. and Tracey looked at each other in bewilderment.

For several minutes Carolyn alternated between screaming fits of rage, knocking over furniture, and sobbing promises of suicide.

The neighbors began pounding on the walls to shut her up, but that just angered her more. Her screaming and babbling about suicide, Daddy being a terrible father, and that what was going on in her life was none of their damn business, persuaded Tom Jr. that the situation was more than he and Tracey could handle. He picked up the phone and dialed 911.

Tracey stood shaking, watching her beautiful sister having a nervous breakdown right before her eyes, unable to understand what had triggered the emotional fallout.

After her brother called the police, Carolyn, realizing what was about to happen, tried to compose herself and unsuccessfully argued against going to a psychiatric hospital as her brother was insisting. Unable to sway her terrified siblings, she exploded in a new, white-hot rage, smashing glass objects against the walls and screaming as if she were being beaten.

A short time later, four New York City police officers stormed through the door and grabbed the flailing woman, who tried her best to escape. While the cops took their sister downstairs to a waiting ambulance, Tom and Tracey quickly threw some of Carolyn's clothes in a suitcase and hurried after her.

Strapped down in the back of the vehicle, which sped uptown with its siren wailing, Warmus calmed down enough to realize she wasn't about to scream her way out of this mess. Five minutes later, the police took her off the stretcher, grabbed her by the arms, and half-walked, half-carried her into Metropolitan Hospital's psychiatric ward.

An hour later, Dr. Isaac Ramsden listened patiently to Tom Jr. and Tracey as they described Carolyn's behavior and the pressures that were obviously building in her.

They knew nothing, however, of her being a possible suspect in a murder investigation. Nor were they able to tell Ramsden much about Carolyn's personal life. They couldn't answer the doctor's questions about their sister's drug use and had no way of knowing that the cause of her outburst was not being able to see the man with whom she had become obsessed.

After speaking with Carolyn's father on the phone, Ramsden emerged from his office and assured the two frightened siblings that Carolyn would receive the best in counseling and rest at the hospital. He suggested they return home and contact him later in the week after his staff had had a chance to talk with and evaluate her.

Leaving the building and hailing a cab for the airport, Tom and Tracey wondered just how sick their sister really was.

Normally Jimmy Russo liked the noise of the traffic and the shouts of people from the street below his office windows. But today the sounds of the bustling metropolis seemed almost deafening as he sat poised over his worn, IBM typewriter, deciding how much of what he knew he should put on paper. Finally, he grabbed the blank police statement forms Constantino and Sullivan had left for him, inserted one of the pages, and began slowly tapping out his story.

An hour later he finished the last of the four pages and began rereading the document that he knew would propel him into the center of the Betty Jeanne Solomon homicide. He had written:

The following statement in regards to Carolyn Warmus is true and to the best of my knowledge. I first spoke with Ms. Warmus, while I was employed with Vincent Parco & Associates as a Field Investigator. Mr. Parco had assigned me to conduct a surveillance of a boyfriend of Ms. Warmus and had instructed me to take Ms. Warmus along on the surveillance. The only details that Mr. Parco had given to me were that I was to take Ms. Warmus to New Jersey and take photos of her boyfriend "Mat", his car and his home. During the drive to New Jersey Ms. Warmus had stated that her boyfriend Mat, was married lived in either Summerville of Summerset, I cannot recall, and that he worked nights as a bartender at the Ramada Inn, in either Summerville or Summerset and that he drove a black Honda, auto. During the Surveillance, we did not observe her boyfriend Mat, but did take approx. [sic] 36 photos of his car, home and his place of employment. During the evening Ms. Warmus spoke very little as to why she wanted the photos taken, but did express that Mat, had stated to her he would marry her if his wife would give him a divorce. Ms. Warmus further stated that she did not believe that Mat had the guts to tell his wife, but she would have to either wait it out, or she would have to confront Mat's wife, with proof of her affair with Mat. I began to realize that Ms. Warmus wanted the surveillance photos of Mat, his car and his home for the purpose of causing problems between Mat and his wife. At this point I decided to terminate the surveillance and drive Ms. Warmus, back to Mr. Parco's office, where I gave Mr. Parco the roll of film. At this time I left Ms. Warmus with Mr. Parco, at aprox. 10:00 P.M. This was sometime during 1987, Ms. Warmus had come in to see Mr. Parco at aprox. 4:00 P.M. and I was sent out to conduct the surveillance, with Ms. Warmus at aprox. 5:00 P.M.

My second Meeting with Ms. Warmus, was while I was still employed by Parco & Associates, aprox. 3 or 4 days after the first meeting and was sometime between June and September 1987. Mr. Parco had instructed me to go to Ms. Warmus' apartment located somewhere between East 20th, street and East 22nd, street off of 2nd Avenue. Upon arrival I found Ms. Warmus dressed in a see-thru lingerie and wearing a pink wig. I at this time was told by Ms. Warmus that I was to take photos of her in her various outfits. The photo session lasted aprox. 1 hour and during the session Ms. Warmus had appeared in outfits that were nude and semi-nude. Prior to leaving her apartment Ms. Warmus had asked me if she had excited me sexually, when I replied to her that she had not, she appeared to have a sudden change in her personality. Ms. Warmus at this time stated that she was interested in taking me to bed and at this point she jerked her knee with a severe force into my groin and stated "maybe this will get you up." At this point I immediately left Ms. Warmus's apartment and returned to Mr. Parco's office. At this time I expressed to Mr. Parco, that something was not right with Ms. Warmus and told him what had occurred at her apartment and told him I would not continue with any part of any investigation in which Ms. Warmus was involved in.

During the next few months Ms. Warmus had various meetings with Mr. Parco and I had observed them meeting in Mr. Parco's office until I decided to leave my employment with Mr. Parco during January or February of 1988. At this time I along with Gabe Laura, who had worked with Parco, during the same time that I did and left his employment at the same time I did, to open are [sic] own Investigation firm, which we opened during March of 1988. Sometime between July or August of 1988, Ms. Warmus telephoned my office and stated that she would like to come in to discuss our taking on an investigation into the alleged crash of her father's jet in Michigan.

The 1st meeting with Ms. Warmus she stated that her father's jet had been sabotage by an unknown female. At this time, I told Ms. Warmus to get all the News Papers that covered the crash story and after aprox. 30 minutes she left my office.

2nd, meeting again Ms. Warmus telephoned my office and stated that she was coming up to see me. When she arrived I asked her how she knew, that I and Gabe Laura had opened up our own company and how she got our telephone number. She replied that Vincent Parco had told her. During this meeting she stated that her sister, who lives in Washington D.C. was hit by a hit and run driver, while she was riding a bike. She further stated that the driver of the vehicle was described by witnesses as the same female that had been near her father's jet prior to the crash.

Again I told her to give us any documentation as to the crash of her fathers jet and the hit and run accident of her sister. after aprox. 1 hour she left my office.

3rd, meeting again Ms. Warmus had called prior to coming in to see me. During this visit she stated that she knew who the female was that had caused the jet crash and who had attempted to kill her sister.

She stated that she had been conducting her own investigation and knew where the woman worked and lived, she said the woman lived in Westchester and her name was either Jean or Betty Jeanne. At this time she was asked "why do you need us, if you have been conducting your own investigation and you know who caused the accidents." Her reply at this time was I want to buy a Machine Pistol with a silencer. At this time we told her that she better leave and go back and tell who ever sent her, that we are not arms dealers and want no part of what ever is going on. Her reply was that she wanted the weapon for protection. At this point she left our office after aprox. 1 hour and stated that she would call again. At this time after Ms. Warmus had left, we advised sources within the New York City Police Department of what had occurred, in regards to Ms. Warmus looking to buy an illegal weapon. We were advised to inform our sources if Ms. Warmus had contacted us again. We were advised by other sources that Ms. Warmus was still having meetings with Vincent Parco. But Ms. Warmus did not contact us at anytime after the 3rd, meeting. At this time we had no further contact with Ms. Warmus and had not heard any further information in regards to Ms. Warmus, until July 6, 1989, when we received a telephone call from Detectives from the Greenburgh, P.D.

Russo looked over the four typewritten pages and, ignoring the misspellings and bad grammar, signed each of the documents. He checked his calendar and then put August 9, 1989, on each page before making photocopies of the material. Stuffing the original into an envelope, he sealed it and tossed it onto a pile of other letters to be mailed later that day.

"This ought to make those Greenburgh detectives' day," he laughed, as Laura walked into the room. "It'll give them a side of Carolyn that I'm sure they haven't seen yet."

With a self-satisfied smile, Russo pulled out his pack of Kools and leaned back in his chair, lighting up and taking a satisfying drag from the cigarette.

During her stay at Metropolitan Hospital, Carolyn attended the various counseling sessions, read magazines and books, and went to bed at the prescribed time.

She had gotten a grip on her emotions and knew she had to show Dr. Ramsden and his staff that she was psychologically stable. She also realized her father would be getting a report, and she wanted it to be glowing so he would stop worrying and leave her alone.

The place wasn't so bad, after all, and it gave her a chance to rest up. Her father and the doctors had assured her that no one, including her bosses at the Byram Hills School District, where she was scheduled to start work in September, would ever know she had been there. That in itself was a big relief.

From the first day she arrived at the hospital, Carolyn decided her best course of action was to be as friendly as possible with the nurses, doctors, and the rest of the medical staff. Whenever any of them entered her room, or arrived at the boring, never-ending talk sessions, she would paste on her big, wide smile and be just as pleasant as you please.

She even began flirting a little with the male doctors and patients. She knew they liked that, especially from somebody as attractive as she was. It was a little game, but she enjoyed playing it anyway. But at night, when the lights were switched off and she was left alone with her thoughts, Carolyn began to think of Paul. She couldn't help it. She wanted him in the worst way and his keeping her at arm's length was a hurtful thing to do, especially after everything they'd been through.

But she would forgive him. She always did. When her thoughts drifted to Barbara Ballor, she felt the anger bubbling within her again. She suppressed the feeling, knowing that being worked up over that little tramp would only interfere with the secret plan she had been carefully plotting for the past several nights as she lay in the darkness of her hospital room. It was a good plan and she was excited about it.

The withdrawal pangs were less frequent now for Manuel Rodriguez, and he found it was easier to get out of bed and stroll the floor of the psychiatric unit. He couldn't remember exactly what day he'd been brought in, but he was sure it was because he'd flipped out after injecting a bad hit of heroin.

At first, the greasy-haired, skinny Hispanic had frightened her, but Warmus soon found herself entranced by the fast-talking, street-wise patient. Their daily conversations between sessions helped the time pass more quickly.

On Tuesday, August 15, after spending seven restful days in the psychiatric center, Carolyn dressed, packed her suitcase, and signed out of Metropolitan Hospital with the blessing of Dr. Ramsden.

The week-long stay was surely enough time to placate her father, whom she knew would receive a favorable report from the hospital. And now that she was well rested and feeling fine, there was no reason for her not to get on with her life. She hailed a southbound cab and, minutes later, was safely back inside her apartment.

She didn't have much time to enjoy her first day of real freedom, however, because she had to start putting her plan into action. She had some shopping to do, and she had also promised Manuel she would meet him for lunch. When he left the hospital a few days before her, they had promised each other to hook up.

She checked the cabinet under her bathroom sink and saw she was out of suntan oil. Carolyn made a mental note to pick some up along with the other things she would need. Locking her apartment behind her, she took the elevator to the ground floor and walked out into the warm sunshine.

When she finally hailed a cab, she told the driver to take her to First Avenue and 116th Street. Minutes later, the cabbie slammed to a stop along the curb. Warmus handed him the fare and a dollar tip as she flung open her door and walked into the Delightful Restaurant, a coffee shop that Manuel had told her made good bacon and eggs.

Rodriguez sat in a back booth and waved Warmus over. After only a few minutes, they left together, and another short cab ride took them back to her apartment.

Five minutes later, Rodriguez walked down the three flights of stairs leading out of Warmus's building, a smile on his face. He patted his coat pocket to make sure the thick wad of cash was still there. Reassured, he strolled down the busy sidewalk, looking over his shoulder every few minutes as had become his habit.

With Manuel gone, Carolyn began cleaning up the mess in her apartment, which hadn't been touched since her explosive episode the week before. Her heart was racing by the time she finished drying the last dish, and she sat down on the sofa next to the telephone.

She pulled a sheaf of papers from her purse and fumbled through them until she came to the page of phone numbers she was looking for. Glancing down the list, she found the right number and began dialing.

Tammy Rogers was sitting at home reading a newspaper when the ringing telephone made her jump. She was always a little nervous when her roommate was away, but she laughed to herself when she realized how silly she was being. She looked at her watch on the way to the telephone. It was 8:29 P.M.

"Hello," she said.

"Hi, Barbara?" the friendly female voice responded.

"No, this is her roommate Tammy. Barb's not here right now. Can I help you?"

After a slight pause, the woman said, "Oh, hi. This is Madlyn. I'm a friend of Barbara's. I understand from her that you may be needing a new roommate soon because Barbara is planning to move, and I thought I'd call to check it out. I'm a teacher too at the Greenville School where Barb works and that's how we got to know each other. To be honest, this is a bad time for me to be doing this because I'm leaving tomorrow for a vacation in France. Do you have any idea when Barb might be back?"

Rogers listened to the rambling conversation and was strangely confused. She knew a teacher named Madlyn Newman who taught with Barbara at Greenville and who was getting ready to leave on a trip to France. In fact, she and Madlyn had met in February 1988 on a vacation to Cancun, Mexico, and struck up a friendship. It wasn't until later that

Tammy learned Madlyn and Barbara worked at the same school in Westchester.

Bewildered, Rogers decided to say nothing about her confusion.

"Barbara won't be returning for a few days. Is there any message?"

"Well, can you tell me if she is vacationing with Paul Solomon?"

Deciding that only a close friend of Barbara's would know she had gone on a trip with Paul, Rogers hesitated only a second before telling the caller, "Yes. They're in Puerto Rico already. Do you want to leave your name and number and I'll have her get back to you?"

The woman sounded miffed. "No, thanks, but I'll call her back later." Hanging up the phone, Rogers went back to her newspaper.

Six minutes later, the phone rang again.

"Hello."

"Hi, my name is Carolyn. Are you Tammy Rogers?"

"Yes, I am. Who did you say you were?"

Rogers thought the voice sounded exactly like that of the woman named Madlyn who had just called. She shook her head, thinking she must be getting punchy.

"Oh, you don't know me, but my friend Madlyn just told me she talked with you a little while ago. The reason I'm calling is that I'm living in Michigan right now, but I'm going to be moving to New York fairly soon. I'm here now looking for an apartment and a roommate and Madlyn told me you might be interested. She's a friend of your roommate, Barbara Ballor."

Rogers couldn't shake the feeling that something definitely strange was happening with these calls, but she couldn't figure out exactly what.

For the next twenty-three minutes, the woman who now called herself Carolyn chatted on in a happy tone, mixing in questions about Barbara with stories about the excitement of moving to New York, her career as a teacher, and the prospects for meeting sexy hunks in the Big Apple.

"I'm twenty-six and looking forward to everything," Carolyn told the ever-more-confused Rogers, who nonetheless answered most of the caller's questions about Barbara.

Finally tiring of the conversation, Rogers pulled a small note pad from a drawer and offered to take the woman's name and phone number to give to Barbara upon her return.

"Sure, that's fine. Just tell her Carolyn called. Thanks."

Rogers wrote down Carolyn's number, hung up the phone, threw the note on the counter, and went back to the sofa.

Carolyn placed the receiver back on the hook. While she hadn't been able to find out exactly where Ballor and Paul were in Puerto Rico, at least she knew they were there. The information disturbed her. She sat back on the sofa and smiled. Phase two of her plan should give her all the information she needed. She jumped off the sofa and spent the rest of the evening cleaning her apartment and watching television.

The next day, Tammy Rogers finished cleaning up the lunch dishes and decided to prove to herself that she wasn't going crazy. She grabbed her address book from her purse and dialed Madlyn Newman's number.

"Hi, Madlyn? This is Tammy. How are you doing?"

Caught in the middle of packing her last suitcase before she left for Kennedy Airport, Madlyn was frazzled, but made time for her friend.

"Hi, Tammy. I'm glad you called," she lied. "I'm just about ready to walk out the door. I'm so excited. I can't wait to see Paris!"

Rogers took the hint. "I won't keep you long. I really hope you have a great time. The reason I called, and I know this will sound a little strange, is I wanted to ask you if you called me yesterday."

"No, I didn't call you," Madlyn responded, hearing the note of concern in her friend's voice. "Is something wrong?"

"No, I guess not. Somebody called me yesterday and said her name was Madlyn and she was looking for a roommate. She also said she was getting ready to leave for a trip to France. It didn't sound like you and I thought it was strange, so I figured I'd just make sure it wasn't you."

Cradling the phone on one shoulder and bouncing on a tightly packed suitcase to force it to close, Madlyn didn't give much thought to the story. "That is strange, but it was probably nothing. Listen, I have to run."

Rogers wished her friend a safe and enjoyable trip and hung up. It was good to know she wasn't cracking up, but the calls still made her wonder. With a shrug she pushed the thoughts aside, figuring Barbara would be able to explain everything when she got back.

8

THE NEXT DAY, Carolyn awoke early and hurried through her morning chores. At about 9 A.M., she looked at her watch and realized she would have to hurry if she were going to make it on time. She gathered an armful of newly ironed summer clothes and rushed into her bedroom.

Traffic on 278 was light that afternoon and the cab driver expertly pulled off the highway and drove her through the La Guardia Airport complex, depositing her in plenty of time to make her flight. Carolyn waved off a baggage handler as she walked through the electronically controlled doors.

As she set her suitcase down while waiting in line, she looked at the flight board and saw that her plane to San Juan, Puerto Rico, was expected to be boarding on time. She hadn't had time to have her travel agent mail her the ticket, but she knew the desk clerk would have one reserved for her.

Carolyn's expressive eyes lit up and a smile came to her face as she pictured Paul's reaction when he first saw her. Twenty minutes later she boarded her flight and settled in for the long ride.

The screeching tires and the quick deceleration woke Carolyn from a light sleep. She looked out one of the small porthole windows of the 727 and stared into the bright Puerto Rican sunshine.

Grabbing her luggage as soon as it appeared on the carousel, she walked out the main terminal door, flipped designer sunglasses down over her blue eyes, and waved for a taxi.

"The Caribe Hilton, please," she told the driver, and settled back for the ride.

"By the way, driver, how far is the Condado Plaza Hotel from the Caribe Hilton?"

When he informed her the two were only a few miles apart, Carolyn smiled.

After checking in at 1:30 P.M. and eating a late lunch in one of the hotel restaurants, Carolyn walked back to her room and opened the drapes, allowing the sun to come streaming in. The room was festive in its bright, floral decor, but she had no time to enjoy it right now.

She pulled the folded sheaf of papers from her purse and searched the list of phone numbers printed on them. She picked up the phone and once again placed a call to Tammy Rogers.

When Rogers answered, Carolyn didn't try to disguise her voice. Parco had told her a number of times that very few people could remember a specific voice and that the trick in making fake calls was to sound authoritative and like you knew what you were talking about.

"Hello, this is the desk clerk at the Condado Plaza Hotel in Puerto Rico. I'm calling to confirm the whereabouts of one Barbara Ballor and Paul Solomon. We're holding a room for them and they have not shown up. This is the number I was given with the reservation and I was wondering if you could tell me where they are?"

Despite Parco's professional opinion, Rogers knew instantly that once again she was talking with Madlyn/Carolyn or whoever the hell it was. "Listen, I don't know where they are. I'm sorry. I can't help you," Rogers said, quickly hanging up the phone.

This last call had convinced her that something was seriously wrong. She forced herself to calm down and decided that she would call Puerto Rico later that evening and tell Paul what was happening. He'd know what to do about this wacky caller without scaring Barbara. She prayed it didn't mean trouble for her friend.

Carolyn hung up. It was no use trying to get any more information from Ballor's roommate. She had asked Parco for help in finding out where Paul and Ballor were staying and he had pulled one of his telephone scams with the airlines to learn what flight they were taking and then did the same thing with San Juan hotels. Parco had told her Solomon and Ballor would be at the Condado Plaza Hotel & Casino. But she had to be sure.

Carolyn decided a more direct approach was in order. She pulled out the San Juan phone book and found the main number for the Condado. The desk clerk tried to ring Solomon's room, but there was no answer.

For the next few hours, a frustrated Warmus continued to call the hotel in an effort to reach Paul. She began to snap at the by-now-exasperated clerk, finally accusing him of purposely not putting her calls through. Since the woman was getting progressively angrier, the clerk notified the front-desk manager, who in turn decided to cover his ass by calling security.

Ali Baez had been security director for the Condado Plaza for a number of years, and by now he believed he'd dealt with just about every kind of problem there was. A large man, standing well over six-feet tall, he prided himself on keeping order in the peaceful resort and calming the many security fears of the various hotel guests.

The call from the front-desk manager informing him of an angry and determined young woman named Carolyn Warmus who was jamming up their switchboard with calls to one of the hotel guests didn't sound particularly bad. Baez's experience told him it was probably a jealous wife or girl friend, but he also knew that these types of situations could turn into unpleasant problems not just for those involved, but for the other guests as well. He told the manager to route the pesty caller to him if she should call again.

A short time later, as Baez sat at his desk doing some paperwork, his phone rang, and to his surprise the woman identified herself as Carolyn Warmus. She told him she had called the front desk and was trying to reach a guest by the name of Paul Solomon, but had been switched to him. Baez was glad to know the desk clerks were following his instructions.

"Miss Warmus, I'm sorry. But the hotel guest you are trying to reach just has not been in his room to receive your calls. And as our operator has informed you, we cannot give out room numbers to anyone. If you leave a message with a phone number I'm sure Mr. Solomon will call you when he is able. I'm sorry I cannot help you further."

He hung up, thinking the woman sounded calm and rational and did not appear threatening in any way. He went back to his paperwork.

An hour later his phone rang again and once more it was Carolyn Warmus. Telling her he still did not know where Solomon was, Baez again suggested she leave a phone number where she could be reached.

"If he wishes to return your calls, I'm sure he will do so," Baez said politely, but sternly.

Carolyn hung up, frustrated that no one would help her find Paul, or better yet, confirm whether he was with another woman.

Only minutes later, she once again telephoned Baez and this time identified herself as Sharon. Baez immediately recognized the voice and gruffly told her to stop bothering him and the guests of the hotel. He slammed the phone down without waiting for a response.

Realizing the situation might be more complicated than he had first thought, he quickly dialed Solomon's room and listened as the phone kept ringing. He made a mental note to himself to keep trying to reach the man to see what he had to say about his ardent caller.

Several miles away, and seething at the treatment she was receiving, Carolyn decided to take matters into her own hands. She grabbed a piece of hotel stationary and jotted down the words she was sure would entice Paul back to her.

Looking around the room, she spied the extra key she had tossed on top of the television. Quickly folding the note around the plastic, punch-card key, she placed the package in an envelope and slowly licked it. Seconds before walking out the door to deliver the note personally to the Condado's front desk, another wonderful idea struck her.

Pulling open the desk drawer, she hauled out the island telephone book and flipped the Yellow Pages until she came to the listing for messenger services.

Thomas Alvarez, a forty-three-year-old machinist from the Bronx, strolled down the Condado's ornate hall on the way to his room, feeling very relaxed after an afternoon of sunbathing by the hotel pool. The deliciously hot Caribbean sun had sapped most of his energy and he was looking forward to a nice, long nap before an evening of dining and dancing.

When he opened the door to his room he caught sight of the piece of paper that had been jammed underneath it. He picked it up and saw it was a hotel message asking him to call his sister Haydee. When he plopped on the bed and reached for the phone, he noticed the blinking light for the first time, a signal telling him to call the front desk for another message. Before he could pick up the receiver, the phone jangled to life.

"Hi. Is this Thomas Alvarez?"

The burly vacationer didn't recognize the voice. "Yes, that's me. Who's this?"

"Mr. Alvarez, my name is Carolyn Warmus. I'm a friend of your sister

Haydee. She suggested I call you to see if you could help me out. I called Haydee where she works at the messenger service to see if she could get an envelope delivered for me, but apparently everyone at her office is busy. I've got a message that really needs to be sent, and you're my last hope. I know this is an imposition, but I'm down in the hotel bar in your lobby. Can you come down and meet me there in a few minutes. It would really help me out."

Alvarez stretched his arms and yawned as he listened to this stranger's problem. He hesitated a second before answering. He was tired and didn't feel like traipsing all over hell to deliver somebody's message. But the fact that this was apparently one of Haydee's friends prompted him to agree to the meeting.

Throwing on a pair of slacks and a T-shirt, he took the elevator down to the lobby.

He, his wife, and a group of friends had come down to Puerto Rico to celebrate his forty-third birthday, and everyone was having a great time. The beautiful island was home to his parents and sister. Alvarez himself had been born and raised in Manhattan but always loved visiting his family. This trip had so far been tremendously relaxing, and he hadn't once thought about all the problems awaiting him at home.

When the elevator slowed to a halt, he slipped through the opening doors and walked past the plant-filled lobby to the bar. He spotted his caller immediately standing at the bar. When he called her name, she turned and smiled, her thin, white summer dress hugging her ample curves.

"Hi, Tom. Thanks so much for coming down. Can I buy you a drink?"

Alvarez waved off the offer and suggested they sit at a nearby table. Carolyn grabbed her fruity drink and hurried over to him.

"I'll try not to take up much of your time," Carolyn said, a warm smile crossing her face as she tried to put her tablemate at ease.

"My boyfriend is staying at this very hotel. He came down here for a vacation and I wasn't able to go with him when he left. I finally persuaded my boss to give me some time off so I could come down here to surprise him. He doesn't know I'm here. What I want you to do is deliver this to him."

Carolyn reached into her purse and pulled out the envelope containing her note and room key. Alvarez took the package and looked it over.

"How come you don't just have someone from the hotel do this?" he asked.

"I tried, but they said they can't do that sort of thing. Some kind of policy or something, I don't know. Can you help me out? Since you're a guest at the hotel, I'm sure they won't give you any trouble."

Alvarez stood, thinking the whole thing very silly, but he was willing to help out. As he stood, Carolyn thanked him. "My boyfriend's name is Paul Solomon," she said.

Carolyn watched from the doorway as Alvarez walked to the front desk.

Catching the eye of the young girl working behind the counter, he asked politely, "Is there a Paul Solomon registered here?"

The girl checked her guest list and spotted the name. "Yes, sir, there is."

Placing the envelope on the countertop, he said, "My name is Thomas Alvarez and I have a package for Paul Solomon."

"I'm sorry, sir," the clerk responded. "I can't give you his room number, but I'd be happy to call his room for you."

Alvarez nodded, telling her that would be fine.

When a male voice answered her call, the clerk said, "I have a man down here with a package for Paul Solomon." A moment later, she handed the phone to Alvarez. "He'd like to speak with you, sir."

Taking the phone, the Bronx machinist said, "Mr. Solomon, I'm down in the lobby with a package for you from a friend and I was wondering if you could come down to get it?"

There was a long silence, finally broken by Solomon's uneasy voice.

"Can't you just leave it in my mailbox at the front desk? I can get it later."

"This is a personal package, Mr. Solomon, and I was asked to give it to you directly. Can you come down?"

Solomon hesitated and then agreed.

Alvarez left the envelope on the counter and walked back to the bar.

"All right, he's coming down to get it," he told the pretty blonde, who was still perched at the same table.

"Oh, I can't thank you enough," Carolyn said excitedly, again reaching into her purse and yanking out her wallet. She pulled out a crisp $50 bill.

"Oh no, you don't pay me, you pay Haydee," Alvarez said. "I left the envelope at the front desk. I can wait until he comes, but I've really got to get back to my room. My wife will be wondering where I am."

"There's really no need for you to wait if he's coming right down. I'll wait to see that he gets it," she said, her voice dancing with delight.

□   □   □   □

Solomon was sprawled out on his bed, wrapped in a towel. The call from the strange man at the front desk unnerved him. Only a handful of his closest friends knew where he was staying, and none of them would have delivered a package to him at the hotel, he was sure of that. The call bothered him, but he couldn't explain why. In any case, he was in no hurry to go downstairs and pick it up. Besides, he was waiting for another call.

He and Barbara had just finished an afternoon at the pool, and the heat and a couple of drinks had zapped them both. She was showering and then they would rest before dinner. For now he was just waiting for 6 P.M. When he and Barbara had returned to the room, they found a piece of paper stuffed under the door telling him to be in his room at 6 P.M. to receive a call from the United States. Neither one knew what the call was about, and they both hoped nothing was wrong with either of their families.

When the phone finally rang, he reached over and snatched it up. He was surprised to hear Tammy Rogers's frightened voice on the other end.

"Paul, I really didn't want to bother you and Barbara, but something's happened that has me scared. I don't know if it's anything or not, but I felt I had to tell you what's been going on."

Solomon listened intently as his nervous caller began describing the phone calls she had received from a woman obviously desperate to track him and Barbara down. Paul was puzzled by the events, and upset when Tammy mentioned one of the names the female caller had used. Shortly after hanging up, his puzzlement turned to fright as he recalled the "personal package" waiting for him at the front desk.

Seconds later, another phone call confirmed his worst fears.

"Mr. Solomon, this is Ali Baez from hotel security. I'm calling to let you know that a woman has been calling the hotel all day long trying to reach you. Her name is Carolyn Warmus and she has been quite insistent about getting hold of you. She wouldn't leave a number. I'm sure she'll call again. Please call me if there's anything I can do for you."

Frightened by the quickly unfolding events, Solomon told Baez that he and Barbara needed to see him immediately.

"We'll be right down. Please don't leave."

Without a word, Solomon hung up the phone. He had no idea whether Carolyn was on the island or had just tracked him down and was phoning him from New York.

Stifling a shiver that ran down his spine, he quickly got dressed and then waited for Barbara to finish drying her hair before he hit her with only a fraction of the unsettling news.

As they took the elevator down to the security office, Solomon had no idea what was going on. Cautiously poking his head out of the hotel elevator and not seeing anyone who resembled Carolyn, Solomon pulled on Ballor's hand to make her hurry. Unsure of what was happening, she was becoming more scared by the minute.

She realized she had good reason to be fearful when, almost an hour later, Solomon had finished telling Baez his tale of murder and obsession involving Carolyn Warmus.

Solomon then mentioned the package and Baez stood up. He told Ballor to wait while he and Paul went to the front desk.

When they reached the desk, Solomon asked for his message. The clerk fumbled through a stack of notes he had taken down that day for the hotel patrons.

"Ah, here it is," he said. "I have a phone message and a letter for you. The message is, "Call me. I'm here just as we planned. Caribe Hilton, Room 1574. Love C.""

The clerk then handed him an envelope, which he immediately tore open. It took two minutes to finish reading the one-page letter and only a moment to realize the plastic card that came with it was Carolyn's hotel-room key.

Ashen-faced, Solomon hurried back with Baez to his office. The burly security man told the couple to return to their room and he would follow shortly.

After watching Paul pick up her envelope and then leave, Carolyn paid her tab and hurried back to her hotel. Solomon sat on the corner of the bed, the note and room key from Carolyn still clutched tightly in his hand. He realized Barbara would have to be told all that had happened. He had never felt it necessary to tell her about his relationship with Carolyn, but now that events were spinning out of control, he knew he'd have to tell her everything. Through no fault of his or her own, she was involved in a situation that could possibly put her life in jeopardy. He began to fill her in on the details he had skipped over with Baez.

Solomon thought about Carolyn, his wife's murder, and Barbara, and prayed that what he was thinking was not true. But the developments of the last few hours had convinced him that the horrible picture forming in his mind could well be more than just a slim possibility. What Carolyn was doing went beyond strange, and while he was fearful for his own safety, he was even more frightened for the unsuspecting Barbara. Hearing Baez's knock, Solomon almost ran to open the door.

"Why don't we start again from the beginning and you tell me what this is all about," Baez said, sitting in one of the chairs near the window.

Solomon's mind raced through several thoughts at once. Carolyn's being late for their date that night in January, her repeated efforts to persuade him to divorce Betty Jeanne, and the indescribable horror of the bloodied corpse that once had been his wife.

He began telling his story to the awestruck security man, several times grabbing a tissue from the desk top to wipe his sweaty brow in the air-conditioned room.

Not caring whether he sounded overdramatic, Solomon told Baez that he couldn't be sure Carolyn wouldn't try to do something to him or Barbara, since she now apparently knew they were down here together. He hadn't realized Carolyn had become so obsessed with him that she would follow him all the way down to Puerto Rico. He was scared and didn't know where to turn.

Ballor, too, was afraid. Without telling Paul, she decided to end their relationship. Seeing the fear in Paul's eyes, she was relieved when he finally said they should leave the island that night.

Baez agreed, but first he insisted on calling the San Juan police. For what seemed like an eternity, the trio waited.

Solomon and Ballor both jumped when they heard a knock on the door. Peering through the peephole, Baez saw a uniformed cop standing outside. He opened the door and shook the man's hand, at the same time pulling him gently into the room.

Once more telling the story of his wife's murder and that day's events frazzled Solomon's nerves even more. Ballor sat across the room trembling, wondering how this terrible nightmare could be happening to her. The Puerto Rican detective agreed that their plan to catch the next flight off the island was a good one. He listened as Solomon called the front desk and made arrangements to check out, securing a promise from the hotel manager to tell anyone who called that he had already paid his bill and was gone.

Next he called Detective Sergeant Thomas Lind. "Please. We're flying out tonight," Solomon told Lind. "The police are giving us an escort to the airport here. Can you have someone meet our flight in New York and give us an escort home?"

Lind assured him he would be taken care of but stopped short of giving an actual promise.

Finishing that call, Solomon hurriedly dialed the number of his lawyer and friend, Gary Pillersdorf, and filled him in on what was happening. He made the attorney promise to call the Greenburgh police.

During all this time, Ballor sat across the room, chewing her fingernails and trying to maintain her sanity.

Through the next several hours, Solomon's fear grew uncontrollably. By the time the darkness of the summer evening finally fell, his hands visibly shook and he trembled at the thought of simply making his way to the airport. When the hour arrived, he phoned the front desk and asked for a bellman.

At the Condado's front doors, he hurriedly tossed the luggage into the open trunk of their taxi and quickly followed Barbara into the back seat. Peering over his shoulder, he saw two marked police cars. Both the detective and Baez had been true to their word. Solomon hoped they would stay on the job until their flight boarded.

Once on the plane, he felt safer, but he jerked his head around to be sure Carolyn was nowhere in sight. When their jet touched down at La Guardia, Solomon looked around but saw neither Lind nor any other cops waiting to follow them home. Nerves on edge, he hustled to a bank of pay phones and telephoned Pillersdorf.

"Gary, hi, it's me. Are the Greenburgh cops coming? I don't see them here."

"Sorry, Paul. I spoke with them but they said they wouldn't be sending anyone down. I talked with Sullivan and filled him in again about Rosenbaum's call about Carolyn's mental problems and her family's concern that she might commit suicide. They want to talk to you tomorrow, but there won't be any escort. Do you want me to come get you?"

Solomon thanked his friend, but declined the offer. "Thanks anyway, Gary, I'll call you later tonight."

Ballor sat in silence during the drive home, her thoughts concentrated on putting the whole terrible episode behind her as quickly as possible. When they arrived back at Paul's condo, she helped him carry in his bags. The blinking light on the telephone answering machine caught his eye, and he pushed the button to get his messages. His heart almost stopped when he heard Carolyn's unmistakable voice.

"Hello, it's Carolyn calling. It's about 8:15 on Thursday evening and I have received your message on my answering machine, and as you know, I called you in Puerto Rico, um, Thursday morning, this morning, and let you know what time I was coming in and I don't quite understand what's going on. Um, you know, when I got your message on my machine, I was in Detroit and I got a ticket. It cost me an absolute fortune to fly down here and see you for the one last day when you said you still were going to be here and then, you know, they are telling me, you know, first you're at the hotel where you tell me you are at, this Condado Plaza Casino thingamabobber and then they said you checked out. I mean, I don't know what's going on. But I am down in Puerto Rico now, not pleased, is the fact that I'm down here, supposedly to be seeing you and you are nowhere around. Would you please be kind enough to leave, if you get this message, call my answering machine in New York, and explain to me what is going on so that I have some idea. Thank you. Good-bye."

Paul stared at Ballor, a sickening queasiness moving through his stomach. He had never called Carolyn to invite her down there, yet here she was pretending that he had. "This is madness," he said, unable to control the quaver in his voice.

Ballor stared at him. She wanted out of this place and out of this entire soap opera . . . now.

August 18 was a warm, breezy day in San Juan and Carolyn still had a few tricks up her sleeve to end Paul's fling with Barbara Ballor and bring him back to her.

The thought of her Paul in the arms of another woman made her see red. She pulled from her purse the list of people and their telephone numbers that Parco had obtained for her and found the ones she needed.

For the remainder of the morning, Warmus stayed in her room, making calls to her own phone in New York, Solomon's home, TWA, American Express, and the Condado Plaza.

Hours later, tired and thwarted in her efforts to find the man for whom she had come looking, she decided to try another tack. She rifled through her purse and pulled out the small address book that contained Gary Pillersdorf's home phone number. She had never liked the bumbling lawyer—she was sure he and his bitchy wife didn't like her— but it was worth a try.

"Hi, Gary? This is Carolyn Warmus," she said in her sweetest voice. "The strangest thing has happened. Paul invited me down to Puerto Rico and I was supposed to meet him here, but now I can't seem to find him. He's not in the Condado Hotel, where he told me to come. I can't figure him out. I think he may be on his way back home. Why would he invite me down here and then just leave when I arrive? Do you have any idea what's happening? Have you heard from him or know where I can reach him?"

Pillersdorf was stunned. He knew that Paul was back home primarily because of her. He also knew that Paul would never have told Carolyn he was down there, let alone invite her along. The whole thing just didn't make sense. The woman was really nuts, he decided.

"Carolyn, I don't know what to tell you," he lied. "I haven't heard from Paul and I don't really know where he is. If he calls me I'll tell him you're looking for him."

Warmus began seething. She knew she was being brushed off by Pillersdorf and it made her furious that he thought she could be so easily dismissed.

"Gary, you better listen. I'm very, very angry. Now tell me where he is this minute."

The harsh pitch of her voice made him jump. "I'm sorry, Carolyn. I just don't know. Now I've got to go. Good-bye."

With that he slammed the receiver down. With her frame of mind, Pillersdorf prayed Carolyn would never find out Paul was back home. He was now deeply worried for Paul and Kristan's safety, not to mention Barbara Ballor's.

Warmus tried to compose herself as she figured out her next move. She checked herself in the mirror and finally decided to go out for a late breakfast and then a few hours on the beach. As long as she was here she might as well get working on her tan, she decided, pushing her momentary troubles out of her mind.

The next morning, she once again burned up the telephone lines, still vainly searching for Solomon. Then another wicked idea struck, as she looked up the one number she had yet to call.

"Hello," said the woman's voice.

"Hello, is this Mrs. Marie Ballor of Lynwood, Michigan?"

"Yes it is. May I help you?"

"Mrs. Ballor, this is Detective Susan Ball from the Greenburgh Police Department in New York. The reason I'm calling is that I'm investigating the murder of a woman named Betty Jeanne Solomon. It has come to our attention that your daughter, Barbara Ballor, has begun dating a man named Paul Solomon, the victim's husband.

"Mrs. Ballor, the reason I'm calling is to let you know that Paul Solomon is our prime suspect in this murder case and we believe he killed his wife by shooting her eight or nine times with a small-caliber gun. I thought you would like to know that your daughter may be in some danger and that you might want to help persuade her to end her relationship with this murder suspect."

"Oh my God, of course I will," Mrs. Ballor said, trying to catch her breath and sounding as if someone had just punched her in the stomach.

She thanked her caller and seconds later called her daughter's apartment in Yonkers. When no one answered after several tries, she became even more frightened.

In New York, Solomon wasted little time in calling the Greenburgh Police Department to tell them he and his lawyer were coming in. When Constantino hung up the phone, he was disturbed by his suspect's frightened voice. Lind had briefly filled him in, but he couldn't wait to hear the story straight from the horse's own mouth.

Singer, too, wanted to see Solomon. After describing for Constantino and Sullivan the events of the past two days, Paul was ushered into the chief's office.

"The detectives have filled me in on what happened," Singer said. "The reason I wanted to see you is just to ask you a couple of questions. I understand you have a young daughter. What I wanted to know was whether, with Carolyn Warmus out there, you've made arrangements to have your daughter taken care of financially in case something happens to you? Is all your insurance paid up?"

The blood rushed from Solomon's face as he listened to the chief. "But, but . . ." he stammered, "I want protection. Isn't there anything you can do?"

Singer looked at his detectives, who were standing behind Solomon. They knew the old man was just stirring things up, and they were enjoying the show.

"Look, our job is to protect you, but I can't have my men on you around the clock. If we're called and it's legitimate, we'll send someone over. But nobody can protect you twenty-four hours around the clock. That's all I'm saying. I'm not saying anything is going to happen, just that if it does, I want to make sure that you've provided for your daughter. That's all."

Singer picked up the report he had been reading before the men entered, signaling the end of the meeting. Solomon almost stumbled as he left the office, more scared than when he left Puerto Rico. He went home and bolted shut his door.

After Paul had dropped her off, Ballor walked into her apartment and for the first time in a long while finally felt safe. Tammy Rogers greeted her with a look of concern, a million questions, and a handful of messages from her mother.

"My God, Barb, what's going on? I was scared to death something was going to happen to you and Paul. Are you okay?" Rogers asked, her voice straining to hide the very real terror she had felt for the last forty-eight hours.

"I'm all right. I'm all right," Ballor responded, giving her friend a quick hug.

Barbara called her mother immediately. After listening to Mrs. Ballor's recitation of the warning from the New York detective, she realized for the first time the depth of her dilemma. It was no longer her own safety she had to worry about, now her family could be in peril as well!

She tried to explain the situation as calmly as she was able, but the more she said, the more upset her mother became. When the call finally ended, Ballor found herself almost as scared as Paul had been when they left San Juan. She called information and got the number for the Greenburgh Police Department.

The dispatcher transferred the 8 p.m. call to Detective James Teahan, who told Ballor the two detectives on the Solomon case were not around. He pulled out a piece of paper and grabbed a pen to take her message. When she had finished her story, Teahan knew the information was important.

Ballor had said the mysterious detective who had called her mother mentioned that Betty Jeanne Solomon had been shot eight or nine times with a small-caliber gun. That information had never been made public. Only the killer and the police knew about it.

When Constantino arrived back at the station, Teahan dropped Ballor's message in front of him.

"If I have to solve all your cases for you, you're going to owe me big time!" he said, watching Constantino's eyes grow big as the meaning of the young woman's information hit home. Lind came into the room and plopped himself in his chair. The anxious and excited look on his partner's face as he flipped the paperwork in front of him meant something was up. Quickly scanning the message, Lind immediately realized its significance.

They both knew, even before they checked, that no detective would have phoned Ballor's mother. The fact that the caller had mentioned almost the exact number of shots was important, even if it was only circumstantial evidence.

Constantino called the number that Ballor had left with Teahan. Between Solomon's tale of terror in the Caribbean and now this, Constantino felt it was a pretty safe bet that the one person at the bottom of it all could only be Carolyn Warmus.

When Ballor answered, he made an appointment to see her and Tammy Rogers at their apartment the next day. After hanging up, Constantino gave a toothy grin to Lind, who had just walked into the squad room.

"Pack your bikini, pal." He laughed. "We may just have won ourselves a trip to Puerto Rico."

On August 21, in the early evening, Pillersdorf was relaxing at home with his wife and children when the phone rang. The voice on the other end sent chills up and down his spine.

"Gary, it's Carolyn," she said happily. "I'm sorry to bother you again, but I think you and I really need to get together to discuss Paul and what's been going on. I think for some reason you're interfering in our relationship and I'd like to talk this out in your office. Could you set up a time for us to meet?"

Pillersdorf shook his head. He couldn't believe this woman. One thing he knew for sure. No way in hell was he going to meet with her, not in his office or anywhere else.

"Listen, Carolyn. I really don't think there's anything to talk about. Why don't you just let things cool down a bit and maybe we'll talk sometime later. I'll let you know."

The next day in his office, Pillersdorf telephoned Paul Rosenbaum in Michigan.

"Look, Paul. You've got to do something about Carolyn. She's got a lot of people worried out here. You're the one who said she's mentally unstable, what with the suicide threats and all."

He went on to explain what happened in Puerto Rico, the strange message on Solomon's machine, and her calling to set up a meeting with him to discuss the problem.

"Can't you get her father to do something? This is getting frightening."

Rosenbaum listened, knowing that Carolyn's problems required more than a stern lecture from him or her father.

"I'll speak with Mr. Warmus and we'll try to come up with something," was all he said.

Pillersdorf hung up knowing that Carolyn Warmus would continue to haunt all their lives for some time to come.

He didn't have to wait long to share these new developments with the police.

On August 30, Constantino and Detective Sergeant Vincent LoGiudice paid another visit to his home to meet with him and Solomon.

Once again, Solomon provided a new twist.

"After I got back from Puerto Rico, Carolyn finally got hold of me on the phone. She told me that she knew Barbara and I had been escorted to the airport under police guard and that I had told the police she killed my wife.

"She sounded very scared, why, I don't know. When I asked her how she found all these things out, she told me because 'I know people.' Gentlemen, I don't mind telling you she has me scared to death."

"I have another question for you," Constantino said, looking at Pillersdorf. "You told us at one point that you knew Betty Jeanne had been shot eight times. What made you think that?"

The lawyer looked up quickly and then relaxed. "It's really no big secret. Betty Jeanne's brother-in-law, William Green, is the person who made the funeral arrangements. He told me that the funeral director mentioned that while he was preparing the body, he noted that she had been shot eight times. That's how I knew. But I've never shared that with anyone, including Paul. Up to now he's always thought she was shot five or six times."

Constantino just grunted. Fifteen minutes later, he and LoGiudice thanked the men, leaving them to wonder what would happen next.

The funny thing was, Constantino told his cohort, even he didn't know what it all meant. But he had some pretty good ideas.

9

THE DESK SERGEANT at Manhattan's 19th Precinct looked up in time to see the voluptuous blonde storm through the door. Several of the uniformed cops passing the time of day with their cohorts stopped and stared at the attractive figure gracing their lobby. Not many good-looking women ever paid them a visit, and the few that did usually came because they'd just been beaten up by their pimps or ripped off by their johns.

"I want to report an armed robbery," Warmus almost shouted as she pressed against the tall counter surrounding the sergeant. After being told to calm down and giving her full name and address, Warmus was directed to a nearby chair to wait for a detective.

James Ryan had been a cop for as long as he could remember. Now a detective with the 19th, the ruddy-faced investigator was used to handling anything that was thrown his way. Two minutes after meeting her, Ryan knew that Carolyn Warmus was a long-awaited bonus. She followed the well-built cop up the stairs to an empty office.

"Like I told the police officer downstairs, I want to report an armed robbery," she said, sounding like a poor little girl innocent to the ways of the big city.

"Tell me what happened and when," Ryan said, trying desperately to keep his eyes locked on those of the sexy woman in front of him.

"On August 15, a man I had just met named Manuel Rodriguez came to my apartment, and after I opened the door, he pulled out a large, black handgun and forced me back inside. He ransacked my home and ended up stealing $15,000 in cash I had in my bedroom."

Ryan slowly wrote down Warmus's complaint. His eyebrows raised slightly when she mentioned Rodriguez's name and the amount of money that had been taken.

"A couple of things, Miss Warmus. It is 'miss,' isn't it? First of all, if I'm not mistaken, today is September 11. You say this armed robbery took place on August 15. Why have you waited so long to report this?"

Warmus put on her most charming smile. "I've been away on a trip to Puerto Rico. I left shortly after the incident, and there really wasn't any time to report it then, so I'm doing it now."

The broad, warm smile from the tanned, well-built woman stirred him, and Ryan felt that some sort of electric bond was beginning to connect them. "I have to ask you, what were you doing with $15,000 in cash in your apartment? That's an awful lot of money to have lying around."

Explaining that the money was for her trip, bills, and other expenses, Warmus also told the detective that she had met Rodriguez while she was hospitalized in early August. She decided to leave out that it was a psychiatric stay.

An hour later, with the report taken, Ryan promised Warmus that a warrant would be issued for Rodriguez's arrest. She stood and shook his hand, thanking him for his time, allowing her hand to remain in his for an extra second. Warmus liked the power she held over men, and Ryan had definite possibilities.

Almost a month later, on October 4—and after several telephone calls from Ryan—the police arrested Rodriguez outside the home of his ex-wife, who lived with her family just down the street from the Delightful Restaurant, where Warmus and he had met after their stay at Metropolitan Hospital. Rodriguez, a well-known drug user–dealer and street person, offered no resistance. But once back at the 19th Precinct, when he was told who had pressed charges against him, Rodriguez became angry, loudly telling Ryan that he never ripped off Warmus.

"Oh man, what really happened was that bitch gave me $15,000 to buy her some cocaine," he said, almost pleading with Ryan to believe him. "I was the middleman. I paid some dudes the cash and they were supposed to supply me with the powder, but I haven't seen them since I gave them the money. But no way did I rip her off. I never had no gun. You guys know me. You ever busted me with a gun? No way. This is bullshit. I'm being set up."

After hearing the same story over and over, Ryan wrote down the man's statements, but, unknown to Rodriguez and everyone else, his feelings for Warmus had by now transcended the professional.

Thrown into a dank holding cell overnight, Rodriguez was arraigned the next day and, unable to post bond, remained in jail to await his trial.

The tormented history of an unhappy, angry, and obsessive young woman lay spread out on a desk, one tragic tale after another buried within the various documents gleaned from the archives of Michigan courthouses, police stations, and even the Secret Service.

Detectives Lind and Constantino stared down at the papers, unable to believe the portrait they painted of a troubled, privileged youth who apparently had learned to hide her deep-seated problems behind the mask of a well-adjusted schoolteacher. They had spent almost every day since mid-August investigating the secret and not-so-secret past of their now-prime murder suspect, Carolyn Warmus.

Ever since Constantino learned of the Puerto Rico affair from Solomon and Barbara Ballor—he and his partner had gotten to fly there for two sun-filled days of investigation—they had spared no effort to find out more about the attractive heiress whose penchant for unattainable men knew no bounds. It was the Puerto Rico trip and Warmus's obvious obsession with Solomon that had turned them away from him and toward her as their most likely killer.

The investigators pulled up two chairs around the paper-laden table, and each picked up a file. They had read every one of them a dozen times before, but on this September afternoon they decided to pour over the paperwork once again in an effort to convince themselves that Warmus was indeed capable of coldly staring into Betty Jeanne Solomon's eyes and blowing her away. Neither one needed much convincing at that moment.

Constantino opened the file folder filled with his notes and began reading.

Thomas Aloisous Warmus and Elizabeth Navickas were married in a church ceremony on February 18, 1961, in Saint Clair Shores, Michigan. Three years later, their first child, Carolyn, was born on January, 8, 1964. Later that same year—on December 28—they had another daughter, Tracey. The family lived in a well-kept suburban Detroit home located at Avonhurst in Troy.

While Elizabeth stayed home and took care of the children, Tom

Warmus threw himself into his work, and friends and relatives often characterized him as a workaholic. A driven, successful insurance man, who would later come to be named chief executive officer for the Michigan Benefit Plans Inc., in Southfield, Michigan, he appeared to prefer late nights at the office to the home life his wife had made for them and their children. On October 13, 1968, the couple had another child, this time a son, who was named after his father.

Friends and relatives said the next two years brought much pain and unhappiness for Elizabeth as marital bickering turned to never-ending, heated arguments over Tom Warmus's work. He blamed his wife's drinking for their problems. She blamed his working habits.

The strain became too much for Elizabeth, and she separated from her husband on July 31, 1970. She then filed for divorce in Oakland County Circuit Court on November 24, 1970, claiming Tom Warmus had committed acts of extreme and repeated cruelty toward her. He was served with the divorce papers the next day but did not move out of the Troy home until January 7, 1971, when he purchased a $60,000 house on Edgewood Road in Union Lake, Michigan.

During the next six months, Tom Warmus would arrive back at the couple's Troy home unexpectedly, sometimes in the early morning hours, and announce he was staying overnight. All three children, but especially Carolyn, took the separation very hard, according to family members and friends.

On those occasions when Tom Warmus showed up at the house unannounced, Elizabeth would often be entertaining friends and family. She claimed that her spouse would not miss many opportunities to ridicule and embarrass his wife in front of them.

On July 8, 1971, Tom Warmus stormed back into the Avonhurst home and announced that he was moving back in and his wife would have to find another room to sleep in and to keep her clothes. Although he never attempted to bring his clothes and other personal possessions back into the house, he sporadically spent many nights there, until finally neither Elizabeth nor her torn children could take any more and she asked for, and was granted, a court order to force him to vacate the premises. The judge granted the request after learning that, besides his new home in Union Lake, Tom Warmus also owned another house in Saint Clair Shores and a condominium in Scottsdale, Arizona.

Additionally, Oakland County Circuit Court Judge James Thorburn also ordered Tom Warmus to make temporary support and child custody payments to his estranged wife. The divorce battle dragged on for almost a year and a half, primarily over the issue of dividing up the lucrative family assets, until finally, on March 16, 1972, Thorburn granted the divorce and awarded custody of the three children to Elizabeth.

Along with being awarded alimony and child support payments, Elizabeth was allowed to keep the Troy home and a 1972 station wagon with air conditioning. Tom Warmus kept controlling interest in the various businesses he owned, his homes in Union Lake and Saint Clair Shores, the condo in Arizona, a snowmobile, and a nineteen-foot boat with a motor and trailer.

An incident which family members said disturbed the children very much, causing them nightmares for many weeks, occurred on a Sunday night in June 1972. Tom Warmus was returning the children to his ex-wife after they had spent a week with him. When he dropped them off, he told Elizabeth that he was taking his son back with him for the remainder of the summer months. Elizabeth argued with him and pulled her three-year-old son into the house. The children watched from the living-room window as their mother and father stood swearing and yelling at each other in the driveway.

Suddenly, Tom Warmus grabbed his wife and threw her to the ground. He ran into the house, grabbed his son's arm, and pulled the screaming child into his car, and drove off. It took another court order to force Warmus to return the child to his mother.

A short time later, Tom Warmus married his secretary, Nancy Dailey, a beautiful woman who made no bones about liking minks, fast, expensive cars, and tight, sequined dresses. In commemoration of their new marriage, Tom Warmus built for his wife a palatial, six-bedroom, $500,000 home overlooking a well-manicured five-acre estate in the posh suburb of Franklin, Michigan.

Elizabeth's legal battles with her former husband were far from over, as she had to return to court numerous times to force him to make his child support payments.

In 1974, after hiring a private investigator to follow his ex-wife and photograph her entertaining men in her home, Tom Warmus unsuccessfully attempted to get the court to give him custody of the three children and to put an end to his child support and alimony payments. In 1976, Tom Warmus owed as much as $35,000, in child support, which he finally paid, but only after Judge Thorburn ordered his assets attached.

On October 1, 1979, after Elizabeth had remarried and made plans to move east, despite being told by her attorney that the court would frown on her taking the children from their home and schools in Michigan, Judge Thorburn granted Tom Warmus's request for custody. He moved the children into his lavish, sprawling—and as Carolyn herself once described for a friend—empty Franklin home, where they each remained until they went away to college.

To say Tom Warmus had done quite well for himself would have been an understatement. In 1989, Warmus was owner and president of the American Way Service Corporation, and his estimated wealth was in excess of $150 million, including the Southfield, Michigan–based American Way Life Insurance Company—a subsidiary of his corporation, worth about $107 million—eight airplanes, at least twenty antique cars, plus his lucrative land holdings.

Schoolwork came easily to Carolyn and she received high grades during her time at Derby Junior High and Seaholm High School, both located in trendy Birmingham, Michigan. She was a member of the girls' basketball team and was considered a fairly good, but not great, player.

Her high-school friends remember that she was always eager to please all the boys and would often try to use her never-ending supply of money from Daddy as a way to buy popularity. According to one report, she once paid her best friend $100 to set her up for a date with a certain boy.

Socially unsure of herself, Carolyn tried unsuccessfully to emulate her very popular sister, Tracey. Some said Carolyn was torn by a love-hate conflict, and was jealous of her slightly younger sibling's natural ease in social situations.

As an example, her friends said, almost every high-school party thrown at the Warmus house was hosted by both girls, but most of those who attended were, more often than not, in Tracey's circle. While Carolyn did have some flashy, expensive parties of her own, she constantly feared rejection, privately telling girl friends that she was afraid no one would show up.

Her insecurity, coupled with her desire to impress her friends with her father's money, often led her to hand out overly generous invitations for weekend shopping trips to New York or plane rides down to her father's estate in Florida.

In 1981, Carolyn enrolled at the University of Michigan with the intention of becoming a psychologist or teacher. Michigan offered the three things she had decided were most important to her: a great place to get an education, it was a noted party school, and it was less than an hour from home. She did well in school and carried a B+, A– average in most of her courses.

In her junior year she first began exhibiting the strange behavior that Detective Constantino would find so interesting six years later. In February 1983, she met a graduate teaching assistant named Paul Laven.

The lovely coed had caught his eye and her continual, obvious efforts to make him notice her finally paid off. In June of that year they began dating.

While Laven took the shapely student to concerts, dinners, the movies, and occasionally to synagogue, unknown to her he also dated others. Friends of both characterized Carolyn as a love-struck girl who couldn't even get a haircut or buy a new pair of shoes without asking her girl friends whether they thought Paul would like them. Her world revolved around the young teaching assistant, but he, apparently, considered her only a passing fancy.

In November of that year, Laven started seriously dating a woman named Wendy Siegel, and in early December, he took Carolyn out for the last time. Over dinner, he told her that he didn't feel they were right for each other, assuring her she would soon find someone else. Still in tears when he dropped her off at her apartment, Carolyn vowed to find out who it was that had come between her and her lover. It didn't take long.

Keeping watch on his apartment, she angrily looked on as night after night Laven returned home with the same woman. Within three weeks, he and Wendy Siegel were engaged. They planned their wedding for the following July.

When Carolyn found out, she went berserk. Every day for the next several weeks she filled Laven's answering machine with messages of love, hate, and threats, until he finally had to disconnect it. She lied to a Michigan Bell Telephone employee to obtain Siegel's unlisted number and began harassing her.

Meanwhile, Laven began receiving letter after letter from Carolyn, each one more pitiful than the last, all professing deep love and a willingness to take him back. She would show up in the classroom when he was teaching, wait for him to finish, and try to convince him to renew the relationship.

It was during this time that Carolyn had her first run-in with the law. On February 5, 1984, she walked into an Oak Park pawnshop with four pieces of gold and diamond jewelry: a 1.15-carat diamond necklace; a tennis-racket charm; a pin in the shape of the word *Love* spelled out with twenty-two diamonds, and a pair of exquisite diamond earrings. She walked out of the shop with a smile and $3,000.

The next day, the wary pawnbroker telephoned the Royal Oak police, telling them he had purchased the expensive items from a twenty-year-old named Carolyn Marie Warmus.

"She told me the jewelry belonged to her mother and that her mother had given her permission to sell it," the broker said in filling out a report. "Hell, the whole lot is really worth about $7,250."

Checking out the address the young woman had given the distressed broker, Royal Oak police called their counterparts in Franklin, who in turn called Thomas Warmus. A quick check determined that the jewelry had been stolen.

According to the Royal Oak police report of the incident, "He stated that he wanted no prosecution of his daughter, but would buy the items back from the dealer."

A few hours later, an angry and embarrassed Thomas Warmus arrived at the pawnshop and repurchased the valuables Carolyn had stolen from her stepmother. What he ever said or did to his daughter was never reported.

Paul Laven knew nothing of Carolyn's thievery. He knew only that when he moved in with Siegel that spring, his former girl friend's harassment continued and took a slightly uglier tone. Although both Laven and Siegel had initially been sympathetic, they now grew angry, and finally afraid.

On April 10, 1984, Carolyn lost control. She went to the home of Laven and Siegel and began pounding on the door, screaming and yelling threats when they refused to answer. The couple called the Southfield Police Department, and several terrifying minutes later she was pulled away by police.

Soon after, at spring college break, Carolyn traveled to Pompano, Florida, and spent the week sunning herself at another of her father's many houses and sailing off the coast on one of his two 42-foot sailboats. When she returned from vacation, she picked up where she had left off. She typed the following note—filled with misspelled words—and mailed it to Siegel.

Wendy,
I really hope you enjoyed this past week of not being bothered by me, because now that Im back from vacation you can start

worrying all over again. And lit me tell you, with the tan I have now, you've got even more to compete with! Of coarse with a body like mine, I'm sure you relized what tough competetion you were up against even before I went to Florida. In fact, your just about out of the running completly now! I hope you enjoyed having Paul all to yourself this past week, because it will be a long time before it happens again. Of coarse, knowing Paul's devotion to me, he probably spent as little time as possible with you thes past week and weekend. I guess as long as you keep letting him live in your apartment with you, he'll just continue to pretend to care about you. Go right on fooling yourself, Wendy—your just making Paul's job of fooling you even easier for him.

C—

Two months went by and Carolyn's reign of terror continued. Then, on May 30, 1984, she tried a new tack. That day Laven found a note under the windshield wiper of his car.

P—
I'm 2½ months
pregnant. Call me!!! Please!
Love,
C

She then went around telling anyone who would listen that she had become pregnant and that Paul Laven was the father. Laven and Siegel had had enough. They were afraid to pick up their own telephone or walk to their cars. Their worst fear was that Carolyn was planning to show up and disrupt their wedding.

They hired attorney Sheldon G. Larky to obtain a court-ordered injunction barring Carolyn from coming near them or attending their wedding, and also to sue her for invasion of privacy.

Larky filed the civil complaint on June 20, 1984. That day, Oakland County Circuit Judge Frederick C. Ziem signed a temporary restraining order to keep Carolyn away from the betrothed couple and ordered her to stop all communication with them.

On July 23, 1984, in exchange for Laven and Siegel dropping their invasion of privacy suit, Carolyn signed a permanent restraining order prepared by Judge Ziem, agreeing never to contact either Laven or Siegel again. She also promised to stay away from their wedding. Laven and Siegel were married without incident and never heard any more from Carolyn Warmus.

Many of Carolyn's friends have said that she tried to justify Laven's actions by saying he left her because she wasn't Jewish. Some felt she was trying to rectify that situation during her senior year at Michigan, when the Catholic Carolyn decided to convert to Judaism. She visited the Congregation Beth Shalom in Oak Park, and persuaded Rabbi David Nelson to sponsor her conversion.

Months later, when Carolyn had completed her religious studies, she attended the mikvah, the ritual immersion that marked her conversion to Judaism. Rabbi Nelson, who thought it odd that no family members or friends attended the usually joyous celebration with Carolyn, believed she had chosen to convert because she wanted to marry a Jewish man. As part of the ritual celebration, Carolyn chose a Jewish name, Chana Ariela, which means "gracious lioness of God."

The physical and emotional turmoil caused by Carolyn's inability to accept the inevitable, resulted in her father's deciding that his daughter was going off the deep end.

Her sporadic crying jags, rapid mood swings, and talk of suicide, scared Tom Warmus to the point that he forced his daughter into psychiatric therapy. Fighting with her family became almost a daily ritual after that. Apparently embarrassed to be in therapy, Carolyn never talked about it with her friends.

Upon her 1986 graduation from the University of Michigan with a B.A. in psychology, Carolyn moved her belongings back into her father's home and made her plans to move to New York, where she would attend the fall session at Columbia University's Teachers College.

She was convinced the teaching profession was for her, and she wanted her master's degree from a well-known and well-respected university. But first she wanted to have some fun and make a few extra dollars' spending money during the summer of 1985. A waitressing job at a popular watering hole for college students in Royal Oak, called the Jukebox, provided just what she was looking for.

Carolyn loved the attention she received from the usually drunk— and perpetually horny—college boys who frequented the Jukebox, a 1950s version of a beer-and-burger bar.

The always-crowded saloon was a well-known pick-up joint and a favorite meeting place for the wealthy, well-to-do Birmingham/Bloomfield/Franklin college set looking for a place to hang out during summer break. Classic rock 'n' roll, cheap drinks, and attractive, friendly waitresses decked out in jeans and saddle shoes combined to make the place irresistible to the college crowd.

Carolyn was a particular favorite of many of the regulars, who liked her quick, flirting style and outrageous body. She dated several of them —usually only once—until she met Brian "Buddy" Fetter. Then the old Carolyn emerged.

Fetter fancied himself a ladies' man and enjoyed the fast life, whether it was having a few beers at the Jukebox or grabbing some pals and cruising along the Eight Mile Road strip in Detroit looking for a good topless bar. Cash had never been much of a problem for Fetter, whose father was very generous with the money he made from his million-dollar carpet business.

When Brian first met Carolyn, he was enamored of her good looks and terrific build and the pair spent many nights in each other's arms. But, the last thing Fetter wanted was to be tied down to any one woman, and when he tried to distance himself from the Jukebox waitress, she left scores of messages on his answering machine, finally forcing him to change his number.

Fetter would also find her waiting for him when he returned home on nights he didn't want to see her. Finally he'd had enough. Trying to get rid of her, he introduced Carolyn to a married friend who had shown an interest in her. Apparently it worked, for she finally left him alone, but the whole affair left a bad taste in his mouth.

Carolyn's problems with men didn't appear to affect her social life much. Joseph Cohen, a Birmingham lawyer and owner of another Warmus hangout—the Rikshaw Inn located in West Bloomfield Township—frequently saw the tall blonde having drinks and dinner, usually with a pack of girl friends.

Carolyn would often grab the bill, delighted with the opportunity to display her wealth and generosity. On one occasion, Cohen recalled, she asked him to make a special case purchase of Dom Perignon so it would be on hand should she want to buy a bottle or two for her friends.

Cohen also recalled that this was the summer when Carolyn began dating his manager at the Rikshaw Inn.

"He was very nervous about the relationship because she was kind of possessive," Cohen later told friends. "At least that's what he indicated to me. She made him a little nervous. They may have dated a month to six weeks. She was around here a lot. As I recall, he broke it off."

During that same summer, Carolyn became enmeshed in a new scandal, one that not only cost her the Jukebox waitressing job, but brought the force of the U.S. Secret Service down on her. The bar's owner, Mark Papazian, for the first time ever, had begun receiving "a stack of complaints" from American Express. Customers were screaming to the credit card company that they had been double-billed at the Jukebox, and they demanded action.

What Papazian found after he began his own investigation surprised him.

"I was stunned," Papazian, a Birmingham lawyer, told several friends. "I had never received a complaint from a customer before about an improper charge, then all of a sudden in late summer of 1985, I received a multitude of complaints from American Express, a stack about four inches high. The amount stolen was between $5,700 and $10,000. It cost me double because I had to reimburse the customer, so I lost all of that."

Papazian's probe kept leading to only one suspect: Carolyn Warmus.

Checking the receipts, he found that Carolyn was the waitress each time. The scam was pretty simple. Carolyn had apparently run off a customer's card twice and then used the fake invoice to replace another customer's cash payment on a later night, pocketing the money. He couldn't understand why a young woman with a multimillionaire father needed to stoop to thievery to augment her income, but he was convinced that she had.

"I confronted her with it," Papazian said. "She denied it. She was very composed. She said some other waitress was probably jealous of her and was blaming her for something she had nothing to do with."

Disbelieving every word, he fired her that very moment.

Papazian contacted the local authorities who in turn alerted the Secret Service, the agency responsible for credit card fraud. Although she was never prosecuted for the crime—insufficient evidence, they claimed —the Secret Service report of the incident remained in the agency's file until a request by New York authorities brought it to light once again.

Carolyn spent what was left of the summer planning her fall wardrobe, working on her tan, and partying with a few close friends. She never went back to the Jukebox to say good-bye to the other waitresses or regulars.

After a couple of trips to New York to find an apartment, she finally found one on East Twenty-second Street. Later, she found an even better apartment on First Avenue between Seventy-eighth and Seventy-ninth streets.

Her master's program was demanding, but not enough so she couldn't enjoy the night life she loved so much in New York.

A few weeks after watching the lighted ball drop down in Times Square, ringing in 1987, she went out bar hopping and met a tall, good-looking Italian named Matthew Nicolosi. Although he lived in Newton, New Jersey, the two saw each other whenever possible. It wasn't until after the third or fourth date that Nicolosi told Carolyn he was married, and he was delighted when she told him it didn't really matter to her. After that they had secret rendezvous at the Sandalwood Lounge where he worked part time at night.

Occasionally Carolyn would surprise her new lover by renting a room at the Ramada Inn in Somerset, where the lounge was located. She would then sit at the bar and make small talk with him until closing time, when she would wrap a napkin around her room key and leave it on the bar. He would snatch the napkin as if cleaning up, and slyly slip the key into his pocket.

After closing the bar, he would go out the front door, waving to his friends at the front desk, and then quickly run around to an open back door. He would find the room Carolyn had rented and the two would spend hours in passionate lovemaking until he had to go home to his wife.

This scene was played out several times during the next few months, until Carolyn began pressuring him to divorce his wife for her. Fed up with the pressure, Nicolosi began seeing less of Carolyn, often making up excuses to keep her from coming to the lounge.

One night Carolyn secretly followed him as he drove home in his black Honda CRX, and then made several return visits during the next few weeks to see what her lover's wife looked like.

Frustrated at his blowing her off time after time, Carolyn began calling him both at home and at the bar, repeatedly professing her love and demanding that he see her. Occasionally he would give in, when the thought of her wild lovemaking became too much for him to resist, but for the most part he persisted in making up excuses not to see her.

Up to that time, Nicolosi had managed to hide his affair with Carolyn from his wife, but he feared that if she persisted in making phone calls, it wouldn't take long for his marriage to explode.

Carolyn's pressuring him to leave his wife for her struck him as ludicrous. Although he had told Carolyn he loved her—hell, during a night in the sack he would have said just about anything she wanted to hear—

he also knew he had made it clear that he would never get divorced. He couldn't understand why Carolyn couldn't get that through her head.

He became nervous and irritable both at home and at work, and soon found himself nervously scanning the lounge parking lot for Carolyn's red Hyundai.

It was after one particularly bad argument in early June that Carolyn had gone home and called Vincent Parco, whose agency she had found listed in the Yellow Pages.

While both Lind and Constantino knew that Carolyn Warmus's background wasn't enough to get her convicted in a court of law, it was enough to convince them that the woman was unstable and probably, under the right circumstances, capable of murder.

When Sullivan finished reading the DD2 reports sent to him from the New York City police files about Warmus's latest problems, he yelled for his secretary to ask Constantino and Lind come to his office.

Within seconds there was a knock on his door. Both men walked in and, after once more quickly scanning the reports, Sullivan flipped them to the detectives. It took Constantino only a minute before he broke out in a belly laugh. Within the past several weeks, in two separate incidents, Warmus had reported her car stolen, and had claimed she was the victim of an armed robbery in her home. It was the robbery that Constantino found humorous.

The other incident wasn't so amusing. Warmus had reported her red Hyundai stolen. Someone had swiped it while it was parked on East Seventy-eighth Street. She had a slot in a monthly parking garage a few blocks away, but she had told police she had gotten home late the night before and didn't want to risk the walk to her apartment.

The questions that crossed the minds of Constantino and Sullivan at the same time were identical. Had someone actually stolen the car, or had she made arrangements to have it swiped, knowing it might contain evidence related to Betty Jeanne Solomon's murder?

Up to that point, the detectives hadn't gathered enough evidence to persuade a judge to give them a search warrant for the vehicle, but that was now changing. Did Warmus know they were starting to focus on her as a suspect and fear that her car might hold some valuable evidence that could be used against her?

On the other hand, scores of cars were stolen every day in New York City, and maybe this was nothing more than a coincidence. There was that word again that kept popping up, *coincidence*. It had reared its head just once too often in this case and Constantino was getting frazzled by it.

He didn't believe Warmus was just a victim of some random car theft. He was operating on the premise that she was a very intelligent foe and knew just enough about police investigation procedures to keep one step ahead of them. Her luck couldn't hold out forever, he mused more to himself than to the others in the room.

While he had begun to believe that Warmus was their shooter, he hadn't completely ruled out the possibility that she had committed the murder with the help of Paul Solomon. None of the principal players had a free pass just yet.

During the next several days, Constantino and Lind hashed over all the evidence they had uncovered up to that time. When they finished, they went to Sullivan's office and told him their theories. They were both sure Warmus was the killer. They were less sure about Solomon's involvement, but they felt the time had come to push the investigation to a new level.

"Here's the way I see it happening," Constantino said. "Carolyn knows Paul will be out of the condo on his way to see her about 7:15 P.M. that night because of the telephone conversation they had that morning. Hell, she may even have been sitting in her car in the parking lot and watched him leave. Carolyn also knows that Kristan is gone for the weekend because Paul told her that, too. Sometime after Paul leaves, Betty Jeanne gets a knock on the door. She doesn't like Carolyn, but she doesn't have a problem letting her come inside. As Betty Jeanne leads the way to the living room, Carolyn whacks her on the back of the head twice, either with the gun or maybe some object she happened to grab. Betty Jeanne doesn't go down, and she struggles with Warmus, maybe even knocking the gun out of her hand. Betty Jeanne has a few seconds to pick up the phone and call 911, and that's when the operator, Linda Viana, hears the screaming and yelling. By that time, Carolyn has the gun in her hand, and forces Betty Jeanne back into the living room, at the same time she takes the phone clip out of the wall to disconnect the call. While Betty Jeanne is backing up into the living room, Carolyn begins plugging her. To make sure she's dead, Carolyn puts the gun against her back and blasts her four times. With the silencer, there's no noise. Afterward, Carolyn slips out the door and drives away to go meet Paul. Well, what do you think?"

The detectives watched Sullivan lean back in his chair, digesting what he had been told. "I can buy it, but now we gotta prove it."

Sullivan asked the pair what they thought their next step should be, and both quickly replied that a court-ordered wiretap on Warmus's home telephone could get them the evidence they needed to put her away.

Certain that they had enough evidence to convince the assistant district attorney to go to a judge, Sullivan gave them the green light. They had hit a dead end on most of their other leads in the case and it was time to try something else.

They discussed a plan to start putting the heat on Solomon and Warmus by requestioning them and then making sure they both knew that the detectives were talking to their families, friends, and work associates. That kind of heat just might make Warmus a little more anxious to talk on the telephone with her friends, and hopefully her accomplices—if there were any—while the police secretly listened in.

The following week Constantino called Kennedy and asked him to set aside some time for a meeting. Several days later, with bulging file folders tucked under their arms, the detectives walked into the county courthouse building in downtown White Plains, passed through the security screening, and took the elevator to the third floor, where a busy secretary waved them through to Kennedy's office.

Two hours later, when Constantino and Lind had finished their presentation, Kennedy smiled. It had been more than eight months since the murder, and he'd been waiting not so patiently for the detectives to bring him something—anything—to go on. Even though he had been assigned the case right from the start, and the detectives had briefed him regularly on their progress, he knew his hands were effectively tied until they handed their case over to him.

Kennedy liked the presentation they had just made and felt that even though the evidence was so far circumstantial and still shaky, it might just be enough to persuade one of the black robes to put his John Hancock on a wiretap order.

He finished reading the last of the written reports that made up the Betty Jeanne Solomon murder file and set the paperwork down on his desk. "Gentlemen, I'll have to check this with Bob Neary, our chief of the homicide bureau, and then with Bill McKenna, our chief of investigations, before a decision is made," he said. But between you and me, I think we have a shot. A damn good shot. Nice work. Richie, I'm going to need an affidavit from you to present to the judge. It should contain just about everything you just told me we have so far that points to Warmus being our girl. All this is going to take a couple of weeks and we should start working on that right away.

"Oh, by the way," Kennedy added, "there's a good shot we may get a search warrant out of all this for Warmus's apartment. Might as well start doing the groundwork now. Can you find the time one day to check out the building where she lives; you know, what floor she's on, how many doors, the basic layout. We'll need that for the warrant and for logistical purposes when we hit the place."

Pulling out his pocket calendar, Constantino thumbed through the pages. "Tell you what, me and Detective Teahan will take care of that on September 26. I'll have a report ready for you the next day."

The detectives stood up, shaking Kennedy's hand. It was nice to know they had somebody on their side, they said, as they turned and walked out the door.

10

VISIONS OF CLOWNS, pirates, witches, and goblins danced before Constantino's eyes as he daydreamed about what costumes his children would be wearing for their night of trick or treating. Halloween was only six days away and already his kids were excited about how many candy bars they could cram into their little plastic orange pumpkins with the black handles. Kennedy's loud cough brought him back to the present.

The prosecutor was going over his affidavit one last time before he filed it with the court along with a request for the wiretap on Carolyn Warmus's telephone. His bosses had already approved it, but since this was his first murder case as a member of the district attorney's homicide bureau, he wanted to make sure there were no last-minute hang-ups. They had worked hard on preparing the legal statement, and Constantino felt it made a compelling argument that any judge would be hard pressed to turn down. While Kennedy continued to read his copy, the detective forgot about the pending holiday and, for what seemed like the millionth time, began rereading portions of his statement:

Based on the foregoing, I have probable cause to believe that Carolyn Warmus committed, or aided and abetted the commission of, the homicide of Betty Jeanne Solomon. The facts and circumstances uncovered by the investigation set forth a compelling circumstantial case against Miss Warmus. It is apparent, especially when reviewing those events of August set forth within the instant affidavit, that Carolyn Warmus is a woman obsessed with Paul Solomon. This obsession supplies the motive to the killing, the circumstances of which most resemble a gangland hit.

Constantino thought that paragraph would get across quite clearly to the judge that they felt they had a *Fatal Attraction* nut case on their hands. He liked the part about the gangland hit. That was his idea. He thought it added a little color to give the judge an idea of how methodical their suspect had been in plotting and carrying out the murder of the woman she believed stood between her and total happiness. He continued reading:

Further, based upon the foregoing and my experience in criminal investigations, I have reasonable cause to believe that Carolyn Warmus has utilized, is willing and will utilize, [her] telephone . . . to conduct conversations concerning the Solomon homicide. Based on my interviews with Vincent Parco and Barbara and Marie Ballor, Warmus has made statements in person and over the telephone inconsistent with innocence. It is to be noted that if your affiant's request for the eavesdropping warrant is approved, your affiant and fellow investigators intend to intensify the investigation and conduct massive re-interviews of Warmus's peers, associates, and friends in an effort to generate telephone conversations concerning the homicide.

With a loud sigh, Kennedy laid the seventeen-page document on his desk and slumped back in his chair. "It looks good to me," he said. He grabbed the affidavit and motioned for Constantino to follow him. He stopped at the desk of Priscilla Patrincs and had her notarize the detective's signature.

Ten minutes later, the smiling investigator was driving back to his office. Lind was busy filling out a report when his partner came strolling into the squad room. The look on his face told Lind the visit to the District Attorney's office had gone well. They slapped a high-five and walked down the hall to Sullivan's office to fill him in.

The next day—October 26—Constantino and Kennedy drove into Manhattan and pulled up outside the supreme court building at 100 Centre Street. They made their way to room 1100 and asked a harried law clerk to tell Judge Brenda Soloff they had arrived.

The clerk buzzed his boss and a moment later the judge opened her office door and beckoned the men inside. She took her time reading Constantino's affidavit and the wiretap request signed by Westchester County District Attorney Carl Vergari. After asking a few questions and getting satisfactory replies, Soloff asked the detective to once again swear to the truth of his statement. When he finished, she signed the thirty-day eavesdropping warrant that would allow the police to tap into Warmus's home phone line.

Before they left, the judge reminded Kennedy that she wanted a weekly oral progress report on what they were finding out.

Later that afternoon, after a series of aggravating phone calls, Kennedy discovered that it would take a few days to set up the tap with the telephone company's security agents. Greenburgh police officers with expertise in monitoring phone calls had to rearrange their schedules so the tap could be manned around the clock.

The wiretap laws contained a minimization rule that required the police to cease monitoring a call once it was determined that the conversation did not deal with the criminal act they were investigating. Log books had to be kept for each intercepted conversation, detailing the person the suspect was talking to—if he or she could be identified—and the time of the call. One mistake and a judge could throw the whole case out of court.

It could be a boring, tedious assignment if the person being monitored didn't use the phone for hours, or even days at a time. But Kennedy, Constantino, and Lind all agreed that would not be the case with Carolyn Warmus. Having seen the telephone records that led them to Parco, the trio was convinced she would be yakking whenever she got the chance. With the added pressure they were preparing to put on Warmus, her friends, and associates, the likelihood of her not using the phone was almost nonexistent.

Six days later, on November 1, Constantino walked across the hall from the squad room into a small, almost-empty office in the far corner of the building and watched as the switch was thrown to start the tap on their heiress's home phone.

The next day, Vergari received a call from Soloff's law clerk, Frank Linatti, voicing the judge's concern that she hadn't yet received an oral progress report on the Warmus wiretap. Vergari explained the problems they'd had and assured Linatti that the wiretap hadn't actually been in operation until the day before. When he got off the phone, he prepared a confidential letter for the judge, reiterating his conversation with the law clerk and promising to provide her with an oral report the following week.

The first useful piece of information the police obtained, from one of Warmus's conversations with a girl friend, was picked up a few days later, but it wasn't anything the detectives or the district attorney's office had expected.

During the call, Warmus bragged to her friend how great her latest conquest was in bed. She described in vivid detail the sexual prowess of her most recent lover, and when the girl friend asked how they had met, she dropped the bombshell that caused ripples of laughter to spread throughout the Greenburgh Police Department.

Warmus explained to her friend that the man she had been having great sex with for the past several nights was a New York City detective whom she met when she filed an armed robbery complaint two months earlier. He was the one, Warmus explained, who had investigated the complaint involving Manuel Rodriguez, her old buddy from the funny farm.

And true to form, Constantino thought when told of the conversation, it turned out that Detective James Ryan was a married man. Singer and Sullivan just shook their heads in disbelief when their subordinate filled them in. The woman was simply incredible.

But when the laughter died down, the seriousness of this new problem became apparent. The detectives, with Kennedy, had already decided that the goal of the wiretap was to obtain enough evidence to persuade a judge to sign a search warrant that would allow them to rummage through Warmus's apartment.

The news that she had started bopping a cop couldn't have come at a worse time. One of the things they were listening for was any mention of her having a gun in her apartment. It was a safety measure, if nothing else. They'd all heard the horror stories of cops who had to bash into somebody's apartment with a search warrant only to be staring down the muzzle of a loaded gun.

Constantino played the scenario out in his head. They'd get to Warmus's door with the "no-knock" warrant, having ascertained that she was inside. They'd then proceed to use a master key from the building superintendent—or better yet break the sucker down with a steel battering ram they kept for just such a purpose—and rush inside to secure the premises. They'd storm into the place and find Warmus screwing her new cop boyfriend, only he might not immediately realize it was a police raid and pull out his service revolver, maybe thinking it was a burglary or something, and possibly open fire.

What a scene that would be. Constantino shuddered as he picked up the phone to call Kennedy with the latest bit of information. But Lind grabbed his hand and gently forced him to return the phone to its cradle.

"Listen, I know this is serious, but I don't want to get this guy in any trouble with his bosses," Lind told his partner. "He's a fellow cop and maybe we can come up with some way to work this out so he won't be there if and when we get a search warrant. Maybe we can talk to him privately or something."

Constantino shook his head. He was willing to discuss the matter with the chief and Sullivan before he called Kennedy, but he knew his superiors wouldn't go for the idea of letting Warmus's new boyfriend know what was coming down, even if he was a cop.

What if the guy started thinking with his pecker instead of his brains and told Warmus she was about to be hit with a subpoena? Cops weren't stupid, and Ryan would probably realize they had a tap going on her phone as well. If she got wind of that it could blow the whole thing. Lind sat fuming as Sullivan told Constantino to call Kennedy and tell him what had happened.

"Safety considerations come first," Sullivan told the detectives. "I understand the concern about this guy, but I don't see risking our entire case because he's decided to share the sack with Warmus. The D.A.'s office will have to decide this one."

Constantino got up and placed the call. When he hung up, he could still hear the young man's laughter echoing through the phone lines. A decision didn't have to be made for a while, he told his pissed-off partner, who knew full well what the ultimate outcome would be.

Lind didn't like seeing a fellow cop get hurt over something as stupid as screwing a broad on the side. His bosses would probably get internal affairs involved and that would most likely put a cap on the guy's career. Well, it was out of his hands, he told himself as he went back to work.

Several days later, Sullivan decided to handle the matter his own way. He called Ryan and asked him to come up to the Greenburgh Police Department for a chat. Sensing he was in some kind of trouble, but unable to figure exactly why, Ryan made the twenty-five-mile trip in record time.

After almost an hour of conversation with Sullivan, Ryan prayed for two things: One was never to hear from Carolyn Warmus again, and the second was that nothing of what happened, especially his relationship with her, would ever come out in court. He knew he would have one hell of a time explaining to his superiors—not to mention his wife—why he had visited Warmus's apartment at night just a few days before.

Especially since his investigation of her complaint against Rodriguez had officially ended with his arrest back in October.

Parco angrily threw the pen on his desk and muttered a string of profanities as he pushed his chair out and stood up. He took several deep breaths to compose himself. When were these motherfuckers going to leave him alone, he thought, as he walked toward the door, straightening his new Ralph Lauren tie and readjusting his gold tie bar. He glanced at his desk calendar. Under the November 6 date, he saw several appointments. This was not a good day for unannounced visitors, he fumed.

He pasted on the best smile he could muster and walked to the reception area where Constantino and Lind were thumbing through a couple of aged editions of *Sports Illustrated*. Parco politely, but brusquely, welcomed the pair and waved them toward an unoccupied conference room.

"I'm very busy today, Detectives, so if you don't mind, I'd like this to be brief," he said, taking the chair at the head of the table for himself. "I can't think of anything I haven't already told you. What's today's visit all about?"

Constantino noted the barely concealed anger in Parco's voice and knew that, once again, they had hit a nerve. The purpose of the visit was to keep the private eye off-balance and under pressure now that the wiretap was running on Warmus's phone.

Outside of Warmus's phone records, which showed several calls to Parco, they really had nothing on him, certainly nothing connecting him to Betty Jeanne Solomon's murder. But the plan was to keep the hammer on everyone associated with their prime suspect in the hopes that they could shake someone up enough to make that first mistake.

"Sorry to bother you again so soon, Mr. Parco, but we've developed some new evidence in the case and wanted to recheck your earlier statements to us," Lind said, realizing the way he presented his carefully chosen words would put their man on the defensive.

For the next hour the pair asked him scores of questions, and when the interrogation was over, Parco realized they were the very same questions they had asked him back in July and again in August. He knew from experience they would compare his answers today with his earlier statements and try to find some inconsistency. He was confident they would not, but their surprise visit had unnerved him. Another thought crossed his mind, and he decided to tell it his way before they asked him about it.

"Something else you guys may have heard, I thought I'd clear up for you," Parco said, trying to keep his voice as nonchalant as possible. "A lot of people thought Carolyn and I were fooling around, but it just never happened. She was always over here or calling me up, but that's because she got some idea in her head that she wanted to become a private detective.

"To be honest, I humored her a lot and let her do a little work around here, a couple of surveillances and things like that, nothing too important, just to keep her happy. Once in a while if my wife was too busy I'd take Carolyn to a party I'd be invited to, or if I was really bored I'd take her out to dinner or a nightclub. We'd go to places like Mumbles or the Hard Rock Cafe or some place like that. There was nothing between us, she was just kind of infatuated with me because of the kind of work I do. Just thought I'd mention it. I have a lot of women friends I do stuff with, and I don't want you guys to get the wrong idea in case somebody was passing stories on me."

The detectives looked at each other and then back at Parco. Constantino had picked up some rumors about the pair, but they weren't solid enough yet to confront him with them. He found it interesting that Parco felt it necessary to bring the issue out in the open. Constantino tucked the information in the back of his mind just in case the relationship between Parco and Warmus became a bigger issue. He had the uneasy feeling it just might.

When his two unwelcome visitors finally departed, Parco hurried back to his office and flipped to the M section of his Rolodex. He found the card he was looking for and jotted down the number. He silently hoped Melucci would be home.

Meanwhile, the detectives drove south through the crowded streets, with Constantino checking a map to help locate the address they would be visiting next: Avenue J in Brooklyn. They hoped Melucci would be home as well.

Rocco Lovetere, Jr., hung up his phone and stared out the window of his Bakersfield, California, apartment. November 7 was sunny, as usual, a cool wind blowing through the planted flowers dotting the complex's well-manicured lawn.

But the handsome private detective wasn't in the mood to enjoy nature's treasures. The call from his old pal Ray Melucci had triggered a deep-rooted fear that he couldn't shake. While he considered Melucci a friend, he really didn't trust him. They had gotten to know one another when they worked for Parco. They were both private detectives, but Melucci had an additional specialty that put him in great demand not only by their former boss, but by many less-than-savory characters in New York as well. These people had good reasons to use Melucci's electronic eavesdropping talents and were willing to pay good money for the kind of information that could be picked up by an illegal tap.

Both men had split from Parco, but Lovetere knew that Melucci had stayed in touch with him. Now the wheels in Lovetere's head spun as his mind replayed their just-ended conversation.

"Hey, Rocco, how ya doing?" Melucci had asked, trying to keep the nervousness out of his voice.

"Listen, I talked with Vinnie the other day and I picked up something I think you should know about. Remember that Carolyn Warmus broad, the girl who was built like a brick shithouse that Parco had Russo take out on some surveillance of her boyfriend? Well, anyway, it seems that the cops were talking to Vinnie and he tells me they've questioned him about some upstate murder that happened in January that they think she's involved with. Seems the wife of some guy Warmus was seeing was shot with a .25-caliber and they were asking Vinnie what he knew about Warmus and what the firm did for her. Vinnie seemed kind of shaken up by the visit. You know anything about any of this?"

Melucci decided not to tell his friend that the Greenburgh detectives had also questioned him the day before.

Keeping his voice even and suspecting Melucci was taping the whole conversation, Lovetere responded that he didn't know anything about it at all and didn't want to get involved in any murder case. A few minutes later the call ended.

Lovetere spent the next several minutes trying to figure out what was happening and why Melucci had called him out of the blue. His best guess was that Melucci had called at Parco's request and was trying to pump him for information. Fat chance, he thought. He wasn't about to tell Melucci about the times Parco had also ordered him to take Warmus on routine surveillances, even though they had nothing to do with her.

At the time, he figured Vinnie was just trying to impress her enough to get into her pants. He remembered that when Carolyn went out on assignments with him she seemed to really get off on hearing about private detective work. She sure as shit enjoyed the covert surveillances they went on. He had just figured her for a private-eye groupie—their business had them like a lot of others—and figured that besides the sex angle, Vinnie probably had his eye on her old man's money. But Parco's relationship with Warmus wasn't what was worrying him at that moment.

Lovetere knew he had some vital information to provide the police investigating the woman's murder, but his instincts told him not to get involved. He had moved out to California to get away from this kind of bullshit, but the more he thought of his former employer, the more anxious he became.

For the next two days he wondered and worried about what kind of trouble he might be in. If the police discovered what he knew from someone else, it might appear that he was somehow involved. He knew well enough that if Parco and Melucci's feet were held to the fire, they wouldn't hesitate to try and implicate him as a way of saving themselves.

It was this thought that finally persuaded him to pick up the phone. On November 9, he dialed information for the 914 area code and asked for the number of the Rockland County Sheriff's Department. Melucci hadn't said specifically where in upstate New York the murder investigation was going on, but for some reason Rockland County came to Lovetere's mind.

"Rockland County Sheriff's Department. May I help you?"

"Yes, I'd like to talk to one of your detectives about a murder case I believe you're investigating."

When Lovetere heard the quiet buzz of the phone line as he was placed on hold, he decided to play his hand cautiously.

"This is Lieutenant Stan Greenberg. Can I help you?"

"Yeah, listen. I don't want to give my name, but I have some information for you regarding a homicide investigation. I think you should know that a private investigator from Manhattan named Vincent Parco sold Carolyn Warmus a .25-caliber handgun equipped with a silencer which she used to kill her lover's wife. That's it."

Before the stunned lieutenant could utter a word, Lovetere slammed down the phone. He sat in his living room and was surprised to find himself sweating and breathing quickly.

For the next ten minutes he thought about what he had done and suddenly realized he had made a tragic mistake. There was always the possibility that the sheriff's department had the equipment to trace his call, even though he hadn't been on the phone that long. What bothered him more, though, was the thought that even though he had given them the information, they didn't know who had called and he could still be in hot water should Parco decide to finger him.

Cursing himself, Lovetere decided the only thing to do was call back. When the dispatcher transferred him to the familiar voice once again, he drew a deep breath.

"This is Rocco Lovetere, the guy who just called a few minutes ago about the homicide case. I decided I better call back and give you my name in case you needed some more information."

After once more going over the story he had to share—only more slowly this time—and giving his name, address, and telephone number, Lovetere listened as the man informed him that this particular murder case wasn't being handled by his department.

After a few minutes of checking his records, Greenberg came back on the line, told him the Greenburgh Police Department in Westchester County was looking into the murder, and said he would pass along Lovetere's name and the information to them. Lovetere thanked him and hung up.

He knew it wouldn't be long before the Greenburgh police contacted him. He got up, wrote a note to his wife, Venus, grabbed his car keys off the kitchen counter, and headed out to the two-man office he shared with his partner. Meanwhile, Greenberg placed a call to Sullivan.

After thanking his Rockland County counterpart for the information, Sullivan walked into the squad room looking for Constantino and Lind. But they had left for the day, and he decided not to bother them that night.

At about the same time, five miles away, Kennedy walked into his office and telephoned Judge Soloff's office. When the judge finally came on the line, he gave her an update on what had so far been obtained from the Warmus wiretap. The conversation lasted only a few minutes, but it was enough to satisfy the judge's requirement that they keep her filled in.

The next morning, Constantino threw his jacket over the back of a chair and grabbed a coffee cup from the edge of his desk, wiping the inside with his finger to clear out the inevitable dust that always seemed to find its way in there.

Coffee usually kicked his motor into gear on a cold day like this. There wasn't any snow yet, but the biting wind made him glad he had a nice, warm office out of which to work, at least for a while. He poured himself a cupful of freshly brewed coffee and went back to his work space, quickly thumbing through his phone messages. His forehead wrinkled as Sullivan stuck his head through the squad-room door and told him to come into his office.

An hour later Lind sauntered into the squad room, bitching loudly about the weather and how long it had taken him to start his car. When he looked up, he saw his young partner with a grin stretching from ear to ear.

"What're you so happy about?" Lind grumbled, as he plopped his tired body into a protesting chair.

"How about the biggest break we've had so far in the Solomon murder?" Constantino responded, unable to contain his pleasure. "I just got off the phone with a private eye by the name of Rocco Lovetere from California. Seems he used to work for our friend Vincent Parco until he left this past summer to set up his own shop out west.

"Anyway, Mr. Lovetere said he just heard the other day about our murder investigation involving Carolyn Warmus and decided to shed a little light on a few things that might help us. He first called up to Rockland anonymously and gave them the info, but then he called them back to give his name. Said he was afraid he was going to get tangled up in all of it even though he had nothing to do with it.

"You're going to love this part," Constantino went on. "Lovetere tells me that some time in December 1988, shortly before Christmas and a few weeks before the murder, Parco pulled him aside and asked him if he knew how to make a silencer. Lovetere told him he didn't but that Parco was in luck, because a few months before he had picked up a brochure in one of those spy shops in Las Vegas that showed how to make one. He says he gave it to Parco and then forgot about it.

"A few days later, Lovetere's at his desk and gets a call from Parco to come into his office. When he gets there he sees Parco and a guy named George Peters, who used to work there several years before. You'll never guess what Lovetere sees in Parco's hand. Don't guess, I'll save you the trouble: a .25-caliber Beretta automatic with the nicest little silencer you ever did see attached to the end of it. He says Parco was like a kid with a new toy, the way he was handling that gun and looking at it. Lovetere said Parco handed it to him to look at, and when he took it back, the guy walks out onto a balcony that overlooks a courtyard, right off his office. You following me so far?"

Lind nodded numbly, his mouth open, as Constantino continued.

"Lovetere says Parco walks onto that balcony with the gun and all of a sudden aims it at a tree and fires off a shot. All he says he heard was the whoosh and figured the silencer worked perfectly. After a few minutes he leaves the office and says he didn't think much more about it.

"Several days after that, he says, he went back to Parco's office and told him he had a friend who wanted to see the gun and check out the silencer, and did he mind letting him borrow it for a while. Lovetere says Parco looked like he was going to freak and got real nervous.

"Now, you ready for this? Lovetere then says Parco told him he had sold the gun and silencer to a girl who got nervous with it and threw it in the East River. Lovetere said he figured Parco had just taken the weapon home and had probably gotten scared knowing it was illegal and didn't want him to see it again.

"Lovetere said he went back to work and forgot about the whole thing until the other day when our pal Ray Melucci called him. You know him. Sullivan and I spoke to him the other day trying to stir things up. Melucci used to work for Parco and does some wire jobs, you know, heavy into electronic eavesdropping.

"Anyway, Lovetere said Melucci told him about our investigating the case and he didn't want us to think he was in any way tied up in this with Parco should we learn about the gun. He said as soon as Melucci told him the weapon was a .25-caliber with a silencer he knew right away what must have happened.

"Lovetere told Lieutenant Stan Greenberg in Rockland when he first called that Parco had sold the gun to Carolyn Warmus and she used it to kill her lover's wife. But after talking to him [Lovetere], he tells me he really doesn't know if Parco gave the gun to Carolyn or not, just that Parco said he gave it to some girl who tossed it into the river.

"Now, the new questions for the day are did Parco give or sell the gun to Warmus, and if so, did he know what she was going to do with it? Or is it possible that Parco pulled the job himself or contracted it out at the request of Warmus in return for a few of Daddy's big bucks? Either way, Mr. Lovetere just made my day and I can't wait for our next little meeting with Parco."

Constantino paused to catch his breath and enjoy the look on his flabbergasted partner's face.

"Holy shit! I think we're almost home, pal."

"I think it's time we tried to get our wiretap order to include one Vincent Parco, so if he calls Carolyn or vice versa we can record the entire thing. I also think that we should think about hitting Parco the same day we get the search warrant for Warmus's apartment and see what we can squeeze out of him. Are we going to get a written statement from this guy, Lovetere?"

Constantino nodded, and with a sly grin held up a cassette tape he pulled from the tape recorder pushed off to a corner on his desk. "We'll get Mr. Lovetere's signed statement soon enough," he said. "But this" —and he waved the tape in front of Lind's face—"guarantees that he won't be trying to change his story."

The cold, wintry day forgotten, Constantino felt great as he tossed his tape-recorded conversation with Lovetere into the Betty Jeanne Solomon murder file. "Hey, don't forget that you, me, and LoGiudice got an appointment with that neighbor of Warmus's in a little while," he yelled across the room to his partner.

Lind nodded and grabbed his coat.

The three detectives couldn't get a good read on Ellen Inkelis as she ushered them into her apartment and quickly closed the door. She lived two floors below Warmus and appeared pretty normal, but there was something in the way she talked so fast and darted her eyes around the room while speaking that bothered them.

"Miss Inkelis, we understand from some other people we spoke with in the building here that you know Carolyn Warmus pretty well," Lind began. "We're investigating a homicide of the wife of the man Miss Warmus was dating at the time. Anything you can tell us about that?"

Inkelis nervously twisted the loose ends of an old afghan blanket that covered the chair she was sitting in. "I think I have something that may be of interest to you," the dark-haired woman replied. "During July or August of this year Carolyn happened to see me in the hallway and asked me to take a walk with her, which I did. During the walk, she told me that she was involved with a married man and that on a Sunday evening they were out on a date. Carolyn said that after the date she left him and he went home to find his wife had been shot nine times. She said her and her boyfriend were now under investigation by the police."

Inkelis watched as all three detectives wrote down her statement. Satisfied they had gotten it all, she continued, "Carolyn told me she loved this guy Paul very much, but that he didn't want to see her anymore, although she mentioned that he had come by to see her about six months after the murder."

LoGiudice held up his hand to slow her down. His writing was like chicken scratch anyway, and he wanted to make sure it was legible enough to read later on.

"Here's the part I think you'll be interested in," she went on. "In

August, Carolyn's sister and brother were here because something had happened to her. I don't know exactly what it was. What her sister told me was that Carolyn was writing suicide notes to her attorney because her boyfriend Paul wanted nothing to do with her.

"I then spoke with Carolyn's brother, who told me that there was a witness willing to testify about the homicide and that Carolyn offered $2,000 for a person to do it, but Carolyn's sister denied that. They both said, though, that Carolyn had cocaine and psychiatric problems."

Constantino kept the surprise he felt off his face. Here was a witness who not only had Warmus saying Betty Jeanne had been shot nine times—that was still not publicly known—but also telling them that her very own brother knew about some witness and her offering someone money to perform the hit.

He didn't need a conference with Lind and LoGiudice to know that they would never be able to get Tom Warmus, Jr., to admit what he'd told Inkelis. Neither would Tracey willingly discuss her sister's drug and mental problems. Still, it was good info and Kennedy might be able to do something with it.

Later, reflecting on the day, Constantino felt it was one of the most productive they'd had throughout the entire case.

At two o'clock on November 14, Kennedy and Constantino arrived again at the door of Judge Soloff's Manhattan office. Once inside, the assistant district attorney handed her Constantino's amended affidavit and also an amended eavesdropping warrant for her to sign.

The judge carefully read the documents and noted that the only change from the original request was that the name Vincent Parco had been added. Soloff picked up a pen from her desk and quickly initialed the request.

Kennedy took the papers back and shoved them inside his briefcase. They could now legally tape-record any conversation Warmus had on her telephone with Parco. There was still one more set of papers they needed a judge to sign that day, perhaps the most important set of papers so far drawn up in this murder case.

Kennedy had spent the last couple of days drafting the search warrant request that would allow them to search Carolyn Warmus's apartment for a .25-caliber gun; ammunition; and blood, hair, and fiber samples. The plan was to hit her place with the search warrant the next night, after making sure she was home. Constantino and Lind wanted

Warmus there in the hope that her fear would make her crack and maybe break down and say something they could later use against her.

They both knew it was an old cop trick, but it wouldn't be the first time someone broke after a dozen cops with guns drawn crashed through the door and ransacked their home.

Once back at the Richard J. Daronco Courthouse in White Plains, Kennedy and Constantino strode into the office of acting New York Supreme Court Justice Francis A. Nicolai and handed him the papers for the search warrant. After taking the better part of a half hour to read the detective's affidavit and hear Kennedy outline their case, Nicolai signed the order authorizing a search of Warmus's apartment between 6 A.M. and 9 P.M. on November 15.

The order gave authority to the Greenburgh police, New York State police, and any investigator of the Westchester County District Attorney's Office to conduct the search. The two men happily left the judge's chambers and walked back to Kennedy's office, where they immediately got down to planning the next day's activities. It had been decided—based on the new information that had fallen into their laps—that Constantino and Lind would revisit Parco in the morning. The plan was to hit him hard and not to give him any choice but to come clean.

Handled just the right way, Parco could be the linchpin to the entire case. If he balked, perhaps after the detectives left, he would try to phone Warmus at home to warn her, and possibly discuss the crime.

Of course they would check the tree that Lovetere had told them contained the bullet Parco had fired when he tested the silencer-equipped gun from his office. If they could find it, and possibly a shell casing that wasn't too badly damaged, they could let the ballistics guys check to see if it matched the shell casings and spent bullets found at the murder scene.

Once their interrogation of Parco was over, they would move on Warmus's apartment at about seven o'clock. To ensure the right measure of fear, they decided that somewhere in the neighborhood of ten armed officers should conduct the raid. Sullivan would be there to supervise the search, and Kennedy would be available at his home in case any questions arose.

The sun was just peeking over the horizon on Wednesday, November 15, when the two unmarked cars pulled onto the quiet street in the lower-middle-class Long Island neighborhood of North Bellmore.

There wasn't anyone around so early on a chilly morning, but that was why they had chosen to show up at 7:30 A.M.

While Lind went to check on the address on Waltoffer Avenue, Constantino went over the plan with his team, Westchester County District Attorney Investigators Joe Knapp and Mark Del Vecchio and the two Nassau County detectives they had snared into coming with them.

Ten minutes later the men were at the front door. Lind began ringing the doorbell.

George Peters shuffled down the hallway and peeked through the security hole. Wondering what all those men were doing on his porch, he opened the door a crack and was met with a stream of bodies brushing past him.

"Mr. Peters, we have a search warrant for your house, allowing us to look for any .25-caliber firearms, .25-caliber ammunition, and any silencers, tools, or materials used in the manufacture of silencers or other firearms," Lind said, watching the man's expression.

Taking the piece of paper, Peters exploded in a fit of coughing and hacking that told Lind the man was really sick.

"Please excuse me," the machinist said when he was able to catch his breath. "I've got emphysema and I'm not very well."

Lind stepped back, trying to remember if the condition was contagious.

"We're here because we have information that you manufactured a silencer last year for a Manhattan private investigator by the name of Vincent Parco," Lind continued, as the other men spread out through the small, seven-room house.

Just then, Peters's two sons, Ferdinand and Phillip, came downstairs and asked their father what was happening.

Telling them to go back to their bedrooms, he grabbed Lind's arm and directed him into the kitchen. "I'll tell you what you want to know," he said between coughs. "Vinnie paid me $1,000 in cash last winter to make a silencer and fit it on a .25-caliber automatic Beretta Jetfire."

For the next half hour, Peters told the detective how Parco had called him up in early December 1988 to discuss the job. At a later meeting, Parco gave him a pamphlet that showed him how to do it. He then described what tools he used at his workplace in Brooklyn to make the illegal weapon.

"I never would have done it, but I needed the money," he finally said, agreeing to Lind's request that he provide them with a signed statement.

Several minutes later, Steven Carey, one of the Nassau County detectives, walked into the kitchen carrying a .25-caliber Beretta and a boxful of .25-caliber ammunition.

Constantino and Lind looked at each other, both noting the coincidence.

"I found these up in his room," Carey said, handing them to Lind.

Peters quickly butted in. "That's not the same gun. It's one that I carry, and I have a permit for it. It's all legal. You'll find that out when you test it."

His next coughing fit lasted more than two minutes. When he finished, he signed a piece of paper shoved at him by Constantino, giving the detectives permission to search his 1983 Cadillac parked in the driveway.

Two hours later, with the search completed, Peters stood on his front porch watching the men who had just ransacked his home drive off. He was relieved they hadn't arrested him on the spot, especially after he admitted to making the silencer for Parco. But he was sure he hadn't heard the last of this and wondered if he should call Parco, or better yet, a lawyer.

11

NEITHER SULLIVAN nor Greenburgh Police Detective John Park had called Parco this time to let him know they were coming. Surprise always worked in favor of the cops, and besides, in the pecking order of law enforcement, private detectives ranked somewhere near the bottom of the barrel, as far as they were concerned, and didn't merit any professional courtesy. Especially Parco and especially this morning.

Pulling up in front of Parco's now-familiar building, Sullivan and Park got out and walked over to the car that had been tailing them since they left Greenburgh. Westchester County District Attorney Investigators John O'Donnell and Pete Slivka and New York State Police Investigator Bill O'Leary quickly went over their plan of action with the two detectives.

The plan was to wait for Constantino and Lind to finish up at Peters's place and then join them for the big party at Parco's.

Satisfied the wheels were turning, Sullivan nodded for Park to follow him inside.

This time, the private detective made no pretense of appearing happy to see the two cops. But, regardless of his displeasure, Parco started right in telling another of his never-ending war stories. Sullivan took the opportunity to glance out through the glass-paneled balcony doors.

He could see the giant tree centered in the middle of the enclosed space, but was too far away to notice any bullet holes. They would check into that before they left.

Finally finished with his third "Magnum P.I." story, Parco brought his attention back to his visitors. "Well, what brings you here today?" he asked, checking his Rolex, hoping the two detectives would realize he didn't have much more time for them this afternoon.

Sullivan decided to make the cocky private eye roast on the spit a bit before carving him up. He didn't like the guy and consciously refused to keep the scorn out of his voice. "Mr. Parco, we're here because we've received information that leads us to believe you haven't been fully truthful with us concerning your involvement in the Betty Jeanne Solomon homicide. Now, before we begin, I'm going to read you your rights."

The comment snapped Parco's head back as if someone had hit him with an uppercut. "What—what—just what do you mean by that?" he stammered, picking up a pen and nervously tapping the desk with it, a habit that Sullivan had seen enough times to know he had his quarry scared shitless.

"Just a minute." Parco buzzed his secretary on the intercom and asked her to bring him the Warmus file. A minute later, the unsmiling receptionist walked in, handed a thick file to her boss, and left.

"I'm sorry. Please tell me what it is you think I haven't told you," Parco said, as he opened the folder and pretended to study its contents.

The small beads of sweat slowly dripping off Parco's balding dome told Sullivan he had hit a nerve.

Noticing that the clock on Parco's desk read 10:30 A.M., Sullivan checked his own watch and decided he didn't have time to play cat and mouse.

At that moment, Constantino and Lind appeared on the scene and Sullivan excused himself as his two detectives walked in the office to take over the conversation with Parco. All of this was, of course, part of the script they had carefully devised.

Watching the scene, Parco must have known something was up, but he continued his bantering with the two new arrivals.

Meanwhile, Sullivan walked down the street, where he met O'Donnell, Slivka, and O'Leary, who now had been joined by D.A. Investigators Joe Knapp and Mark Del Vecchio. Once more the team went over their plans for searching Parco's office.

At 11 A.M., Sullivan gave everyone the green light and they entered the building, briskly walking past the receptionist before she had a chance to protest. The look on Parco's face was worth every minute of planning they had endured.

"What—what's going on?" he blurted. "Am I under arrest?"

Sullivan said nothing as he reached inside of his suit coat pocket and pulled out the search warrant, tossing it in front of his flustered foe.

"I'll get right to the point, sir," Sullivan responded with mock respect. "We understand that you had a .25-caliber handgun fitted with a silencer shortly before the murder of Betty Jeanne Solomon. We believe that that gun was the murder weapon.

"Now, the way I see it, one of three things happened. You either gave or sold the weapon to Carolyn Warmus, who used it to kill Betty Jeanne Solomon herself, or she paid you to commit the murder, or Carolyn Warmus set you up with the victim's husband and he ended up with the gun and offed his wife.

"Either way, we have you tied directly to a homicide through that weapon and I'll give you one chance to tell me exactly what went down. Otherwise, we can take a ride right now to the station, where I can just about guarantee you'll be booked on a murder charge. It's either you, her, or her and the husband, and how it goes from here is up to you."

The blood drained from Parco's face, and he could feel his chest tightening. He didn't waste time trying to figure out who had snitched to the cops. They had him by the balls and he knew it.

He nervously cleared his throat.

"Listen, guys, I'm glad this is finally over. I want to get this off my chest. There may be something I know that can help you out in your case," Parco said. "I'll tell you right now that I didn't have anything to do with that murder and I don't know anything about it. What you heard about the gun and silencer is true. I had one made because Carolyn asked me for one. I had a guy I know, George Peters, make the silencer and fit it on a .25-caliber Beretta I had in my safe that I got as a gift a while back.

"Carolyn paid me $2,500 for it, and I brought it to her at her apartment some time in early January, a week or so before the murder. I can check on that. I honestly didn't have any idea she was planning to use it to kill anybody. She told me she wanted it for protection. That's all I knew."

The sweat was now a stream and the detectives revelled in Parco's discomfort. They didn't believe for a minute that he had no idea Warmus wanted a silencer-equipped gun to kill someone. The only question now was how much he really did know and was involved in the homicide.

"Am I going to be arrested?" Parco asked again.

Sullivan shook his head. "Mr. Parco, you're not under arrest. You're free to walk out of here any time you want. But we will be seizing some of your records."

Constantino stood nearby, not missing a word. He wished he could share his excitement with his partner, but held his tongue. There'd be plenty of time for that later.

Parco interrupted his thoughts. "Before I say anything else, I want to call my lawyer. I think we can work something out," he said.

The detectives watched as Parco hit the intercom switch once again and asked his secretary to get his lawyer on the phone. The calm, cool, and cocky facade had crumbled. Parco was now a frightened man.

Meanwhile, the team of detectives and investigators were already busy tearing through the office, reading files, desk calendars, and computer screens to see what they could grab under the terms of the search warrant. They also went outside and checked the tree, quickly finding a bullet hole in the trunk.

Constantino pulled Sullivan aside and told him the good news about Peters folding like a hundred-year-old accordion. The young detective couldn't stifle a grin as he turned his attention back to Parco.

He wanted to drag their fat quarry back to Greenburgh as soon as possible. Any deals Parco and his lawyer wanted to cut would be handled by the D.A.'s office, and that could take days or weeks.

The detectives' main concern at the moment was to seize all documents linking Warmus, Parco, Peters, and anyone else who may have been involved in any way with Betty Jeanne Solomon's murder.

As strange as it sounded, they all wanted Parco back in circulation as soon as possible. It would work to their advantage to have him on the street now that they had dropped their big bomb.

Their goal was to shake him up enough to give Warmus a call on her tapped line, maybe in an effort to keep their stories straight. From the look of the man across the desk nervously waiting for his call to go through, their plan was working to perfection so far.

When Parco finished talking with his lawyer, Constantino took over.

"Vinnie, we'd like you to drive back to the station with us so we can get a signed statement from you. You don't have to go. It's up to you."

Parco nodded. "Listen, I'll go back with you. But you can take a written statement from me here. I don't want any tape recording made, but after we're finished I'll take a ride with you to Greenburgh." Giving it a second thought, Parco nervously asked, "If I go to the police station with you, am I going to be arrested there?"

"No," Sullivan piped in. "You aren't going to be arrested here and you won't be arrested there. You'll be free to go whenever you wish."

Sitting back down in his expensive chair, Parco pushed the button on his intercom.

"JoAnne, you help these gentlemen find whatever it is they want, and tell everyone else in the office I said to cooperate with them fully."

For the next forty-five minutes he spilled his guts about Carolyn Warmus, a silencer-equipped, .25-caliber Beretta Jetfire, and a twisted obsession.

Then, completely wrung out, he slumped back in his chair.

"I think I'm ready to go back to your office," he said. "I'll feel more relaxed there. I don't want my employees to find out exactly why you're here."

Constantino stood up and motioned toward the door. Trying to regain some degree of composure before he walked out of the office, Parco stood and took several deep breaths, and smoothed out the sleeves of his shirt.

The squad room crackled with excitement as Sullivan and Kennedy went over last-minute instructions with the detectives, uniformed officers, and district attorney investigators who, in the next several hours, would be giving Carolyn Warmus a most unexpected surprise.

The chief of detectives and assistant district attorney were both pleased with Constantino's rendition of the meetings with Peters and Parco. Kennedy knew he would be hearing from the private detective's lawyer very soon, but for now his energy was directed toward that evening's performance.

The young assistant district attorney realized that even with Parco's admissions, the case was far from airtight. One problem was whether to charge Parco as Warmus's accomplice. If Parco was charged, he could not be forced to testify against Warmus because he would, in effect, be admitting his own criminal acts. The Constitution protected him from that. The district attorney would then have to produce additional, corroborating testimony or evidence against Warmus from someone other than Parco.

Even if they could use his testimony, it was still a circumstantial case, and while that was often good enough to persuade a jury to convict, hard, physical evidence, such as finding the murder weapon in Warmus's apartment, would make the case unbreakable. Kennedy hoped to obtain that evidence tonight.

An hour later, with everyone fully briefed, Sullivan and his crew hopped in their cars and headed for Manhattan, while Kennedy pointed his car toward home.

On the drive to the city, Sullivan mentally calculated the risks of the venture. He knew the problem of Carolyn's most recent fling, with the New York City detective, had been taken care of. He felt sorry for the guy, but he understood why the D.A.'s office had notified his superiors.

He knew the New York City police had been notified that Greenburgh would be executing a search warrant in their town tonight. Confident that all the loose ends had been tied up, he sat back and felt the rush of adrenaline pump through his veins.

He was surprised at himself for being so excited, but realized this was turning into a major murder case, something like that movie he had seen a while back, *Fatal Attraction*. He could see the headlines now. The media was going to love a juicy case like this. He kept his poker face for the remainder of the trip.

The police parked their cars directly in front of, and across the street from, Warmus's apartment building. They calmly got out and met in a group inside the doorway, crowded into the small outer hallway that led to the security door.

Constantino peeked at his watch: 7:45 P.M. They were right on schedule. They knew Warmus was inside. The surveillance team that had kept tabs on her most of that day had provided them with that information. One of the detectives buzzed the apartment of the building's landlady, who cautiously walked out into the hallway and opened the security door.

The group quietly climbed the stairs to the fourth floor and took up positions on either side of Warmus's door. When everyone was ready, the landlady knocked on the door.

When Warmus looked through her peephole, she immediately recognized the woman and opened the door. The moment they heard the dead bolt pulled back and saw the door begin to swing open, the uniformed officers and detectives poured through, waving their guns menacingly in the air. The look of surprise and fear on Warmus's face was exactly what Constantino was hoping for.

"Miss Warmus, we have a warrant here to search your apartment for items connected to the murder of Betty Jeanne Solomon."

With that, Constantino slapped the legal paper into her hands and watched her eyes as they followed the men who were tearing through her home like human tornadoes. Her mouth formed the words to protest, but fear kept the sound from coming.

She stood unmoving for several seconds, obviously confused and scared at the onslaught of armed people invading her home. She was dressed in a pair of tight blue jeans and a large, white T-shirt, and for a moment she looked like a lost little child searching for someone she knew.

Sullivan took her by the arm and led her to the sofa. Meanwhile, Lind was busy scouring the apartment for any places where she might have stowed the gun. Although the warrant was specific in what they could look for and seize—a gun, bullets, and hair and carpet fiber samples—a .25-caliber handgun was small enough to be hidden just about anywhere. So as far as Kennedy was concerned, they had carte blanche to look any place they chose.

Lind rummaged through Warmus's dresser drawers, closet shelves, and under her queen-size mattress. It took him about five minutes before he made his way to the desk unit that held a personal computer. A brown paper bag sitting atop some books caught his eye and he didn't hesitate to pull it open and peer inside.

Reaching in, he pulled out a stack of typewritten pages, bills, and other assorted items. Taking a minute to read through them, Lind let out a low whistle and called Constantino over. The young detective grabbed the two sheets of paper from his partner and shook his head. The first sheet was headed "Dear Paul."

"I just can't believe what's happened," Carolyn had written to her lover. "As I've said before, the only thing getting me through these last seven months was knowing that we would always be friends and that, in time, some sort of normalcy and stability would return."

She went on to tell him how important he was to her, how nothing in her life was significant without him in it, and how shocked she was that he didn't want to see her again. "I honestly still can't believe that you really mean it." Paul had Kristan, she went on, to help him get through each day and give him some hope for the future. "Without you, I don't have that, and it's just too painful for me to go through this alone."

She told him he was making a big mistake, completely destroying the time they'd had together, and she berated him for breaking his promise not to cut her out of his life.

And finally, to prove that all she wanted was his happiness, Carolyn offered to take the fall for Betty Jeanne's murder. The "plan," as she outlined it, involved her writing what amounted to a letter of confession

—or rather, to be sure she got all the facts right, sending him blank sheets of paper that she had signed and had notarized, so that he could type the letter himself, consulting, if he wished, with either his or her attorney.

"I do have a few concerns, however, that you will need to consider. In the letter that you write, you should probably give me a motive. But please consider that if this letter ever became public, it might hurt you more by admitting in writing that I had been dating you."

A second concern was that she had volunteered to take and had passed a series of polygraphs clearing her of the crime. Maybe Paul could "convince the police" that the polygraph was neither reliable nor admissible in court.

She assured him that the police would accept her letter of confession because "being as egotistical and selfish as they are," they would want to close the case. But, having offered herself up as the sacrificial lamb, she begged him to be sure Kristan knew she "had nothing to do with any of this." And she closed by once more declaring her love and her hope that her "idea can help bring some peace back into both your lives."

When Constantino finished reading, Lind handed him another two pieces of paper that Carolyn had typed up. At the top of the first page were the words "Things to Do."

The detective's eyebrows almost knitted together as he read the contents. When he finished, he just stared at his partner, both men wondering just how bad a head case Carolyn Warmus actually was.

"This is a fucking instruction list of things to do after she kills herself," Constantino finally said, shaking the sheets of paper in front of Lind's face. "She lists the people she wants to be at her funeral and then gives another list of people she doesn't want there. You noticed that Paul and Kristan Solomon are right at the top of the invited guests."

Lind nodded and snatched the papers back. "Yeah, and did you see some of the instructions she left? Listen to this. 'Please bury me in a very cute and sexy outfit. It should probably be pants or a jumpsuit since I don't usually wear skirts. Something in pastel colors would be very nice. I'll try to choose a few options.' "

Lind's face screwed up in disbelief. "Wait, here's another couple of gems. 'Please do not do strange things to my hair and make-up. My hair color is perfect just the way it is. Please leave the shape and color of my eyebrows the same, too.' Jesus Christ, listen to this. 'Here is a list of items I would like to have buried with me in the casket. My two favorite stuffed animals, Mortimer Alfonse and Little Fluff. All my pictures of

Paul and Kristan that are in my apartment. All the notes and letters that Paul and Kristan have written to me.' "

Lind could barely contain his laughter. He kept his voice low so Warmus, who was in the other room, could not hear.

Ignoring the fact that Constantino had already read the strange letter, Lind said, "Richie, get a load of this one. 'No autopsy is necessary or allowed. If there are any questions, I overdosed on a variety of sleeping pills. If I am still able to donate any body organs, I would like to do so. I paid for a 26-week New York LOTTO subscription by mail. If I should win anything but the grand prize, please make sure the money goes to Paul Solomon. If I win the grand prize, I would like all the money split equally among the following people: Paul Rosenbaum, Paul Solomon, Elizabeth Schmidt, John Schmidt, Tom Warmus, Nancy Dailey, Tracey Warmus, Tommy Warmus.' "

Handing the pages back to Constantino, Lind stood in the middle of the room just shaking his head. As his partner began walking away, the older man realized he was still holding a piece of paper in his hand.

"Richie, take this. It was with those papers."

Constantino came back and took the offering. It was a four-page document entitled, "Confidential Will Questionnaire."

Walking into the next room, Constantino handed the paperwork to Sullivan, who scanned the pages quickly then read them more slowly, a second time. When he saw the will forms, his eyebrows shot up.

When he finished, he told the detective to put the papers back where he'd found them. The search warrant did not allow them to seize these things, and he wanted to talk with Kennedy about how to proceed.

Another detective soon discovered a pile of photocopied Gannett-Westchester newspaper clippings detailing their investigation into the murder of Betty Jeanne Solomon. Then, seconds later, he found a check made out to Vincent Parco for $100.

Nearby, there were copies of records from the New York State Department of Motor Vehicles and the New York Telephone Company giving detailed information about Barbara Ballor. There was a letter, dated September 7, 1989, to Warmus from the Metropolitan Hospital. Someone else brought him two spring 1989 curriculum schedules from Columbia University with the written-in names of their unappreciative host and Paul Solomon.

In Warmus's living room, Constantino found more papers, one of which caught his interest. Calling Lind over, he showed the find to his partner and watched his reaction. It was a letter from one of Carolyn's doctors indicating that Warmus had recently requested an AIDS test.

The correspondence revealed that she had tested negative for both AIDS and HIV, but the detectives wondered what had prompted Warmus to have herself checked out at that time. They agreed that her obviously promiscuous lifestyle was probably the reason, and Lind wondered out loud whether any of her sexual partners, including Solomon, knew she had been worried about having AIDS.

The phone rang at about 10 P.M., startling Sullivan. He reached over and picked it up before Warmus thought to do it herself. When an operator asked if he would accept a collect call from a Kevin Kennedy, Sullivan agreed and quickly warned the assistant district attorney they were talking on a "live wire."

He knew the wiretap guys were recording everything and didn't want Kennedy unintentionally to say anything that would be damaging to their case. After Kennedy indicated he understood, Sullivan detailed for him the items they had so far uncovered, including the possible suicide note and the check to Parco.

Kennedy hesitated a few minutes, trying to decide how to proceed, and then told Sullivan he would draw up a new search warrant that would allow them to seize all the paperwork they had found. He advised Sullivan to sit tight until he called back.

The assistant D.A. would have to get Judge Nicolai's signature on any new search warrant request, so he immediately decided to call Nicolai at his home to alert him.

The judge answered after the second ring and said he would wait up. Relieved, Kennedy pulled out a copy of the original search warrant order, cut off the top, which contained the legal phrasing with which all search warrant orders began, and pasted it on a clean piece of paper.

When it came to the part that read, "Proof by affidavit having been made before me this day by Detective Richard Constantino of the Greenburgh Police," Kennedy crossed out the detective's name and wrote in his own. Then, in a hurried scrawl, he wrote:

You are therefore commanded at any hour of the day or night to make a search of the above-captioned premises for the following property: Any and all notes, papers, memoranda, lists, letters, pertaining to Paul Solomon, Betty Jeanne Solomon, or any facet of the investigation into the homicide of Betty Jeanne Solomon; any newspaper clippings pertaining to the homicide investigation concerning Betty Jeanne Solomon; any passports, travel itineraries, reworded arrangements concerning travel plans; any other evidence tending to connect Carolyn Warmus to the homicide of Betty Jeanne Solomon. And if you find same bring it before a term of this court at White Plains, New York, without unnecessary delay. This warrant is valid for ten (10) days and any property secured pursuant thereto shall be returned and delivered to the court without any unnecessary delay.

Kennedy congratulated himself on his quick, scribbled legal work and began the task of putting together a handwritten affidavit, laying out as succinctly as possible the evidence and information that would persuade the judge they had valid reason to seize the additional items the cops had found in Warmus's apartment that night.

It was late—11:59 P.M.—when he finally got Nicolai's signature, and he asked permission to use the judge's phone. Once again he called collect and Sullivan accepted the charges, not once thinking about whether it was proper to have Warmus foot the bills for their conversations.

When Kennedy relayed the fact that the new search warrant had been approved, Sullivan hung up and quietly told his men to start gathering the items they had so far found. Within the hour the task was completed and Sullivan decided it was finally time to let Warmus call her lawyer.

Her initial fear had been replaced with a fuming anger. It was the delayed reaction for which they had been waiting. Now it was time to let phase two of the operation go into effect: the wiretap.

Told she could use the phone, Warmus stormed up to her bedroom and dialed her father's attorney, Paul Rosenbaum, in Michigan. When his answering service told her they would try and reach the lawyer, Warmus hung up the phone and stomped back down to the living room to wait.

Minutes later the phone rang. After listening to Carolyn, the attorney asked to speak to Sullivan. The lawyer told him that he was not allowing his client to make a statement and that he would expect a copy of the search warrant and notice of the items seized. Sullivan handed the phone back to Warmus and smiled to himself.

While their target talked in an ever-escalating tone of voice to her lawyer, Sullivan strode around the large apartment for a last look. His people hadn't found the gun or ammunition, but maybe what they had gotten their hands on would be just as good.

He let his mind drift back to the contents of that supposed suicide letter she had written Solomon. He didn't believe for a minute that she ever really intended to kill herself, but the letter did pose some interesting questions. His instincts told him it was a fake, something she had created to throw the police off the trail should a search ever be conducted. It certainly wouldn't be the first time a sharp lawyer had suggested a client have something around his home that would point the finger in another direction should it be discovered.

Sullivan didn't know very much about Rosenbaum except that he appeared to be a corporate attorney for Warmus's father rather than a criminal lawyer. It had surprised him when Warmus placed her first call to Rosenbaum. He would have guessed that with all of Daddy's big bucks they'd have hired some hot-shot, legal barracuda by now.

In any case, Sullivan knew Rosenbaum would tell Warmus to keep her big mouth shut until he could get there or have somebody handle things from the New York end. But watching her face as she bellowed into the mouthpiece, he was betting the girl wasn't in the mood to heed any such advice, and that she planned on talking to whomever she damn well pleased.

The items discovered so far in her apartment painted a pretty solid picture for Sullivan of Warmus's guilt. It wasn't one particular thing necessarily, but all of them together. Now he wanted more tangible proof of her obsession with Paul Solomon.

When Constantino got a hold of the phone records from Warmus's room at the Caribe Hilton, a few weeks back, and verified that she had made those calls to the roommate and mother of Paul Solomon's new girl friend, Barbara Ballor, that had pretty much clinched it for him. But now they had the actual Department of Motor Vehicles and telephone company records on Ballor that Warmus had obtained to keep track of her rival. For a brief second Sullivan wondered if this investigation might not have saved Ballor's life as well.

He shook off the thought and continued to assess the new evidence. The newspaper clippings didn't mean anything by themselves, but his police experience reminded him that many killers kept newspaper and magazine stories about murders they had committed. Maybe Warmus fit that profile, he thought.

For the first time that night Sullivan glanced at his watch and realized it was already well past midnight, time for him and his men to go.

Looking at his two lead detectives, Lind and Constantino, Sullivan saw their disappointment. He knew they both had hoped to find the gun or ammunition. They figured anyone who paid for a gun and silencer would be a little hesitant to just throw it away. An experienced criminal would know better than to keep incriminating evidence around him, but a twenty-five-year-old schoolteacher possibly involved in a crime of passion might just be stupid enough to do so. But if she had kept it in the apartment, it wasn't there now.

Sullivan called his troops together to leave. As a parting shot, Lind walked up to Warmus and told her they'd be back sometime soon. He figured it couldn't hurt to give her something else to think about.

Once back at the station, Sullivan called the two detectives into his office. He told Constantino to draw up a list of the seized items and send a copy to Kennedy. Then, for the next twenty minutes, they rehashed the evening and the entire case and finally all agreed that Warmus was definitely involved. They just needed to tie up a few more loose ends before they could bring the curtain down on her. What they weren't so certain of was what role, if any, Paul Solomon had played or what Vincent Parco's involvement was besides supplying the murder weapon.

Sullivan noticed the contemplative look on Lind's face and asked him what his problem was.

"I'm convinced Warmus was involved in the murder," he said firmly. "I just have this feeling, though, that Paul Solomon played some part in it as well. Just something about the guy. His wife's body isn't even cold and he's off dicking some new broad. I don't know, it's just a feeling. I saw him when we had to just about carry him out of Singer's office the day he got back from Puerto Rico, and I believe sure as shit that he was really scared of what Warmus might do. So, who knows? It's just a feeling I have." He got up to leave, ending the thought.

Constantino followed his partner into the squad room and threw himself into his swivel chair. His desk was piled high with all the papers and books taken earlier that evening.

He enviously watched as his colleagues one by one called it a night and headed home. He had at least a couple more hours of work to do, but he really didn't mind. Everything from here on out would put one more strand in the noose that would soon be placed around Carolyn Warmus's neck. Now convinced she had murdered Betty Jeanne Solomon, he was comfortable with that thought.

Five days later, Constantino and Kennedy sat watching Judge Nicolai as he slowly and carefully checked the evidence seized from Carolyn Warmus's apartment against a list the detective had prepared. Nicolai was a thorough judge who prided himself on doing things right. He picked up the detective's return sheet and began reading.

SUPREME COURT : WESTCHESTER COUNTY
STATE OF NEW YORK

IN THE MATTER
OF
THE APPLICATION FOR AN ORDER OF SEARCH AND SEIZURE
(AMENDED)

I, DETECTIVE RICHARD CONSTANTINO, of the Greenburgh Police Department, state that on November 15 and 16, 1989, the annexed warrant was executed upon the above-captioned premises and hereby return the following property before the court.

1. Two page typewritten letter entitled "Things to Do"
2. Two 2-page letters to Paul Solomon
3. Four page "Confidential Will Questionnaire"
4. One 5" × 8" yellow pad with five pages of writing
5. One personal check register from 11/18/88 through 11/15/89 (checks 1574 to 1738)
6. One passport in the name of Carolyn Warmus
7. One letter from Metropolitan Hospital, New York, dated 9/7/89
8. Two curriculum schedules from Columbia University for Carolyn Warmus and Paul Solomon
9. Telephone book and address book for Carolyn Warmus
10. One 1989–1990 calendar planner
11. Manufacturers bank credit card statement, closing 9/16/89
12. Citibank MasterCard Statement
13. American Express Platinum Card, statement with corresponding xerox copies of credit card charges dated 1/6/89
14. American Express Platinum Card, statement account, with corresponding xerox copies of credit card charges dated 9/6/89
15. Four Citibank account statements, dated 10/10/88, 1/9/89, 2/7/89, and 10/9/89
16. Department of Motor Vehicles and Telephone Company information for Barbara Ballor
17. Numerous photocopies of newspaper articles pertaining to the homicide of Betty Jeanne Solomon
18. Personal check #1601 of Carolyn Warmus to Vincent Parco for $100.00.

Detective R.J. Constantino
Greenburgh Police Department

When he found everything in order, Nicolai asked Constantino to swear that the list was a true and accurate description of everything taken from Warmus's apartment. Then the judge signed the document.

Kennedy had heard that Warmus's father had hired for his daughter a sharp criminal lawyer from New York and he wanted to avoid any foul-ups down the line.

Parco's lawyer, John Jacobs, had called Kennedy to set up an appointment. He said his client wanted to cooperate once a few side matters were cleared up. The young assistant D.A. had filled in his boss, Bob Neary, chief of the homicide bureau, and both were anxious to meet with the private detective and his lawyer on November 30. Kennedy knew they would have to be careful. From what Constantino and Lind had told him, Parco was as slippery as an eel and smart enough to try to pull a fast one on them. They needed him, but it was very possible he also was involved in the murder plot. They would have to assure themselves he wasn't, or Mr. Parco could well be facing life in prison.

The anticipation of locking Parco into testifying against Warmus put some renewed vigor into Constantino, too. Parco had already opened up the biggest door of all for them, and he might well be the key to Warmus's conviction. Kennedy had already started talking about the possibility of putting the case before a grand jury once the Parco matter was taken care of. Although the case might be winding down for them, Constantino reminded himself not to quit looking for evidence. So far this case had been full of unbelievable twists and turns, and there was no telling how many more surprises there were in store. He wanted to do a little more checking on Parco's background before the meeting. If he could find a few skeletons in the guy's closet—and he was positive there were plenty—they just might come in handy when it was time to start squeezing his oranges.

Constantino decided Parco's old employee, Ray Melucci, might just know about a few of those skeletons.

The November 22 return trip to Melucci's Brooklyn home took more than two hours, as Constantino and Lind found themselves snarled in New York's noontime rush hour.

When the short, shifty-eyed private eye let them in, he apologized again for having little to offer in the way of information. "I know you guys are just doing your job with these reinterviews, but like I told you before, I don't know nothing about any of this. All I know about that

Warmus broad is what I told you when you came here back in June. I still think she's a flake, a schizophrenic, and a *Fatal Attraction* case. I don't know how much simpler I can make it for you."

The ringing phone stopped his speech.

"Yeah, hi, Bob. How ya doing? Listen, can I call you back? I got some cops over here talking to me about that murder case Vinnie's involved in with that Carolyn Warmus."

The two detectives could hear only Melucci's side of the conversation and when he stopped talking for almost two minutes and kept glancing their way, they got curious.

"Hey, Bob. They're right here. Why don't you just tell them what you told me."

With that, Melucci handed the phone to Lind.

"Hi, Detective. My name's Bob Carroll. I'm an old business associate of Vinnie Parco's. What I was telling Ray was that I heard about that murder case Vinnie was involved in and that the killing was done with a .25-caliber gun. I thought maybe you'd like to know that back in 1987, I gave Vinnie a .25-caliber Beretta Jetfire as a gift 'cuz we was going into business together. I don't know if it was the same gun or not, but it got me thinking."

It got Lind thinking as well, and he couldn't believe their luck. He pulled out his note pad and wrote down the information. When he finished with his questions, he made arrangements for a meeting at Carroll's home in two days so they could get a signed statement from him.

Constantino watched his partner hang up the phone and knew they had hit some kind of pay dirt.

"Glad I could be of some help to you guys," Melucci said, waving at the two detectives as they sped out of his driveway.

12

THE FLOOR of the welding room at the J. B. Slattery Company in Brooklyn was cluttered with boxes, tools, and metal shavings, and whenever the two detectives moved something out of their way, George Peters looked at them nervously. Lind and Constantino didn't care.

They had Peters by the balls and the not-too-bright machinist knew it. He was even helping them search his own workplace to find some evidence that would tie him, Parco, and Warmus to the silencer-equipped .25-caliber Beretta that had been used to fill Betty Jeanne Solomon full of holes.

The look on Peters's face alone when he walked into his job on the morning of November 28 was worth the price of admission, Lind thought. Even though they didn't have a search warrant with them, Peters was so worried about his bosses finding out what he had done, that he had quickly ushered them upstairs and virtually begged them not to let his supervisors know what they were doing.

"I made the damn thing out of two pieces of metal and some stove insulation," Peters squirmed, looking around to see if any of his co-workers were getting suspicious. "Vinnie had given me some brochure that showed you how to do it. After I was done I test-fired it a few times into a piece of wood, but I'm sure that was thrown out a long time ago. Hell, it was almost a year ago that I did all that."

Looking at the two detectives, Peters began to plead with them. "I'll help you guys any way I can. I'll even help you look for whatever it is you need. Only thing is, I need this job and if anyone finds out, they'll can me in a second. I don't know where in the building my bosses are, so could you please hurry. If you need more time maybe I can get you back in on Saturday when almost nobody's around."

Constantino felt a twinge of sympathy for the distressed machinist, but it quickly passed when he remembered the stone-cold body of Betty Jeanne Solomon. Lind didn't appear to be bothered either as the three men made their way to the welding room.

Besides, the chief had a plan where Parco might still have to answer to someone else for his involvement in having silencers manufactured, even though the Westchester and Manhattan district attorney had discussed giving him immunity. The feds weren't bound by any state agreement and after Parco's testimony in front of a grand jury about Warmus, you could never tell who might get a little telephone call.

Because Peters was being helpful now, they'd probably be able to work out an immunity deal in exchange for his testimony against Parco, who in turn would hand them Warmus. Constantino thought the immunity agreements might come back to haunt them, but it was the district attorney's call, so he tried not to worry about it.

A few minutes later, Constantino heard his name being called. He walked over to where Peters was standing, and without a word, the machinist pointed toward his feet. "This is the piece of two-by-four that I test-fired the gun into after I made the silencer," he said, shaking his head as Constantino picked up the board. "You can see where I shot into it three times." Lind had come over by then to see what was going on, and he had to force himself to keep from grinning.

"Look, guys, you found what you were looking for. Can you go now before my bosses come in here? They always make their rounds in the morning and they could be here any minute."

The look on Peters's face was one of the most pathetic that either man had seen in a long time.

"We'll have to come back to complete our search, but I guess we can do that. When did you say would be better, Saturday?" Lind asked.

Looking relieved, Peters replied, "Yeah. Yeah, Saturday I can get you in and just about nobody comes in that day. You can look around all you want."

Lind shot a look at Constantino, who shrugged his shoulders, leaving the decision up to his higher-ranking partner.

"All right. We'll be back here Saturday morning at 9 A.M. You be here."

With that, the two detectives walked down the stairs and out of the building, Constantino carrying the evidence they both hoped would link Carolyn Warmus to the slaying.

Four days later, Constantino arrived back at the gritty, dirty machine shop, this time with Detective Dan Genet in tow. True to his word, Peters was waiting for them in the parking lot.

Constantino had learned his lesson the hard way, and this time he wore a pair of old jeans and a raggedy sweatshirt. Being a pal, he'd warned Genet to wear similar clothing. The cost of the ruined pair of suit pants in which he had been stupid enough to go crawling around on Tuesday would come out of his own pocket, a thought that didn't sit well with him or his wife.

For the next several hours, the men searched every nook and cranny of the large work space: crowded shelves lined with half-filled jars and coffee cans, machines spattered with grease and grime, and a floor covered with so much junk that Constantino seriously thought about calling a fire inspector.

Just when he was about to call it a day, a glint of something shiny caught his eye. He got back on his hands and knees, and there it was, under an industrial drill press. He pulled a pen out of his pocket and used it as a tool to pick up the brass jacket of what appeared to be the shell of a .25-caliber bullet. He yanked his handkerchief out and used it to wrap the shell casing.

If the markings on this shell casing matched those found on the casings scattered around the murder scene, Parco's gun, which he now claimed he had sold to Warmus, would be positively linked to the murder weapon.

Constantino folded the white linen around his treasure and stuffed it into his pocket.

John Jacobs reached across the table and offered his hand to the young assistant district attorney with whom he had just finished an hour's bargaining session on behalf of his client. It was December 6, and their agreement was the result of intense discussions that had begun on November 30.

Kennedy wasn't fully convinced that the man sitting next to Jacobs was going to tell the complete truth, especially about his involvement in the Solomon case, but he had just promised him immunity from any possible gun-selling charges in exchange for his testimony before a grand jury and during any trial.

Assistant District Attorney John Fried of the Manhattan D.A.'s office had gone along with Westchester's request to give Parco a free ride on the gun charges, provided he passed certain tests. To the surprise of quite a few people, he had passed the required polygraph. He had also provided alibi evidence, promised to waive immunity before the grand jury, and agreed to testify against Warmus before the grand jury.

The idea of promising Parco immunity from prosecution on gun charges and then allowing him to testify before the grand jury that he was waiving immunity struck Kennedy as absurd, but he had checked with the office's lead appellate lawyer, Richard Weill, who gave him the applicable case law to look at and, after extensive research, he decided it could be done.

There was no immunity for murder, however, should they ever discover that Vincent Parco played a greater role in the killing of Betty Jeanne Solomon. But Jacobs had assured him that was definitely not the case.

When all the agreements had been discussed, it was time for Parco to give his statement. Kennedy looked over and nodded to the stenographer sitting next to him in the district attorney's main conference room.

"All right, Mr. Parco, once more. Why don't you begin."

Parco looked at his lawyer, who told him to go ahead. The private detective began his long story about how Carolyn Warmus had come to his office in the summer of 1987 to hire his firm to do some surveillance of her married boyfriend in New Jersey. Twenty minutes later he got to the part Kennedy had been waiting to hear.

"Well, it's like this. Carolyn came to me one day and told me that she was scared because some woman was after her family. She told me about this hit-and-run incident involving her sister in Washington, D.C., and the crash of one of her father's planes. She convinced me there was this woman who was causing all the problems and that she was genuinely scared for her safety.

"When she asked me if I could get her a gun for her protection, I told her sure. She wanted a small gun with a silencer. I know a silencer is illegal, but she said she was willing to pay for it, so I said what the hell. I told her it was going to cost $1,500 for the gun and $1,000 for the silencer, and she agreed to pay it. I told her it would take a little time to get it and she said no problem.

"I had a .25-caliber Beretta in the wall safe in my office. I received it as a gift several months before from a guy named Bob Carroll, full name is Sheldon Robert Carroll, from Brooklyn. A few months before all this happened, Bob was interested in buying a franchise of my detective business and starting an office in Florida. When the paperwork was completed and the office was set up, Bob gave me the gun as a present to mark the beginning of our working together.

"I never used it and stuck it in my safe. Anyway, that's the gun I used. I didn't know anything about silencers, so I got a hold of a guy I know named George Peters. He used to do some work for me years ago and I knew he was a machinist and could possibly make one for me.

"I called him up and he said sure, he could make it at work if I got him the gun. I did and a while later, he shows up at my office with the gun and attached silencer. I don't know who all saw it, I think it was just me and him and a guy who used to work for me named Rocco Lovetere. I test-fired the weapon from there. There's a little courtyard outside my office and I fired the gun into a tree. It worked fine. George told me he had also test-fired it at his workplace and that it had worked with no problem.

"This all happened around Christmas 1988 or somewhere right in there. In the next couple of weeks I called Carolyn and told her I had the item she had asked for. We made plans for me to go over to her apartment one night and that's when I delivered it to her. That was some time in the first week in January. It was either nine or ten days before the murder. She paid me the $2,500 in cash and I told her to be careful with it.

"I showed her how to use it, but she seemed to be pretty familiar with guns already. She was really into being a private detective. That's the last time I ever saw the gun or that she mentioned it to me."

Parco caught his breath and started wiping his brow, which had begun beading with perspiration.

"I had no idea that she would ever use it to kill somebody. I honestly thought she just wanted it for protection. The first time I heard anything about the murder was on January 16 when Carolyn called and told me the police had questioned her about it, but she said she had nothing to do with it and that she wasn't involved with that guy Solomon.

"I didn't put two and two together and never thought that Carolyn could have murdered somebody. After the cops called me in and asked me some questions, I got scared because I knew I had sold her the gun and silencer and I didn't want to become tangled up in a murder case. That's all I know. I swear."

Kennedy looked up at his stenographer again. "You got all this?"

The young lady assured him it had all been taken down.

"Mr. Parco, where were you on the night of January 15, 1989?"

Once more receiving the go-ahead from his attorney, Parco told Kennedy that he had been at the bedside of his father, who had been hospitalized with a serious illness. "Any number of people can vouch for my alibi. My wife, the nurses, and I'm sure several others saw me there."

Making a notation on his yellow legal pad, the assistant district attorney wrote down the names of the hospital and his father's doctor. Parco's alibi would definitely be checked out.

Kennedy looked up once again. His gut told him not to trust the silvery-tongued private eye. Someone with Parco's background would surely have known that a person who wanted a silencer had something more than self-protection on her mind. A plain gun would have given her all the protection that was necessary.

Something about the whole story stank, but he couldn't figure out specifically where the smell was coming from. It was too late now anyway, he thought. Parco had been given his immunity deal because Kennedy's bosses had decided that the evidence pointed most strongly to Warmus as their shooter and only Parco, through his testimony, could place the actual murder weapon in Warmus's hand.

The wiretap on Warmus's phone had been shut down on November 24, so no further evidence would be obtained from that quarter. No, without Parco's testimony, the case against Warmus fell flat on its face.

Kennedy felt sorry for the assistant district attorney who would inherit this case. A good defense attorney would waste no time—and would probably have no trouble—in trying to rip to shreds the credibility of Vincent Parco.

When they finished for the day, Kennedy showed Jacobs a draft of the immunity agreement. Jacobs scanned the paperwork and nodded his approval of the wording.

It is hereby agreed and understood among and between the undersigned that, in consideration for Vincent Parco tendering full and truthful cooperation; which includes, but is not limited to, testimony before that grand jury and the Superior Court of Westchester County; to the Westchester County District Attorney's Office in the investigation and prosecution of the matter of the death of Betty Jeanne Solomon, Vincent Parco shall, at the conclusion of the trial of aforementioned matter, be extended immunity from any prosecution arising from facts, circumstances, and occurrences concerning

Vincent Parco's alleged act of supplying and/or otherwise facilitating the supply of a firearm to Carolyn Warmus.

Jacobs handed it back to Kennedy, who told him that once an official sheet was typed up, he would sign it and send it to Fried, the Manhattan assistant district attorney, for his signature. Fried, in turn, would send it to Jacobs for him to sign.

Jacobs and his client left the District Attorney's office knowing a grand jury would soon be impaneled to hear evidence in the Betty Jeanne Solomon murder case. Kennedy had told Parco to keep himself available for most of January, and the private detective planned on heeding the request.

For Constantino and Lind, the next several weeks were a whirl of meetings, organizing evidence, and constant briefings to ensure everyone involved was up to speed on what had been obtained in the case.

Although Kennedy had been involved with the case from the beginning, he, like his police counterparts, had worked on many other matters as well. He wanted to be sure he was up to speed on every facet of the developments, and, like everyone else, he turned to Constantino, who was considered the human library on the Betty Jeanne Solomon homicide. A day didn't go by when a handful of detectives or prosecutors didn't stop by his desk or call him up to check one last detail. He didn't mind. The adrenaline was pumping again and he knew it probably wouldn't stop until they indicted Carolyn Warmus.

Sullivan had a special reason to delight in the way the case had shaped up. The Betty Jeanne Solomon investigation was his first murder case since taking over as chief of detectives, and it was a rite of passage for him. There had been other murders since January 15, 1989, but this one held a special place in his soul. And although they had never discussed it, Sullivan was sure Constantino felt the same way. He'd be damn glad once they got the conviction. Anything could happen once a case was turned over to the district attorney and the vicissitudes of the judicial system. Wacky judges, crazy decisions, and mind-boggling verdicts were par for the course, and Sullivan wasn't willing to bet that this crazy case was a surefire winner. He hoped and knew it should be, but he wouldn't bet.

Lind took it all in stride. This wasn't his first murder case, not by a long shot, but it sure as hell had been the most interesting. He had already told Sullivan and Singer that he was retiring right after this case went through the grand jury and Carolyn Warmus was indicted.

He had lined up a private sector job as part of the security team with the Fabrikant & Sons jewelry company in Manhattan, and while he realized it may not be as exciting as his twenty years of police work, the money would be a lot better and the hours more regular. Of course, he'd be available to testify when and if he was needed, but for right now the excitement of the new challenge in his life held most of his interest.

Kennedy felt pulled in several directions as he prepared the case. It seemed as if his bosses, Neary and McKenna, were taking turns coming up with questions to which he had to find answers. But overall, they were pretty much staying out of his hair. This case was his to win, lose, or draw with the grand jury and he liked it.

He looked forward to standing in front of the grand jurors and laying out as little of his case as necessary, but enough to ensure an indictment.

One of the cardinal rules of grand jury presentations is to prevent a zealous defense attorney from discovering what your ace in the hole is. That way, he or she couldn't come up with an argument to suppress it. Nothing was prettier to Kennedy than when a prosecutor caught a defense attorney by complete surprise by laying out a bombshell of undiscovered evidence during trial.

Although his job wasn't to present the D.A.'s case in court, he was expected to hand the trial prosecutor as ready-made and airtight a presentation as possible. He knew he had done his best and felt he was good at his job.

Carolyn Warmus arrived back at the Byram Hills school on January 2, 1990, fresh from her Christmas vacation. She sported a deep, rich tan from the days of sunbathing and sailing she had enjoyed the past week at her father's estate in Pompano, Florida.

Her new winter wardrobe had been meticulously selected and it was sensational, even if she did say so herself, and she looked forward to the envious stares of the other female teachers and the admiring looks of the male instructors.

She felt stronger both mentally and physically and more relaxed than she had in a long time, mostly because she hadn't heard of any more developments in the Betty Jeanne Solomon murder case and the police had stopped questioning her friends and family.

The fright, anger, and then embarrassment of that day in November when those storm troopers invaded her home with their search warrant had begun to fade. When she entered her classroom, she checked the computers her young charges would soon be tapping away on and she promised herself that 1990 was going to be a very good year.

Wednesday, January 24, 1990, was a brisk, winter's day and it took Westchester County Court Judge Francis A. Nicolai a few moments to shake the chill from his bones as he removed his overcoat and carefully hung it in the small closet within his chambers. This was the day the grand jury was scheduled to begin hearing evidence in the murder case against Carolyn Warmus.

At 9:30 A.M., Nicolai took the elevator down to the third floor, where Kennedy waited with twenty-three grand jurors. When he entered the room, everyone stopped talking.

After introducing himself and thanking the men and women for their time and commitment to the criminal justice process, Nicolai asked Kennedy if each person had received the small printed pamphlet that detailed the duties and responsibilities of a grand juror. Assured they had, the judge continued with the instructions required by law.

"The statutory requirements for a valid indictment or other action by a grand jury require a concurring vote by at least twelve jurors, each of whom has heard all the critical and essential evidence presented and the legal instructions and charge given in the case."

Nicolai looked around the room and found he had the rapt attention of all his grand jurors. For the next hour, he provided them with the legal instructions they would need to decide whether Carolyn Warmus should be indicted for murder. When he was finished, he left the room and went back to his chambers. Since the grand jury was run by the District Attorney's office, he was not required to stay.

After the jurist had left, Kennedy checked with his stenographer to ensure everything was being properly recorded and he once again counted his twenty-three grand jurors, the requisite number to begin the proceedings.

"During the next week you'll hear the testimony of police officers, witnesses, and be presented various documents you can use to determine whether Carolyn Warmus should be indicted on charges of second-degree murder and criminal possession of a weapon in the second degree," he said.

After fielding several questions, Kennedy told his group that after all the evidence had been presented, he would instruct them in the law that would bind them in how they would make their decisions. Confident with his case and comfortable with the grand jurors that had been randomly selected to hear his evidence, Kennedy called his first witness.

David Lewis sat back in his chair and stared out at the panoramic view of lower Manhattan that spread out beyond the window of his thirty-third-floor office on Broadway. Out of habit more than anything else, he stroked his thick, brown beard and quietly planned his strategy for the defense of his client, Carolyn Warmus. He had spent the last couple of months, with the help of two private investigators, Victor Ruggiero and Michael DiSalvatore, learning everything he could about the case.

The thirty-five-year-old attorney wasn't among the best-known in New York, but his reputation as an exceptional legal mind coupled with his untiring pursuit of any evidence, witness, or potential loophole that might help a client, had earned him the respect of his colleagues and a degree of financial success.

A large man with a quick wit who could tell a joke with the best of them, Lewis delighted in hearing himself compared to a gentle teddy bear with a wonderful sense of humor.

In his initial meetings with Carolyn Warmus, he had watched and listened and decided that the self-confident woman was very convincing in her blanket assertions that she had not murdered Betty Jeanne Solomon. Warmus spoke deliberately, with the assuredness of a woman who was used to telling people what she thought and, in some cases, what they should think.

After several meetings, he decided she was angry, visibly unconcerned about the torrent of legal trouble she faced, and very intelligent. For the moment, Lewis wasn't interested in her protestations of innocence. He was more concerned with the potential evidence pointing to her as the murderer and whether or not her alleged guilt could be legally proven in court.

He obtained from her everything she could remember having told the police and then asked her to slowly relate to him the events that had led to her being a suspect. He cautioned Warmus that if she were untruthful, or kept anything from him, there was little he could do to protect her.

During the following weeks, she provided him with a detailed picture of her relationship with Paul, Betty Jeanne, and Kristan Solomon, what she knew of the murder either from talks with police or through newspaper articles, her relationships with the various private eyes she had come to employ, and why she had hired them.

He took her back through her life's history, knowing that the police and district attorney would find and exploit any skeletons there might be in her personal closet.

Lewis took copious notes on everything she told him and, as quickly as possible, had his private detectives check out her story. On those occasions when her temper would flash, Lewis weathered the storm and dove back in. He quickly realized that her strong and sometimes abrasive personality could work to her detriment, especially in a courtroom, but that was a concern for a later day, if the case even got to a jury.

When on January 24, Lewis's sources informed him that a grand jury had finally been impaneled to decide whether or not his client should be indicted for murder, he didn't waste time worrying about whether the Westchester County District Attorney would be successful. There was no doubt in his mind that an indictment would be returned, and then the real work would begin.

While he had no way of knowing at that moment when the grand jury would vote, Lewis did his best to prepare Warmus for the inevitable. He counseled her to continue teaching her computer classes in the Byram Hills School District and to refrain from talking to anyone about the case.

13

THE SCREAMING HEADLINE splashed across the top of the local newspaper quickly caught the eye of Carl Vergari as he sat down to breakfast on February 3.

BYRAM HILLS TEACHER SOUGHT
IN 1989 SLAYING, LAWYER SAYS

The sixty-seven-year-old, silver-haired district attorney could feel his anger rising with each paragraph as he carefully read the exclusive report. There, laid out in black and white, for the 200,000 or so readers of the Gannett Westchester Newspapers, was his office's entire case against Carolyn Warmus. The article contained specific information about the evidence, and worst of all, correctly detailed the supposedly secret grand jury vote handed up the night before and then sealed.

It was a felony crime for a public official to leak grand jury information, and most of the judges in his circuit would soon be yelling for him to hand them somebody's head on a platter.

Grand jury leaks were something that the legal profession just didn't tolerate. Now, fourteen hours after a grand jury vote, the press had not only got hold of and printed their entire case, but, worst of all, the splashy arrest he'd planned for the schoolteacher was probably down the drain. He threw the paper down in disgust and vowed to find the person who had leaked the story. His Saturday now ruined, he decided to call his homicide bureau chief and the chief of investigations to see what they had to say about the article.

He looked out the kitchen window at the sunless, graying skies that now matched his mood. A tough, year-long investigation had finally culminated in a murder indictment against the lover of the victim's husband, and now, one day later, with a single news story the whole case might be jeopardized.

Twenty miles away, David Lewis opened the front door of his Hastings-on-Hudson home and stooped to grab the rolled newspaper from his porch. It took him only a second to find the article he was expecting to see. The reporter had called him the night before, apparently only minutes after the grand jury voted to indict Carolyn, and told him the story would appear in the next day's editions.

Lewis recalled the events of the previous evening. He had telephoned Kennedy and McKenna after learning of the indictment in an effort to find out if an arrest warrant had indeed been issued for Warmus. He had offered to make arrangements to surrender his client voluntarily to spare her the embarrassment and potential media onslaught should reporters and photographers be waiting for the police to drag her in. But the prosecutors had refused even to acknowledge that she had been indicted. In an instant he had realized the District Attorney's office wanted to make a much-publicized arrest and had no intention of allowing Carolyn to turn herself in.

"If that's the way they want to play this game," Lewis told his law partner, Charles Fiore, "I'll be more than happy to oblige them. But we'll play by my rules, not theirs."

Since the prosecutors had refused to say whether or not there was an outstanding arrest warrant for Carolyn Warmus, he was not legally obligated to produce her.

After a quick telephone call to tell his client to make herself scarce and not spend the next few nights at her apartment, he quietly made plans to sneak her into the courtroom of Judge John Carey for her arraignment the following Monday.

Lewis told his partner that he was not going to allow the Westchester D.A.'s office to make a spectacle of his client for their own interests. It was usual for the lawyer—if he was willing and able—to bring his client in voluntarily. It saved tax dollars and more often than not prevented a media circus. But if Kennedy and McKenna wanted to play it another way, hell, he was willing.

Now, he smiled as he continued to read the specific case the district attorney had against Carolyn. When he had finished, he walked over to a desk and pulled out a yellow legal pad and a pen and began jotting down notes. Freedom of the press was a great thing, he chuckled to himself.

At that very moment, Police Chief Singer grabbed the ringing phone off the hook and wasn't surprised to hear his chief of detective's unsteady voice at the other end. "Chief, have you seen a copy of today's paper?"

When Singer's answer came back in a low, sharp growl, Sullivan knew he probably hadn't been the first one to call that morning.

"I don't know where the reporter got all his information from, but the story's right on target," Sullivan said. "The D.A.'s office is going to be pissed. I'm trying to get a call through to Kennedy right now."

After ordering his chief of detectives to keep him posted, Singer hung up the phone. As a trained lawyer himself, he knew that Lewis would be reading the story with relish, using every last detail to help him with his case.

The chief retied the belt of his blue, terry-cloth robe and headed for the bathroom. He liked, and often admired the work of the press and prided himself on understanding the rules of their game. But on days like this, he mumbled out loud, reporters could be a big pain in the ass.

It was unseasonably warm on Monday, February 5, and traffic was light on Martine Avenue in downtown White Plains as Charles Fiore cautiously steered his car into a dark corner of the public parking garage located only a block from the county courthouse. Lewis had warned him that the police or district attorney's investigators might have the courthouse staked out, but no one approached them. His law partner had to be in court in Manhattan that morning or it would have been him taking Carolyn to her arraignment.

Fiore glanced over at his temporary client and thought she seemed very calm for someone about to be arraigned on a murder charge. Carolyn had asked a few questions about the arraignment procedures on the drive up, but she didn't seem particularly interested in knowing how the case would be handled after that, only perturbed that she had to miss a day of work. Fiore shrugged his shoulders and silently figured that Lewis had briefed her the day before.

When the pair walked into the courthouse at about 10:30 A.M., they took a slow-moving elevator to the tenth floor, and quietly entered Judge Carey's courtroom.

Looking around, Fiore noticed only a few people seated in the long pews. The judge was in the middle of an arraignment, so he motioned

for Carolyn to sit down. Several minutes later, a man entered the courtroom and walked straight toward the pair. Reaching down and grabbing her arm, the man quickly identified himself and began pulling her
down the aisle. Fiore yelled for him to let her go. Warmus fought back,
locking her feet and dipping her weight backwards to thwart his efforts.

Carey looked up from his perch behind the massive, elevated pine
bench. Offended by the outburst, the judge repeatedly rapped his gavel
on the small, wooden disk on the bench as a court officer from the back
of the room made his way to the disturbance.

While he had never seen the trio before, Carey knew the man who
accompanied the woman was a lawyer by the well-tailored, silver-gray
suit and his telltale briefcase. The woman who was being pulled from
her seat wore a pair of brown slacks and a tight, white angora sweater.

"What exactly is going on here?" Carey boomed from the bench, his
face turning red with anger.

The unknown man pulled his wallet from his suit pocket and opened
it, revealing a silver badge, which he flashed toward the court officer
and then the judge. He said, "Your honor, I'm an investigator with the
District Attorney's office and I am arresting this woman. There is a
warrant out for her arrest on a murder charge and I'm taking her into
custody."

Fiore did not wait for the judge to respond. "Your honor, my name is
Charles Fiore and I represent Miss Warmus. We came here today to
surrender her to you and have her arraigned on this warrant. This
man, for whatever reason, is attempting to drag my client from your
court to effect an arrest, even though she has appeared voluntarily to
turn herself in."

Carey took a moment to assess what was happening. Then, in a voice
dripping with controlled anger, he ordered Fiore and Warmus to seat
themselves and told the D.A. investigator to leave his courtroom.

The man stood for a moment, as if unsure of what to do next, but a
less-than-gentle tug on his arm by the court officer helped him decide.
He stalked out of the courtroom and took the elevator down to the
fourth floor to inform his bosses of what had happened.

Fifteen minutes later, Kennedy was seated before the judge, at the
prosecutor's table, preparing for Warmus's arraignment. Within the
hour, Constantino, accompanied by Detective Ronald Elsasser, strode
into the courtroom. They had practically flown there after receiving a
hurried call from the D.A.'s office, telling them Warmus had popped up
in court.

When Carey finished with his paperwork from the previous case, he nodded toward Kennedy, who stood and identified himself.

"Your honor, a grand jury on February 2 has voted an indictment against Carolyn Warmus, charging her with murder in the second degree and criminal possession of a weapon in the second degree in connection with the January 15, 1989, murder of Betty Jeanne Solomon. The people are here to proceed with her arraignment."

Hearing no objections from Fiore, the judge commenced with the routine procedural paperwork that was a part of every arraignment. When he was finished, he asked Kennedy for a recommendation on bond.

"Your honor, the people would ask that Ms. Warmus be held on no bail. Not only because of the seriousness of the offense, but because of the fact that Miss Warmus has the resources to set up residence anywhere in the world and as a result poses a definite threat to flee to avoid prosecution."

Fiore was on his feet in an instant, arguing that his client was a law-abiding resident of Manhattan, who had a secure job as a schoolteacher in Westchester County, and who had appeared voluntarily for arraignment.

Carey pondered the matter for only a moment before ordering Warmus held on a $250,000 bond. As he remanded her to the custody of the county police, Warmus's face showed the first sign of emotion that morning. She cringed when the court officer took her arm and led her through a door in the back of the courtroom.

She was deposited in a holding cell in the courthouse, from where she would be taken to the Westchester County Jail for processing. She really hadn't prepared herself for the indignity of the fingerprinting and mug shots that Fiore had tried to warn her about before they arrived.

When the processing was finally completed, John O'Donnell, a Westchester County district attorney investigator, put Warmus in the back seat of his car and drove her to the women's unit at the county jail in Valhalla.

Meanwhile, after Warmus had been led away, Kennedy handed Carey and Fiore copies of a two-page request for a temporary order of protection.

An indictment having been filed on February 2, 1990, charging the defendant Carolyn Warmus with the crime of murder in the second degree under section 125.25 of the penal law.

It appearing that a temporary order of protection is necessary and desirable;

Now, therefore, upon all the proceedings had herein, it is;

Ordered that Carolyn Warmus, defendant; shall observe the following conditions of behavior: that she, or anyone acting on her behalf, shall not contact, annoy, harass, disturb, threaten or be offensive to the following persons:

> Paul Solomon
> Town of Greenburgh, New York
>
> Kristan Solomon
> (same as above)
>
> Barbara Ballor
> Yonkers, New York

That she shall not annoy, harass, disturb, threaten, or otherwise contact Paul Solomon, Kristan Solomon, and Barbara Ballor, either at their home, place of business or school.

That she shall stay away from the vicinity of [their residences in] Town of Greenburgh, New York, and City of Yonkers, New York.

It is provided by law that the presentation by any of the above-named complainants of this order to any peace officer shall constitute authority for said peace officer to arrest the person charged with violating the terms of such temporary order of protection and bring said person to this court and otherwise so far as lies within his power to aid the above-named person in securing the protection which order was intended to afford.

This order shall remain in effect pending the disposition of the case.

Carey picked up a pen and signed his name, warning Fiore to be sure his client was made aware of the penalties should she violate the order.

Several hours later, Fiore entered the visitors' area of the jail and waited while a female corrections officer brought Warmus to him. He could see the fright and anger in her eyes as she was led into the room.

Visibly shaken and trying to control the emotion in her voice, Warmus told her lawyer she had been waiting all day for one of the guards to come and tell her the bond had been posted and she was free to go. She was dirty, tired, and scared.

When she finished her burning diatribe against the judge, prosecutor, and police, Fiore reluctantly told Warmus she would have to spend the night in jail because a $250,000 check sent by her father had not been accepted by the court employees who handled such matters.

"Don't these people know how much my father is worth and that the check was surely good?" she asked the apologetic lawyer, who repeatedly tried to explain that nothing more could be done until morning.

Led back to her cell, Warmus sat alone with her thoughts. She refused to eat the jailhouse food and curled up on her pillowless cot to wait out the night.

The next day, a courier arrived at the courthouse with a certified check from Tom Warmus. An hour after posting the bond, Fiore picked up his distraught client from the jailhouse and drove back to Manhattan, the silence broken only by her intermittent outbursts of rage at being thrown in jail like a common criminal.

Fiore held his tongue, and thought about what his partner would have to do next to unravel Carolyn Warmus from the serious predicament in which she had become entangled. The first step would be to find out through discovery exactly what the prosecution held in the way of evidence against her. Once that was determined, they could intelligently devise a defense that would perhaps explain any inconsistencies in her story.

Fiore knew that Warmus had no real alibi for the afternoon and evening of the murder and that the first time anyone could vouch for her presence was when she arrived at the restaurant where she met Paul Solomon. While he was sure most single people spent many of their Sundays alone, it was unfortunate for her that she had not been with other people, especially at about 7:12 that evening.

Once Fiore deposited her at home, Carolyn, facing the inevitable, placed a call her father.

When she had finished, she sat on her bed and thought of Paul. She wanted desperately to call and let him know she still loved him and that things could still work out.

As a sidelight to the main event, one benefactor of Carolyn's indictment was Manuel Rodriguez, whom she had earlier accused of armed robbery and who had been cooling his heels in jail for the past four months.

It seemed the Manhattan District Attorney's office decided to drop the armed robbery charges against him on February 5, 1990, feeling that they might have a little trouble getting a conviction based on the word of an accused murderess.

Tommy Lind took a last stroll around headquarters on March 5, shaking hands with the young patrolmen and older detectives who had been his family away from home for so many years. There'd be a going-away party for him later on at Patrick's Pub in White Plains, but for now he just wanted to savor his last day on the job. He saved his last handshake for Constantino, telling the little general how much the last big homicide case had meant to him.

"Just setting up a meeting on March 8 with our old friend Jim Ryan," Constantino volunteered. "Remember him? The city detective with the thing for Warmus. We're going to talk with him again to see what he can tell us about Warmus being dragged off to the booby hatch by some of the cops in his precinct. I'm sure he'll be cooperative."

Lind smiled as he thought back to Ryan's involvement in the case. "Just do me a favor and keep me posted on anything that pops up, okay?"

His former partner nodded and shook his hand.

Lind was a popular guy around the station and there was a genuine feeling of sadness among his colleagues when he finally turned in his badge at the end of the day. He wanted to go out a winner, and the Carolyn Warmus indictment had allowed him to do just that.

During the next two months, the New York tabloids, Gannett Westchester Newspapers, and even the *New York Times* combined to keep David Lewis's gastric juice's flowing by detonating one bombshell after another, in articles detailing the sex-filled, and sometimes kinky, private life of Carolyn Warmus.

The amount and detail of the coverage surprised even the cynical Lewis, who, when not preparing for the murder trial or handling any one of his dozens of other clients, was busy fielding scores of telephone calls from Carolyn. Every time a new story broke—and it seemed as if that were every other day—she would call up and scream at him to do something, even to let her hold a press conference to try and counter the stories she felt were making her look like a murderous, nymphomaniac/adultress. Lewis would always try to calm her down, and he warned her repeatedly against talking to the press, who, he privately felt, would tear her to shreds if given a chance.

As a lawyer, he knew that any statement she uttered would be memorialized in print, or worse yet, on tape, and could possibly be used against her in court. He had his secretary cut out all the articles he could find and place them in a manila folder. Any time he had a free moment at the end of a long day, he would pull the clippings out and read them.

The headlines never ceased to amaze him. Those in the *New York Post* were the worst:

Feb. 6   **Westchester
teacher nabbed
in murder of
her lover's wife
FATAL ATTRACTION**

Feb. 8   **SECRETS
OF 'SEX
TIGRESS'
Suspected
teacher-killer
obsessed with
married men**

Feb. 9   **SLAY SUSPECT WAS
A WOMAN OBSESSED**

Feb. 12 **SLAY SUSPECT'S
LIFE OF TWISTED
OBSESSIONS**

The press was having a field day, and the best Lewis could do for the moment was to read each new article carefully just in case any one of them contained some smidgen of information he might use to defend his client or to obtain some new insight into the prosecution's case against her.

While it was easy to follow the stories in the New York papers, it was harder keeping up with all the television stations, magazines, and newspapers around the country that had picked up on the now-famous *Fatal Attraction* murder case in Westchester County.

To make matters worse, he and his private detectives had heard of book and movie deals being negotiated. A Los Angeles–based film company called Citadel was apparently trying to buy the rights to Paul Solomon's version of events, through his attorney Gary Pillersdorf, for a possible deal with HBO. And Tommy Lind, one of the detectives on the case, had retired and then sold his rights to Citadel.

That last bit of information could come in handy if Lind ever took the stand to testify against Warmus. Lewis could probably tie Lind up in knots in front of the jury by attempting to show that the detective was far more interested in making money than in protecting the constitutional rights of the accused. He could picture Lind squirming as he asked him whether his greed might have caused him to view the evidence against Carolyn Warmus with a jaundiced eye.

One thing Lewis and his team had learned was that private eye James Russo, who used to work for Parco, had been paid $10,000 to appear on a segment of "Inside Edition" to tell his sordid tales about Warmus. One story, he said on camera, was that Warmus had tried to buy a gun and silencer from him in summer 1988. Russo had already provided that information to Constantino.

Russo had shared juicy tidbits about how he had helped Warmus track down and keep under surveillance the married man with whom she was obsessed, and of the time he had taken the half-naked pictures of Carolyn in her various costumes. That information would help Lewis discredit Russo's testimony against Carolyn should he ever be put on the witness stand.

One of Lewis's greatest enemies was time. He would appear in court during the day and still be hard at work preparing for upcoming cases when most people were heading off to bed at night. He was a tireless worker who knew that his greatest strength was being better prepared than his adversaries, and he drove himself hard.

After being hired to defend Warmus, he was also offered—and had accepted—a slot on the defense team for former Panamanian strongman Manuel Noriega, whose trial on drug charges would soon be held in Miami.

Although denying it publicly, Lewis enjoyed the media coverage his cases attracted and felt he handled reporters well, attributing this to his brief stint as a radio reporter years before. His law practice was booming and would only get better if and when he won his two most publicized cases. If the stress of the battles didn't kill him first, life would be good, he promised himself.

The strain created by Carolyn's indictment only added to Tom Warmus's burgeoning troubles. His own most recent legal problems had begun only a few months before, in December 1989, when he decided to refuse to make payments to 280 people who had bought his credit insurance, which promised to make payments on installment loans if the borrower became disabled and could not work, through fifteen Michigan credit unions.

He had warned the credit unions earlier in 1989 that his company,

American Way Life Insurance, would soon cease honoring the policies it had sold. While the premiums for this type of insurance were lucrative, he had decided to stop making the payments on some of the policies because many of the credit unions had told him they were going to switch their business to other insurance companies because of the poor service they had been receiving from American Way.

Michigan Attorney General Frank J. Kelley had just launched an investigation into the matter, and the *Detroit News* and *Detroit Free Press* were slowly killing Warmus's company with their stories about poor, sick people whose loans weren't being paid even though they had purchased American Way insurance to protect them from just such a problem.

Warmus felt he was being made to look like Simon Legree and he didn't like it. But this recent run-in with the attorney general wasn't his first. In winter of 1988, Kelley had filed a suit to appoint a conservator to take over American Way, claiming the giant insurance company had refused to allow state examiners access to its records and had violated an Oakland County Circuit Court order to stop selling one controversial line of insurance, while marketing another without the approval of the state's insurance bureau. A state judge had denied the request, but had ordered Warmus and his company to cooperate with state auditors.

Warmus was used to letting his high-priced lawyers handle all the legal headaches, while he busied himself with the task of making more and more millions. Money was power, he knew, and he was good at accumulating both. But his problems were growing by leaps and bounds. First Carolyn and now another state insurance investigation. Kelley was now also after him for potentially illegal ownership of several auto dealerships that marketed his policies.

These new legal problems gave him little time to take a direct hand in Carolyn's defense. That was why he hired lawyers, and the recommendations and reports he had received from Rosenbaum about David Lewis had been excellent.

14

THE SOFT VOICE on the other end of the phone whispered the words so quietly that Michael DiSalvatore had to ask the woman to repeat herself. He quickly grabbed a pad of paper and his gold Cross pen and wrote down the anonymous woman's message. Assuring her he had gotten it all, he heard the crisp crackle as the line went dead.

He tore off the page that contained his notes and placed it on top of a stack of other notes and memos detailing tips from concerned citizens, con men, and the usual crackpots who always came crawling out of the woodwork when a case hit the newspapers. His experience as a former cop and a longtime private investigator usually gave him a sixth sense about a legitimate lead, and this one sounded like it could wait.

Besides, Lewis had a ton of other assignments for him and Ruggiero to complete before they could even begin to sift through the hundreds of tips people had called or written.

Once Lewis's name appeared in the tabloids, the phone hadn't stopped ringing. Most of the tips were like this one—anonymous. DiSalvatore once more picked up the piece of paper and reread the message: "If you want to know Vincent Parco's real involvement in the Westchester murder case check this out. LISELA."

The last was apparently a vanity license plate. Once he had a few moments, he could have it run through the state Department of Motor Vehicles' computers. Lewis had already made it very clear to both him and his partner that each and every tip, no matter how trivial or ludicrous it sounded, would have to be run down eventually. It was now

March, and Lewis didn't expect pretrial hearings to begin until June, so they still had plenty of time to complete their work.

Lewis meanwhile was busy preparing his motions for discovery and suppression of the prosecution's evidence, along with requests that Judge Carey dismiss the indictment entirely.

The lawyer was confident that he had a good chance of proving that, among several issues of prosecutorial misconduct, there had been illegal grand jury leaks to the media and that, as a result, he could legitimately ask the judge to dismiss the case against Carolyn. Nobody in Lewis's office could remember the last time a judge had ever granted a motion for dismissal of a murder indictment, but one had to try.

On April 2, a seventy-seven-page "Notice of Motions" and an "Affidavit in Support of Defendant's Pretrial Motions" were delivered to Carey's office by Ruggiero and DiSalvatore and placed under seal by the judge.

The paperwork was the first shot fired by Lewis, and he wanted to make it a powerful one. He had tried for about two months to open a dialogue with the District Attorney's office in an effort to obtain copies of their records, to which he was entitled by law. In New York City there usually wasn't any problem getting the documents you wanted and needed, and the prosecutors were more often than not friendly and accommodating. Thus Lewis had been amazed by the hostility he encountered from the first day he called the Westchester District Attorney's office. The circus they had created trying to drag Carolyn from the courtroom when she had shown up to be arraigned in February was ridiculous and showed the depths to which they would sink.

"If this is the way they want to operate, so be it," he told Charles Fiore one night when they finally had time for dinner at one of Lewis's favorite Japanese restaurants. "I'm going to file so many motions it's going to make their heads spin, and I'm going to make them work their fat asses off. I can make it as hard for them as they're trying to make it for me."

Fiore didn't smile at Lewis's promise. He had known his partner for far too long not to take him seriously. For a second he felt a twinge of compassion for the unsuspecting assistant district attorneys who had decided to cross swords with the man seated across from him. They had no way of knowing they had just awakened a sleeping giant.

On April 30, Lewis sat at his desk and read with delight the decision Judge Carey had handed down earlier that day. The judge had granted him the pretrial hearings he had requested in order to try and prove there actually had been prosecutorial misconduct sufficient to merit dismissal of the indictment.

Lewis pounded his massive fist on the desk. He had his shot and he intended to make the most of it.

Roland Rinsland couldn't imagine why two Greenburgh detectives had appeared in his office unannounced on May 23. "Please, gentlemen, take a seat," said the Columbia University administrator as he returned to the swivel chair behind his pine desk.

Constantino and Detective Dan Genet both began speaking at the same time. They stopped and grinned at each other before Constantino continued.

"Mr. Rinsland, we understand you're the assistant dean for student affairs, registrar, and director of doctoral studies here at Columbia. We'd like you to take a look at two university class schedules for the Teachers College and tell us if these are actual documents from the university."

Reaching into a manila folder, Constantino pulled out the two sheets of paper and handed them to Rinsland.

After looking at the documents only a few seconds, he shook his head. "No. These are not the forms utilized by Columbia University. Here let me show you."

Rinsland turned around in his chair and yanked at a stack of papers that sat on a shelf behind his desk. "These are ours," he said, handing a schedule to each of the detectives. "You can see how they're different. The ones you showed me look like they were made on a home computer. The information contained in them could have been obtained by looking at the directory of classes, which is made available to anyone wishing to take courses at the school."

What the detectives had shown Rinsland were the two official-looking, fall 1989 class schedules made out in the names of Carolyn Marie Warmus and Paul John Solomon, which they had seized from Warmus's apartment back on November 15, 1989.

Constantino remembered the long discussion he had had with Sullivan about the schedules. At that time, they believed that Warmus and Solomon planned to go to school together the summer after Betty Jeanne's murder. While they now believed Warmus was the killer, they were still checking to see if Solomon might have played a part in his wife's death. The schedules had led them to believe that the two were still involved.

This new development made Constantino shudder, for Warmus had apparently manufactured the documents on her home computer, apparently playing out some sick fantasy that she and her former lover would go off hand-in-hand back to school.

Turning his attention back to Rinsland, Constantino asked, "There are identification numbers on each of the schedules we just showed you. Could you run those through your records to see who they are assigned to?"

Rinsland stood up. "It will only take me a minute. Please make yourselves comfortable."

Fifty-eight seconds later he was back.

"The identification number on the first form, Z03405, belongs to a Ms. Carolyn Marie Warmus. Our records show she graduated from our Teachers College on May 13, 1987, with a master's degree as a teaching major for elementary childhood education. It also says here that Miss Warmus registered for, but withdrew from classes for the 1989 spring term. Her last registration was in summer and fall of 1989, but she did not attend classes during either session.

"Now, the second identification number, which was on the other form you showed me, Z03719, does not correspond with the name Paul John Solomon. In fact, I ran Mr. Solomon's name through the computer and he has never registered here for any courses. That I.D. number belongs to someone else. That's about all I can tell you, gentlemen."

Genet reached over and took the phony schedules from Rinsland. The detectives thanked him for his time and departed.

Crossing over the Willis Avenue Bridge on the way back home, Genet and Constantino discussed their feelings about Warmus's mental state.

"She's a fucking Looney-Tune, no question about it," Genet said. "Who in their right mind does something like this? When her trial comes up, that broad better plead insanity, 'cuz it's her only chance."

"She needs some kind of professional help. A lot of it," Constantino agreed.

Twenty-eight-year-old Steven Szeman lay on the paper-thin mattress of his bunk bed, hands clasped under his head, and stared at the rectangular pattern made by the metal coils supporting the mattress above him. He paid little attention to the pictures of the beautiful naked and seminaked women cut out of *Playboy* and *Hustler* magazines that he'd taped to the wall next to his pillow.

Instead, he let his mind drift back three years to the time he'd rented a room in affluent West Bloomfield Township in Michigan, and he soon became sexually aroused remembering the excitement he felt while raping nine women and a twelve-year-old girl, all of whom had so easily become his prey.

At twenty-four, he'd been a smooth-talking, handsome but moody loner, who never had much trouble attracting good-looking women in the college bars and smoke-filled dives where he liked to hang out. But he was never much interested in the ones who tried to strike up a conversation or who batted their eyes at him from across a bar.

For some reason even he couldn't explain, his sexual thrills came from stalking, cornering, and raping frightened, screaming women and young girls. Almost as much as the rapes, Szeman found he enjoyed the challenge of outthinking and outmaneuvering the hordes of local cops, state police, and FBI agents who tracked him like an animal almost immediately after he began his reign of terror in April 1987.

He even liked the name that had been slapped on him by the police and the media. The mask had been a last-minute brainstorm right before his first attack. But after the newspapers started referring to him as the "Oakland County ski mask rapist," he decided to keep the black wool mask as part of his criminal ensemble.

He had been too smart for all those Michigan cops. They never even had a clue, and after moving back to Ohio, a small city called Rocky River, in the spring of 1988, he knew he was safe. If only he hadn't gotten caught for raping that one twenty-four-year-old bitch in North Olmsted, Ohio, in November 1988, he wouldn't be where he was now: a young man looking at 140 years behind bars in a crummy little two-man cell in the Orient Reception Center in Orient, Ohio, just a stone's throw from Columbus.

He'd learned one very valuable lesson since they'd thrown his ass in here. A rapist, especially a guy who had raped a little girl, was considered the lowest piece of scum there was in the wacky and dangerous hierarchy of the prison world. He had to be constantly on guard so as not to learn what it felt like to have a small, sharpened, steel shank shoved into his back or to be held down by a couple of 250-pound assholes while their buddy rammed his faggot cock into him. Even in a supposedly protected area of the prison, he was vulnerable and afraid every waking moment.

The clanking of his cell door interrupted his thoughts, and he rolled off the bed to face his visitor.

"The warden's administrative assistant is going to be coming down in a few minutes to talk with you, so get yourself cleaned up," the craggy-faced guard half growled at him. "Don't know why," he added quickly, cutting off the question before it was asked.

Even the guards hated kiddy rapists and never missed a chance to let him know it. Szeman shrugged and sat back down.

Marty Thornsberry had pulled Szeman's file to familiarize himself with the inmate, even though the young man's case history was still pretty fresh in his mind. Now, stopping outside the opened cell, he called out Szeman's name and watched as the inmate stood up from his bed with a look of discomfort etched in his face.

"Hello, Steve," Thornsberry said, resting his elbow on the top bunk. "I got a call this morning from the Michigan state police, a guy named Sergeant David Haire. He was calling on behalf of the Greenburgh Police Department in New York.

"Seems they have a murder case out there and your name has come up in it. They had a couple of questions they wanted me to ask you. They said if you didn't want to answer them, they'd have to come out here themselves and have a talk with you. It's up to you."

"Go ahead. Ask me whatever you want," Szeman replied, as he sat back down on his bed.

"Well, they tell me a woman by the name of Carolyn Warmus has been charged with murdering the wife of a man she was having an affair with. They got word that you might have had some connection with this woman while you were up in Michigan a couple of years ago. They want to know what, if anything, you have in common with her."

Szeman consciously let his body relax now that he knew he wasn't in any trouble—at least not any new trouble—and he decided to cooperate. "Well, sir, I do know Carolyn Warmus, but I don't know anything about the trouble she's got herself into in New York," he said with the proper amount of respect one learned in prison.

"I used to be a caretaker for one of her father's properties in Michigan. You know, like cut the grass, rake the leaves, and take out the trash, things like that. His name was Tom Warmus. Some big-shot insurance guy with a lot of bucks. In fact, I was paid by the company he owned.

"As far as Carolyn goes, I met her while I was working for her father and saw her around on maybe two, three occasions. I think I remember even seeing her at a bar one time. But I never really knew her that well and we never dated or anything like that. She was a little bit strange, kind of flighty, if you know what I mean. Nice body, but that's all I know. I knew her brother, Tom, and her sister, Tracey, better than I did her."

The story Szeman told sounded sincere, but Thornsberry had been around the prison system long enough to know that some of the best actors in the world weren't in Hollywood. He thought about probing for more details, but just as quickly decided to let the New York detectives ask any further questions if they felt the need.

Szeman interrupted his thoughts. "Listen, I don't know anything about Carolyn or that murder case, but I'll be happy to talk with the officers involved in the investigation if they want."

Thornsberry thanked Szeman and walked out of the cell, shaking his head at the thought of how small the world really was.

On May 18, 1990, Jim Delaney and his wife, Laurie, sat squirming in their chairs as Michigan State Police Sergeant David Haire waited for the couple to answer his question.

Their apparent anxiety and discomfort was enough to convince the detective that they were not the slightest bit pleased at being dragged into the sleazy homicide case involving Laurie's friend, Carolyn Warmus.

Their lawyer sat on the sofa with Haire and watched the spinning reels of the tape recorder the detective had brought along to make a permanent record of their conversation.

Jim Delaney kept shaking his head and, in a stage whisper, reminded his wife that he had always predicted that their relationship with Warmus would come to no good. He was a bartender at the Jukebox and well remembered all the problems Warmus had caused herself there.

As Delaney's wife shot him a withering glance, Haire looked at his watch and noticed he had only an hour or so to drive back to his office, call Lieutenant Sullivan in New York, and then get his butt home to his family. He had already spent several weeks talking with Warmus's friends, family, and former employers scattered around the state, as a favor to his Greenburgh counterparts.

"Well?" he said, making his voice as exasperated as possible. He was tired of the little cat-and-mouse game the Delaneys were playing with him, ostensibly to protect their troubled friend.

Noticing the detective's obvious displeasure, Laurie Delaney finally piped up. "Carolyn did say something strange to me once," she began. "It was in February 1987 and I was out in New York visiting her. At the time she told me that she was seeing a man named Matt from New Jersey, who was married to a girl named Lisa who was pregnant."

The woman glanced at her lawyer, who nodded for her to continue.

"Carolyn then told me that she could get someone to arrange for a hit on Lisa for $10,000. With Lisa out of the way she could be with Matt. You never knew with Carolyn if she was telling the truth or making something up. So when this other thing came up, I just didn't know what to think."

Haire sat back on the sofa, putting on his best poker face. He knew this statement would probably erase any doubt the New York cops may have had that Carolyn Warmus was the killer of her lover's wife.

"You did the right thing in telling us about this," Haire told the upset woman, as he got up to leave.

Later that evening, back at his desk, he reassembled for what seemed like the millionth time all the pieces of the Betty Jeanne Solomon murder puzzle the Greenburgh cops had shared with him. He knew he didn't know it all, but what he had so far learned made for a very compelling story.

He had been disappointed to hear from the Ohio prison that Steve Szeman claimed he didn't have much of a relationship with Warmus. Haire didn't know if he really believed that, but even if Szeman and Warmus did know each other better, it was something the prosecutor would probably be unable to get in front of a jury anyway. It just made Warmus that much more interesting as a subject.

Haire told another detective sitting nearby that he found it fascinating how diverse were the lives of the people Carolyn Warmus knew— some as frightening and sick as Szeman and some fairly nice like the couple he just left, the Delaneys.

After making his call to Sullivan, he got in his car and punched the accelerator. He was tired and needed some sleep. Murder cases wore him out.

During the first week in June, Carey issued a press release announcing that the pretrial hearings requested by Lewis would start on Friday, June 15. Soon after, he ordered his law clerk, David Daniels—a bright, studious, and reserved young man, very similar in temperament to himself, he thought—to clear his court calendar for a September 4 trial.

The sixty-six-year-old jurist had reviewed all the weighty motion papers submitted by the defense lawyer in the past several months, and he was impressed with the man's arguments.

He was not quite so enamored of the district attorney's responses to Lewis's numerous allegations of prosecutorial misconduct involving, among other things: grand jury leaks to the media; improperly opened, subpoenaed documents that should have been immediately turned over to the court; misleading the grand jury by failing to disclose a secret immunity agreement given to a key witness against the defendant and illegally obtaining credit history information about the defendant from another state.

Carey looked forward to the pretrial hearings and to asking a few questions of the prosecutor himself. He was troubled by some of the records he had so far reviewed, which revealed some of the police and district attorney's actions during the murder probe.

The minutes of the grand jury hearings and the way Kennedy had led the grand jurors needed further examination, he told Daniels, who knew the judge had little tolerance for shoddy work, by either the defense or the prosecution.

Carey's reputation was well-known to the members of the local Bar Association. While some considered him eccentric at times, he viewed himself as a staunch protector of the rights of the accused and didn't give a damn whether anyone liked or disliked his high-handed courtroom demeanor.

He had a vision of himself as a champion of the underdog and secretly enjoyed media attention. He would often tell reporters that he was guided most by several passages from the Bible. One of his favorites, he said, was "Blessed are they which are persecuted for righteousness' sake, for theirs is the kingdom of heaven."

Born June 11, 1924, in a lower-middle-class neighborhood in Philadelphia, Carey enjoyed his formative school years and soon fell in love with history and the law. Music was another passion, and as a college student he could often be found listening to the music of his favorite composer, Vivaldi.

Carey lived out his dream of becoming a lawyer by graduating Phi Beta Kappa from Yale University and then distinguishing himself at Harvard Law School. After an unremarkable four-year stint in the Navy, he began his career as an assistant district attorney in his hometown.

He later joined the 360-member law firm of Coudert Brothers in Manhattan, where he handled corporate law and litigation for thirty-one years. Five years after he came on board, he was named a partner.

In 1966, prompted by lessons his parents had taught him—namely to help the less fortunate—he joined the United Nations Subcommission on Human Rights, a job he took on with vigor and from which he developed an expertise in the area of law dealing with the illegal detention of prisoners.

Later, when he moved to Rye, New York, he felt the need to jump into the political arena and, surprising everyone but himself, was elected the city's first Democratic mayor in 1973, an unpaid position in which he served until 1981. As a result of his popularity and political experience Carey, by then the father of four, was appointed to the state supreme court in 1987 and elected the following year to the Westchester County Court.

Unlike many lawyers, he chose not to shy away from controversy and publicity, especially when he felt he was acting for the public's own good, and he was willing to engage in some fairly flamboyant and controversial activities in order to make his points.

For example, following a fatal train accident on Long Island in December 1974, Carey called the press, who watched in disbelief as he shoved an artificial leg into a Metro-North Commuter Railroad train door at the Rye station to show the hazards of the train's fast-closing doors.

Another time, in May 1976, the Rye City police chief ordered a ban on skateboarding in the stuffy community. To show his opposition to the move—legally, Carey felt, it was an unenforceable rule—the then-mayor called a press conference and proceeded to skateboard all around town, smiling for the flashing cameras. His inflammatory style didn't change when he took the bench.

An aloof man whom some lawyers and court staff considered arrogant, Carey drew heavy criticism for his unusual sentence in May 1990 of three teen-agers who had written anti-Semitic graffiti on the walls of Ardsley High School.

Carey, a Presbyterian whose brother was killed in combat during World War II, sentenced the youths to learn about the Holocaust by reading several books, including *The Diary of Anne Frank* and one chapter in James Michener's *Poland*. He then ordered them to return to court from time to time during their year-long probation to be quizzed by a panel of judges, including himself.

In an earlier case in April 1990, Carey stunned even his fellow judges when he ordered the District Attorney's office to produce several men who resembled a robbery suspect for an unusual in-court lineup to see if a victim could pick out the right man!

On another occasion he had ordered that Sherman Krisher, a former curator of the Museum of Cartoon Art in Rye Brook, New York, who had been convicted of stealing thousands of dollars worth of rare cartoon artwork, help make restitution for the thefts by working there once again, his salary going toward paying for the museum's losses. The museum director, along with many angry and vocal residents, were outraged over his sentence, with several unsuccessfully calling for his removal from the bench.

Undeterred by criticism, Carey believed his novel ways of handling judicial responsibilities were justified so long as they were for the public's good.

The Warmus case, he believed, with all its widespread media coverage, would give him a forum for addressing the possibly improper and illegal flaunting of the criminal justice system's rules by the District Attorney's office. He wanted some answers and he was determined to get them, regardless of the outcome.

Seven floors below him, Assistant District Attorneys James McCarty and Douglas FitzMorris had no inkling of the buzz saw into which they were about to walk.

On June 30, Warmus sat down at her home computer and began writing a letter of resignation to the Byram Hills School District. A telephone call she received the day before from a school administrator, asking her to resign or face being fired, didn't come as a shock, but it was an emotional blow, nonetheless. When she was done, she stuck the letter in her purse and hurried out the door to find a mailbox.

Reporters from all the local and New York City newspapers and television stations had started gathering early outside the locked doors of courtroom 1000 to ensure they got good seats for the opening day of Carolyn Warmus's pretrial hearings.

Word had spread quickly that Carey had denied Lewis's request that his client not have to appear, and the reporters wanted to get their first good look at the attractive woman whose sexual exploits had become the source of many newsroom jokes.

It was Friday, June 15, 1990, and a friendly, armed court officer stood in front of the locked doors with his arms crossed, politely answering the media's questions and telling them the docket would begin shortly and the courtroom would then be opened.

The banter of the reporters in the hallway centered on current media gossip: Donald and Ivana Trump's marital woes, Marla Maples's figure, John Gotti's legal troubles, and the latest antics of the Reverend Al Sharpton.

At 10:15 A.M., the doors of the courtroom swung open and the press slowly sauntered in, plopping down on the hard, oak benches reserved for them in the first three rows. Notebooks were flipped open, pens readied and set down next to them.

Soon a blanket of silence fell on the room as all eyes were fixed on the woman who had just entered from behind the judge's bench. Carolyn Warmus sashayed toward the defense table, taking in the appreciative stares of the mostly male crowd crammed into the room to watch her.

Wearing a skin-tight, peach miniskirt and matching, low-cut jacket, Warmus stopped and reached down to run a hand over her sheer, black nylons, which, along with two-inch, black high heels, emphasized the curve of her legs.

Ruggiero moved ahead and pulled out her chair at the table, and when she bent down to place her shiny, black leather purse on the floor, her breasts poured against the blouseless jacket. Then she removed the black, designer sunglasses and a wide-brimmed peach hat that made her look more like a Hollywood starlet than a cold-blooded murder suspect.

While Lewis sat down next to her and began pulling reams of paper from his overfilled briefcase, Warmus sat facing the front of the court and distractedly played with the gold-beaded necklace draped around her neck. When Carey entered the room in a swirl of black robes, Warmus's wide, doe-like eyes watched him intently while she brushed the bangs of her blond hair out of her eyes.

Several of the reporters looked at each other in amazement, rolling their eyes and making sexual comments at a decibel level low enough to prevent the judge from overhearing.

Peter Moses, a bearded, overweight reporter for the *New York Post,* jabbed a colleague sitting next to him, saying, "Watch this."

When Warmus turned around once more to check out her following, Moses winked and grinned broadly. The defendant, who obviously recognized the reporter from the times he had tried to stake out her apartment, sneered and quickly turned her back.

Carey asked the courtroom to come to order and for a moment stared out into his crowded, silent gallery. Three of the pretrial motions, which he had earlier ruled would be heard one right after another, dealt with dismissal of the indictment. Should he deny those, the remaining four were requests to suppress some of the prosecution's key evidence. Today's hearing would begin with Lewis's claim that the detectives and an assistant district attorney had illegally subpoenaed documents.

Then, in what appeared to be more a soliloquy than an opening statement, Carey began reading from his prepared notes. For the next fifteen minutes he described his role as a judge in the proceedings. Looking at the reporters in the back of the room, Carey said he considered his responsibilities to include not only ensuring a fair trial for the defendant, but watching for any instances of abuse and illegalities by the prosecution or police.

Apparently satisfied with his speech, Carey sat back in his chair, straightened his judicial robes, and nodded for the prosecutor to begin.

The first witness called to the stand was Detective Constantino, who nervously walked up and raised his hand to take the oath. When he sat down in the witness chair, the lead prosecutor, James McCarty, rose from his seat and walked over to a lectern, on which he placed his file of notes. He then began quietly asking the detective if he had received a package of financial records from Manufacturers National Bank of Detroit.

Constantino carefully explained. "We determined we needed Miss Warmus's savings and checking account and credit card records to see whether she withdrew a certain amount of money at or around the time of the murder.

"We knew from Vincent Parco that the amount of money paid to him by Miss Warmus was $2,500 for the silencer and gun, and we were looking into her banking history to see where she had gotten the money from, which account. So we subpoenaed her records from Michigan as that's where she lived and had done most of her banking before she moved to New York. We checked the few New York accounts she had, but found she maintained most of her credit from Michigan."

McCarty let his witness describe in more detail the need for Warmus's records before getting to the heart of the problem.

"There came a time, Detective, when you were given a subpoena to serve on those financial institutions. What happened with that?"

Constantino leaned forward in his chair, trying to remember this one event among so many other developments in the case.

"I believe we received the subpoena for those bank and credit card records from Mr. Kennedy and served it on the various financial institutions in Michigan so we could get our information."

"And did they honor the subpoena?"

"Yeah. Every one of them sent us their stuff. No problem."

"Did any Michigan institution balk at or refuse to provide the subpoenaed material?" McCarty pressed.

"No. None that I can recall."

When McCarty finally took his seat, the smiling defense attorney quietly stood and began his bombardment. For more than an hour, Lewis hammered at the detective, repeatedly asking him about the financial records and his understanding of the law. Tired of the game, he got to the crux of the prosecution's problem.

"Detective Constantino, in what state was the subpoena issued that you served on Manufacturers National Bank of Detroit?"

Surprised by the seemingly innocent question, whose answer was obvious, he responded, "New York, of course."

"Of course, New York," Lewis said, his voice dripping with sarcasm. Constantino knew instantly he had given the wrong answer, but he didn't know why. He was quickly educated.

"Don't you know that a subpoena from New York is invalid when served in another state, that its only legal authority is within the state it is issued from? Didn't you know, Detective, that in order to obtain Miss Warmus's Michigan banking records you needed to have a subpoena signed and issued by a Michigan judge?"

Constantino looked confused. This wasn't the line of questioning he'd expected. His answer came out as unsure as Lewis had hoped.

"Well, to tell you the truth, I uh, let me say this," he stammered, searching for the right answer and finally deciding that the person who had handled that decision should answer for it.

"Kevin Kennedy got those subpoenas for us and we just delivered them," he finally said. "I didn't question them, I thought he knew what he was doing."

An hour later, mentally and physically drained from Lewis's verbal pounding, Constantino was excused from the witness stand.

The little general tried to walk past the throng of reporters with a confident air, but those who had stayed through the day knew he had been crushed by a talented and well-prepared attorney, with the help of an apparently angry judge.

McCarty glanced over at Warmus, who was doodling on a legal pad with a black felt marker. During Lewis's questioning of Constantino she had appeared to perch on the edge her chair, casting mocking looks at the judge and her private investigators, both of whom doubled as her personal bodyguards. She was really a piece of work, McCarty thought.

Kevin Kennedy passed Constantino in the hallway as a court officer called him to the stand. He noticed the detective's pained expression and averted eyes and wondered exactly what had happened to his feisty and confident investigator. He understood as soon as he took the stand. After McCarty asked him only a few questions, Lewis began firing at him.

"Isn't it true that you knew, or should have known as a lawyer, that a New York subpoena was no good in another state? Isn't that true, Mr. Kennedy?"

The young assistant D.A. wasn't used to being in the hot seat and his eyes burned fire into his colleague sitting at the prosecution's table, apparently unable or unwilling to object.

"Let's go on to something easier," Lewis said, the note of disdain obvious in his voice. "How many homicide investigations have you been the lead prosecutor on?"

Kennedy was at the boiling point, and even McCarty's futile efforts to object didn't quench the flames of anger that lapped inside the ADA. This fat-ass son of a bitch was trying to rip apart their case by tearing him to shreds and making him look like a snot-nosed neophyte.

"This was the first homicide case that I was assigned to handle," came his answer.

McCarty didn't miss Carey's soft "hrumph" when he heard the answer.

Two hours later, mentally battered and bruised, Kennedy was allowed to step down, but McCarty knew that the damage had already been done.

Storming into an elevator, Kennedy punched the fourth-floor button. He had never been madder or more worried about his job in his entire life. Lewis had successfully made him look like the biggest fuckup with a law degree who had ever managed to wriggle his way into the Bar Association. Sure, maybe some mistakes had been made, he told himself, but none as bad as the defense lawyer had tried to paint.

As the elevator came to a stop, a new thought crossed the angry man's mind.

"They're going to hang me out to dry on this one in an effort to convince Carey that the case shouldn't be dismissed because of the screw-ups of a novice ADA," Kennedy said to himself out loud, as a couple of prosecutors walking by shot him quizzical looks.

The slamming of his office door could be heard on the next floor.

Meanwhile, as the day's proceedings drew to a close, McCarty stared in disbelief first at Carey and then at the judge's law clerk. If this were how the rest of the hearings went, he'd be in for a hell of a lot of trouble.

He gathered his files and placed them in the black rectangular briefcase he used to cart around heavy paperwork. He wasn't looking forward to the pending conversation with his bosses, who would certainly want to know how the day's session had gone.

For a moment McCarty felt sorry for Constantino and Kennedy, but then he thought better of it and decided to save some sympathy for himself.

15

THE NEXT SEVEN WEEKS were like something out of a bad horror movie for the Greenburgh detectives and the members of the Westchester County District Attorney's Office, all of whom felt they had been bashed, slashed, and fed to the sharks by Carey.

Constantino sat in McCarty's office on a hot, sweltering day during the first week in August, and the pair replayed all the issues and testimony that had so far been brought out during the trying and tiring pretrial hearings.

How Carey could have let the issues go so far afield still baffled him, McCarty told his distraught visitor. Although they both privately admitted that mistakes—some serious—had been made, there had been nothing brought out in court that would warrant dismissal of the indictment.

McCarty ran through all the pretrial issues out loud and decided they had scored a victory, although a small one, when Lewis told the judge he had information that there actually existed an E911 tape of the chilling call for help from the Solomons' apartment on the night of the murder. There was no tape and never had been, and the fact that Lewis had wasted the court's time on that issue surely was in their favor.

The other issues Lewis was using to get the case dismissed seemed minor on the surface, but McCarty was wary of Carey's seeming indifference to just about every one of the legal arguments that he had tried to raise to offset the defense lawyer's assertions.

If anyone had bothered to keep count of the number of times Carey had overruled his objections to Lewis's countless courtroom improprieties, the total would be mind-boggling, he told Constantino, who was by now convinced that an off-the-wall judge was systematically destroying his hard-worked murder case.

"You want to know something?" the exhausted and steamed detective asked. "I'm tired of getting upset over Carey's rulings. There isn't a doubt in my mind that Carolyn Warmus was involved in Betty Jeanne Solomon's murder. What should be important here isn't whether somebody mistakenly opened up an envelope or whether a grand jury should have been given more information about a witness's background.

"It's about truth and whether or not Carolyn Warmus murdered another human being. Let a jury of her peers decide the truth of what happened that night, and no judge should ever keep from that jury facts that help prove she executed that woman.

"If Carey allows some legal technicality to result in a murderer walking away scot-free, the public should sweep him out of office, because I'm convinced she'll kill again. It's the public who'll pay for that judge's mistakes simply because he's trying to get everyone to believe he's some knight riding a white horse who's boldly defending and protecting the criminal justice system from us."

McCarty, amazed at the outburst of his usually circumspect investigator, said nothing. Both men agreed they had done their best and would continue fighting regardless of any decision by Carey.

Besides, the judge so far had only ruled that some financial records they had obtained on Warmus from Michigan could be suppressed. In the overall case, both men knew those records were of little importance. There were other secrets they had uncovered during the past several months that would surely convince any jury of Warmus's involvement in the killing—assuming they were ever allowed to get that far.

McCarty thought back to July 5 and 6, when the judge had ordered one of McCarty's bosses, Bill McKenna, to the stand to testify about alleged grand jury leaks to the media and what his office had done about them.

He had never seen McKenna so mad as when he found out he would have to testify. Once he was in court, Carey had backed him into a corner and made McKenna admit under oath that he had never really done any formal investigation into the leaks. The judge had read aloud part of the district attorney's press release, which was handed out on February 5, three days after the murder indictment:

Until an indictment is unsealed, the disclosure of its existence is prohibited by law. Recent newspaper reports indicate that there was a premature disclosure to the print media of certain portions of the police reports and the fact that an indictment had been found. Since the violation of several Penal Law statutes may be involved, this matter is also under inquiry by the District Attorney's Office. Members of the press are not the targets of this investigation.

The judge had repeatedly forced McKenna to admit that all his inquiry really consisted of was asking two members of his staff, Kennedy and Neary, whether they had ever talked to reporters. McKenna told the judge that he had decided not to proceed with the leaks investigation at that time because it was possible their inquiries would lead to Greenburgh detectives or their superiors. He did not want to jeopardize the murder case by launching another investigation that could possibly entangle the investigating detectives and their bosses. He admitted, however, that there was no evidence to prove one way or another who had given the media the information.

It hadn't taken Lewis more than a second to jump to his feet and, with just the right amount of righteous indignation, try to get McKenna to entrap himself by admitting that the District Attorney's office obviously felt there were some criminal violations that could be ignored while others had to be prosecuted.

Now Lewis was pumping the judge to get him to order the district attorney himself, Carl Vergari, to the stand in an effort to make him reveal what, if anything, he knew about the leaks or how his own office had handled the leaks investigation.

There had been several long meetings to discuss their strategy on that one, and McCarty knew the last thing in the world Vergari wanted to do was testify publicly.

The hundreds of files, law books, and papers scattered around Lewis's small office made it look like a trampled battleground, but the lawyer usually had no trouble finding whatever he was looking for. Occasionally he had to call in one of his overworked secretaries for help, but more often than not, the misplaced item turned out to be right under his nose.

With the Vergari decision still pending, investigators Ruggiero and DiSalvatore were standing in the midst of this chaos waiting to tell their boss what they had found out that day.

Lewis sat stunned as his older investigator laid the developments out chronologically. A few months before, DiSalvatore said, he had received a telephone call from their anonymous woman friend who worked in Parco's office and frequently called them with dirt on her boss. While some of her information wasn't very useful, this time they had hit pay dirt. She told him they could find out about Parco's involvement in the *Fatal Attraction* murder case by checking what turned out to be a license plate she provided them.

Lewis grimaced slightly when his detectives told him they had put the tip in a file with scores of others and had only recently gotten around to checking it out.

They had eventually run the plate through the DMV and had found the guy it belonged to in East Hartland, Connecticut. DiSalvatore had then paid the gentleman an unexpected visit, not really sure what, if anything, he would have to offer their case.

The man had been very uncooperative at first and said he didn't want anything to do with any murder case. Finally, however, he broke.

"It seems," DiSalvatore told his silent employer, "that this guy says he got lost coming back from Atlantic City and ended up driving along on South Central Avenue on January 15, 1989, when he had to stop and take a piss and grab a hamburger. He gets out of his car at the Brunswick bowling alley in Yonkers and walks in to order a meal and use the john. While he's in the crapper, he hears these two guys come in and start talking. He says he hears one of the guys telling the other, 'Here's the $20,000. You want to count it?' He says he then hears the other guy say, 'No. If it ain't all here, you know you'll end up just like your wife.'

"The guy says he decided to get the hell out of there so he zips up and walks out, right past the two guys. He says as he walks out the door, he sees one guy handing the other one a white envelope. Not wanting to get involved in anything like what he thinks is going on, our boy says he quickly goes to his car and starts to pull out, but in his rearview mirror he sees one of the two guys had followed him out to the parking lot and was writing down his license plate as he drives away.

"He says he never said anything to anybody and that we were the first ones to ever confront him with what happened. The guy says he doesn't want any money for his information, so it doesn't look like he's trying to run a con job on us. He said he's scared and doesn't want to testify and just wants to be left alone. I pulled out one of those magazine articles about the case, you know, I think it was *New York* magazine. Anyway, we open it up and ask him whether he recognizes anyone in the pictures they ran with the article. He right away points to a picture of Parco and said he was the guy who was handed the envelope and who took down his license plate as he drove away. He then points to Paul Solomon's picture, but hesitates and says that that looks like the other guy except the guy he saw on January 15, 1989, had a beard, and in the picture of Solomon we showed in the magazine he was shaved with a moustache. I checked back and Paul Solomon had a full beard the night his wife was whacked. Well, that's it. What do you think, Dave?"

Lewis's instincts told him that everything about this supposedly secret witness was just too good to be true. The guy never goes to the police to report what he heard, he just happens to be out driving in the vicinity of the murder scene that night, and he picks out Parco and Solomon as the two guys he heard and saw in what he says looked like a payoff for murdering the one guy's wife.

The attorney asked his men whether they had run a criminal history check on the new witness, and when they told him it had come back with only a few minor incidents, Lewis pondered the new development.

Maybe their potential witness hadn't asked them for money yet, but it certainly wouldn't be the first time in this case that somebody had volunteered to provide information in exchange for a few bucks. Every con man in the city knew by now that Carolyn Warmus's old man was a multimillionaire, and the lure of trying to make a score at her expense had proven too tempting to many of them.

Luckily he and his partners were usually smart enough to know when someone was trying to run a game on them, and the rule they followed was that not one single penny would ever go to anyone trying to sell their information. Not only was it 99.9 percent likely the info was phony, but even the clownish Westchester County assistant district attorneys could impeach and discredit the testimony of a defense witness who had been paid to tell what he or she allegedly knew. Maybe this was an elaborate scheme by one of Parco's enemies to tie him up in the murder. Maybe Tom Warmus had spread some money around to try and help out his little girl.

Lewis told his investigators to keep a line of communication open with the guy and to start running a more thorough background check.

It was possible that if the guy didn't turn out to be a hoaxster, they would be able to use him as a surprise witness in an effort to place more smoke before the jury and convince them there were other, more believable murder suspects in this soap opera than Carolyn Warmus.

□ □ □ □

Carey's thirty-eight-page decision, released to the lawyers in the case and the media on Monday, August 6, took everyone by complete surprise. The irrepressible judge, who had been expected to rule that day only on whether a particular reporter and the district attorney should have to testify about leaks, instead dismissed the entire murder indictment against Carolyn Warmus.

Try as he might, James McCarty could not recall another instance in which a murder indictment had been thrown out by a judge. It just never happened, he told himself. If there were problems on the part of the prosecution, maybe a judge would take the drastic step of suppressing some evidence, but never, never would a murder indictment be dismissed. The more McCarty thought about the decision, the clearer it became that he should have anticipated Carey's move. A dismissal was right up his alley, a way to generate some more controversy and publicity for himself.

Calming down, McCarty realized the only good thing about the decision was that the judge had graciously given them the opportunity to reindict Warmus by reintroducing their case before another grand jury. He could have dismissed it "with prejudice," which, barring an appellate reversal, would have meant they could never again charge Warmus for the murder of Betty Jeanne Solomon.

He decided to put himself through the pain of rereading the decision to be sure he could answer the questions that would be thrown his way by men probably far angrier than he. There were certain portions he found particularly intriguing.

COUNTY COURT   :   STATE OF NEW YORK
WESTCHESTER COUNTY

THE PEOPLE OF THE STATE OF NEW YORK
–against–
CAROLYN WARMUS
IND. # 90-0061

The main charge is murder, premeditated, deliberate and without pity, cold-blooded and brutal. An innocent mother was mercilessly gunned down in her own home, it is alleged, her body torn by repeated shots from a silencer-equipped pistol.

Anyone properly charged must be brought to trial as swiftly and surely as is consistent with the high standards of criminal justice which are cherished as a basic value of American life.

This requires of all concerned the performance of duties beyond reproach. Inadequate grand jury proceedings are unacceptable in any case; this case is no exception. The reasons are not simply matters of principle. Any ticking bomb of reversible error must be disarmed without delay.

Any errors must be promptly and forthrightly corrected, if not by prosecutorial volition then by judicial compulsion.

Otherwise the ends of justice may be delayed, thwarted or even defeated.

Undue haste to get on with trial can make for the waste of repeated trials. A trial begun on a shaky legal foundation is like a house built on sand instead of rock. A gale of appellate advocacy can blow it down. The law-abiding residents of this county deserve better than that. They are entitled to the highest skills and effort that the legal profession can bring to bear.

The legal machinery by which this case is pursued must be precisely fine-tuned. Impatience has no place here if it means ignoring defects that could disrupt an otherwise valid conviction.

McCarty then turned to the section where the judge began discussing the issue of Parco's secret immunity agreement and the later "show" when he pretended to waive his rights before the grand jury before testifying on January 26, thus, as Lewis maintained, making him a more credible witness. The prosecutor knew this issue was a very big sticking point with Carey, and he wasn't surprised to see that the judge had built his dismissal order around the incident. He found the part he was looking for on page three, and continued reading:

If grand jurors are actively and deliberately deceived as to the veracity of an indispensible prosecution witness, or if they are left to flounder without adequate instructions to guide them intelligently through a legal thicket, the prosecutor is usurping their function and impairing the integrity of their proceedings. When such an impairment results from failure to conform to CPL Article 190 and may prejudice a defendant, the indictment may be dismissed.

Just as a defendant must not be brought to trial on a defective indictment, so also judicial and prosecutorial resources must not be expended on a trial over which hangs a significant and avoidable threat of reversal. Such a threat should be removed at a relatively early stage when mistakes can be rectified at little cost in comparison with that of trying a case more than once. Not to do so would be reckless.

McCarty read with interest other points in Carey's decision:

• That Kennedy had failed to tell the grand jury that New York Telephone operator Linda Viana had initially told him that the words she heard screamed into the phone when she took the call were "He is trying to kill me." Viana later said she hadn't really been sure whether the words used by the terrified woman were he or she, but Lewis had smothered Carey with legal reasons why Kennedy should have told the grand jurors about that first statement and how by not doing so he had kept important information from them. Apparently Carey agreed with the defense lawyer.

· That Kennedy should have warned the grand jurors to disregard any media accounts they may have read or heard about the case and to consider only legal evidence presented to them during the proceeding.

· That Kennedy failed to give the grand jurors adequate "accomplice corroboration instructions."

Carey had ruled that if the grand jury had found Parco to be Warmus's accomplice because he had provided her with the alleged murder weapon, New York law would not have allowed them to indict her without other, possibly circumstantial, evidence from an independent source that she did, in fact, possess the gun.

The judge had also found that Kennedy failed to give the grand jurors adequate instructions when he didn't inform them that Peters, who testified he had manufactured the silencer for Parco, had received immunity from prosecution merely by being called to testify before them. Under New York law, Carey pointed out, a person who does not formally waive immunity and testifies before a grand jury, automatically receives immunity against prosecution for the crimes to which he or she testifies.

Disgusted, McCarty read on:

· That Kennedy also failed to give the grand jurors adequate legal instructions on what constitutes circumstantial evidence. Addressing that point in his ruling, Carey wrote:

Given that the prosecution's case before the grand jury on crucial issues admittedly consisted entirely of circumstantial evidence, the absence of any mention of that subject by Kennedy was a failure to conform to [the law].

More and more upset at the way Carey had shredded his colleague's handling of the grand jury, McCarty flipped to the judge's conclusions and read:

The effect, both separate and cumulative, of the faulty grand jury instructions and of the concealment from the grand jury of Parco's immunity agreement and prior statements constituted failure to conform with the requirements of CPL Article 190 to such a degree that the integrity of the grand jury proceeding was impaired and prejudice to defendant may result.

Accordingly, . . . it is ordered that the indictment is dismissed, with leave to the District Attorney upon application to present to a new grand jury evidence against the defendant in a manner consistent herewith; And it is ordered: That the defendant shall be permitted to remain at liberty upon the bail conditions fixed by the court on February 5, 1990, which conditions shall remain in effect in accordance with CPL 210.45(9).

Dated: White Plains, New York   JOHN CAREY
   August 6, 1990   County Court Judge

McCarty rubbed his eyes and wondered how Kennedy was going to take the news. For a young assistant district attorney trying to make a name for himself in the legal community, this decision could well be the kiss of death. He knew Kennedy was already upset by the way Lewis and the judge had made him look like an incompetent, first-year law student when he'd been forced to take the stand during the pretrial hearings.

It was the consensus of everyone who had witnessed that courtroom debacle that Kennedy had been made to look ridiculous, the powers that be in the D.A.'s office held him personally responsible for the case's screw-ups. The fact that no seasoned prosecutor was assigned or even volunteered to work with him during the preparation of the case, held little sway with the likes of Neary, McKenna, or Vergari.

Well, what had happened was Kevin's problem, McCarty thought, knowing that what happened from there on would be his.

Singer kept the receiver pressed to his ear as he watched his nervous chief of detectives walk into his office and shut the door. Sullivan grabbed one of the plastic chairs scattered throughout the office and waited for the chief to finish his phone call, and when Singer finally hung up, quietly began to fill him in on Carey's decision earlier that day.

Shaking his head in disbelief, Singer tried to comfort his subordinate by saying their murder suspect wasn't out of reach yet. He couldn't believe Carey had thrown out the indictment, and for a minute wondered whether the jurist had completely lost his mind.

"Listen, Sullivan, don't worry about this. The D.A.'s office will bring the case back before a new grand jury and, who knows, maybe they can correct the mistakes they made earlier and the case will be stronger than before. It doesn't make any sense to me why he would dismiss the indictment, but with some of the decisions he's made throughout this thing, nothing really surprises me anymore. I still believe when this thing is all said and done Carolyn Warmus will be convicted."

Noticing his words seemed to have little impact on his unhappy detective, Singer asked how Constantino was taking the news.

"He's mad, but I think he's okay. Like everybody else, he doesn't understand why the judge took such an extreme action, but he's still ready to go with the case whenever it's brought back up. I just hope that the D.A.'s office plans on trying to reindict her. I don't know why they wouldn't, but you never can tell what's going to happen with this thing."

Telling Sullivan to keep Constantino reassured, Singer waved him out of the office.

While the judge's ruling caused the police and district attorney to seethe, David Lewis couldn't have been happier. Reading Judge Carey's decision, he couldn't help but smile. A dismissal was more than he had hoped for, and he realized that Carey must have been even angrier about the police and prosecution screw-ups than he had thought. It didn't take a sharp criminal attorney to know that the Westchester County District Attorney's Office would quickly seek to reindict his client. But he had a few more surprises up his sleeve that just might make that job a lot tougher than they expected.

He would have to put in a couple more weeks of long, hard work to get it prepared, but he was in the driver's seat now and there was certainly the possibility that Carey would see his way clear to keeping a tighter lid on any new grand jury. If Lewis played his cards just right, Carey just might go along with his motions to force the prosecution to submit their evidence before the grand jury. If he could swing that, it was possible there would be no reindictment of Carolyn Warmus.

16

WITHIN HOURS of Carey's ruling the phone lines of the district attorney's secretary were swamped with calls from the media requesting an interview or, at the very least, a statement from the man in charge.

Vergari knew he couldn't dodge them forever, but before he issued any statement he wanted to meet with all his key players, to sound them out about plans for proceeding and how the case now stacked up. He badly wanted Carolyn Warmus to be tried for the crime he was sure she had committed.

When the meeting concluded, and his angry prosecutors had filed out of the office, Vergari began returning the reporters' phone calls to announce that his office would be seeking to reindict Carolyn Warmus on the second-degree murder charge and felony weapons possession as soon as possible, probably the first week in September.

When pushed by one reporter to share his feelings about the way Carey had summarily dismissed the indictment, he stated simply, "All I'll say is that I did not and do not agree with all of Judge Carey's decisions, but right now the most important thing to do is proceed with the murder case. My office will not appeal Judge Carey's dismissal ruling, as we feel that will delay justice in this matter. We will reindict and go on from there."

The next ten days found McCarty bringing FitzMorris up to speed on the Betty Jeanne Solomon murder case. A young, brash assistant D.A. who was considered a real go-getter, FitzMorris was very well versed in the nuts and bolts of criminal law, and had been selected by his bosses to work with McCarty to ensure there was no repeat of the Kennedy fiasco. While FitzMorris had sat through most of the pretrial hearings, he still needed McCarty's insight into the nuances of such a highly charged case, and his professionalism mandated that he completely familiarize himself with file 90-0061.

While McCarty soon grew to know the explosive personality of his new partner, even he was surprised when FitzMorris flew into his office on August 17, waving that morning's Gannett newspaper, the *Reporter Dispatch*. McCarty read with growing disbelief the paper's lead, copyrighted story.

INVESTIGATORS LINK WARMUS TO BULLETS

Telephone records and a stolen driver's license were used by Greenburgh detectives to link Carolyn Warmus to the bullets they believe killed Betty Jeanne Solomon, Gannett Westchester Newspapers has learned.

The new information was uncovered after Warmus, 26, was indicted Feb. 2 on a charge of second-degree murder in the killing. Mrs. Solomon's husband, Paul, 41, was Warmus' lover.

Warmus has denied any involvement in the killing.

Westchester County Judge John Carey on Aug. 6 dismissed the indictment, which also charged Warmus with felony weapons possession, citing several procedural mistakes by assistant district attorneys. Carey ruled Warmus could be reindicted.

The Westchester District Attorney's Office will try to reindict the former grade-school teacher on a second-degree murder charge early next month.

Records at the District Attorney's Office show that a box of .25-caliber bullets was purchased at Ray's Sport Shop in North Plainfield, N.J., on Jan. 15, 1989, hours before Mrs. Solomon, 40, was shot nine times in her Greenburgh home with a silencer-equipped .25-caliber Beretta.

According to Warmus' subpoenaed MCI telephone records, sent to Assistant District Attorney Kevin Kennedy on April 10, a call was made the day of the slaying from Warmus' Manhattan home to the sports shop.

Greenburgh Detective Richard Constantino investigated the call and learned that a woman used the driver's license of a Liisa Kattai, a former co-worker of Warmus', for identification to buy .25-caliber bullets on the day of the killing. Police records show that Kattai had reported her license stolen in August 1989.

New Jersey law requires businesses selling ammunition to maintain an "ammo book," where information from a customer's license, including name, address, date of birth and license number, must be recorded. Purchasers also must sign for the ammunition.

Detectives have determined that the person who purchased the bullets on Jan. 15, 1989, forged Kattai's name, according to reports in police files.

Constantino interviewed Kattai in April and discovered that she knew Warmus when they were both employed at the ROLM Co., in Manhattan in summer 1988. She told Constantino that Warmus—who worked for ROLM from July 14 to Aug. 26, 1988—would have had access to her purse when the license was stolen, according to a police report detailing the interview.

Diane Santabara of South Plainfield, N.J., the clerk at Ray's Sport Shop who sold the bullets on Jan. 15, 1989, told authorities that she did not know if she could identify the woman who bought them because the sale was more than a year earlier.

Warmus' attorney, David Lewis, on Tuesday confirmed that a call had been placed from his client's home to the sports shop on the afternoon of Mrs. Solomon's killing.

"We don't know why she made the call," Lewis said. "When we asked her, Carolyn said she didn't remember making it."

The call came shortly after Warmus telephoned Mr. Solomon at his home at 1:37 p.m. and the couple made plans to meet at 7:30 at the Treetops Restaurant in Yonkers, according to district attorney records.

Warmus and Mr. Solomon each told police they spoke on the telephone on the day of the killing.

Police and the District Attorney's Office have said that during that telephone conversation, Warmus learned that the Solomons' daughter, Kristan, was on a ski trip and that Mrs. Solomon would be home alone.

Lewis said he became aware of the sports shop's connection to the case only a few weeks ago, when he received a copy of Kennedy's "diary reminder," a notebook the assistant district attorney had on his office desk to keep track of appointments and things to do.

Lewis said Kennedy mistakenly scribbled notes about the sports shop in the diary on April 12, making the notation "Ray's firearm appraisal, requested invest."

"When Kennedy wrote that note to himself he obviously never expected me to see it," Lewis said. Lewis obtained a copy of the diary after Carey made it available during recent pretrial hearings in County Court in White Plains.

The District Attorney's Office had no comment when asked about Kennedy's notation.

Lewis said that when his own private investigators went to the sports shop to talk with Santabara and review company records, they were refused permission to review the ammo book.

"The owner of the shop told me he always cooperates with police in these types of matters and that we couldn't see his records," Lewis said.

The District Attorney's Office did not subpoena Warmus' MCI records until March 29, about 15 months after the slaying, because they were un-aware she used the long-distance company service, police records show.

The call to Ray's Sport Shop was not on her New York Telephone records initially reviewed by detectives and Kennedy, according to the subpoenaed documents.

Greenburgh police Lt. Cornelius Sullivan said yesterday that he could not comment about the new evidence. Assistant District Attorney James Mc-Carty also declined to comment about developments in the case.

McCarty tossed the newspaper to the side of his desk and wondered what Vergari, McKenna, and Neary would have to say about this new development. He knew they were already incensed at Gannett for put-ting their entire case on the front page for everyone, including Lewis, to see. With this, most of their secrets—or what they had thought to be secrets—were now in the public domain.

Two days before, on August 15, Lewis had filed a five-inch-thick set of motions with Judge Carey in an unveiled attempt to persuade him to more or less take over the re-presentation of the district attorney's evi-dence to the new, soon-to-be-impaneled grand jury.

Lewis also wanted Carey to suppress the defendant's MCI records, claiming that Kennedy had improperly obtained, read, and then acted on the information contained in them, knowing full well they should have been sent to the court first and not the D.A.'s office.

Lewis claimed that since Kennedy had violated the law by his han-dling of the MCI records, any evidence obtained as a result of his having read them should be considered fruit of the poisoned tree and there-fore should not be allowed into the case.

The judge would have to be very careful with this one and let both sides present to him any case law they could dig up to support their respective positions.

It didn't take any legal genius to see why Lewis was going all out to keep the MCI records out of the trial. If the Gannett story was accurate, the phone records tied his client to the gun shop that had apparently sold the bullets that were used to kill Betty Jeanne Solomon. It was circumstantial evidence to be sure, but damn strong evidence against her.

And it was quite possible that the police and D.A.'s office had learned of Warmus's connection to the gun shop without the help of the MCI records. If that were the case, Miss Warmus had a lot of explaining to do, or more correctly, her lawyer had his work cut out for him in trying to defend and explain her actions.

Carey's order, drafted in response to Lewis's motions, read as follows:

At noon on August 15, 1990, defendant filed with the court under seal two copies of papers entitled "Notice of Motion for Stay and Other Grand Jury Relief and Affidavit in Support Thereof."

Later that day, a conference call took place among David L. Lewis, attorney for the defendant, Richard E. Weill, Assistant District Attorney, and the court at which the issue of whether defendant's papers should remain under seal was discussed.

After due consideration, it is:

ORDERED, that defendant's papers shall remain under seal until the motion's return date, September 4, 1990, at which time the court will consider any further presentations on this issue as well as on the merits; and it is:

ORDERED, that any written response the District Attorney may make to defendant's motion on or before such return date shall to the same extent be under seal, and it is:

ORDERED, that the parties address on the return date the following issues, in writing and/or orally:

1. Whether this court or the Supreme Court Justice currently assigned to grand juries can impanel and initially instruct any grand jury to which evidence against this defendant is presented in the future;

2. Whether this court or that justice can decide what to instruct such grand jury as their options;

3. Whether this court or that justice can decide in advance what to instruct such grand jury as to circumstantial evidence;

4. Whether this court or that justice can monitor the prosecutor's presentation to such grand jury;

5. Whether any party other than such grand jury or the prosecutor can determine what evidence is put before such grand jury;

6. Whether a determination can be made by this court or that justice of the suppressibility before such grand jury of any evidence derived from materials obtained by subpoena from MCI which are alleged by David L. Lewis in paragraphs 25–47 of his affidavit of August 14, 1990, to have been obtained and used improperly by the District Attorney's Office;

7. Whether this court or that justice can determine whether to screen prospective grand jurors by a voir dire process to identify any that may have been excessively tainted by media coverage;

8. Whether this court or that justice can decide in advance whether any witness should receive a copy of his or her previous grand jury testimony;

9. Whether there is any basis for defendant's request that the prosecution be ordered to file an affidavit agreeing to conduct re-presentation consis-

Anyone who watched the extensive television news coverage will remember this image of a fresh-faced Carolyn seated at the defense table during her first trial, which resulted in a hung jury. (*New York Daily News* photo)

On the night of January 15, 1989, Betty Jeanne Solomon was
brutally murdered—shot nine times at close range—in the living
room of her suburban Westchester condominium.
(Gannett Suburban Newspapers)

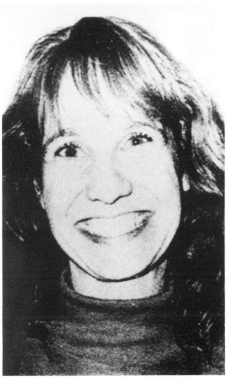

A smiling Carolyn
Warmus, shown here in a
1990 yearbook photo.
(AP/Wide World Photos)

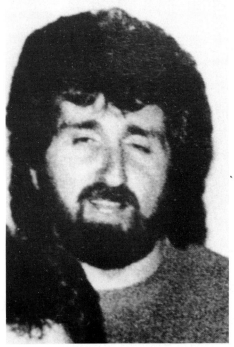

Paul Solomon, as he
looked in 1987, the year
he and Carolyn met.

Carolyn's father made millions in the insurance business and raised his children in this luxurious home in Franklin, Michigan. (*Detroit News* photo by Diane Weiss)

Greenburgh, New York, Police Detective Richard J. Constantino carried out much of the investigation that resulted in Carolyn's arrest. (Alan Zale/*New York Times*)

Prosecutors Douglas FitzMorris and James McCarty
(*right*) had the job of proving her guilt beyond a
reasonable doubt at the second, all-important trial.
(Joe Larese/Gannett Suburban Newspapers)

Defense attorney David Lewis was persuasive enough to
win his client a mistrial. (Alan Zale/*New York Times*)

William I. Aronwald (pictured here with private investigator Vic Ruggiero, *right*) was unable to convince the jury of her innocence a second time. (Seth Harrison/Gannett Suburban Newspapers)

Judge John Carey presided over both of the Warmus trials.
(AP/Wide World Photos)

Private investigator
Vincent Parco testified
that he had sold Carolyn a
.25-caliber Beretta
equipped with a silencer.
(Associated Press)

Paul Solomon, who found his wife's body, testified that he had lied
to her about his infidelities. (Wendy Vissar/Gannett Suburban
Newspapers)

Carolyn Warmus's stylish and revealing pink suit drew a lot of attention as she arrived at the Westchester County Courthouse, where she was being tried for murder.
(Gannett Suburban Newspapers)

By the end of the trial, however, she was hiding from the press behind voluminous coats and concealing scarves.
(AP/Wide World Photos)

tently with this court's decision and order of August 6, 1990, and any subsequent order, and it is:

ORDERED, that presentation to such grand jury of any and all evidence referred to in paragraphs 25–47 of the affidavit of David L. Lewis, sworn to August 14, 1990, is stayed pending decision on the issue referred to in subparagraph 6 hereinabove.

The judge's order would prevent the district attorney from rushing through an indictment, and would give Carey the opportunity to find out exactly what he or another justice could or could not do with a grand jury.

The September 4 hearing wasn't going at all as Lewis had planned. Carey had called the in-court session to discuss his motions and the first words out of the jurist's mouth told him he would have to be very persuasive that day.

"Mr. Lewis, I feel I have to tell you that after reviewing your motions and the relevant case law, I am very skeptical whether I have the authority to rule on your motions. I believe the judge whose turn it is this month to impanel grand juries is the proper person to decide these issues."

Lewis slowly rose from his chair and for the next twenty minutes stroked, cajoled, and pleaded with Carey to retain control of the various requests he had made. He knew his best shot at keeping Carolyn from having to go through a trial was to keep Carey involved in every possible decision. For whatever reason, Carey had bought almost 100 percent of every argument he had presented so far.

When he was done, Carey pondered for a moment the enormity and technical nature of the requests and wondered out loud whether it was fair for another judge to have to tackle so much complex decision making without benefit of knowing anything about the case.

Turning to McCarty, who was listening impassively to his tablemate, Diane Selker, one of the district attorney's key appellate lawyers, Carey asked a question that caused the young prosecutor once more to shake his head in disbelief.

"Mr. McCarty, do you have any objection if I was to write a letter to the administrative judge of this court, David Ritter, and let him decide whether I should be appointed as the one to rule on these motions instead of the impaneling judge for the grand jury that will be convened to hear evidence against Miss Warmus?"

Carey's abrupt turnaround didn't really surprise McCarty, it just frustrated him once more.

Lewis was good, very good. His adversary knew how to use just the right amount of boot-licking to persuade Carey to agree to his requests. It was obvious to McCarty that, for whatever reason, Carey desperately wanted to hold on to every decision-making aspect of this case, regardless of case law or traditional legal procedures.

McCarty finally rose to speak. "Your honor, the people have no objection to you writing a letter to Judge Ritter. We would, however, like to reserve our right to challenge any decision that is made."

Carey nodded and told the lawyers he would try to expedite the process by sending the letter that afternoon. He stood up and retreated to his chambers.

Warmus looked up at her smiling attorney and knew the session had gone well. Lewis had told her that he felt Carey was in their corner and they couldn't have gotten a better judge to preside over the case if they had hand-picked him themselves.

She stood up and grabbed her purse, gently tugging down the bottom of her snug, black knit skirt. She followed Lewis out of the courtroom, her two private detectives, DiSalvatore and Ruggiero, falling in behind.

Just hours later, quietly working at his cluttered desk, Lewis received perhaps the first real disappointing news since he had taken the Warmus case.

Judge Ritter had received Carey's letter and quickly ruled that that month's grand jury impaneling judge in Westchester County—State Supreme Court Justice Peter Rosato—should decide his motions, unless some "extremely thorny issue" arose.

Muttering to himself, Lewis knew he had just lost his best chance of getting the new grand jury to vote not to indict his client. He wasn't going to give up, but he knew his very successful batting average with Carey had been his greatest shot.

A couple of quick phone calls informed him that Rosato's reputation was that of a pro-prosecution, anti-defendant judge, a decided disadvantage for a defense lawyer trying to push through some innovative and novel legal arguments in an effort to save his client.

He went back to work believing Carolyn Warmus stood a very good chance of being reindicted, despite his best efforts.

□   □   □   □

The principal of Greenville School had called Paul Solomon to tell him not to report for the opening of school. He'd be paid, but the bottom line was that the school officials didn't want him back until the whole mess was over.

What with a new grand jury being convened, more pretrial hearings, and then a possibly lengthy trial, it could be several months before he would even see the inside of a classroom and begin getting his life back in order. To make matters worse, he had a new problem to report to the Greenburgh Police Department.

He had awakened the day before, a warm, sunny Monday morning, and found that some son of a bitch had broken into his 1988 Plymouth parked right outside his building. The car's right rear window had been smashed and the thief had stolen his $300 AM-FM cassette player and a pair of $180 glasses.

When he first saw his damaged car, he couldn't help but wonder if Carolyn had paid him an unannounced Sunday-night visit. He had looked around and saw that none of the other cars in the lot seemed to have suffered any similar damage, and he wondered whether his former paramour had gone off the deep end again or if he was just the only unlucky bastard to have gotten ripped off.

He struggled to control a shiver that ran through his body.

When word of Solomon's complaint got back to Constantino, he couldn't help asking the same questions. Although he had no proof, the skeptical detective decided that the word *coincidence* just didn't apply so long as Carolyn Warmus was walking around free.

On September 11, McCarty received Judge Peter Rosato's seven-page decision virtually shooting down each and every motion Lewis had filed.

The biggest victory for the prosecution was that the grand jury would be allowed to hear the evidence linking Warmus with the .25-caliber bullets purchased from the New Jersey gun shop on the day of Betty Jeanne Solomon's murder. Rosato had ruled that Lewis's motion to suppress his client's home telephone records was "premature" and that the grand jurors had the right to review the records so they could make up their own minds about Warmus's guilt or innocence.

Another victory for the good guys, Sullivan told an ecstatic Constantino when he received the news from McCarty, was that Rosato had refused Lewis's request that items of evidence he contended were favorable to the defense also be presented to the grand jury. The judge had ruled that the district attorney was not obligated to search for such evidence and that failure to produce that evidence would not materially influence the grand jury investigation. Lewis's attempt to get the judge to order the prosecutors to call certain defense witnesses to testify before the grand jurors had also been struck down by Rosato's ruling.

"We couldn't have gotten a better decision," McCarty told Sullivan, finally glad to have something positive to report.

But the news of Rosato's decision wasn't the only good news McCarty had to share. The judge had also sworn in the new grand jury that day, and McCarty was determined that there would be no repeat of Kennedy's earlier problems.

He and FitzMorris had pored over their case and reviewed every piece of evidence, testimony, and report that had been accumulated during the past year and eight months. No stone was left unturned in an effort to guarantee that they would obtain another murder indictment against Carolyn Warmus, and more importantly, one that would stick. With Carey still holding the reins, both men knew they would have to be especially conscientious and prepared.

McCarty was confident, despite the formidable threat that Lewis's legal talents presented. The new evidence they had uncovered linking Warmus to the gun shop and the bullets that killed Betty Jeanne Solomon was their new ace in the hole. Their case now wasn't built solely on the wobbly circumstantial testimony of Vincent Parco, who everybody knew was an easy target for Lewis to try to discredit.

17

SCREECHING TIRES echoed throughout the cavernous lower level of the parking garage as the late model, royal blue Lincoln Continental lurched to a stop in front of the doorway. Blue-jeaned cameramen jumped to their feet and grabbed their heavy equipment, flicking on their powerful overhead lights. Print journalists whipped out their notebooks while the television reporters grabbed their microphones and sprinted toward the car.

Carolyn pulled out a gold-colored compact, checking her makeup in the small mirror and running her fingers through her hair one last time. She tossed the compact back in her black leather purse and pulled out a pair of dark sunglasses. She slipped the glasses on and nervously waited for DiSalvatore to jump out of the front seat and open her door.

She had expected this media onslaught after a second grand jury had reindicted her only days before, on September 25. Now, as she arrived to be arraigned again on the murder charge, the bastards were surrounding her car.

When the door opened, Carolyn stepped from the car and stood waiting for Ruggiero to join his partner and form a human shield to protect her from the screaming media throng.

"Miss Warmus, any comment on the grand jury's reindicting you for the murder of Betty Jeanne Solomon?" said an NBC reporter, sticking his foot-long microphone under her nose.

The other television reporters reacted instantly, stabbing at her with their own equipment like a pack of hungry vultures. Their screamed questions blended into one indiscernible, deafening sound that echoed off the walls of the garage. It was their only chance, since cameras weren't allowed anywhere inside the courthouse.

Ruggiero ran around the car and grabbed her arm, pulling her toward the open doorway that would lead them to the escalator, and the four armed court officers standing by to escort her to the courtroom.

Once inside the small, tenth-floor courtroom, Warmus took her seat at the defense table and waited for Lewis. She occasionally beckoned Ruggiero over to her seat and whispered in his ear as the throng of print reporters noisily made their way into the room.

Pulling open the heavy door, Lewis was not surprised to find the few rows of gallery seats filled to capacity. The press credentials dangling around the spectators' necks convinced him his client's second arraignment would receive a hell of a lot more coverage than her first.

He hadn't failed to notice the pack of television cameras perched outside the courthouse and he made a mental note to tell Ruggiero and DiSalvatore they should begin making plans to sneak their client out of the building.

He tossed his black briefcase on the defense table and smiled at Warmus, who, apparently annoyed at being kept waiting, failed to return the greeting. Lewis ignored her icy stare. Before this case was finished, there would be other, more important matters for her to be upset about.

The court clerk strode into the room and bellowed the familiar "all rise" only seconds before Carey emerged from the doorway behind the bench. Warmus sat writing notes on a yellow legal pad as the judge proceeded to unseal and read aloud her second murder indictment. When he mentioned the name Betty Jeanne Solomon, Warmus looked up, and then around the courtroom, her squinting facial ticks noticeable even to the court officer sitting on a chair against the door in the back of the room.

Lewis sat reviewing the 'notes he had made at his kitchen table the night before, at the same time listening intently to Carey's recitation. The next several months would make or break his case, and his private investigators would be asked to comb the streets harder than they had up to this point to come up with some new evidence to discredit further the case of the assistant district attorney sitting across the aisle.

Lewis couldn't count on getting Carey to dismiss this second indictment, although he would certainly try. The key, however, would be to diminish the importance of all the evidence the prosecution had so far made public, most significantly Carolyn's MCI records, which to date presented the greatest threat to his defense. Every effort would have to be made to prevent those records from being admitted as evidence, and failing that, at least to come up with some plausible explanation for the jury as to why that New Jersey gun shop phone number was listed on Carolyn's MCI bills for the day of the murder.

When the hour hearing had finished, Lewis nodded at Ruggiero, who took the cue to escort Carolyn hurriedly from the courtroom. The lawyer watched as his client slipped out the door behind the judge's bench and began stuffing paperwork back into his briefcase.

He had been as successful as any lawyer could have been up to that point. But now, with this second indictment, the stakes were higher. McCarty's reputation as a fair but tough prosecutor would make him a foe with whom to be reckoned.

Lewis clicked his briefcase shut and rubbed his hand over his beard. He turned to face the crowd of reporters, who were waiting impatiently for him to provide a statement they could use for that night's newscast and the next day's paper. After he had answered several of the usual questions, a television reporter shouted from the back of the room, asking who had pulled the trigger of the gun that killed Betty Jeanne Solomon.

"Not Carolyn Warmus," he replied with conviction.

"What's your defense strategy if this goes to trial?" the reporter followed up.

Lewis smiled mischievously, the twinkle in his eye noticeable enough to prompt a spattering of laughter from the crowd. "You'll just have to wait until the trial to see what surprises we have."

18

HER TIGHT black-and-white checked outfit caught the eye of several appreciative male reporters as Warmus strolled to the defense table with her two private protectors on either side.

Gone were the long, flowing, ankle-length dresses and bulky wool sweaters that had been Warmus's wardrobe during the lengthy jury selection process. Now, on the first day of the actual trial, she was back in her form-fitting clothes, and the reporters were taking bets how long it would be before Lewis saw her and suffered his first stroke. While the dark sunglasses had disappeared, she now wore a pair of large, bookish spectacles, which more than one courtroom observer guessed were her one concession to her concerned lawyer.

She handed her coat to DiSalvatore, patted her hair, and sat down. As she waited, she began doodling on her yellow legal pad, writing the date, January 14, 1991, in small block letters at the top.

Lewis pushed open the courtroom door and ambled down the center aisle, taking in the throng of reporters and spectators, pretending not to notice the buzz that his entrance had sparked.

He exchanged good mornings with his client and seated himself at the defense table, where he was busily pulling reams of papers from his overstuffed briefcase when McCarty and FitzMorris walked in.

All three men stood as the judge entered the courtroom, his long, black robe rustling as he mounted the steps to his bench.

"Good morning, gentlemen, Miss Warmus," Carey said, as he slipped into his chair. "Are we ready to begin?"

Noting the nodding heads of the two legal adversaries before him, Carey turned to one of his court officers and ordered the jury into the room. Several minutes later, the eight-woman, four-man group, along with four female alternates, found their seats and waited expectantly for the judge to continue.

Explaining to the jurors that they would now have to be sworn in, he asked them to rise. The court clerk, Dennis Murphy, also rose and recited the oath. When the jury was once more seated, Carey looked out over the group that had been chosen during the process of prescreening and voir dire that had begun December 10, 1990. It had taken more than four weeks and hundreds of 25-page questionnaires, but he was confident a fair and impartial jury was now seated before him.

When the courtroom grew quiet, Carey instructed the jury on their responsibilities and how the law must be applied. He explained that the prosecution, which had the burden of proving its case against the defendant, would present its case first.

"At no time is the defendant required to testify or even put on a defense if she chooses not to," the judge explained. "The burden of proving guilt always rests with the prosecution."

When Carey had finished his lecture, he told McCarty to proceed with his opening statement.

The confident, but somewhat nervous prosecutor had been practicing his remarks for a week. Although his opening statement wouldn't be long by murder-trial standards, he wanted it powerful and complete. Taking a file of papers to the lectern, McCarty maneuvered the wooden box so he could face the twelve jurors and four alternates in whose hands his case now rested. He spoke slowly and deliberately, starting with the thought that was on everyone's mind.

President Bush had set the next day—January 15, 1991—as the deadline for Iraq to end its almost five-month occupation of Kuwait. The United States was on the brink of war, and McCarty chose not to ignore it.

"As we all know, tomorrow marks a very significant day in this country's history, perhaps in this country in the future and the future of the world.

"But it also marks the second anniversary of the death of Betty Jeanne Solomon, ladies and gentlemen. For it was on January 15, 1989, that Paul Solomon came home to his apartment at around 11:40 P.M. and found his wife dead on the living-room floor of their home.

"It was a home that they had saved to purchase. It was a home that she had lived in for two years prior to that point. It was a home that she had lived in together with their daughter Kristan, who was fifteen at the time.

"The evidence will show, ladies and gentlemen, that the person who shot Betty Jeanne Solomon nine times on January 15, 1989, was neither a burglar nor a thief. There was no sign of forced entry. There was no sign of any property having been taken. The evidence instead will point to the conclusion that the person who went there on that day, went there with the specific intent to kill Betty Jeanne Solomon. And the wounds that Mrs. Solomon sustained during the course of that attack clearly demonstrate that point.

"As I indicated to you, the evidence will show that she was shot a total of nine times from a .25-caliber Beretta automatic. She sustained gunshot wounds to her shoulder, her arm, two gunshot wounds to her left leg, a grazed gunshot wound to the back of the left portion of her head as well as blunt trauma to her head in that area and around her ear and, finally, four shots delivered to her back which, the evidence will show, she sustained while lying face down on her living-room floor.

"The person, ladies and gentlemen, who did this, who committed this crime on January 15, 1989, had the motive on January 15 to kill Betty Jeanne Solomon and had the opportunity on that day to kill Betty Jeanne Solomon."

Pausing for effect, McCarty walked over toward the defense table and pointed at Warmus, who sat with her back to him, ignoring his speech.

"That person, ladies and gentlemen, we will prove to you is seated in this courtroom right over here. That person, the evidence will reveal, is the defendant, Carolyn Warmus."

Shooting a look to her right, Warmus caught her attorney's eye, and he gently raised his left hand ever so slightly, gesturing her to be calm.

The jurors sat quietly in their swivel chairs, often glancing past McCarty to see the defendant. If they were puzzled by how this attractive, doe-eyed young lady could ever be a cold-blooded murderess, they would have to withhold judgment until all the evidence had been presented.

"In the next few weeks, Mr. FitzMorris and myself will be bringing to you in this courtroom witnesses who will testify and introduce items of evidence that will prove beyond a reasonable doubt that Carolyn Warmus is responsible for the death of Betty Jeanne Solomon.

"Now recognize that no one witness and no single piece of evidence will prove that conclusively. Like pieces of a puzzle, when each and every one of the witnesses' testimony is put together, when each and every piece of evidence is compiled in this courtroom, that is when they will reveal a clear picture of the killer of Mrs. Betty Jeanne Solomon—the defendant Carolyn Warmus.

"We will show to you that the defendant had the motive, the means, and the opportunity to kill Betty Jeanne Solomon on January 15, 1989. We will demonstrate through the testimony that that motive derived from a year-and-a-half-long affair that she was carrying on with Mrs. Solomon's husband, Paul Solomon. From that affair the evidence will show that the defendant developed a consuming desire to possess Paul Solomon to herself."

His voice rising, McCarty slowly emphasized each of his next words to ensure the jury did not miss the point. "And Betty Jeanne Solomon got squarely in the way of this defendant's desires to have that man to herself!

"We will demonstrate to you during the course of this trial that the defendant had the means to carry out this crime. You will hear testimony from an individual by the name of Vincent Parco, and he will tell you that a week prior to this homicide he, a friend of hers, an associate of hers, gave her—in return for $2,500—a .25-caliber Beretta automatic equipped with a silencer.

"You will also hear that on the day of the crime, the circumstantial evidence will point to the conclusion that this defendant purchased ammunition of the kind and type used to kill Betty Jeanne Solomon. That on the day of the crime she purchased .25-caliber Winchester automatic ammunition from a gun shop in Plainfield, New Jersey, after it was revealed to her during the afternoon hours of January 15 that she would have a window of opportunity to commit this crime. You will hear testimony that on January 15, she learned from the victim's husband that later on in the evening Betty Jeanne Solomon would be home alone and that this would give her the opportunity to get rid of the obstacle that stood in the way of her and Paul Solomon."

For the next twenty minutes, McCarty outlined his case, describing in detail the witnesses he planned to call and the stories each of them would tell. He talked again of the "window of opportunity" that opened for Warmus after she telephoned Paul Solomon on the afternoon of the murder and learned through that conversation that Kristan was on a ski trip and Betty Jeanne would be home alone once Paul left to meet her at the Treetops Restaurant.

He took the jury through the trials and tribulations of the Solomons' marriage, their arguments over money. "But despite the couple's troubles," McCarty persuasively told them, "Paul and Betty Jeanne's marriage was far from over.

"You will find, ladies and gentlemen, that while their marriage appeared to be good on the outside, it certainly, like many marriages, had its ups and downs through the years. Paul Solomon will come into this courtroom and tell you about those various ups and downs that they had. Paul Solomon will tell you that some of the expectations that they had when they were married in the early 1970s were never quite realized.

"Of course you will hear testimony about an affair that Paul Solomon had with this defendant, but you will also hear that Mrs. Solomon had an affair as well. These are some of the problems they had during the course of their marriage, but you will also hear—and I ask you to accept —that through the thick and thin, through the ups and downs, they still stuck together; that in 1989 no matter what had passed before, they were not ready to call it quits on each other.

"In fact, you will hear testimony that on January 15, 1989, they were looking at retirement materials, looking at brochures of retirement communities and continuing to plan their lives together."

McCarty stopped for a moment, giving the jurors a chance to think about his words. He realized that many of his key witnesses, including Solomon, were starting out of the blocks as immoral, deceitful individuals—a notion that Lewis no doubt would play up to the hilt—so he had to try to make them appear to be regular people with regular problems, and to persuade the jurors to find even a little compassion in their hearts for them.

The jurors sat silently, their eyes glued to the slow-talking prosecutor, who then began to discuss some of the specifics of the defendant's affair with the victim's husband.

"You will hear that by mid- to late fall in 1987, a romantic interest was developing for the defendant and Paul Solomon. You will hear that this relationship began to take on a physical proportion late in the fall of 1987, and you will hear testimony that soon thereafter they began to make arrangements to meet each other, to spend time with each other in addition to the time they were already spending in school.

"Mr. Solomon will come into this court, ladies and gentlemen, and admit to you that while he was married in the fall of 1987 and through the winter of 1988 he would make plans to meet this defendant at her apartment in New York City, to meet this defendant at a bowling alley where he bowled on Sunday nights, and at times to meet this defendant at restaurants in the Westchester area while, needless to say, not in the company of his wife. They were carrying on an affair, plain and simple.

"And you will hear from Paul Solomon that during the spring of 1988 he was having trouble with this affair, that he was, to some extent, guilt-ridden by what he was doing and he was not comfortable. As a result, he will tell you that as the school year was about to end in 1988, he took steps to at least end the physical portion of this affair. It was apparent to each of them that Miss Warmus would not be coming back to the Greenville School District and Mr. Solomon saw this as an opportunity to break off the relationship.

"You will hear that during the summer of 1988 it was indeed broken off for all intents and purposes. But while they did not see each other during that time period, we will introduce evidence to you to show you that the passions that had arisen in Miss Warmus had not subsided. That although she did not see Paul Solomon, she still yearned for his company and still wanted his attention."

Describing once again the obsessiveness of Warmus for Paul Solomon, McCarty told the jurors that several friends of hers would testify that she had told them she loved Paul and would do anything to make him hers forever.

"You will also hear testimony from an individual who was a friend of this defendant from her days at the University of Michigan. You will hear from this person that he, too, spoke with her in the summer of 1988 and that she expressed to him her thoughts and feelings about Paul Solomon.

"She told him, as well, that she was in love with Paul Solomon and she went further to say that Paul Solomon was the perfect person for her. He already had a ready-made family, his daughter and him, and with her money they could make the perfect family down the road. The only obstacle to overcome was the wife.

"And you will hear this witness testify that Miss Warmus said to him that she would do anything to get Betty Jeanne Solomon out of the picture so that she could take her place in the Solomon household."

Pausing to let that statement sink in, McCarty walked slowly in front of the jurors, careful to make eye contact with each and every one. He then began to summarize how Warmus had tried to insert herself into Paul and Kristan Solomon's life as a way of preparing for the future she had planned for all of them.

Satisfied that the jury was following his story, the prosecutor began recounting the events that led Warmus to the murder scene on January 15, 1989. For the next fifteen minutes, he walked the jurors through Warmus's relationship with Parco and her purchase of the silencer-equipped handgun a week before the slaying. He detailed the date Paul Solomon and Warmus shared the night of the murder, careful to describe the dinner, the oral sex in Warmus's car in the parking lot of the Yonkers Holiday Inn.

Assured of the jurors rapt attention, McCarty then described in graphic detail the horrible scene that had played itself out in the Solomons' home that fateful winter's night.

In conclusion, he promised the jury that by the end of the trial he would prove to them that Warmus had callously pulled the trigger of the gun that had ended Betty Jeanne Solomon's life. "This is what the evidence will show, ladies and gentlemen. This is what the evidence will demonstrate. I have attempted to outline for you some of the evidence that we intend to introduce during the course of this trial. Needless to say, it is not my role at this point in time to discuss with you each and every witness that we will call to the stand and each and every item of evidence that we will introduce during the course of this trial.

"Our witnesses will come from all walks of life, from teachers to police officers to regular people to forensic scientists. Some of them will demonstrate to you that they have had experience testifying on this witness stand and for others, perhaps, it will be the first time. When they testify here it will be the first time that they ever walked into a courtroom."

Walking to the center of the jury box, McCarty placed his hands on the rail and slowly looked at the men and women who for the next several weeks would be his and Lewis's captive audience.

"What I ask of you, ladies and gentlemen, is to listen to all the testimony, consider all the evidence, and be realistic in your assessment of it. Use your common sense to evaluate it, piece it together to find the truth. Use your common sense to follow the credible evidence to the truth, and if you do that I'm confident that you will find that the truth fits that on January 15, 1989, Carolyn Warmus killed Betty Jeanne Solomon, and we will demonstrate that to you during the course of this trial. Thank you."

With that, McCarty turned and walked back to the lectern and gathered up his paperwork. When he returned to his seat, FitzMorris flashed a brief smile, telling him he'd done well in covering all the essential points that needed to be brought out.

McCarty was satisfied he had provided the jury not only the parameters of the case he intended to prove, but a side of Carolyn Warmus that none of them could possibly see as they now looked at her across the room. The judge may have tied his hands with a decision made shortly before the trial began—that the prosecution would not be allowed to tell the jury about Warmus's pattern of obsessive behavior with other married men from Michigan and her similar destructive relationship with the New Jersey bartender—but he was determined to make the most of what he could present.

"The table's set, now let's see what Lewis has to offer," he whispered in his colleague's ear.

David Lewis rose slowly from his chair and carried his own file folder to the now-vacated podium. He took his time removing several sheets of paper, giving the jury some time to push aside their thoughts about McCarty's speech and start to focus on him. After several long seconds, he walked away from his notes and stood directly in front of the jury box.

"This is a trial about murder. Not passion. Not love. Not feelings. This is about whether or not Carolyn Warmus—whether or not they can prove Carolyn Warmus—shot and killed Betty Jeanne Solomon on January 15, 1989.

"This is not a trial about whether she loved Paul Solomon or how much or whether it was right or wrong or appropriate. Love, passion are not on trial in this courtroom."

Lewis began strolling before the jurors, his voice confident and strong. "Now, this was and still is a horrible, terrible, cold-blooded, vicious crime and their proof to name Carolyn the murderer should be as strong as the viciousness of the crime. But you'll see it's not anywhere near close."

The burly lawyer carefully began to unfold his defense, watching the jurors' faces for the slightest look of uncertainty or disbelief.

Describing his client as a love-struck, but naïve young woman of the eighties, Lewis railed against the evil forces that had come together to frame her for the murder of her lover's wife.

"The evidence will show you that there are people, I don't mean Mr. FitzMorris or Mr. McCarty, but there are people out there feeding information, feeding data, feeding stuff along the way to ensure that Carolyn Warmus is framed for this murder."

Stopping to look at his client and then each of the jurors, Lewis let the next several seconds tick by without a word, hoping the next thing he said would remain with them throughout the long days ahead. With a deep, eloquent voice, he continued:

"Not only are there people who are doing it, but we will put in your hand a piece of evidence that you can look at and hold and talk to each other about and know from that piece of evidence that she has been framed. And it's deliberate and it's malicious and it's with tremendous forethought. And the people who did it, the people who are engaged in it, some of them you will see here before you, will take the witness stand and try and sell you the story. That is the frame and they are doing it to conceal a greater story, a greater level of criminal acts. And they are doing it for their own purposes. The malevolence of these witnesses will be shown to you."

Walking over behind Warmus's chair, Lewis's voice softened as he turned his head back toward the jury.

"How does Carolyn come to be here before you? She's not used to being in a courtroom. You learned she's used to attention, but it's attention of a schoolteacher and it comes from standing in front of a classroom teaching students. She's not used to sitting in a courtroom as a defendant. That's not who she is or what her life is."

Slowly strolling back to the jury box, on his face the expression of a man deep in thought, Lewis continued.

"You will also know, the evidence will teach you, that she's a human being. There are people that will tell you that she laughs, that she cries, that she lives and breathes."

With a scowl and booming voice, the attorney then bellowed, "The evidence will show you that she does not kill. In part, this case is an attack on her lifestyle. Why is that? This is the way that she lived. She had this relationship with Paul Solomon, imperfections of character, but it is not the stuff of which murder is made.

"We must be careful not to be swayed by our moral judgments about the sexual activity of a young girl in this day and age. We also have to be sure that we're not swayed because she loves a man and goes to find him.

"Now, let's talk about the affair with Paul Solomon," he went on. "The evidence will show you that she had this affair, she's never denied it. This fact, when the police came to talk to her the very first night after the murder and asked her, she tells them. Not like Paul Solomon. When the first patrolman asked him questions he, in this terrible state that he was in, lies about where he was. His first response.

"Carolyn was in love with Paul Solomon, a married man. Carolyn also at times, you'll learn, hoped that he would marry her. It's not such an odd dream for a young girl. Nor is it so odd that she would dream that and dream that this man who meant something to her, who loved her too, that he would marry her. That was her dream. And you are innocent when you dream, even about something like that."

A look of disappointment flashed across the jurors' faces with Lewis's next words. "She's not going to testify," he said, pointing at the defense table. "She doesn't have to. She has said everything she has to say to you by saying, standing up before the court and saying Not Guilty. When she does that she says to you, 'I did not do it. I did not murder Betty Jeanne Solomon,' says Carolyn. 'I did not possess a weapon.' You'll learn also she's going to talk to you in a different way because she gave statements to the police telling where she was that night and what she did. She's going to admit in that statement that she had this affair. But the question is why is she here, and she's here in part before you to clear her name, because that's part of this process too."

Shifting gears, Lewis began to focus his attack on Paul Solomon, his words dripping with disgust every time he spoke the name.

"You're going to learn on the night of the murder about six o'clock, Paul Solomon goes out to the parking lot where his car is, gets a charge for the battery, runs the charge from the battery up to the second floor where he lives, and from his sliding door porch runs the charge into the house and disables his car. He then takes her car, his wife's car, out to meet Carolyn. Paul Solomon ensures by doing that that Betty Jeanne Solomon cannot leave her home.

"You also will learn from the evidence that while he leaves the car charging, inside the car is a key, a key to his house, a key left in the car in plain sight where the police find it later that night. Now, we talked in the jury selection about shoddy police work, and Mr. McCarty admits some of it. But here's something you may not know. That key is picked up by the police from the car. They take it, they look at it, and instead of preserving it to see if anybody touched it, if there are any prints on it like if the killer used it to gain entry, they take the key up to the door and they put it in the door and they try it and it works, obscuring all evidence, obscuring fingerprints or whether fingerprints were wiped off."

Lewis then switched his verbal attack from the police and back to Solomon:

"Let's go back to Paul Solomon. I told you he lied to the patrolman about where he was. He didn't tell them he was out with Carolyn

Warmus, he told them he was bowling. You have to ask yourself why. If he needs a cover for that affair, needs to tell his wife he's going bowling, why does he show up to the bowling alley where he hasn't been for months and stand around? He told the cops the reason he did it was maybe they were shorthanded, maybe they needed help bowling. It's a story that doesn't make sense unless you want to establish an alibi."

If Lewis were to be successful in turning the jury's attention away from Warmus as the killer, he would have to create another monster for them to hate. Perhaps his next words would contribute to that creation.

"You will also learn that until summer and fall of 1988, Paul Solomon had in his home the guns he took from the service, guns that were not registered and not licensed that he kept there for twenty years. And in the summer of 1988 he suddenly decides that he should take all those weapons and give them to his brother. When he does that he disarms the house, so if there is any chance of even somebody trying to defend themselves there are no weapons in the house."

Pausing to let his self-described "time bombs" sink in with the jury, Lewis—aware that courtroom theatrics are part of any good presentation—put a look of incredulous disbelief on his face, saying: "Now, maybe it's all a coincidence, maybe every single one is a coincidence. Then you have to ask yourselves, when it comes time for him to testify in this case in the grand jury, why is it he demands from the prosecution and gets a deal that gives him total immunity from any prosecution, from anything including the murder? What does he need it for? But he demands it so he could never be prosecuted for the murder no matter what happens!"

Continuing his stroll before the jury box, Lewis gathered his thoughts. "Well, what else do we know?" he asked the jurors, as if they were now all members of the same team together trying to work out the clues from some mystery novel. "You're going to hear about his conduct at the murder scene, about what he did and didn't do. You're also going to hear that he has never moved out of the house, he never left the scene of that murder."

Perhaps at least some of the jurors would consider reprehensible a father who would force his precious daughter to remain in the very home where her mother had been so brutally killed, forcing her to walk daily over the very spot where her mother had taken her last breath.

"You have to ask yourself about his activity, what he did," the bearded lawyer continued. "Mr. McCarty tells you he has character flaws, that he can't resist Carolyn. There is also something else.

"This is a man who lied to his wife, supposedly the person with whom he's still so involved with regularly. Lied to her, to her face, and he lied for his own purposes so he could be out with Carolyn and maybe others before Carolyn. That's Paul Solomon."

Lewis began to talk about the problems the Solomons had had over money, separate vacations, and their fragile marriage.

"You're going to have to make some important decisions about Paul Solomon, about his credibility and about whether or not he played a role in this murder. I'm not telling you what the answer is. But there are things to watch for," he counseled.

His voice dripping with venom now, Lewis switched to another person he hoped to persuade the jury might have had a hand in Betty Jeanne Solomon's death.

"Let's turn to another actor in this play, Vinnie Parco. He's going to tell you a story about Carolyn Warmus and he's going to tell you a story about getting Carolyn a gun and giving Carolyn a gun and it's a marvelous, lovely tale, and there isn't a single soul in the world that backs him up and the story he tells about how the gun gets to Carolyn."

Rhetorically asking why Parco would point the finger of guilt at Warmus, he then answers, "Because the police came to him and said, 'Look, Vinnie. It's either you or Warmus,' and suddenly he began to change his story. If you don't believe Vinnie Parco, she never got that murder weapon. And the question is, can you believe Vinnie Parco?"

Pointing to his scribbling client, Lewis's voice once again began to rise, and his face took on a pained expression of disbelief.

"Now why do we know that Parco is laying it over on Carolyn instead of taking the heat or telling the truth? He's going to come in and tell you that for $2,500 from her he risked one of the most successful and wealthy private investigation companies in the state of New York just to get her a gun and a silencer. Just for her for $2,500. Is it believable? Or is it more likely that he's concealing something bigger? You'll learn that during the course of this case that Parco is using Carolyn as a shield.

"Now we told you that this was a frame. We told you it was a deliberate lie, malicious and with forethought. Who is the framer that makes the frame? The evidence will show you that it's Parco and Associates. You'll learn that they have some expertise. For example, they have some real good expertise in falsifying evidence, that Vincent Parco is the master in setting people up to take a fall for acts that he committed, that he won't own up to.

"You see, the problem with Vincent Parco, ladies and gentlemen, is that you have to make a decision, and part of that decision is how are you going to know when he's telling you the truth. He's such a good actor! You'll learn also that he's capable of saying anything. The problem is we may never know if he's telling the truth. He lied to the police four times, a number of them under oath, and they believed him each time, at least they went away. You'll see Parco come in here under oath and he will lie, he will tell you a tale."

Trying to downplay Warmus's escapades in Puerto Rico, Lewis again described the relationship she'd had with Solomon. He then summed up the Caribbean scenario for the jurors.

"The whole Puerto Rico evidence comes down to something very important for your purposes," Lewis said, again strolling before the jury as if he were a college professor lecturing to a class of interested, yet naïve students. "Carolyn never threatened anybody, never did anything harmful to anybody, never did anything except go down to Puerto Rico because she wanted to be with him. How does that prove that she killed Betty Jeanne Solomon, that she was going to do to Barbara Ballor what she did to Betty Jeanne Solomon when nothing happened except she was there? And you'll learn that being there, if you don't know, is not a crime. She goes to Puerto Rico and doesn't threaten a soul."

Once more pointing at Warmus, Lewis said, "Decide for yourself if she is an hysterical woman."

For the next several minutes, Lewis entranced the jury with his own version of the prosecution's witnesses and the stories they were soon to tell. Branding most of them liars fearful of retribution for their own crimes, he dismissed each one with a wave of his hand. Concluding his opening remarks with eloquent demands for justice, Lewis paused to lock eyes with each juror.

Quietly asserting that the prosecution would be unable to prove their case beyond the legally required reasonable doubt, he began to scoop up his notes, saying: "What is the issue here? Is Carolyn Warmus guilty beyond a reasonable doubt? Was she there at the Solomon apartment on that night, and did she fire nine bullets into Betty Jeanne Solomon?

"The evidence will show that they cannot prove that, and they cannot prove it because she did not do it. The evidence will show you that someone else killed Betty Jeanne Solomon, and the evidence will show you that there is a doubt, a reasonable doubt, a reason to vote not guilty in this case.

"Well, when I'm done we're going to start taking testimony, the pageant of evidence begins. Watch the testimony. Watch the direct first, then the cross. Watch all of it, because truth lies in there somewhere and we rely on you to find it. We're going to work together, all of us, from our different sides of the room, to find out if the facts are what the district attorney claims them to be.

"In the end, when all the evidence is in and when it has been tested in the crucible of this courtroom before you, I will return to you and ask you for a verdict, a verdict based on the evidence and, in part, on the lack of evidence. I will return to you and ask you for a verdict of not guilty and I will tell you then, as I tell you now, that we believe justice demands it and the law requires it."

Thanking the jurors, Lewis returned to his seat and whispered in Warmus's ear. He then looked over as McCarty rose from his seat and said, "The People of the State of New York call Marshall Tilden to the stand."

The tall, attractive, gray-haired man looked at his wife quickly when the court officer yelled his name outside the courtroom door. He strode to the witness box and swore to tell the truth before sitting down in the leather-bound chair.

Asked by the court clerk to state his full name, address, and occupation for the record, Tilden responded, "Marshall Tilden, Jr. I live with my wife, Josette, and two sons, Craig and Marshall, in Scarsdale. I work at Met Life in Manhattan."

"Mr. Tilden, how do you know Paul Solomon?" McCarty began.

"I met Paul through the Edgemont Recreation Program in 1981. He was the director of the sports program, you know, he handled the scheduling, setting up the draft situations for the boys' baseball teams, things like that. Paul was also one of my sons' teachers and his daughter Kristan was on the baseball team that I coached. My wife and I also socialized with Paul and Betty Jeanne. We'd often get together with some mutual friends of ours, Gary and Diane Pillersdorf. In fact, New Year's Day before the murder, we all had gotten together at the Pillersdorfs' to watch the Syracuse-LSU football game. I'm a big Syracuse fan."

Bringing Tilden's attention to the night of January 14, 1989, McCarty asked him to recall what he had done that evening.

"My wife and I went to a bar mitzvah for the son of some friends of ours, the Orloffs. All the couples who we are close with were there, including Paul and Betty Jeanne."

McCarty held up his hand, prompting Tilden to pause. "Tell us, please, what you remember of Paul and Betty Jeanne Solomon that night, will you?"

Tilden sat back in his chair and glanced up at the ceiling, as if trying to picture the gay, festive night. "It was really nice," he finally answered. "Paul and Betty Jeanne were behaving as they always did when we'd see them. That night they were dancing, holding hands, and laughing with each other. That's the way I always remember them being."

"Now then, Mr. Tilden, if I can bring your attention to the next day, January 15, 1989. Did you have occasion to speak with anyone besides your family that day?"

Leaning forward once again, Tilden appeared uncomfortable as the memory of the day his good friend was murdered darkened his thoughts. He cleared his throat before continuing.

"Paul called me up that Sunday at about 6, 6:15 P.M. We were discussing going to the Knicks basketball game the next day and that he was going to drive his car and we were all going down together. That was about it. Just some talk about the Knicks game. I don't recall anything else."

Crossing his arms as he walked toward the witness stand, McCarty took on a solemn tone as he asked, "Mr. Tilden, when did you first learn that Betty Jeanne Solomon had been murdered?"

"I learned the next day, on Monday morning about 5 or 6 A.M., that Betty Jeanne was dead," he said, staring directly at the prosecutor, his hands folded in his lap.

"What has your relationship with Paul Solomon and Kristan been since that time?" McCarty asked.

"Since the death, our relationship with Paul and Kristan has become so much stronger. We wanted to be there for them. I think the tragedy has brought all of our friends closer," Tilden added, a hint of sadness creeping into his voice.

"Do you know a woman named Barbara Ballor?" McCarty asked.

"Yes. I met Barbara sometime in the summer of 1989. Paul had told us he had begun dating her, and we invited them over to the house. We were happy he was beginning to see someone after all he'd been through."

McCarty walked back over to his chair and sat down. "No more questions, your honor."

Lewis took his cue to begin cross-examination. "Hello, Mr. Tilden. I'm David Lewis. I only have a couple of questions for you. To begin with, did Paul ever tell you he was having an affair when his wife was still alive?"

Tilden winced at the direct question, but answered, "No. I had no idea."

"Also, you said it was in summer 1989 that you were first introduced to Barbara Ballor by Paul Solomon. Can you be more specific as to when that occurred?"

Tilden once again looked upward, trying to recall the exact date. "I believe it was in May or June 1989 when I first met her. That's the best I can recall."

Thanking the witness, Lewis sat down. Warmus leaned over once again to whisper in his ear.

"The state next calls Josette Tilden to the stand," McCarty said, glancing back as the slim, well-dressed woman made her way to the front of the courtroom.

The jurors watched silently as the witness took her oath and then sat down, smoothing out her dress and pulling herself closer to the microphone.

"I'm a sixth-grade teacher in Yonkers, School 18, and will have taught there sixteen years this February. I live in Scarsdale and I'm married to Marshall Tilden and have two sons. I've been married twenty-two years," Tilden said, responding to McCarty's questions.

"Mrs. Tilden, can you describe your relationship with Paul Solomon?"

"I met Paul eleven years ago. My oldest son, Marshall, and Kristan Solomon were in school together. Initially I would see Paul at PTA meetings, sports events, things like that. In the spring of 1987, when the Solomons moved to Edgemont, we began to see them more frequently. I was a member of the Edgemont Recreation Committee which Paul was involved with."

McCarty let the well-spoken teacher continue describing her relationship with Paul Solomon, and then interrupted. "Mrs. Tilden, let me bring you to the night of January 14, 1989. Do you recall what you were doing that evening?"

Hesitating only a moment, Tilden leaned into the microphone. "We were at the Orloffs' bar mitzvah. Most of the people that we were friends with were there: the Pillersdorfs, the Solomons, and the Feinsteins."

"Do you recall what the Solomons were doing that night? Were they upset with each other, or enjoying themselves?"

"Paul and Betty Jeanne were very happy," she replied. "They were holding hands and dancing, the way they always were when we were out together."

Turning to look at the jury, McCarty folded his left arm across his chest and rubbed his chin with his right hand, a habit he had picked up long ago. "Now, Mrs. Tilden, please think about the next day, Sunday, January 15. Did you speak to Betty Jeanne Solomon that day?"

For the first time during her testimony, Tilden looked uncomfortable, but she continued on in a steady voice.

"Yes, I did. I made a phone call to Betty and we discussed Andrew Pillersdorf taking my son's place at the basketball game that our husbands were going to attend on Monday. My son was ill, so I didn't think he could go. We also talked about the wonderful time we had at the bar mitzvah. During that call I told her that I would check with Gary and Diane to see if Andrew could take my son's place and that I would call her back when I found out."

"Did you speak to her again?" McCarty asked.

"Yes. I called Betty to confirm that Andrew Pillersdorf could use the ticket. That was the last I spoke to her. It was a short phone call."

"Do you recall the specific time you made those two calls to Betty Jeanne Solomon?"

Taking a moment to answer, Tilden looked at McCarty apologetically. "To the best of my knowledge the first call might have been sometime around 7 P.M. and the second one might have been about 7:30 P.M."

"Is it fair to say you don't really know exactly when you called Betty Jeanne Solomon that night?" McCarty asked.

"Yes, that's fair. I'm fairly certain about the first one, but I don't really remember when I placed the second call. I think it was around 7:30 P.M., but I don't really recall."

Once again returning to the prosecution table, McCarty looked at the judge. "No more questions, your honor."

Lewis smiled at the witness as he opened his notebook. "Mrs. Tilden, would you say you were closer to Paul Solomon or his wife?"

"We were friendly with Betty, but initially we were closer to Paul. We socialized in their home many times."

Lewis didn't hesitate to try and find out what Tilden knew of the various relationships the Solomons had been involved in.

"Were you aware that Paul Solomon was having an affair during the time you were socializing with them?"

Tilden shook her head. "No, I wasn't."

"Did you know that Betty Jeanne Solomon was having an affair?"

Again shaking her head, the witness responded, "No. Not at all."

Lewis left her answers hanging in the air for a brief moment and then pursued Tilden's telephone conversation with the victim.

"Did Betty Jeanne mention whether there was anyone there with her when you called either time? Whether Paul was with her?"

"During the conversation, Betty told me that Paul was out. I remember that. And I knew that Paul bowled on Sunday nights."

"Did she tell you that he was out during the first or second conversation? Do you remember?" Lewis probed.

"No, I don't."

When Lewis walked away from the lectern, Carey looked up and nodded toward Tilden. "Thank you for your time. You may step down."

Looking at the clock at the far end of the courtroom and then down at the lawyers seated before him, Carey put down his pen. "Gentlemen, I think we'll call it a day," he said.

Turning toward the jurors, he warned them not to speak with anyone about the case and to refrain from reading any newspapers or watching any television news broadcasts about the trial. "Have a good evening and we'll see you back here tomorrow morning," he told them.

McCarty and FitzMorris began gathering up their files and loading them on a metal pushcart. Across the aisle, Lewis huddled with Warmus and his two private investigators.

Their bags packed, the lawyers then walked single file out of the courtroom and into the midst of the waiting newsmen.

19

GREENBURGH PATROLMAN Michael P. Cotter squirmed in the witness chair as he waited for the assistant district attorney to start tossing him some softball questions.

The twenty-nine-year-old cop had been the first one at the Solomon murder scene and for the first time since then he regretted it. Word had spread quickly through the station house about how tough the defense lawyer was going to be on the prosecution's witnesses—especially the cops. He had known since the previous night when McCarty called him that he would be the first witness on the second day of the trial, and while he was anxious to get off the stand as quickly as possible, he also wanted to do well. McCarty had assured him he wouldn't be up there long. He thought about his birthday, which was three days away, to try and calm down.

"Patrolman Cotter, could you please tell the jury the events that brought you to the Solomon residence on January 15, 1989, and what happened after you arrived," McCarty finally asked.

Cotter took a deep breath. "About 11:48 P.M. I was radioed to go to South Central Avenue. The call came in as an 80 case, which means a medical emergency. An unconcious woman down and bleeding. I was on Tarrytown Road, two or three miles from the Solomon home when the call came in. When I arrived there I hurried out of the car and opened the trunk to get out my oxygen unit and first aid kit. While I was doing that, a guy on a balcony was yelling at me to hurry and saying something like 'She couldn't be dead.'

"I ran up the stairs and the man met me there. The door to the apartment was open. I went in and saw a woman laying on the floor face up, covered with blood. I told the man to go outside and wait for the paramedics. I then went over to the body to check for a pulse. Her arms felt stiff. This only took about thirty seconds and it appeared to me the woman was already dead. I then got up and looked around the apartment to see if anyone else was still there."

McCarty glanced at the jurors and noted they were all listening intently. He nodded at Cotter to proceed.

"At that time Detective Ronald Stern, a paramedic, arrived, and I walked back out on the stairwell outside the front door where Paul Solomon was waiting. He asked me, 'Is she dead?' And I said I believed she was. He started crying. I asked him what had happened and he said he came home and found his wife. He said he turned her over and saw the blood. He then looked down at the blood on his hands and started to cry again. I asked him where he had been and he said the Brunswick Bowling Alley in Yonkers. Right after that I went back inside the apartment and Detective Stern pointed out several spent bullet casings laying around. After that, more detectives came and I went back outside."

Cotter paused, reaching for a glass of water.

"Did you notice anything else about the murder scene?" McCarty asked, trying to paint a more complete picture for the jury.

"Yes, when I looked around the apartment I noticed that a closet light in a bedroom was on. Also the living room light was on and the television set was turned on."

McCarty left his spot by the jury box and looked at Lewis. "Your witness."

Pasting a puzzled expression on his face, Lewis stared at the obviously nervous young patrolman.

"Officer Cotter, isn't it true that in your first written statement to detectives that you never mentioned that those lights and the television were on when you arrived?"

Fidgeting in his seat, Cotter agreed that it was true.

"And you will agree, Patrolman Cotter, that as the first officer on the scene it is your job to not only remember and record everything you see, but also to secure the crime scene to make sure nothing is changed or touched, isn't that true?"

Cotter's voice quavered. "Yes, that is true."

Pulling a sheet of paper from his voluminous files, Lewis turned toward Cotter. "In your signed statement you gave to the detectives

investigating the case shortly after the murder, you never mention anything about the lights or television set being turned on, do you?"

Cotter shook his head. "No, I didn't. I don't know why I didn't
include that."

Lewis again quickly scanned the patrolman's written statement. "According to your records, Patrolman Cotter, as the officer responsible for
securing the crime scene, you logged twelve people into that area while
you were there."

"That's true," Cotter replied. "But not all twelve entered the apartment. The people I did let in were detectives and they were there to do
their job."

Lewis rested his arm on the wooden podium and, after looking along
the two rows of jurors, asked Cotter the question he was sure would
show how sloppy the police had been that night.

"When you testified about talking with Paul Solomon that night, you
mentioned he had blood on his hands. Isn't it true that you allowed him
to go into the bathroom to wash his hands?"

"Yes, I did, and that was a mistake," Cotter said, nervously wringing
his own hands as he leaned forward in the witness chair. "I shouldn't
have allowed him to do that."

"Because you know that he could be destroying vital evidence that
could link him to the murder, isn't that right, Patrolman Cotter?" Lewis
asked sarcastically.

"Yes," Cotter answered. "That could have happened."

Lewis relentlessly continued to pound home his point, hoping every
mistake he got the inexperienced cop to admit to would help the jurors
more readily believe his opening statement promise to show them how
shoddy police work had resulted in the wrong person being charged
with the murder. The savvy defense lawyer also got Cotter to admit that
the search he and his fellow officers conducted of the area around the
Solomons' condo was random, with no set pattern to their efforts.

"Do you know what a spiral search is? Or a grid search?" Lewis
inquired. "Do you know these are specific search techniques that have
been proven to be the most effective means of locating evidence at a
crime scene?"

"No," Cotter responded, looking exhausted.

Lewis spent the next ten minutes tying Cotter up in verbal knots
until, finally satisfied with his work, the lawyer sat down.

Deciding he had to salvage what he could by showing the jury that
Cotter's mistakes stemmed more from inexperience than incompe-

tence, McCarty rose and asked his witness, "Was this the first murder scene you had ever been to and was it the first time you had ever had the responsibility of securing a crime scene for a homicide, Patrolman?"

Cotter's whispered "yes" was barely audible.

Several minutes later, Detective Ronald Stern passed his downcast colleague as he was called into the courtroom.

After prompting Stern to tell the jury about his ten years of service as a paramedic for the Greenburgh police, McCarty turned the questioning to the night of the slaying.

"I was at headquarters at about 11:45 P.M. when I was told to go to South Central Avenue. I got there around midnight. When I arrived, I saw a police vehicle, but I didn't see the officer at first. I then heard a male's voice, who was later identified to me as Paul Solomon, yelling at me to hurry up. I grabbed my equipment and ran up the stairs and I passed Patrolman Cotter in the hallway."

"What did you do when you reached the body?" McCarty asked.

"The body was cool. I checked the pupils, and they were fixed and dilated. Her arms were in a bent-up position. I tried to straighten them out, but they were quite stiff. There was a lot of resistance. There was a tremendous amount of blood. It was my opinion that the woman was dead and had been for a period of time. After checking the body, I helped Patrolman Cotter and Detective Enrique Cancel search the premises. There were several shell casings on the floor. I then went out to speak with Paul Solomon."

McCarty interrupted Stern's testimony to show the jurors a picture of the outside of the Solomons' building and a second, more gruesome shot of Betty Jeanne Solomon's bloodied, lifeless body lying on her living-room floor. The jurors passed the photos slowly from one to the other. When they had finished, Stern continued.

"When I went out to Paul Solomon, he appeared upset, but he wasn't irrational. I only spoke to him for a few minutes. He said he'd been bowling that night. Later me, Cotter, and a sergeant checked around the perimeter of the building for anything that could have been connected to the crime, a gun, bloody clothes, anything. I remember there was a wire on the side of the house, but I didn't know where it went. We then recorded all the license plates of the cars in the parking lot outside the building and then had both of the Solomons' cars towed to our police garage."

Lewis opened his cross-examination by making Stern take him step by step through his examination of Betty Jeanne Solomon's body.

"Isn't it true that by pulling on the victim's arms during your examination to try and detect whether rigor mortis had set in you were altering the crime scene, that you moved vital evidence?"

Stern thought about the question for a moment and responded, "It was part of my duties as a paramedic. My first concern is to find out if the victim is still alive so I can administer help."

"But she wasn't alive, was she, Detective Stern?"

"No. I don't believe she was."

Lewis then turned his questioning to Stern's conversation with Paul Solomon that night.

"After your talk with him, what were your thoughts, Detective? Did you believe he was telling you the truth about what he knew?"

Stern hesitated before responding. "Paul Solomon told me that he went to the Brunswick Bowling Alley and that he had a few drinks with some friends. I thought that he was possibly involved in the murder."

Lewis pried deeper. "Did Paul Solomon tell you that he had turned over his wife's body when he arrived home? Were you aware of that when you conducted your investigation?"

"No. He never told me he had moved the body," Stern said.

Ryan Attenson was well dressed and handsome. He carried himself with an air of confidence as he walked to the witness stand. Educated and articulate were the first impressions one might have gathered of the Southfield, Michigan, real estate broker. Yuppie might also have come to mind.

McCarty watched his witness being sworn in and prayed the man's anger at being summoned to White Plains to testify in the trial against Carolyn Warmus wouldn't cause him to lose control. The conversations they had had over the past couple of days had gone well, but there was an underlying current of hostility even toward the District Attorney's office. Attenson had made it very clear he did not want his name associated with the celebrated murder case, but that was a promise McCarty couldn't honestly make. He dove into the questioning, hoping for the best.

"Mr. Attenson, can you tell us how you know the defendant, Carolyn Warmus?"

Attenson glanced over at the defense table. Warmus, decked out in a knee-length black skirt with matching jacket, a pink low-cut blouse, and black high-heel pumps, refused to look at him.

"I first met Carolyn on January 8, 1981, at a bar at the University of

Michigan. I remember the date because it happens to be both our birthdays. I was a junior and she told me she was a sophomore. I didn't know it at the time, but we had attended the same high school together. Our friendship grew as a result of that meeting. I would see her around campus, at parties. I spoke to her often."

Attenson then told the jury that he and Carolyn had stayed friends through the years and that she had even attended a Christmas party at the company he worked for in Chicago one year. McCarty soon brought him to the important part of his testimony.

"Mr. Attenson, did there come a time when Carolyn Warmus would call you and tell you about her relationships?"

In a slow, deliberate voice, the twenty-eight-year-old witness began telling a story that caused a hush to fall over the entire courtroom.

"Carolyn called in the fall of 1987 and told me she was very excited because she had secured a teaching position. She called me up on the phone to tell me that she was going to be able to teach and that she was very excited because she had met someone at the school, and she was very interested in him romantically and that she hoped that this relationship would develop. But there were a couple of drawbacks. Although the gentleman was married, she felt that he would in time be separated or divorced from his wife at the time and that she could see him."

Trying to give the jury a time reference for that call, McCarty asked, "Can you pinpoint to any degree when this phone call occurred?"

Attenson thought for a moment and then said, "September, October of '87, early in the fall, I believe."

McCarty slowly drew out the information he knew the jury would need to hear.

"Did she tell you the name of this individual at that point in time?"

"She mentioned his first name," Attenson responded. "She mentioned his name was Paul and I had a conversation with her about that name."

McCarty asked his witness to remember the next time he spoke with Warmus.

"I would say the next time that I had a conversation with her would be in and around my birthday or our birthday time, in January 1988. During that call, Carolyn mentioned that things were beginning to progress a little. She had high aspirations to being able to have a relationship with this gentleman and that things were progressing in her favor, that eventually they would be separated or divorced and she would be able to go out with this guy."

"When was the next time that you saw or heard from her?" McCarty asked.

"The next time after that would be in August of '88. The circumstances were, I was at my apartment and Carolyn stopped by to visit me, and she just dropped by to say hi and she stayed for a couple of hours at least, and she discussed her relationship with this gentleman and what was going on in her life. Things weren't progressing in a manner in which she was comfortable with. She had expected things to be different at this point."

Warmus's fixation with Paul Solomon would have to be brought out if the jury were to get a sense of how obsessed she had become with her lover.

"How long did she stay in your apartment that time?" McCarty asked.

"It seemed like a couple of hours," the witness replied.

"And during that time period, about what percentage of it was she speaking about a relationship with this man?"

Attenson chuckled out loud. "About 98 percent. I mean, the conversation was based on her. Most of the conversations I have had with her were always what was going on in her life, her relationships, et cetera."

Stepping to the end of the jury box, McCarty turned to his witness and asked him to describe more fully Warmus's problem with her relationship with the man named Paul.

"Well, she was a little distraught that the relationship didn't move in a positive way at the time," Attenson said. "She felt that by now this gentleman would have been divorced or separated from his wife and that she had to take it upon herself to do something about it to kind of move things along."

"And did she tell you what it is that she would do?"

Once again Attenson smiled, as if remembering a silly childhood prank. "Yes, she told me that she was going to hire a private investigator to prove that the gentleman's wife was cheating on him, and if she could prove that, he would leave her then and Carolyn would be able to have a relationship with him."

The prosecutor maneuvered Attenson's testimony to produce the response he wanted the jurors to hear.

"Do you recall whether or not she said anything about his family beyond that during this conversation?"

"Well, the interesting thing at the time was that she felt that given her resources and him having a ready-made family, everything would work out together for the two of them."

"Now you used the term resources. What did you mean by that?"

"Financial, money," Attenson replied. "She said with her money and his family they would have a perfect life together."

McCarty stole a look at the jurors, who appeared to be riveted to his witness's testimony. Lewis was feverishly writing down notes as Attenson's story unfolded.

"I heard from her again around Thanksgiving 1988. She called me at home. This conversation was a bit different than the other conversations inasmuch that in the previous conversation she was very upbeat, very excited, and that she had a certain air of confidence to her, that she knew she was going to eventually end up with Paul Solomon. In this conversation she was very tense, very uptight, and just focused on one thing and that was she wanted to make sure that she would end up with this guy.

"The conversation consisted of that she would take it upon herself to make sure that she ended up with this other gentleman Paul Solomon. She would then end up with the family that she wanted and live happily ever after, so to speak, with Paul Solomon."

Attenson calmly reached for a cup of water on a shelf in the witness box. McCarty paused, allowing him to finish drinking, and then asked him to recall the next time he heard from Warmus.

In the same assured voice, he continued, "Like clockwork, she called again on my birthday or in and around my birthday 1989, and it was a very short conversation."

"Was there any discussion about Paul Solomon?"

"A little, and the reference was in this conversation that she wasn't . . . I guess things hadn't gone her way and she was still working toward that end."

Prompted by McCarty's questions, Attenson recalled that Warmus next called him in late summer or early fall of 1989. "I didn't hear from her again until later that year—late summer, early fall, and we had a conversation about the fact that Mr. Solomon and her were going to end up together now, everything had been taken care of and that this woman was no longer an obstacle in their lives together."

With those words, several spectators gasped aloud. Carey looked up, and the jurors continued staring at Attenson as McCarty took his seat.

"I have nothing further, your honor," he said.

The moment Lewis positioned himself behind the podium, Attenson's eyes narrowed. He had been warned by McCarty that the defense lawyer would try to prick him with sharp questions designed to confuse him and make him change his story. Attenson was ready.

"Sir, isn't it true that you came here to testify today without being subpoenaed, but that the District Attorney's office told you they could easily get one if necessary?"

Attenson stared into Lewis's eyes. "That is true, sir."

"And isn't it true that when my private investigators called you to discuss this case, you told them that your aunt's a judge and you'd be guided by her and your attorney's advice in July 1990? Do you remember saying that on the telephone? Do you?"

"If you say I said it, I must have said it."

The witness sat straighter in his chair, appearing not the least bit intimidated by his burly interrogator.

"Do you remember telling the investigator that you were sympathetic to Carolyn and her situation? Do you remember saying that on July 13, 1990, as part of the same telephone call?"

"No, sir, that is not true. The answer is I told him never to call again, leave me alone. I remember telling him that I am certain that their side, meaning you and your people, didn't want to hear what I had to say. I don't remember saying I was sympathetic to Carolyn. I don't believe I said that."

Lewis switched course, trying to get Attenson to admit he may not have remembered the exact name of the man Warmus had talked to him about. "Do you remember specifically that Carolyn told you the name of the man she was dating?" he asked.

Attenson again spoke in an angry but controlled voice, showing his utter dislike for the portly lawyer who was trying his best to make him look stupid or dishonest. "Very clearly, and make no mistake about it. Carolyn Warmus told me the man's name was Paul."

During further testimony, Attenson told the court he was unaware, during all his conversations with Warmus, that the wife of the man she had been dating was killed on January 15, 1989.

"I didn't know anything about it at all until a friend of mine showed me a newspaper article, I believe in February 1990, about Carolyn's being arrested and charged for her murder," he said. "That's when I began to realize how important all the things Carolyn had told me were."

For the rest of the afternoon, and into the next morning, Lewis and Attenson continued their verbal sparring match.

As often as Lewis tried to discredit the testimony of the feisty witness, Attenson responded with sharp, crisp answers that gained him the respect of jurors and spectators alike.

Several times during the cross-examination, Lewis's private investigators shot their boss questioning looks, as if to ask why he was continuing to cross swords with an adversary who was obviously hurting their case. The lawyer ignored them.

Frustrated at not being able to "bounce" his opponent—a term he often used for making a witness look silly through careful and baited questioning—Lewis asked Attenson why he had called the authorities.

"I called them, sir, because it scared me what I knew."

Lewis recoiled, knowing the answer was something the jurors would long remember. He tried another tack.

"You had a nickname for Carolyn Warmus, didn't you?"

When Attenson answered no, Lewis thought he had found a tiny flaw with which to work on the witness's credibility.

"Are you telling me, sir, that when talking with police you have never referred to Carolyn Warmus as 'Crazy Carolyn'? Is that what you are asking us to believe?"

Attenson nodded. When Lewis looked back to his notes on the lectern —including a signed police statement where Attenson had supposedly referred to Warmus as "Crazy Carolyn," his sharp-tongued opponent added, "It is very possible, okay, that on many occasions that I told Carolyn that she was crazy. Rest assured I have not, I have not referred to her as Crazy Carolyn."

Lewis blanched at the stinging answer, but continued on. Taking one last swing at the unbreakable witness, he framed his questions to find out if Attenson had ever had a sexual relationship with Warmus.

"No, sir, I never did."

"Now, when she went to this party with you in Chicago, where did she stay in Chicago?"

Attenson saw the sexual innuendo coming and tried to hold his temper. "She stayed in my apartment on the couch."

"And where did you stay?" Lewis asked innocently.

"In my bedroom."

Slapping a look of utter disbelief on his face, Lewis continued. "You didn't give her the bedroom and you didn't sleep on the couch?" he asked, more in jest than as a serious question, evoking a round of laughter from jurors and spectators alike.

There was a bigger laugh, however, when Attenson put his own look of pained disgust on his face and answered, "Nope. It was my bed!"

Lewis shook his head and sat down as Carey excused the witness.

All eyes focused on the pretty seventeen-year-old as she walked to the witness stand to be sworn in. The picture of innocence in a white wool sweater and gray-and-white skirt, Kristan Solomon nervously checked her long, slender gold earrings as she sat down and faced Doug FitzMorris, the assistant district attorney who had worked with her for several weeks preparing her for this day.

The television cameraman and still photographer in the back of the courtroom set their equipment aside, obeying the judge's ruling that Kristan Solomon was not to be photographed during her testimony. While most of the media attending the trial didn't agree with Carey's explanation that her youth merited the ban, they realized there wasn't a heck of a lot they could do about it.

In a soft voice, FitzMorris slowly took Kristan through the early years of her life, allowing the jury to be shown a picture of the Solomon family through the eyes of an only child. It soon became apparent that Kristan was her father's daughter. The love and reverence in her voice when she talked about him bordered on hero worship.

"I've always done everything with my dad for as long as I can remember," she said. "He taught me how to play basketball and all other kinds of sports. We'd go everywhere together. I think he's the most wonderful father in the whole world."

FitzMorris directed her thoughts to Carolyn Warmus and asked her to recall their first meeting. Kristan quickly looked at the defendant and just as quickly turned away. Warmus, who was busy doodling on her yellow legal pad, apparently hadn't noticed the glance.

"I was at an unofficial captain's basketball practice in November, in late fall of 1987, and she walked in with another teacher and played some basketball with us. Later on my father introduced me to her."

FitzMorris nodded. "Did you have further occasions to encounter or run into the defendant?"

"Whenever I went to Greenville, I usually popped my head in her classroom to say hello. Sometimes I sat down and talked with her a little bit. No official meetings, but I would see her a lot. It would usually be me popping in saying hi," Kristan answered.

"At the beginning it was just like, 'Hi, how are you?' Just very friendly, and as the months went on we became better friends. I always talked to her at least three times a week. If she would call we would have conversations and it was very friendly, nothing really significant. She would call, ask how my games were, and hoped that she had the time to come to some of them."

It was time to start showing the jury the slow, but purposeful way Warmus had begun to ease herself into the Solomon family's life, especially with Kristan.

"Around Christmastime 1987, did you attend any special event with Carolyn Warmus?" FitzMorris asked.

Kristan nodded, answering in a shaky, quick voice that reminded jurors and spectators alike that despite her grown-up appearance, they were still listening to a child.

"Yes. We went to see the Radio City Music Hall Christmas Spectacular with her and one of her friends, a Gwen Pasco. Who all went? Me and my father basically met them in the city and we went to the show and dinner after. We went down to Little Italy and had a quick dinner and went home."

Moving her story along, FitzMorris brought Kristan to late January 1988 and a scenario he was sure certain members of the middle- to upper-class jury—especially the women—would not like.

"Did you have any other occasion where you had dinner with the defendant?"

Kristan nodded, staring straight ahead as if picturing the moment in time.

"Carolyn came to dinner at the Candlelight Restaurant in Scarsdale with me, my father, and my mother. It was a last-minute thing, let's go to dinner. No plans. It was just okay, we're going to dinner, why don't we all go.

"At dinner, we were talking about the February school break and how my father was going away, and basically I was pleading to let me go with him, but he was going with one of his friends. We got on the subject of February break and me staying home, my mom working, and then Carolyn said that she was going skiing and maybe I could come. Of course, I jumped at the chance because I wanted to go away so badly and it was 'please, please, please' and basically the trip came from that."

Prompted by FitzMorris's steady stream of questions, Kristan told the court about continually begging her parents for permission to go on the ski trip, the several phone calls from Warmus to see how the family debate was progressing, and finally getting the okay to go.

On a Saturday, about two weeks before the trip, Carolyn called the

Solomons and got permission to stop by later that day. With only Betty Jeanne and her daughter home at the time, she arrived armed with a ski jacket, ski pants, ski suits and gloves, Kristan recalled.

"I had never been skiing before that and I didn't have any of the equipment."

Slowly walking in front of the jury, head bent and hands clasped behind his back, FitzMorris waited for his young witness to finish before attempting to show the jury just how reprehensible Warmus was. He asked Kristan about her new friend's acceptance of a forced dinner invitation.

"Kristan, do you recall the circumstances that led up to Carolyn Warmus having dinner with you and your mother that evening?"

Nodding while running her fingers through her thick, dark hair, Kristan answered: "I was still trying all this stuff on to see if any of it fit, and my mom was making dinner for me. Carolyn was there and my mom asked if she would like to stay for dinner. It was a very quick dinner. It wasn't anything special.

"Well, my mom wasn't too excited about me going off on this weekend and she wasn't really too excited about me going with Carolyn, so basically she was being very polite and asking if she wanted to stay for dinner. At dinner it was too polite and we ate. My dad came home while we were eating dinner and he was kind of startled that Carolyn was sitting there at dinner, because he just thought she was dropping stuff off."

Kristan also recalled that during the month before the trip, Carolyn would call her father at home sometimes three to four times a week and that on the occasions she would answer, the talk always centered around their ski trip.

FitzMorris then steered his questioning to the actual trip and the conversations Warmus had initiated. The prosecutor was hoping the jurors would be as angry as he had been to learn how Warmus had used Kristan to try and squeeze out information about her parents' marital problems.

"Now, Kristan, on the four-hour ride up to Mount Snow, Vermont, what did you and Carolyn talk about?"

"We talked about skiing and how excited I was. We talked about her car, the ski rack that was kind of falling off, and we talked about my dad and my mom. She regularly asked me that weekend, you know, if my mom and dad fought about her regularly. She didn't think my mom liked her very much."

Nodding toward the defense table, FitzMorris asked Kristan, "What led you to believe that she didn't think your mom liked her? What did she say?"

Kristan breathed deeply, as if gathering some inner strength. "Carolyn turned and asked me, 'Your mom doesn't like me, does she?' I said, 'No, no, no, she does like you,' but in the back of my mind, of course, I knew that my mom didn't like her at all, but I was taught to be polite. I was taught to hold back things, not be mean to someone's face."

FitzMorris pressed harder. "What other questions did Carolyn Warmus ask you about your parents?"

"Basically if they fought a lot. Carolyn tried to say compliments to me, would compliment the family and she would say something like, 'You're growing up so well and you're such a great kid you must have this great family life. Your parents must never have any fights, but they must fight.' And I would say, 'They fight like normal parents, but it's few and far between,' and then she would ask me about my dad and how he was teaching and, you know, what people thought about him and stuff like that. She was very interested in if my mom didn't like her and what my dad was doing.

"She asked me at least four other times during the ski trip if my mom liked her. It was kind of strange to me because I kept on saying, 'No, she likes you, don't worry about it.' And she would tell me how wonderful my father was and what a great man he was and what a great teacher he was. I would always say, 'Yes, yes.'"

The next line of questioning bothered FitzMorris, because he knew the answers the young girl was about to give and, more importantly, how she would come across to the jury merely by speaking the cold, harsh words. He pressed on.

"Kristan, what was your relationship with each of your two parents?"

Looking down and smoothing out the front of her sweater, Kristan hesitated for a few moments and then spoke in an even, unemotional tone.

"Well, my father was basically an overprotective father, not wanting his little girl to grow up, and I was very close to my father, I always have been. My mother was basically oblivious toward me. She really didn't want to have anything to do with me. It was very different outside when the public saw it and when I was in private. In public she would be very loving and caring, and behind doors she would be very stern and cold. It was very different between my mom and my dad. My dad in public and in private is a very loving man and very warm, and my mom is not, was not."

There was a murmur in the courtroom at the coldness with which this young girl spoke of a mother who had been brutally murdered.

"Did you love your mom?"

"Yes."

"Did you tell Carolyn Warmus during that ski trip the same thing you just told this jury?"

"No. I'm a very private person and don't tell many things to anyone. I keep it very in. I guess I'm kind of like my mom. I'm very warm and caring on the outside and keep all the stuff that is very personal inside and don't really tell much to anyone."

"Do you miss your mom, Kristan?"

"Yes, very much."

Jumping ahead to Kristan's birthday, August 5, 1988, FitzMorris brought out another incident involving Warmus and the Solomons at their home, an incident that once again was intended to show the lengths to which she would go to insert herself into her lover's family.

"Carolyn came to my home on my birthday to drop off some presents, and I didn't know she was coming. My family didn't know she was coming, and she rang the bell and walked in with all these packages and put them down on the living-room table and was just like 'oh, happy birthday,' and my mom was there. My father wasn't there right at the beginning, but he walked in about five minutes after she had come in.

"Well, I was in shock. I mean I hadn't seen her since that spring. I was kind of drawn back by it because I didn't expect anything. And I was kind of, not frightened, but like hesitant because I knew my mom didn't enjoy her in the house and didn't like her. So I was kind of worried that there would be words spoken to each other."

"What kind of presents did she give you?" FitzMorris asked.

"She bought me a bracelet and two outfits from Le Château. One was a pants outfit and one was a skirt with a shirt."

For the next fifteen minutes, FitzMorris took his witness through her school days and the off-and-on conversations she would have with Warmus during the following months.

Buttoning his gray suit jacket as he walked back to the podium holding his notes, FitzMorris—nicknamed "the choirboy" for his handsome, young, and angelic-looking face—led Kristan up to the weekend of her mother's death.

"Did there come a time in January of 1989, shortly after the holidays of New Year's and Christmas, when you went away on another trip?" he asked.

"Yes. My friend Cassie Stone asked me on a Thursday night if I wanted to go skiing that Friday and on the weekend with her and her parents, Dudley and Sally Stone, on that Martin Luther King weekend, and it was very sudden and I packed that night. I had a basketball game on Friday, so we left after that. My parents said, 'Okay, fine.' It was a very sudden, spur-of-the-moment thing."

Kristan began describing telephone calls to her parents when she arrived at the Thorton, New Hampshire, winter home of Charles and Suzanne Allen, where they were all staying that weekend. The Allens were a Scarsdale couple who were friends of the Stones, Paul Solomon, and the Pillersdorfs. Kristan called Friday night and again Saturday morning, telling her father she was all right.

Kristan then said she remembered talking to both her mom and dad on the day of the murder. "I called them in the afternoon. I was skiing all day, so it was probably around 3 P.M. I was still at the slope and I got into a fight with my friend, and I was more depressed than I was the day before and talked to them for a good half hour probably."

Describing the fight with Cassie as "stupid," Kristan said she first spoke to her father for about fifteen minutes and then her mother got on. "I talked to my mom about fifteen minutes again, and we were talking about how tired she was, and how she was eating popcorn. I remember that, she was eating popcorn and she was chewing and talking at the same time and I could barely hear because I was on a pay phone."

"Everything seem okay?"

"Everything seemed totally normal."

Drawing her attention to the following day, Monday, January 16, 1989, FitzMorris asked Kristan to describe what happened.

"We got back to Westchester later that evening, probably around 9 P.M. The Pillersdorfs, they—someone called where I was staying and said that our heat was broken, which is totally normal for Scarsdale Ridge Apartments, and that winter the heat was on and off a lot, so I stayed over at the Pillersdorfs a lot, so we went straight there."

"Did that seem unusual?"

"No, not at all. I actually laughed about it. We got there and took all my stuff out of the car. Two of the Pillersdorfs' friends that I know walked in front of us and I said, 'Hi, Herb, how are you? What's up?' He walked by me straight in. I walked in and my dad was at the door and he looked like a zombie, he was pale white and looked like he hadn't shaved in a while and was just very, you know, he was shaking. I asked, 'What's wrong?', and Stephanie, who was also one of my best friends, walked in and saw me and turned around and ran down the hallway. I asked my dad, 'What's going on?', and he sat me down and hugged me tight and he told me my mom had been killed and I was just like 'okay, okay.'

"I was basically in shock. I didn't really know what to do, and he was crying and everyone was crying and I was the only one that wasn't crying in the whole entire place. I walked down this hall and Stephanie started crying on my shoulder. I went downstairs and my family was there and they were all crying. It was a very, very weird situation that I was kind of the only one not crying. I was very—I was kind of waiting for my mom to walk in the door and say, 'Ha! It's a joke!' "

"It never happened, though, did it Kristan?"

"No, it didn't."

All eyes in the courtroom were glued to the pretty girl, searching for some type of reaction to having told her heart-wrenching story. But there was none. She only stared straight ahead, awaiting the next question.

A hard-bitten reporter in the second row leaned over to one of his colleagues and whispered, "Someday this is all going to come back to her and she won't be able to keep it all bottled up inside. One day this girl's going to explode." A few other eavesdropping journalists nodded in agreement.

FitzMorris ignored the whispers, even from members of the jury. Kristan's demeanor wasn't normal, or maybe it was. Maybe it was some kind of emotional defense mechanism built into children to help protect them. He pushed on.

"Now, Kristan, do you know a girl named Barbara Ballor?"

"Yes, I do. I met her in June 1989 at my house. My dad introduced her to me."

"Did your dad ever talk to you about Barbara Ballor before you met her in June of '89?"

"Yes, I was telling him, urging him to date more, date at all actually. I would say, 'Dad, you got to go out, go on with your life. It can't be so stagnant. I was urging him to go out because he was still very down about it and everything that had happened. I was trying to get him to live, basically. I knew that he had to get out and do some things before he just couldn't anymore.

"I was going out a lot just to take my mind off of things, and I was leaving him home and I didn't want to leave him home all the time. Before I actually met Barbara, my dad asked me about maybe seeing this person, is it okay? And I was like, 'Yeah, like good, this is great. Bring her over and I'll make dinner.' I was probably more excited than he was. He was reserved about it. He didn't want to move too fast."

FitzMorris knew he had to bring out some emotion from his stoic little witness. He wanted the jurors to feel the family's pain over the loss of Betty Jeanne, but they weren't getting it from Kristan.

"How were you doing at that point in time, Kristan?"

"How was I doing? I was basically holding up. Everyone else around me was a little down, and I always had the opinion, you know, I did my mourning at that point in time and I said, 'You know, it's time to live life again and I can't do anything about it if I sit home and cry or I go out and enjoy myself. So basically I was doing fine. And at that point I was trying to forget as much as you possibly can and still remember the memory of my mother."

FitzMorris again moved Kristan along, asking if she remembered the gift she had received from Carolyn on her sixteenth birthday.

"Yes. It was a beautiful pair of diamond earrings. They looked very expensive."

Getting on with the questioning, he handed his young witness a greeting card and asked her to recite for the jury the words that appeared on it.

Reading out loud the words from the very card that Carolyn had given her along with the earrings in August 1989, Kristan said:

"Happy 16th birthday, Kristan. I hope you don't mind that this gift is about a month early. Believe it or not, I bought it for you at the end of last August and I've been waiting to give it to you ever since. I really wanted to give it to you in person, but you seem to be very busy this summer. I thought you might enjoy receiving your present now because you'll probably get a lot more use out of it during the summer when you're going out with your friends than during the school year when you're always too busy competing in sports. I hope you like it. And please remember that unless you're playing in some sport, this present can and should be used all the time, during the day, at school, et cetera. Not just for fancy occasions.

"And knowing how much you love to save the bags from stores, I folded up this one for you and included it in the box, too. As you probably remember from your last birthday, usually I hold a present over your head and say, 'Heavy, heavy, hang over your head. Is it something you eat, use or wear?'

"But since I'm not there to do this, and since you're going to know where the present is from when you see the bag and the blue suede box, I'll let you off the hook this time. I'm sure you'll know it's not something to eat. Ha, ha. I hope you love it. And I hope you'll get a lot of use out of it. It's a special gift for a very special young lady on her 16th birthday. Love always, Carolyn."

FitzMorris knew from his investigators that Warmus had given the earrings to Kristan in a Tiffany's jewelry box, though they actually had been purchased at a jewelry store on Forty-seventh Street in Manhattan for $225.

At FitzMorris's request, Kristan then read for the jury another letter Carolyn had sent her that summer along with another batch of gifts from Disney World in Florida. When Kristan finished reading, FitzMorris told the judge, "No more questions."

After a quick break for the jury, Lewis rose from his seat and, with his best bearish-but-lovable expression, began asking Kristan in his friendliest tone, a few questions.

"On Sunday, the fifteenth of January, you talked to your mom by phone and she told you she was eating popcorn, right?"

"Yes."

"And she was watching the football game?"

"She didn't tell me anything about watching the football game, but she could have been."

Lewis changed the subject.

"Did the police talk to you at all about the door being open to your house at different times?"

Watching her nod, the defense lawyer began asking questions whose importance would become more readily apparent to the jurors as the case progressed.

"Did you say anything to them about using the bottom lock only after 5:30 P.M.?"

"Not that I recall."

"What about the dead bolt, that it was used only at night?"

"Yes," Kristan replied. "I remember something about that."

Keeping his voice soft and pleasant, Lewis tried to learn more about the Solomons' use of door locks. Showing Kristan a copy of the statement she had given police back on January 18, 1989, Lewis asked her, "Do you remember telling the cops that the door was locked at 5:30 P.M.?"

"No," she replied with conviction. "I recall telling them that our door was usually open and that at night we use the dead bolt, but it was open a lot. The door was wide open many times. We just didn't have any need or . . . didn't think about closing it."

Taking one more unsuccessful stab at trying to get Kristan to say she remembered talking with her mother about a football game, Lewis smiled at the young witness.

"Nothing else, judge," he said, taking his seat at the defense table.

Looking out the courtroom windows at the darkening sky, Carey called it a day.

20

MARIE CONTRI took the oath and sat in the witness chair, looking out at all the faces staring back at her from the courtroom gallery and jury box.

While the prosecutors took a few minutes to consult quietly at their table, she glanced over at Warmus, the woman whose picture had made the front pages of the newspapers and the six o'clock news for the past several months.

The brown horn-rimmed glasses were new, but it was her. Definitely her.

The prosecutor's questions were easy enough.

"Yes, I talked with the police on January 16, 1989," she began. "They showed me a picture and asked me about this man who came into the bar the night before. I told them the guy came in alone, and I served him a vodka Collins and after a while he ordered another one. He was paying cash.

"About a half hour later a woman joined him," Contri recalled, starting to feel at ease telling her story. The dread she had felt for the past few months at having to testify was vanishing.

"She was about five feet seven, blond hair, thin build, about twenty-five years old. She ordered a glass of champagne and they sat drinking for a while. Later they ordered dinner. I believe he ordered a hamburger and she ordered some oysters and some more French fries."

McCarty pulled out a restaurant bill that had been time-dated by a computerized cash register. "Do you mind looking at that receipt and telling us when the bill was closed out that night?" he asked.

Contri peered at the blue-inked markings. "It says 23:14, which means I cashed out their bill at 11:14 P.M."

"Does that mean that was the time the couple left the restaurant?" McCarty asked.

"Not necessarily. You see, sometimes, especially when I'm busy, I may put the bill aside and later, when I have more time, I'll ring it out on the cash register."

Bending down to tug on his pant leg, McCarty tried to listen to his witness's answer, but found himself in a battle with the static-cling that had claimed his trousers that morning. Several jurors watched the perplexed lawyer continue to try and pull down the ever-upward-creeping right pant leg with his left foot, but to no avail. The suppressed smiles and giggles of not only the jury but an amused group of courtroom spectators did little to alleviate the embarrassment McCarty was beginning to feel. Bravely, he pressed on.

"Ms. Contri, how did these two people appear to be acting that evening with each other? Do you recall?"

"They weren't overly affectionate, but seemed intimate with each other. I felt they knew each other well. It seemed to be that she was comfortable with him."

Under cross-examination, Lewis brought out Contri's reasons for remembering the couple.

"He was one of the first people in the bar that night," she said. "Our usual crowd doesn't start coming in until about 8 P.M. or so, so there wasn't many other people in the place when he came in and then she [pointing at Warmus] joined him. Also, it's stayed fresh in my mind because the police talked to me about it the next day. It's made that Sunday stick out in my mind where I otherwise might not have remembered."

Contri appeared surprised when the judge thanked her and asked that she step down. All that buildup for only a few minutes of testifying. She mentally kicked herself for worrying about it for so long.

Jimmy Russo strode down the courtroom aisle, his chest puffed, jet-black hair greased back, and a suave, devil-may-care look plastered on his face for the jury's benefit. He was wearing a black pinstripe suit that he had decided to set off with a blue shirt. His shoes were polished, and he wore just a splash of cologne.

Sworn in, he slowly looked over the sixteen men and women seated in the two rows to his left and then at the television cameras pointed toward him from the rear of the room. He appeared to be delighted at having his moment in the sun.

After giving McCarty his Staten Island address and telling him he was co-owner of All-Tech Investigations in Manhattan, he sat back in the chair, straightening his turquoise tie. He seemed ready to tell his story. And this would be an opportunity to give him and his partner's private investigation firm some much needed publicity.

His cockyness did not allow him to see the wrecking ball slowly starting to swing toward him with Lewis at the controls. For the moment, McCarty was tossing him the softball questions he expected.

Russo told the jury that he had first worked for Vincent Parco as a field investigator in January 1987, adding that he had met Warmus several months later, in late summer 1987, after she had hired the firm to do some work for her.

McCarty began crafting his questions carefully. He knew Judge Carey had already ruled that the jury was not to hear of Warmus's relationship with Matthew Nicolosi, the New Jersey bartender who had been the reason for her hiring Parco in the first place. He wished the jurors could hear even a little about the seminude photographs of Warmus in her pink wig and the attempt at superimposing the pictures, which were to be sent to Nicolosi's wife. These were some of the antics that really showed what kind of person Carolyn Warmus was, but even an inadvertent mention of them might cause Carey to declare a mistrial. Whether or not he thought it was fair, there was nothing he could do about it. He could only hope that Russo's story would be shocking enough.

"Did you continue to see Miss Warmus through the late summer of 1987 and thereafter?" McCarty asked.

"Yes, I did. I would see her visit Mr. Parco's office on a biweekly basis, up until I left, which was February 1988."

"Did there come a time that you saw Miss Warmus in connection with your work at All-Tech?"

Russo nodded, a small smile tugging at the corners of his mouth. "Yes, there was. It was late summer, possibly early fall of 1988 at my office on West Fifty-second Street. I had received a phone call prior to her coming, asking if it would be all right for her to come up. I told her yes."

McCarty continued to ask his questions slowly, knowing he was drawing a picture that would allow the jurors to see what had happened.

Russo's testimony filled only one part of the canvas that would be filled in by others to complete the mural that he hoped would convince the jurors beyond a reasonable doubt that Warmus was a cold-blooded killer.

"Did there come a time that she actually came to your offices?"

"Yes, there was," Russo said, building up to the juicy part of his story. "There were other investigators in the office when she came. Basically Miss Warmus expressed concern about a jet crash that occurred in Michigan involving her father's jet. She said that it was a question of sabotage and that there was a female seen in the vicinity of the hangar. She didn't give me an exact date as to when it happened."

"What did she ask you to do as far as this was concerned?"

"At the time nothing," Russo responded. "I asked for her to furnish me with documentation that there was a jet crash that had occurred."

McCarty moved the story ahead. "Did there come a time after that incident that you heard from her again?"

"Yes. I received a second call asking me if it was all right for her to come up. I said yes and a short time later she returned to my office. During this second visit I was advised there was a hit-and-run accident involving her sister and the female driver was seen by witnesses matching the description of the female that was seen at the airport. She told me this accident happened in Washington, D.C., and that it involved her sister."

"Did she bring any newspaper clippings or any other documents regarding the plane crash that she described in the first meeting?"

"No. I asked her again for the additional documentation concerning the hit-and-run. I was told I would receive it at a later date."

Warmus dropped her pen and crossed her arms over her chest. For the first time since Russo's testimony began, she snuck a look at him. She must have known what was coming and steeled herself against it.

McCarty led Russo into the most important part of his testimony. The grinning private eye was ready.

"Was there a third meeting with the defendant?" the prosecutor asked, looking toward Warmus.

When Russo responded yes, Lewis objected, and—after a side-bar conference with McCarty and the judge—asked that the next item about which Russo was expected to testify be ruled inadmissible.

"Your honor," Lewis whispered, "I believe that this is the conversation in which they are going to seek to elicit that Carolyn Warmus asked Mr. Russo for a gun and silencer. I want to object. That is a prior uncharged act and it's not admissible in this context. This is designed to prove nothing but a predisposition to commit these criminal acts."

Carey listened for several minutes to McCarty's response and finally agreed with the prosecutor that the incident was indeed relevant and related. He overruled the objection.

Once again behind the podium, McCarty looked over the jurors to make sure they were each paying attention.

"Can you tell us, Mr. Russo, what it is that was discussed during this third meeting?"

Russo leaned forward into the microphone as if he didn't want anyone to miss what he was about to say. "She stated that she knew who the unknown female now was. She mentioned the name Jeanne or Betty Jeanne. She had seen the woman up by the school in Westchester. I asked her why she was coming to us. If she wanted protection I suggested bodyguards. Her answer was no. At that point I pushed her and asked, 'Exactly what do you want from us?' and I got the answer 'A machine gun with a silencer.' "

"What was your answer to that?"

"We're not arms dealers."

McCarty needed more. "Is there anything else that you recall about the request for the weapon?"

"Yes, I do," came the reply. "It had to be small enough to conceal within the confines of a handbag. After that, she left when she was told we wouldn't be supplying her a weapon."

Russo went on to say that after Warmus left his office, he immediately called the Midtown North police precinct and informed them of the conversation.

"After that I didn't have any more contact with Miss Warmus."

For the next several minutes McCarty asked his witness about a television movie deal he had signed, selling the rights to his story about the case for $50,000. Russo also disclosed that he had been paid $10,000 by the TV news show 'Inside Edition' and another $3,000 by another nationally syndicated TV show called 'Hard Copy.'

McCarty gathered his papers. "I have nothing further."

Lewis rose from the defense table and cast a heavy-lidded eye on his target. He had to make Russo appear to be one of the slimiest, scummiest human beings God had ever placed on the face of the earth, in order to destroy his credibility with the jury. With Russo's background, the task would not be hard.

Knowing Russo's intense hatred of Parco, Lewis asked, "Did you ever call Mr. Parco a set-up artist?"

"Possibly on occasions," Russo responded. "On occasions when I called him a host of other names besides that."

Lewis toyed with his quarry for the next few hours, pumping him for answers about Parco, his relationship with Warmus, and the records he kept or didn't keep about his conversations with New York and Greenburgh police.

The cross-examination became heated when Lewis asked Russo about a report that Russo had illegally flashed a U.S. Drug Enforcement Administration badge at a woman who caught him taking photographs while on a stakeout.

After denying the incident, Russo was handed a copy of a New York State Attorney General's complaint filed against him for allegedly using the phony badge.

"You're telling us that is not true. Right?" Lewis said, the sarcasm dripping from every word.

"The complaint was false."

Lewis then turned to a report made by Annette Angel, a woman who had come to Russo to do some child custody work.

"Did you inquire at all into her case?" Lewis asked.

"Yes, we did."

"Did you bill her for it at all?"

"No, we did not."

"How much time did you spend?"

"Maybe two hours."

"And what," Lewis pursued, "is two hours of your time worth?"

"Approximately $150."

Lewis moved in for the kill. "And you took the time, the value of your time, from Annette Angel by having sex with her in your office, did you not?"

"That's not true."

Lewis moved on.

"Mr. Russo, you do landlord-tenant-related work, do you not?"

The private eye nodded.

"And one of the landlords you represent, is someone called Park Holding Company, right?"

"I don't know them under that name."

Lewis waved off the flimsy attempt to sidetrack him.

"Well, at some point did you go to an address on East Seventy-seventh Street in Manhattan on behalf of a landlord you represented?"

Russo nodded.

"And, as part of your duties that day, you were doing an investigation into prostitution in that apartment, right?"

"Yes, I did."

"And on behalf of that client, as part of your duties that day, you went in to determine whether or not there was prostitution in that apartment, right?"

Again, Russo answered yes.

"And you remained there about an hour. And during that hour you paid the woman $400, right? You paid her for the sexual act?"

Russo finally smiled as if recalling the moment. "Yes, I did."

"And you know now that what you did was in part the promotion of prostitution, right?"

"That would be up to the Manhattan District Attorney's Office to decide," Russo shot back.

"Is it your testimony that you didn't know while you were doing this that you were committing a criminal act?"

Russo tried to fence with his antagonist, but quickly found he was overmatched.

"Circumstances at the time dictated it," he finally said.

Lewis looked at the jury, scratching his head with a questioning look on his face. "And the circumstances that dictated it were what?"

"It could have been my death."

Lewis's head shot up from the reports he was staring down at. "What?" he nearly shouted. "You mean it was death or sex, Mr. Russo?"

The courtroom erupted in laughter, jurors trying to suppress their guffaws while the spectators did little to hide their delight. Russo sat smiling on the stand, his discomfort apparent.

Lewis drove on, firmly in control, ripping Russo's believability to shreds.

"How many times did you commit this crime in your life as an undercover operator?"

"With regards to fellatio, maybe twice," came the reply.

Lewis saw another opening. "So when you said this particular crime, you're distinguishing it from other crimes, right?"

"I was distinguishing fellatio from intercourse."

The smile on Lewis's face told the entire court he was finding his opponent unarmed in this war of wits.

"How many times did you have intercourse in the course of promoting prostitution as part of your undercover operation?"

"Maybe the most, three times."

"You like your work?" Lewis asked, to another roar of laughter from his growing throng of admirers.

"Yes, I do," Russo responded, and no one doubted him.

Lewis continued his attack. Each episode of unsavory, devious, or immoral behavior he brought to light would increase the possibility that the jurors would be too disgusted to take his word for anything.

When Russo once again fell into the trap of trying to defend his sexual proclivities as part of a private eye's work, Lewis couldn't resist a few barbed sexual innuendos.

"You say the police department won't act on a complaint of prostitution unless someone goes in there and has sex with a prostitute? Is that what you are telling us?"

"No. They are not just going to act on a complaint," Russo stupidly argued.

"Even though you can tell them that?" Lewis asked.

"I have to give them more information. I have to get within the organization itself."

Lewis chortled to himself, unable to pass up the easy sexual reference.

"How deep within the organization do you have to get, Mr. Russo?"

Again, laughter rolled through the courtroom. But this time Russo wanted to play as well.

"As deep as possible."

"And that's what you do. Right?"

"On occasions."

Carey peered down from his bench, a smile creasing his face. Jurors and spectators laughed aloud as he interrupted the two combatants. "Mr. Lewis, we have to adjourn for lunch now."

The meal did little to tire Lewis or stem the tide of legally permissible abuse he continued to heap upon the witness.

The weeks he and his own private detectives had spent preparing to incinerate Russo's integrity and bomb his believability paid off as the afternoon session ended with the man's credibility in shreds.

McCarty and FitzMorris sat shaking their heads as the day wound down, marveling at Lewis's skilled cross-examination, his ability to slit, slice, and then slay their offerings.

While neither was willing to throw in the towel at that point, both realized at that moment they were in for the fight of their lives.

At the end of the day, Warmus left the courtroom with DiSalvatore and Ruggiero in hot pursuit, her trademark smile even broader after the wonderful spectacle she had seen of Russo being skewered.

McCarty picked up his files and left ahead of his partner. He was met in the lobby by the usual horde of reporters.

Pushing the elevator button while dodging some of the tougher questions being thrown at him, McCarty allowed himself a small smile. "Look, guys. You go with what you got," he yelled over his shoulder as the doors opened and he stepped inside.

Once back in his office, McCarty put his feet up on his desk. He'd have a little extra time to go over his case since the trial wouldn't resume until Tuesday, due to Monday's celebration of Martin Luther King, Jr.'s, birthday.

The prosecution's first witness after the long weekend was Richard J. Vizzini, the former Scarsdale Police Department police aide who answered the emergency telephone calls and complaints the night of January 15, 1989.

The twenty-one-year-old looked comfortable on the witness stand, and the jurors appeared to like the clean-cut, polite young man who stood in sharp contrast to Jimmy Russo and his tales of prostitutes, pimps, and blowjobs.

Vizzini took the jurors through New York Telephone operator Linda Viana's report of the strange emergency call she had received from a woman who was screaming that someone was trying to kill her.

"After we got that call and checked the phone number the operator gave us against our [cross-reference] directory, we passed the information on to Greenburgh police when we realized the number the operator had given us was from a location in Greenburgh, not Scarsdale," Vizzini said.

McCarty and FitzMorris had set up a tape recorder on the table and they asked Carey's permission to allow the jurors to put on the earphones that had earlier been placed on their chairs.

"Ladies and gentlemen, the recording you are about to hear is that of New York Telephone operator Linda Viana calling Mr. Vizzini at the Scarsdale Police Department to report the emergency call."

With that, FitzMorris flipped a switch and the jurors, judge, Warmus, her lawyer, private eyes, and the prosecutors sat back and listened intently to the recorded call.

Several minutes later, the headsets came off as McCarty resumed questioning Vizzini.

"I was also the one who took a call shortly before midnight on January 15, 1989, from a man who identified himself as Paul Solomon," Vizzini said.

Once again McCarty asked the jurors to put on their headsets to hear the frightened, terror-filled call from Paul Solomon to the Scarsdale police moments after he arrived home to find his wife brutally shot to death.

Warmus picked up her headset and slowly adjusted the volume. She winced noticeably as the stricken voice of her former lover was sent echoing through her head. Seconds later she tore off the device, throwing it to the table. She had never listened to that tape before. While the judge quietly reviewed some documents, Warmus tugged on Lewis's coat sleeve begging him to let her leave the room.

With Carey's permission, Warmus stood up and turned to leave, momentarily forgetting the cameras in the back of the courtroom that she had so demonstrably tried to avoid by refusing to turn her head during the proceedings.

Hearing Paul's terrified screams and then mistakenly giving the cameras the shots they had waited days to get, proved too much for the defendant. Tears welled in her eyes as she almost sprinted through the courtroom, her private investigator DiSalvatore jogging to catch up with her.

Ten minutes later, Warmus returned, her intermittent sobs loudly filling the courtroom. Everyone turned and stared as she angrily made her way back to her chair. Seconds later, she threw herself down on the defense table, erupting into screams, crying so loudly the judge finally called Lewis to side-bar and asked what was wrong.

"She hasn't been feeling well, judge, and I'm not quite sure what happened here. Maybe if we take our noon recess now she'll have time to compose herself."

Carey agreed, telling the court officers to send the jury to an early lunch.

Two hours later, the courtroom doors were unlocked and as the reporters and spectators made their way back to their favorite seats, their attention was focused on the woman who had now virtually thrown herself across the defense table, her earlier sobs replaced by short gasps and ear-piercing sniffles. Her arms stretched out in front of her as she lay trembling, Warmus appeared to have suffered a complete collapse.

Carey and the lawyers carried on with their discussions for the next twenty minutes with the jurors out of the room. When it came time to bring the panel back in, Lewis jumped to his feet, telling the judge he had been unable to snap his client out of her current emotional state.

The judge looked down at the pathetic woman sprawled before him, clutching handfuls of blue tissue. With a look of resignation, he ordered an end to the day's proceedings.

Before allowing the jurors back in the courtroom to be dismissed, Carey told Lewis to remove his client. DiSalvatore and Ruggiero leapt from their seats and stood on either side of the distressed defendant. Each taking an arm, they practically lifted her out of her seat. Reporters, trial watchers, and court officers looked on in utter disbelief as the stumbling, trembling, and crying woman was half-carried, half-dragged out a back door behind the judge's bench.

After she had departed and the jurors returned to their seats, Carey tried to explain the day's developments.

"We're going to adjourn early today, ladies and gentlemen. The defendant has taken ill, so you all get an early break. Please be back tomorrow at 9:30 A.M. Thank you for your patience."

After the jurors had filed out, McCarty and FitzMorris began once again gathering their files, exhibits, and reports together.

"Who knows," McCarty whispered to his partner. "With the way she looked today we may not have to go through a trial. She was a mess."

FitzMorris grinned. He knew of some of the quiet, side bets being made in the D.A.'s office and the Greenburgh police station that Warmus would flip out long before this trial ever concluded. As he pushed his evidence cart down the aisle, he found himself thinking about how it was his birthday today, and maybe someone up above was giving him a well-deserved gift.

The following morning, Lewis didn't even bother to unpack his briefcase before asking the judge for permission to speak. The two prosecutors looked up, unsure of what was coming.

"Your honor, as you are well aware, my client became very ill yesterday," Lewis began in a grave tone. "This morning after she was picked up at her apartment by one of my investigators and was being driven here, she fainted twice and then began vomiting blood. She was taken to a New York hospital for treatment and as of this moment I am not aware of whether she has yet been treated or has been admitted as a patient. I'm waiting for a call now. Under the circumstances, I would request an adjournment until Miss Warmus is physically able to continue."

The look of fatherly concern on Carey's face was enough to make McCarty think he had probable cause to ask for a mistrial, but the attorney held his tongue as he stood to address the court. "I don't think we should continue until Miss Warmus is able to be here. All I would ask is that your honor be given the medical report of her illness to ensure that she is indeed unable to be here for medical reasons."

Taking his seat, McCarty caught the disbelieving look from his partner.

"Vomiting, my ass," FitzMorris hissed in his ear. "She was having a mental breakdown yesterday and it has nothing to do with the flu, I'll guarantee you that."

Carey called for the jury, and when they were seated, he told them of the defendant's illness.

"Please call into the court tonight after 5 P.M. at the number the court clerk will hand you when you leave to see if we'll need you tomorrow," Carey said. "If the trial will not resume then, please be here Monday morning at 9:30 A.M. Thank you."

The trial did not, in fact, resume the next day. Carolyn Warmus shuffled through the lobby of the courthouse the following Monday, oblivious to the flashing electronic light bulbs attached to the photographers' cameras, her face partially hidden by the ominous-looking black hooded cape she wore to shield herself.

Her two minions, DiSalvatore and Ruggiero, scurried through the metal detectors and gently took her arms, directing her into an empty elevator.

Once inside the courtroom, Ruggiero pulled a small white pillow— the kind used on airplanes—and placed it on the defense table in front of his client. Warmus, her eyes glassy and glazed, wasted no time flopping her head down on it.

Lewis lumbered into the room, shrugging off questions from the media about whether Warmus was drugged, as her appearance and demeanor indicated. "It's just that she's still not feeling well, I'm sure you all can understand that," he told the unbelieving journalists.

Minutes later, Carey entered and told a court officer to bring in the jury. Seeing the defendant resting on her pillow, her arms stretched out before her as if she were enjoying a good night's sleep, they exchanged puzzled looks, but said nothing.

"Is the prosecution ready to proceed?" Carey asked.

"We are, your honor. The people call Linda Viana Newcomb."

The short, pleasant-looking woman took the stand and told the court she had been employed by the New York Telephone Company for the past four years, the last twelve months as a business representative. She proudly told of being recently married.

"Mrs. Newcomb, bringing your attention to the evening of January 15, 1989, can you tell us about an emergency call you received at about 7:15 P.M.?"

Shifting her weight in the uncomfortable chair and leaning into the microphone, the former operator began telling the story she had thought so long and so hard about for the past two years.

"I was working the 2 to 10 P.M. shift. That night like every other night, I had a computer terminal screen and keyboard in front of me and I was wearing a headset," she began. "When someone calls the operator, on the computer screen would appear the number the person was calling to and the number where the person was calling from. In an emergency call, if someone had dialed 911, the letters EMER would appear on the screen, alerting us to a possible emergency situation."

McCarty interrupted. "And did you receive an emergency call that night?"

Newcomb nodded. "I had a tone on my headset and I could see on the screen that somebody had dialed the emergency number. I began my usual greeting, 'New York Telephone. Miss Viana. May I help you?', when all of a sudden I could hear someone screaming.

"The person, it was a woman, screamed someone 'is trying to kill me.' I couldn't make out whether the caller said he or she is trying to kill me."

When she paused for a moment, McCarty spurred her on. "What happened next?"

"Well, all of a sudden the phone line went dead, you know, disconnected. I tried to ring her back while also trying to call the Scarsdale police to let them know I had a possible emergency."

"Were you able to reach anyone?"

"No. I didn't get an answer. It just kept ringing. She didn't pick it back up."

Pulling a sheet of paper from one of the numerous stacks positioned on the prosecution table, McCarty walked over and handed it to Newcomb.

"Please take a look at that and tell the jury what it is."

Taking a moment to scan the document, the witness finally looked up. "This is the ticket I made out after the call. A ticket is like the official report made after an operator gets an emergency call. On this one, it gives the date, the time the call came in, where the number was called from, . . . the number of the Scarsdale police that I called."

McCarty sat down, spurring Lewis to begin his cross-examination. No sooner had the defense lawyer stood up, though, then Warmus let out a loud sob, raising her head slightly and grabbed for a pile of Kleenex in the middle of the table.

Lewis stared at his client. After two long blows into the tissue and a couple of dabs to her red and swollen eyes, she settled her head once again on the pillow.

Shaking his head, Lewis brought his attention back to the witness and the point he hoped to imprint on the jury's memory. "Isn't it true that when you first spoke to the authorities about that phone call, that you said the words you heard were 'he is trying to kill me,' isn't that true?"

"I believe I told the police and Mr. Kennedy that I was never sure whether the woman said he or she. I just don't recall. I've tried so hard to remember because I know how important it is, but I just can't say. I'm sorry."

For the next twenty minutes, Lewis pecked away at Newcomb, hoping to persuade her to admit that the woman screaming into the telephone that fateful night had said "he" and not "she." The simple one syllable word *he* would be enough to free his client, but the harder he pushed, the fiercer Newcomb became in her unyielding replies. Finally, unable to cajole, badger, or break her into submitting to his version of the call, Lewis gave up.

"The people now call Detective Robert Whiting," McCarty announced.

The handsome, supremely confident detective marched to his seat, eager to finish his testimony and be on his way, but silently hoping for a chance to cross swords with Lewis. He wasn't impressed by the lawyer and thought his buildup was nothing more than a lot of hype and self-promotion.

"I've been employed by the Greenburgh police for eleven years, the last five as a detective," he said in response to the prosecutor's question.

Asked to describe the night of the murder, Whiting carefully detailed the steps he had taken in searching for evidence, securing the crime scene, and dealing with Solomon.

"Mr. Solomon appeared upset that night, withdrawn. His eyes were glassy. I believe he was crying. I performed a gunshot residue test on Mr. Solomon's hands, and I turned over the kit to Detective Constantino."

Directed to switch his attention to Warmus, Whiting continued. "My partner and I traveled down to the city to locate Miss Warmus. We rang her doorbell and Miss Warmus answered and then allowed us inside. She had on a robe and some kind of nightclothes. We told her we were conducting a homicide investigation involving Betty Jeanne Solomon."

"How did Miss Warmus react to the news about Mrs. Solomon's murder?" McCarty asked.

"She wasn't taken aback by it," he recalled.

Patrick McGowan, the jury foreman, leaned forward in the jury box, apparently anxious to hear more about the defendant's reactions that night.

"We went into her living room and sat down. We started to talk to her about the events of what we had learned from Mr. Solomon. My partner, Detective Bonaiuto, read her her rights," he said, careful to get on the record the legally required Miranda warning.

"She said she had been out with Solomon that night at a Holiday Inn. They had drinks and she was with him until about 11:30 that night," Whiting said, casting a glance in her direction.

"She admitted having an affair with Mr. Solomon," he continued. "She stated she had sex that night with him before leaving. She also discussed a telephone call with Mr. Solomon earlier that day and said she spoke to him for about forty-five minutes."

McCarty spent the next half hour prompting Whiting to tell the jury about the days following the murder, when he and Bonaiuto had spoken to Warmus at the station, and her later refusal to speak after contacting her lawyer.

Given his turn at the witness, Lewis began to drive home his theme that the Greenburgh police had handled the case like a bad episode of the Keystone Cops. Whiting was difficult to crush, but the attorney did score some points.

"Detective Whiting, isn't it true that when you examined Paul Solomon's car outside the murder scene, the one with the battery charger attached to it, that you found a key on the driver's side floor mat?"

Forewarned of this particular attack, Whiting still found himself unable to defend his actions. The lawyer's questions were too carefully crafted to give him much opportunity.

"Yes, Mr. Lewis, we found a key."

"And isn't it true, Detective, that instead of following proper police procedures for processing a crime scene, you picked up that key, thereby smearing any possible fingerprints that may have been on it?"

Whiting nodded, knowing the direction the cross-examination was heading but helpless to do anything about it.

"And isn't it true, Detective Whiting, that you took that key and tried it in the Solomons' front door and found it was a key that unlocked it?"

The jurors followed the verbal tennis match, looking back and forth from one player to the other.

"Yes, Mr. Lewis, the key fit the Solomons' front door lock."

Lewis smiled as he took a moment to glance slowly from one juror to the next, sharing his victory.

He was sure they all grasped the scenario he was attempting to play out. If Paul Solomon had orchestrated his wife's murder by hiring a hit man, what could have been simpler than his leaving for the night and placing a housekey in his car for the killer to use. Once the deed was done, the murderer would only have had to return it to the floor mat where Solomon could later retrieve it.

And what made this scene even more believable was that Solomon had run the cord of the battery charger to his own car, so the killer would have no trouble finding the right car or the right apartment. Stupid, maybe, but effective.

When Lewis was finished with Whiting, the judge called for lunch.

An hour and a half later, with all the players back in place ready to begin, Bonaiuto took his turn in the hot seat.

Also asked to recall the night he and Whiting visited Warmus's home to check her and Solomon's alibi, the detective described what he called the unsettling conversation he'd initially had with the schoolteacher.

"Once we were inside her living room, I again told Miss Warmus that we were investigating a homicide," Bonaiuto testified.

"She said, 'Is Paul all right?' And I told her he was fine. I then asked her if she knew Betty Jeanne Solomon. She said she did. I told her Betty Jeanne Solomon had been killed. When I told her that, her expression didn't change. All she said was, 'Oh, really.' It was shortly after that that I read her her rights."

When, on cross-examination, Lewis tried to introduce a series of police reports in an effort to refute Bonaiuto's and Whiting's testimony that Warmus had been given her Miranda warnings (the detectives' own reports did not indicate that such a warning had been made), Carey sent the jurors back to their by-now-familiar waiting room.

Twenty minutes later, after hearing arguments from both sides, the jurors returned and Carey allowed Lewis to pursue his line of questioning.

Lewis sidled up to the jury box and leaned against it as the sixteen-member panel made their way to their seats. He looked over at his client and noticed she was also standing, as he had asked her to do. No good lawyer would waste an opportunity for his client to show such a simple display of respect for the jury. It was just one of those little things that might sway a juror or two if the decision were close.

When the group sat down and Bonaiuto had returned to the stand, Lewis began to speak, but then stopped abruptly.

Out of the corner of his eye he caught sight of the defense table and watched in horror as Warmus not only remained standing, but kept her head bent down as if in prayer. She then started swaying as if she were a wobbling bowling pin ready to fall.

The defendant's dilemma didn't go unnoticed by her ever-watchful private eyes. Seeing Warmus begin to lean backwards, DiSalvatore jumped from his bench behind her and stood with his arms outstretched, apparently ready to catch her should she tumble over.

Watching the entire scene—and knowing the jurors hadn't missed a moment of it either—Lewis walked over to his client, placed his hand on her back to steady her, and began whispering in her ear. A moment later he gently helped her to her seat.

Unflustered, he then continued his cross-examination of Bonaiuto for the rest of the afternoon, sniping at the wide-eyed cop and forcing him to admit to more than one blunder during the initial stages of the investigation.

Lewis truly thought the Greenburgh police had botched the case, and he wanted the jury to believe that if the police were stupid enough to make basic investigative mistakes, it stood to reason that they had also charged the wrong person with the crime.

"Detective Bonaiuto, isn't it true that when Miss Warmus was brought to the police station the morning after the slaying that you and Assistant District Attorney Kevin Kennedy questioned her and that you tape-recorded the interview session?"

"Yes, we did. That was routine, to question everyone associated with the case as soon as possible."

"And isn't it true, Detective, that during that session you allowed the tape to run out on the tape player, so only part of the interview was recorded?"

Sheepishly, Bonaiuto tried to explain the mishap. "You see, I was taking notes and listening to Miss Warmus, and I really didn't pay attention to the machine and I guess it did run out of tape before we were finished."

"Do you know at what point during the conversation the tape ran out, Detective? Was it in the middle, the end, what?"

The embarrassed cop looked toward McCarty and FitzMorris for help, but there was none to be offered.

"No . . . I . . . I guess I don't. It was later in the interview that I first noticed it had run out, but I can't say exactly where we were in the talk when it happened. If I had to guess, I'd say it was near the end."

"I don't think we need you to guess any more than you have already," Lewis said with derision over the objections of McCarty.

Saving the most ludicrous for last, Lewis took his time thumbing through his notes.

"Now, Detective, when you spoke to Carolyn that day, didn't you ask her if she knew what color of underwear Paul Solomon had been wearing that night? Was that some kind of standard investigative question?"

Bonaiuto thought the question made perfect sense at the time and failed to note the derision in Lewis's voice.

"She had already told us she had oral sex with Paul Solomon earlier that evening, so I figured she must have seen his underwear," he said in a confident voice. "The reason I asked that question was because I wanted to know if he had changed his underpants before we got to his home. You know, like maybe he had gotten some blood on them and changed them so we wouldn't suspect him."

With a theatrical shake of his head, Lewis wrapped up his questioning shortly before 5 P.M., while Warmus remained motionless upon her airline pillow.

The next day, Warmus remained at home while the judge and the lawyers spent their Tuesday in court listening to Bonaiuto's incomplete tape and trying to agree on a transcript the jury could use as a guide while they listened to the static-filled recording. At the end of the day, neither side was completely happy with the effort, but all agreed it was the best they could do.

Bright and early Wednesday morning, Bonaiuto strode into the courtroom sporting a striking blue suit, a freshly starched shirt, and a dapper blue and yellow tie, which he smoothed down as he once again took the stand.

McCarty had promised him he would be through quickly, and the assistant D.A. was true to his word.

When the jurors had all been handed a set of headphones, FitzMorris cued up the January 16, 1989, recording of Warmus at police headquarters, and everyone settled back to hear the conversation.

21

TRY AS HE MIGHT, Constantino couldn't shake the memory of the beating he'd taken from Lewis during the pretrial hearing the summer before.

But that was then, and this was now. Maybe the coaching he had received from Sullivan and the chief would make him a better witness this time.

McCarty had counseled him to just answer the questions as best he could and to ignore Lewis's pointed jabs and innuendos. The detective took a couple of deep breaths.

"I've been employed by the Greenburgh Police Department for eight years, the last three years as a detective," he said in response to a question from McCarty. "Before that I worked for approximately three and a half years as a patrolman for Elmsford."

The prosecutor took his witness through the early morning hours of January 16, 1989, in order to focus the jury's attention once again on the crime scene.

"Did there come a time when someone from the medical examiner's office responded to the scene?"

"Yes. That was Dr. Jeanty. I observed him bag the victim's hands and then I observed the doctor do a physical examination of the body, removing the clothing, examining the wounds, things of that nature. I believe when he was finished I just might have helped lift the body onto the stretcher."

For the next several hours, McCarty took the young detective through the various stages of his investigation. As tedious as some of the testimony was, such as photographing the crime scene, examining Solomon's Toyota, and putting shell casings into evidence bags, the prosecutor knew it was necessary to offset Lewis's attempts at making the police appear to be bumbling idiots.

"Now, with respect to the phone receiver you found on the floor of the Solomons' home. What did you do with that?"

"When I lifted it off the floor I grabbed it from the connection of the cord and the headset itself and slid it into a paper bag. When I got it back to headquarters, I dusted it. I didn't find any fingerprints on the telephone."

McCarty knew that after Newcomb's testimony, the jurors would probably be thinking that Betty Jeanne's fingerprints—and possibly her killer's—might be on that phone. He wanted to make sure they all knew early in the game that none had been found.

Led by his friend, Constantino took the jurors through the days and weeks after the murder. Then, trying to once and for all dispel the myth that the slaying could have been the result of a burglary, McCarty brought Constantino's testimony back to the night of the killing.

"Can you tell us what types of things you saw in the Solomons' home that night?"

The detective paused for a moment, recalling the scene.

"I saw the victim's pocketbook on a table in the hallway and next to the victim's pocketbook I saw a video camera, and within the living room I observed $300 in cash on the table."

McCarty reached into an evidence box on his desk and pulled out an old-fashioned black rotary phone, and passed it to the witness.

"That was the telephone that was in the den of the Solomon house," Constantino said, turning the device over in his hands.

McCarty then pulled out an old gym bag and handed it over.

"This is a vinyl bag which has the New York Mets logo on it, which was found in the apartment, right by the head of Betty Jeanne Solomon."

Asking Constantino to recall the events of January 19, 1989, McCarty steered his questions to the search for fingerprints in the Solomon home.

"I dusted the walls in the living room, the dining room, and the hallway leading toward the living room and found nothing. I also dusted the stereo glass, which covered the stereo unit, and I recovered latent fingerprints from there. We also lifted a print from under the lock on the front door."

"Did you recover any other prints?" McCarty asked.

"I recovered, well, smudges. I took from the scene the stereo glass and a feather I found in the hallway and a piece of wood chip."

"Is it fair to say you have no idea what the source of this feather is, Detective?"

"That's true."

A short time later, McCarty pulled from the side of his table a large diagram depicting the floor plan of the Solomon home on the night of the slaying, including furniture, the body of Betty Jeanne, and markings to indicate where police and De Forest found shell casings and bullet fragments.

Lewis interrupted and received permission to ask the witness a few questions of his own, took the moment to drive home once again the problems of police screw-ups.

"Detective, this diagram is made from measurements you and Dr. De Forest took, is that correct?"

"Yes, sir."

"Now, what was wrong with the way you took measurements at the crime scene?"

McCarty objected, saying the diagram he was offering showed no specific measurements.

Carey shot down the objection, as McCarty had begun to expect.

Forced to answer, Constantino gave Lewis a withering look. "There was inconsistencies between my measurements and Dr. De Forest's. All the measurements had to be made from a fixed point. I used the sofa and Dr. De Forest used a wall."

"Isn't it fair to say, Detective, that a sofa could be moved or pushed about and thus not really be a fixed point, thereby throwing off all your measurements?"

Constantino wasn't ready to concede anything. "I still don't feel there was anything wrong with the way I took those measurements."

After several more questions, Lewis objected to the diagram being shown to the jury, but Carey overruled him, a small prosecution victory.

Pulling out a set of gruesome police photographs of the bloodied body as it lay in the cluttered living room, McCarty received Carey's permission to show them to the jury.

As the jurors wrinkled up their faces in reaction to the pictures, Mc-Carty knew he had made the right decision. He didn't want them to lose sight of why they were all there. A woman had been murdered and the scene was stomach-turning. He didn't want them to forget it.

After several of the photographs had been passed around, the lawyers met with Carey at side-bar for a few moments.

When they finished, the judge addressed the jury.

"Ladies and gentlemen, it's getting late, past 4:30, and it's a dangerous and foggy afternoon. It's getting dark and we're going to adjourn at this time so you could get a little bit on your way home with some daylight left."

Having been reminded once again not to read anything about the case in the papers or to watch it on TV, the jurors filed out of the room.

The following day, Constantino was back on the stand, taking the jurors through the police investigation, their conversations with Warmus, and how the detectives had finally begun to unravel the mystery surrounding the murder.

By late morning, McCarty had finished with his witness. Now the detective would have to lock horns with Lewis.

Once again, the silver-tongued attorney wasted no time in attacking his prey. His job was to create reasonable doubt, and the questions he asked Constantino during his two days of cross-examination accomplished their purpose.

"Detective, didn't you find a broken door leading onto the Solomons' balcony, a door that anyone could have entered?"

"We found that the door handle of the screen door which was in front of the sliding glass doors in the living room was off, but when we checked the holes made by the screws used in the door handle, we found them rusty, telling us that the door had been that way for quite a while."

On his favorite topic, police inadequacies, Lewis pried from his unwilling witness an admission that Paul and Kristan Solomon, along with their friends, had been allowed into the sealed crime scene to get clothes for the funeral, even though the place was still being processed for evidence.

Grabbing his hair as if in utter frustration and using a tone of voice one would normally save for addressing a mischievous, naughty child, Lewis displayed his incredulity at the detective's stupidity.

"Did it ever occur to you that maybe one of them might tamper with or remove some evidence from the crime scene?" he asked, clearly hoping the jurors would be astute enough to pick up on the suspicion he was attempting to cast on Paul Solomon.

"Well, sir, we were watching them very closely."

Two women jurors seated in the second row shared a look at the less-than-convincing answer.

Lewis moved on to other fertile areas.

"When you obtained fingerprints from Paul and Kristan Solomon, their friends, Vinnie Parco, James Russo, and just about anyone else you could think of in an effort to eliminate them as suspects, why was it that you never thought to ask for Carolyn Warmus's fingerprints until after she was arrested, more than a year after the murder? Can you tell us that, Detective?"

Constantino wiped his forehead, a nervous habit both Singer and Sullivan had warned him to avoid. Apparently remembering their advice a little too late, he quickly clasped his hands together in front of him. "Well, we probably should have taken hers sooner," was all he could muster, playing right into Lewis's hands but unable to avoid it.

For the next hour, the defense lawyer expertly directed Constantino toward the answers he wanted the jury to hear, including a damning explanation of why some things were dusted for prints and others were not.

"That's just the way we do things," the detective finally shot back after a long and pointed string of questions.

Lewis raised his eyebrows and walked over to the defense table, where he grabbed a photograph, which he then handed to a court officer to give to Constantino.

"Do you recognize that photograph?" he asked innocently.

"Yes. It's a photo I took of the victim at the crime scene on the night of the murder."

"Look closely, Detective. Do you see a black glove near the victim's left hand?"

Constantino must have seen the punch coming, but there was no way to duck.

"Yes, sir. That glove was found at the scene and we had a forensic expert test it for blood, but it turned out negative."

Lewis paused, listening in amusement as the detective tried to put the best possible spin on the situation he was about to bring up.

"Detective, where is that glove now?"

"I don't know, Mr. Lewis," he responded. "After it was field tested, it was put aside, and I don't believe anyone retrieved it. I don't know where it is now. At the time I remember thinking that it probably belonged to Betty Jeanne Solomon or her daughter."

Lewis's face became a mask of disbelief. He slapped his forehead and grabbed his sparse hair for additional effect. His theatrics alone caused ripples of laughter throughout the room. The lawyer's next words dripped with sarcasm.

"Do you mean to tell me, Detective, that no police officer investigating that crime scene thought to secure what could have been a crucial piece of evidence? A glove that had been found underneath the victim's body wasn't important enough to seize as potential evidence?"

Like any good lawyer, Lewis knew the answer to the question before Constantino responded. He had learned by reviewing the prosecution's records before trial that the black glove, whatever its evidentiary value, had disappeared. No one had thought to slip it into a plastic evidence bag for safekeeping. That mistake was now just another hammer he could use to bludgeon home his claim that the Greenburgh Police Department had been sloppy and unprofessional in carrying out their investigation.

"All I can tell you, Mr. Lewis, is that apparently no one secured the glove as evidence," Constantino quietly replied.

McCarty put his hands over his face and rubbed his eyes. He didn't even want to look at the jury's reaction.

At the end of the day, Lewis decided to leave the jurors thinking about how desperate the police had become to hang this murder on someone, anyone.

"Can you tell us, Detective Constantino, about a phone call Lieutenant Sullivan asked you to make in an effort to locate a psychic to help you with your case?"

"That was on June 7, 1989," he responded resignedly. "Lieutenant Sullivan asked me to call the New York City police and inquire about their use of psychics to help them solve cases. I spoke with a Detective Ray Pierce about the use of psychics, but it never really went past that. We did not use a psychic in this case."

The titterings from the jury box must have been music to Lewis's ears as he concluded for the day.

When the trial resumed five days later, Constantino was forced to pick up where he'd left off.

This time the defense lawyer wanted to know why Constantino and Lind had failed to continue searching George Peters's workplace after they found the bullet-riddled board on the floor of the welding shop on November 28, 1989.

"That was Sergeant Lind's decision to leave there that night," Constantino said, tired of the verbal beating he was taking. "If you want to know why we agreed to Peters's request that we come back another day, you'll just have to ask him."

Lewis was at his best when his adversary showed anger. "But didn't you tell us you were the lead detective on this case?" he said. "Couldn't you have told Lind to continue searching?"

"I believe Sergeant Lind had somewhere else to go that night. I don't remember where. We didn't feel we were in danger of losing any evidence. We had just found the board."

Lewis moved in for the coup de grace.

"Let me get this straight. A man who admits making a silencer that you believe was used in a homicide, a felony offense, asks you for a favor —that you and your partner come back another day to look for evidence because he's worried his bosses may find out what he's done and you two agree to it. Is that about right, Detective?"

"That about sums it up," the tired witness hurled back.

"Did the thought ever cross your mind that Peters may try to hide evidence, or maybe even plant some new evidence before you returned?"

"No. Mr. Peters was being cooperative."

The semistifled chortle from Lewis was lost on no one as he scooped up his paperwork and plopped back down at the defense table, ending Constantino's misery.

McCarty called Dr. Darly Jeanty to the stand.

"I was an associate medical examiner for Westchester County for twelve years," Jeanty said, with a deep Haitian accent. "Now I'm medical director at the Greenhaven Correctional Facility."

"Doctor, can you tell us about the night you were called to the Scarsdale Ridge Apartments on January 15, 1989?"

"Most certainly," he replied. "I arrived there at about 2 A.M. and examined the body of Betty Jeanne Solomon. I found that there was caked blood on her left cheek and that her body was rigid. There was lividity, which is the blood settling in the lowest portion of a person's body once they are dead. I also checked the thermostat and found the room temperature was 75 degrees."

"Were you able to draw any conclusions from your findings, Doctor?"

The tall physician nodded and turned to the jury as an experienced witness was trained to do.

"Yes, I was able to surmise that Betty Jeanne Solomon had been killed within an hour or two either side of 7 P.M. based on the rigidity of the body, the lividity, and the body temperature."

McCarty turned his witness over to Lewis.

"Dr. Jeanty, were you able to tell the police how many times the victim was shot?" Lewis asked.

"I told them that it was my belief that she had been shot eight or nine times, but that a full autopsy would have to be performed to be sure."

Looking through his file on Jeanty, Lewis read his handwritten notes regarding the doctor's initial findings.

"Isn't it true that you set a preliminary time of death estimate of between 3 and 5 P.M.?"

Jeanty cleared his throat. "That was very preliminary, before any lab testing had been done. I always stress that a complete autopsy must be conducted for a more accurate estimate as to the time of death."

After a few questions, Lewis thanked the witness. "Nothing further, your honor."

Dr. Louis Roh, the deputy county medical examiner, took the stand next and spent the first part of his testimony corroborating the statements of his former colleague. He then added some new, interesting details about the gunshots for the jurors.

Roh watched as FitzMorris set up a chart depicting the front and back views of a person and indicating the location of Betty Jeanne Solomon's wounds. Pointing to a cluster of bullet wounds on the rear-view diagram, he explained their significance.

"These three shots in the back of the victim are in close proximity and were made when the victim was not moving," he said, letting the meaning of his words sink in before he continued.

Bringing the jurors' attention to two head wounds also identified on the rear-view chart, Roh described them in detail.

"These are not gunshot wounds. They were made as a result of blunt trauma. What I mean by that is that someone struck the victim from behind with something, here behind the left ear and again on the left side of the back of the head. Neither wound was sufficient to cause death. There was also an abrasion on the left shoulder."

Roh went on to describe the other gunshot wounds, using layman's terms the jury could understand.

"Take for example this gunshot wound to the leg," he said. "This was made while the victim was lying on the ground. You can see that the bullet entered and traveled up the leg. In my opinion, the only way this could have happened was if the victim was already on the ground when this shot struck her."

McCarty asked the question that must have been going through the mind of each and every juror. "Doctor, what was the actual cause of Betty Jeanne Solomon's death?"

His answer was short and frightening. "The victim's heart, lungs, and liver were perforated."

Moving on, McCarty produced four plastic evidence bags containing small metal objects. "Can you identify these, please?" he asked, handing them to his witness.

"Yes, these are the three complete bullets and one bullet fragment that I removed from the victim's body during the autopsy."

After Carey approved his request to allow the jurors to look at the ballistic evidence, McCarty passed out the plastic bags and took his seat. His mind was already on Paul Solomon, the witness he planned to call the following day.

McCarty wasted no time in trying to lead Solomon to paint a picture of Carolyn Warmus as an obsessed nymphomaniac who just wouldn't let her lover end the affair.

"Mr. Solomon, after the death of your wife, did you speak to the defendant, Carolyn Warmus, about seeing each other?"

"I'm sure we probably did," he answered in a quiet, nervous voice. "I mean, in our phone conversations she might have mentioned 'when can we see each other?' She would ask me how Kristan and I were doing. She would, in the beginning, tell me about how terrible it had been for her at school. She didn't understand why I hadn't called her. She was somewhat broken up on the phone, hysterical. I guess this was probably several weeks after Betty Jeanne died and I tried to explain to her what a difficult time we were having."

He paused, as if remembering the emotional period. "I told her that at that point I hadn't even given that much thought to her and that Kristan and I were just kind of going through each day. I remember the first phone conversation she ended up saying 'thank you' and 'I understand now.' "

McCarty led the questioning to the items he intended to introduce as evidence.

"Did she begin to leave notes or letters for you?"

Solomon nodded as the jurors watched his every move. "There came a point when I said to her, 'Look, we can't talk on the phone, it's proving too difficult for me.' I was at that time trying to get Kristan and myself going forward, trying to get through each day, trying to deal with the police. I said to her, 'Really, we can't talk, it's too difficult for me to talk to you.' Then she asked me, 'Well, can I drop you notes off, can I drop a note to you or can I ask other people how you're doing?' I said fine. And so she started to drop some notes off to me at school. I think she used to go to my school very early and I would get to school and I would find a note in my mailbox or she would send me several notes at home."

McCarty pulled from a folder a Hallmark card and showed it to his witness, who read the words to himself before answering.

"This is a card Carolyn sent me. The sentiment on the card is talking about my sorrow and how she would try to take the pain away from me if she possibly could and how sorry she was she can't shelter me. And it says that she's here if I want to talk to her."

For the next twenty minutes, McCarty showed Solomon a series of cards, notes, and letters all written by Warmus, which, Solomon told the jury, were sent between the night his wife was slain and the following August. The prosecutor asked him to give a synopsis of each one, obviously trying to convince the panel that the correspondence was evidence of Warmus's obsession with her then-lover.

A short time later, several of the reporters sent Judge Carey a handwritten note asking that Warmus's personal letters be released publicly, since they had been entered into evidence.

The judge told the lawyers of the request and called a side-bar conference to discuss the matter. Several minutes later, Carey announced to the reporters that after that day's proceedings, he would remain in the courtroom and read aloud the letters. He would not, however, release copies of them at that time.

Warmus sat seething at the defense table and finally jumped out of her seat, striding past DiSalvatore and hollering, "Don't you follow me!" as he began to rise from his seat.

Fifteen minutes later, her face still twisted in an angry scowl, Warmus returned to her seat and loudly began to berate Lewis, shaking her finger at him while McCarty continued his questioning.

"Now, Mr. Solomon, from the time of your wife's wake until late May 1989, did you see the defendant?"

"No," he replied. "I spoke to her those times on the phone that I mentioned and then just these notes and cards. I never sent her any letters either."

"Did there come a time after June 1989 that you did, indeed, see Miss Warmus?"

Looking as if he had just swallowed a very sour piece of grapefruit, Solomon took a drink of water from the paper cup in front of him before answering, "Yes, I did. As I remember the evening it was some-time in early July or within the first couple weeks of July and I was playing in a basketball league in Manhattan. I was going down for a game one night and Kristan and a friend of hers were supposed to go with me, the idea being that we would go down, I would play the game, they'd watch, and then we would go out and get something to eat. At the last second my daughter decided that maybe she and her friend would go to the movies instead. I guess they decided it wasn't worth watching a bunch of old men play basketball." He smiled.

The attempt at self-deprecating humor didn't elicit a smile from the jurors and, noticing their stony faces, Solomon once again averted his eyes and dropped his voice. "So I went down and I played the game," he went on. "At that point I had known that I would eventually have to see Carolyn and speak to her and deal with some of the things that I was trying to deal with. The fact is that I had cared for her a great deal.

"I guess in my own mind I was convinced the police knew finally that I hadn't had anything to do with the murder and I had to deal with Carolyn because she had meant a great deal to me, and I decided since I was close to where she lived, to stop and see her.

"So I went over by her apartment and I walked into the bar next door and I called her, but there was no answer," he continued, encouraged on by McCarty's nods.

"So I sat down and I had a few drinks and it was around nine o'clock at night. The place was pretty empty. Then I called her again and there was no answer. By that time I had to go to work the next day, so I got up to leave and figured I would ring her bell. She has one of those bells to be buzzed up and so on, so I rang the bell and there was no answer. So I turned to walk out and Carolyn was walking in.

"She was somewhat shocked to see me because we hadn't really seen each other since the wake. I think she was in sweats and she had appar-ently been up to Westchester taking a golf lesson."

Describing how he turned down an offer to go up to her apartment, Solomon said he went back to the bar while Warmus went up to change and later joined him. After several drinks, he said, he gathered enough courage to spit out the one question he knew he had to ask.

"At some point I said to her, 'Carolyn, I have to ask you this question, did you have anything to do with Betty Jeanne's death?' And she said to me, 'I'm so glad you feel comfortable enough to ask me that question. No, I didn't. I never would do anything to hurt you or Kristan.' "

Solomon stopped to rub his eyes.

"We continued to talk and I mentioned that it had been so difficult and how terrible it was and how guilty I felt about the fact that I had been with her that night that Betty Jeanne had died. I always felt if I had been home I could have stopped what had happened."

Testifying that he then went back to Warmus's apartment where they shared a "very passionate kiss," Solomon recalled telling her that they could never see each other again and that the thought had upset them both.

But a few days later, he added, "Carolyn placed a note on my front door asking me to meet her at a golf driving range. I called her and said, 'Carolyn, we can't see each other. I can't deal with that at this point.' She was upset. She told me, 'But, Paul, we're friends and you have to go on with your life. You can't let things that have happened hold you back and stop you and Kristan from living.' "

Warmus not only ignored his request to stop calling and sending him notes, Solomon said, but she also tried to resume a relationship with Kristan as well.

"Kristan's birthday is August 5," he explained. "Sometime late that July, Carolyn had dropped off some presents for both me and Kristan at our front door. She gave Kristan a very expensive pair of diamond earrings and me a copy of a Jack Nicklaus *Golf My Way* tape and a sweater she had made."

McCarty then received permission to show the jurors the numerous cards, notes, and letters the persistent defendant had showered on the man who was trying to dump her.

Finished with their reading, the jurors handed the paperwork back to McCarty and, moments later, were excused for lunch.

With a stern voice, Carey halted Warmus as she also prepared to leave.

"All right, Miss Warmus. I don't know if I ever said this to you, but a defendant, first of all, has a right to be present at all stages of the trial. Not only that, the defendant has an obligation to be present at all stages of the trial. This means you may not leave the room without permission. There are obviously occasions when you will have to leave the room, of course. But you should not just take it upon yourself to leave whenever you feel like it. You should ask Mr. Lewis to call it to my attention."

Warmus sat shaking, her voice filled with contempt. She didn't like being talked down to, not even by a judge. "What if you're at side-bar, do I come up and interrupt you?" she asked with disdain.

Lewis shot her a warning look, while Carey glowered.

"If at any time that you absent yourself willfully, deliberately, that would not prevent us from continuing, because your right to be present at all stages of the trial is a right which can be waived or it can be forfeited. And if sometime you are not here and there's no reason for your absence and it has not been excused, first of all, I would issue what is called a 'bench warrant,' whereby you would be arrested and taken into custody and brought here."

The judge searched Warmus's face to see if his message was getting through. With her next words, Carey must have known it was not.

"If I deliberately stay away willfully, do I have to—" Warmus stopped suddenly as Lewis grabbed her arm and whispered for her to shut up. After several moments of conversation, Lewis glanced at the judge, signaling him to continue.

"Furthermore, Miss Warmus, if I have any apprehension about your not being here, I will greatly increase the amount of your bail, which would probably mean that you would be taken into custody until such time as the increased bail was established."

Warmus's face was red, but she held her tongue.

When the trial resumed at 2 P.M., McCarty began to take Solomon through his first introduction to Barbara Ballor, and their trials and tribulations while on the infamous Puerto Rico vacation.

"Mr. Solomon, as of August 17, 1989, when was the last time you had seen the defendant Carolyn Warmus?"

"The time when I was in the city, in July 1989."

"Did you ever discuss with her that you were going to Puerto Rico on that evening?"

Solomon looked over at Warmus. "No, not at all."

"Did you ever in any way, shape, or form invite her down to meet you at the Condado Plaza?"

"No," he responded with emphasis.

For the next two hours, McCarty pulled from his witness the frightening episode orchestrated by Warmus in the Caribbean: the envelope from Thomas Alvarez containing Warmus's room key; the note under the hotel door telling Solomon to expect a call from the United States; Warmus's numerous calls to Condado Hotel Security Chief Ali Baez; the call from Tammy Rogers; the late-night escape from the island guarded by Puerto Rican police and the puzzling message from Warmus he found on his answering machine when he and Barbara returned home, asking why he had invited her down there and then left when she arrived.

Despite vigorous opposition from Lewis, Carey allowed the jurors to hear that message.

After the jurors had finished listening to the tape on their bulky headsets, McCarty concluded his questioning of Solomon, and Carey called for a ten-minute break.

Once back in session, Lewis sidled up to the lectern and eyed his new adversary. His job would be to break down the quiet, victimized facade of the witness and show the jury it was he, not Warmus, who had kept their relationship alive.

Solomon would also have to be shown as a man who "thought and acted with his penis" and for whom Carolyn was just one of many women to satisfy his sexual needs.

Lewis took his time pulling out his paperwork, playing the game of making the witness believe he had reams and reams of information about him. In this case it was true. The cross-examination of Paul Solomon would be lengthy, but by the time it was over, no one would feel an ounce of sympathy for him and the jury might even believe he was quite capable of killing, or paying someone else to kill, his wife.

Lewis's first order of business was to try and show that Carolyn wasn't obsessed with Solomon, that it was he who kept stringing her along, and that her only fault was in loving him. The lawyer dove in quickly.

"In February 1988 you went to Club Med in the Turks, right?"

Solomon nodded. "That's correct."

"From the Turks in Club Med you sat down at a desk and wrote a postcard to Carolyn, signed by you in the fashion, 'love, me,' right?"

"Could be, yes. I sent her two or three cards that I remember, yes."

From his voluminous files, Lewis pulled out a card Solomon had sent to Warmus in December 1988.

"In this note to Carolyn you tell her that you each bring a certain amount of baggage to your relationship. Tell us what is the baggage you brought to that relationship?"

Solomon tried to be careful in his answer. "I was talking about the kind of people that we both were, the fact that family baggage, the fact that I was married, the fact that she . . ."

"So part of your baggage, sir, was your wife?" Lewis asked, jumping the gun in his effort to get his point across.

"May I finish?" Solomon asked with annoyance.

Carey told him to proceed.

"I was referring [to the fact] that she had spoken about her relation-ship with her father to me, and I also had spoken to her about my relationship with my parents and so on, that we used to talk about what we were and [how] what we had become was a result of the way we had been brought up, and baggage refers to all those things."

Lewis stubbornly pressed his point. "One of the pieces of baggage was your wife and that's what you were telling her in December of that year, right?"

"I think I was telling her that our lives, my life, was what it was," Solomon replied, keeping his voice soft and nonaggressive.

Reading out loud the words Solomon had penned to Warmus during the initial stages of their affair, Lewis made sure the jury would have no doubt about his motives:

"If you're really smart you'll do one of two things, turn away and never see me again and save yourself pain and hurt, or keep on loving me and take the risk of you and I having something together forever. It's a big risk for both you and me."

Looking embarrassed, Solomon knew he had no choice but to re-spond. "We had had a discussion regarding her seeing me or not seeing me and she had been upset because I would not . . . she didn't seem to understand why I could or would not attend a Christmas party with her at her father's home in Michigan, and I felt very bad about that and I gave her this note just before she left. I wanted to make her feel better."

Lewis saw an opening. "How is it that you were making her feel better with this card, by telling her the truth? By those being your real sentiments or were they false?"

"What I'm trying to tell you is I certainly cared for her, and you're asking me to now go back to that point and tell you exactly what I meant by these words. And I'm telling you I cared for her and that there's no question about that."

The next hour showcased Lewis's ability to keep Solomon on the defensive, repeatedly asking him the meaning of the word *love*, the difference between his feelings for Warmus and those he had for his wife, and making him talk about the lies he had told to Betty Jeanne so he could run to the arms of his lover.

"Mr. Solomon, there came a time when you would talk to your wife about you going out and you knew you were going out to meet Carolyn, right?"

"Correct."

"You wouldn't tell her you were going out to meet Carolyn, because you didn't want her to know you were having another relationship, right?"

"Correct," Solomon said, staring back into the eyes of his inquisitor.

"When you faced her and you talked to her and you knew you were going to lie to her, you would look her in the eye and just do it, right?"

Solomon said nothing.

Lewis pursued his quarry. Just one emotional outburst would be enough to show the man's propensity for violence. "Right? Isn't that right?"

In a slow, measured voice, Solomon replied, "Yes, there were times I did."

"And this was someone you loved, right? Someone that you took an oath, a vow to respect, to cherish, right?"

"Yes, when we were married, we did."

Lewis moved in for the kill. "Now, is Carolyn Warmus the first affair you ever had?"

Solomon unwisely tried to stall for time. "Could you define the word affair please?"

Noting the look of sheer disgust on Lewis's face, Solomon added, "I'm being very serious. I'm not being . . . are you referring to sexual relations with another woman?"

Lewis was having none of this game. "You know what adultery is?"

"If you're asking me if adultery is having sexual relations with some-one out of your marriage, then yes, I do know what it means."

"Now will you answer the question?"

Caught in a trap of his own devising, Solomon had no way out. "During my marriage, the nineteen years I was married, I have known a couple other people, yes."

Looking at the jury, who were seeing a man making a pathetic at-tempt at trying to avoid the truth, Lewis turned his steely gaze back on Solomon. "And you use the word *know* in the biblical sense, is that what you're doing?"

"Okay, yes," the witness answered.

"You're having trouble admitting to this, is that the problem?" Lewis shot back, completely in control.

Solomon wrung his hands and responded quickly, "If you're saying is it difficult to stand up here and bare your entire private existence, yes, it is."

As the afternoon wore on, Solomon was forced to admit that from the day he first met Warmus in September 1987 until spring 1988, he'd had "sexual relations" with her approximately ten to fifteen times; that he told Warmus he had no intention of divorcing his wife and would do nothing to jeopardize his relationship with Kristan.

Lewis then began peppering him with various questions designed to make him appear a prowling, lascivious Lothario, a picture that Lewis wanted each juror to take home that night and remember throughout the trial.

"Isn't it true, sir, that you told Carolyn that you were unhappy in your marriage?"

"I told her we had problems, yes," came the answer. "I told her my marriage was not perfect by any stretch of the imagination."

Bringing Solomon's attention to the night of January 15, 1989, while he and Carolyn were tucked snugly inside her small car, Lewis asked, "Even though you felt so guilty about having sex with Carolyn, you found yourself back in the same position that night, right?"

"Uh-hum," he said, looking at the big wall clock in the back of the courtroom. But Lewis wasn't finished.

"In fact, she asked you for permission to perform oral sex on you?"

"Correct."

"Even though you had felt so terribly guilty all the other times, right?"

Solomon nodded. "It's very hard to resist Carolyn."

Lewis scrunched up his face, as if thinking about this response. "One of the ways to resist Carolyn is to stop her from asking your permission to have sex?" he reasoned.

"Actually," Solomon responded, "one of the ways to resist would have been simply not to see her ever."

Lewis pounced on the answer. "But that's not what you did, is it? You saw her, didn't you?"

"Right."

"And when she asked you for your permission that night for oral sex, you gave it to her, right?"

"Uh-hum."

"And you say it's hard to resist her?"

Solomon stopped for a moment to collect his rattled thoughts. "I said it's very hard to resist her, and I stopped her after she started. I was caught up in the moment and I felt guilty."

Bringing Solomon's attention to the night in July 1989 when he surprised Warmus with a visit, Lewis queried, "Isn't it true that after you spent time in the comedy club that you went back to Carolyn's apartment and the two of you had sex?"

Solomon first denied it, then, under relentless questioning from Lewis, changed his response. "I don't recall," he said. "I guess I just don't remember."

Changing tacks again, Lewis directed Solomon's attention to the phone call he'd had with Warmus the afternoon of the murder. "Mr. Solomon, can you tell us whether or not you told Carolyn that Kristan was on a ski trip?"

"I think I may have, but I'm not positive."

"Now additionally, you don't know whether or not you told Carolyn that Betty Jeanne was going to be home alone that night, do you?"

"That was not something that I would have said," he answered determinedly.

At that point, Carey gave Solomon a temporary respite by calling it a day.

During the next five days of trial, Solomon took an emotional beating from Lewis that at times drove him from angry rebellion to resigned ambivalence. With all his secrets being brought forth and his entire life put on display, Solomon could do little but sit in the cushioned witness chair and battle back with what little fight he could do.

Asked why he had allowed his beloved daughter to go on a February 1988 ski trip with his mistress while he traveled to a Caribbean Club Med with a male friend, his response seemed halfhearted. "I felt it would be good for Kristan to go skiing," was the best he could do.

On another occasion, Lewis's pointed questions forced him to admit having "eight to ten sexual encounters with three different women" during the time he was married to Betty Jeanne.

Confronted with the names of women with whom he still worked, Solomon reared back in an angry display of gallantry, shouting at his tormentor, "Is everybody I've ever been a friend with now going to be attacked?"

Lewis seemed to enjoy the fencing match and never failed to go for the jugular, often alluding to Solomon's inability to complete the sex act with his female partners and his repeated lies to his wife, and questioning his relationship with an allegedly homosexual pal.

Warmus watched her former lover carefully during the grueling days of his testimony, often scribbling down notes and passing them to her sometimes annoyed lawyer. She appeared to revel in Solomon's words when he said how much he had cared for her, but would often smile as Lewis ripped into him when the testimony turned to his other girl friends.

Lewis also took Solomon to task for receiving immunity in exchange for testifying before the grand jury that had indicted his client. With carefully crafted questions—and the anticipated answers—Lewis tried to convince the jurors that Solomon had gone looking for immunity to protect him from ever being prosecuted for the murder of his wife. The jury could not have known from the attorney's questions that New York State law gives automatic immunity to any person testifying in such a proceeding.

"You knew that by testifying you would get immunity, right?" Lewis asked.

"Yes, that's what I was told."

"And you would get immunity from being prosecuted as the killer of your wife, right?"

Angered, Solomon shot back, "You mean prosecuted for the crime that was committed, yes."

"That's what you wanted immunity from, right?" Lewis pushed.

With a look of frustration, Solomon answered, "It's hard to want something for something you have not done. If what you're asking me is if I was told I would get immunity by testifying, yes, I was told that and I accepted that."

"You know that you could have waived immunity, right? You could have signed a document and said I don't need immunity. Right?"

"Correct."

"But you didn't do that?"

"No, I did not."

Lewis repeatedly tried to get Solomon to admit to knowing Vinnie Parco, a connection that, if proved, would set the stage for him to try and show a conspiracy between the two men to kill Betty Jeanne and use Carolyn as the naive fall guy. But time after time Solomon steadfastly denied ever meeting the man, finally frustrating even the unflappable Lewis.

"The only time I even heard the man's name was when Carolyn

mentioned him to me, that he was some kind of private eye that she had hired for something," Solomon explained. "I understood he was some Queens kind of guy. That's all I know about him."

Switching tactics, Lewis began to bring out testimony about the television movie deal that Solomon had signed for a six-figure contract. The lawyer knew that any self-respecting juror would be hard pressed to have any sympathy for a man who was trying to make a buck off the recent murder of his own wife.

"You have a deal with Citadel Productions and HBO, right?"

"I believe so, yes," Solomon responded.

"You know that your deal gets you as an initial option for your story $15,000 for the first year. Then you get $10,000 as part of the option. You also get a purchase price, $100,000, if the movie is made and another $30,000 as a consulting fee, right?"

Solomon looked stunned. "I'm kind of interested in hearing this because I don't know the figures," he said.

It was Lewis's turn to look surprised. "You signed the contract?"

"I know I signed the contract."

"You don't know the name of the movie?"

"I have no idea."

Lewis stepped back from the lectern. "You don't know it's called *The Paul Solomon Story?* You don't know that?"

"No."

Solomon went on to explain that his lawyer and friend, Gary Pillersdorf, had actually negotiated the contract and that, while he had signed it, he had never read it.

"The money was to be put in an escrow account for Kristan for college," Solomon added, ignoring Lewis's looks of disbelief. "Money was not a thought at the time. Gary told me he would get an agreement that would keep my name out of it, Kristan's name out of it, and the Edgemont School District's name out of it, and it would be some kind of fictional account.

"At that point I said to Gary, 'Is there any chance that the movie won't be made?', and he said there's always that chance. My great hope was that it wouldn't be made."

Lewis struck another theatrical pose, his face and body language telling the jury how unbelievable he found this response. "Let me get this straight now, Mr. Solomon," he said. "You signed a movie contract for money to not make a movie. Is that what you're telling us?"

Solomon's answer was lost in a roar of laughter from the spectators.

No matter what topic he hit upon, Lewis would always return to one particular line of questioning. Repeatedly asking Solomon about the many lies he'd told his wife in order to sneak off to the arms of his lover, forcing him to admit again and again to his affair, Lewis would usually elicit a sigh from the tired and embarrassed teacher and then his admission of guilt.

But on a few occasions, Solomon would bristle and fight back. After a particularly rough series of questions focusing on infidelity, Solomon snapped at the lawyer, "We've been over that. Why don't I just put a scarlet letter over my chest."

In another heated exchange during which Lewis once again asked Solomon about lying to his friends about his affair with Carolyn Warmus, the frazzled witness barked, "Yes, Mr. Lewis. I had an affair and I lied to them. For the eight-thousandth time!"

When not focusing on Solomon's adulterous relationships, Lewis hammered away at the incompetence of the Greenburgh police.

"Mr. Solomon, do you recall seeing a black glove in your home on the night you found your wife?"

"I found it either . . . it was under Betty Jeanne, I think it was under her when I found it. When I turned Betty Jeanne over I think the glove was there."

"And it's fair to say from the very beginning you knew that the glove did not belong there?"

"Correct," Solomon replied.

McCarty sat back in his chair. The glove issue was a red herring Lewis would be bound to raise. The funny thing was, that looking closely at the crime scene photographs, it appeared to be a long, black woman's glove, not a man's. But without having it to produce as evidence, the prosecution couldn't even suggest that to the jury.

Concluding his cross-examination, Lewis asked Solomon why he had come home so late the night of his wife's slaying. He didn't wait for the widower's response. He provided his own answer. "You didn't get home early because you knew your wife was dead."

Solomon recoiled in horror at the words, his anger finally bursting forth. Visibly seething, he yelled, "For you to sit there and make that statement is so obscene and so horrible. The fact that someone could manipulate facts or words or half-truths or incomplete reports . . . and to throw up this obscure vision of something is so obscene and just so disgusting.

"I'll accept my guilt for this affair," he continued to shout. "But for you to sit there and make that comment and throw that kind of light on me, I only hope to God that when I'm punished and judged, you're punished and judged for what you've done here."

Lewis returned an icy stare. "You know, sir, there is no court of law that will punish or judge you because you made an agreement through immunity."

Solomon rose from his seat, continuing to scream. "The fact that someone was able, and I won't say the name [as he looked and pointed at Warmus] because I don't think that would be in keeping with decorum, the fact that someone went in and shot my wife nine times . . . is obscene."

On February 21, six days after he began, Lewis hurled his last barbed spears at Solomon and allowed the hate-filled, broken-looking man off the stand.

Without a word, the victim's husband stepped down, gathered whatever dignity he had left, and walked out of the courtroom, his rumpled, navy suit hanging from his stooped shoulders.

22

ELIZABETH LANG seemed a little surprised and disappointed when the judge thanked her for her testimony and asked her to step down. The manager of the Manhattan office of the ROLM Company, a telecommunications firm, had thought she would be asked more questions and had found the experience of speaking before a room full of people hanging on her every word very exciting.

The prosecution witness didn't fully understand how her tiny bit of information about Carolyn Warmus was important to the murder case, but she had readily agreed to come to court when Mr. McCarty asked her.

Her testimony was just one part of the giant jigsaw puzzle McCarty and FitzMorris were trying to piece together for the jury.

"Carolyn was a temporary summer employee in 1988 who handled clerical chores, including answering the telephones and filing papers," Lang said. "There was a group of us who worked together pretty closely and that included myself, Carolyn, Denise Bodner, and Liisa Kattai."

Lewis looked up from his paperwork at the mention of Kattai's name. The main reason Lang had been called to the stand was to show how closely Carolyn worked with Liisa, whose stolen driver's license would soon become a focal point in the case.

"Carolyn and Liisa had their desks right next to each other," Lang testified. "It was a pretty small office."

Asked to recall whether Warmus had ever discussed her personal life, Lang smiled and looked over at the defense table.

"Carolyn often told me about how in love with Paul she was. She told me he was married, and I tried to warn her that it was always the woman who got hurt in situations like that."

McCarty brought her attention to the murder.

"I remember that Carolyn called me the day after it happened and asked me to meet her at a coffee shop that we sometimes went to. When we got there Carolyn talked about the night before, you know, the night of the murder, and said she and Paul had gone to dinner, had drinks, and then fooled around in her car out in the parking lot," Lang recalled. "She told me the police had questioned her.

"I asked her whether she should get a lawyer, and she told me that there were people who could say she was with him in the car and there was a camera on a pole in the parking lot. When she was telling me all this I kind of sat back and looked at her and she seemed tired and kind of pale."

McCarty looked over at Lewis. "Your witness."

Lewis shuffled slowly to the podium, and began asking Lang whether there was ever an occasion when she, Carolyn, and Kattai had met Vinnie Parco and Ray Melucci for lunch during summer 1988.

He knew he would have to somehow explain away the prosecution's contention that Warmus had stolen Kattai's license in August 1988 and, five months later, used it as identification to buy bullets from a New Jersey gun shop on the day of the murder. The theory he was going to put forth was that somehow Parco had filched the I.D. from Kattai's purse during some lunch as part of a continuing grand conspiracy to frame Warmus.

When Lewis heard Lang's response, he realized his plan had gone up in smoke.

"No, I don't believe Liisa was with us the time Carolyn and I had lunch with those friends of Carolyn's. I only remember their names being Vinnie and Ray and I didn't care for them very much," Lang said.

Lewis refused to give up. "Isn't it true that you and Carolyn and Liisa and others had lunch at the Rio Grande Restaurant in Manhattan with Vinnie and Ray during the summer of 1988?"

Lang grew more rigid in her replies. "No, Mr. Lewis, I'm sure Liisa was never with us. I believe the only other woman who may have been there was Victoria Abrams, but not Liisa. I know that because I would not have gone out to lunch with Carolyn if Liisa was there. At that time I didn't feel Liisa liked me and I felt uncomfortable around her, so I made it a point not to socialize with her."

Unable to get the stubborn witness to agree to his scenario, Lewis shrugged his shoulders and sat down. He still had a chance to get what he wanted from Kattai, who was scheduled to testify later in the trial.

During that day's lunch break, McCarty picked up his files and took the elevator down to his fourth-floor office. There was a pink phone message slip indicating that Stephanie LaRosa, a teacher who had worked with Carolyn in Pleasantville, wanted to speak with him. When he returned the call, LaRosa said she had phoned at the request of the school nurse, Patricia January, who had information she thought might be important to the prosecution.

McCarty thanked LaRosa and immediately dialed the number she had given him. He didn't expect to learn anything new and was almost ready to hang up when a woman's soft voice answered at the other end.

Fifteen minutes later, McCarty hung up the phone and let out a loud yell that startled FitzMorris just as he walked into his partner's office.

"Sit down, Doug," the bubbling lawyer shouted. "You're not going to believe this."

Vincent Parco strolled through the courtroom on February 21, catching the glances of the many spectators who had crowded into the court-room to hear him tell his story.

After taking the oath, Parco smoothed his red silk tie and tucked it inside his carefully cut gray suit. He squinted out at McCarty, who had risen to begin his questioning, the bright sunlight apparently hurting his eyes.

He appeared nervous, and not without reason. Peeking sideways at Warmus sitting to his right, he couldn't miss her withering glare. He quickly looked down at his Rolex watch, probably wondering how long he would have to endure this.

After several preliminary questions about how he had met Carolyn (McCarty was careful to ensure that his witness wouldn't mention Warmus's affair with Matthew Nicolosi, the married New Jersey bar-tender, as per Carey's orders) the prosecutor zeroed in on the informa-tion he wanted everyone to hear.

Describing various catered garden parties he had thrown for clients at his Manhattan office in summer 1988, Parco recalled a strange con-versation he'd had with Warmus during one of these events. "One occasion, she had discussed with me and another investigator, Ray

Melucci, the possibility of her acquiring a firearm. I told her she could apply for a New York City gun permit, but that it would take about six to eight months to get it."

"What was Miss Warmus's response after you told her all these things?"

"She said something to the effect that that would take too long, she couldn't wait that long. She would want to get it a faster way."

McCarty waited a moment and then continued. "Did she tell you during these conversations why it was that she wanted a gun?" he asked.

"She had mentioned that there was a series of burglaries in her neighborhood, which is very common in New York City, and I believe she mentioned there might have been one burglary in her particular apartment house," Parco responded. "Carolyn also talked about a short, dark-haired woman from Westchester that she was concerned about. She was afraid for herself and she wanted a firearm for protection."

The time had come to start leading Parco to the point of his story. "During the summer of 1988, were you in the possession of a .25-caliber Beretta Jetfire?"

Parco knew by the question that it was time to start pointing the finger of guilt. "Yeah, I did. It's a small black automatic pistol of Italian origin. It's very, very small and can almost fit in the palm of your hand. It holds eight bullets in a magazine and one in the chamber. We had opened an office in Miami in summer 1988 and the partner that was managing that office, S. Robert Carroll, had given me the firearm as a present. I never bothered to register the gun."

Looking over at the defendant, who was busy doodling on her note pad, McCarty asked the private eye, "Did you ever show that gun to Carolyn Warmus?"

Parco let out a small chuckle. "We were at that garden party and I mentioned to her that I had the Beretta in my safe," he began. "I took her to the ground-floor level of my office where I had a safe in the floor, and I took it out and showed it to her. She kind of looked at it and was fascinated by it. She had an expression on her face of glee or happiness. She had a happy look on her face."

Lewis jumped from his seat, objecting to the answer.

Carey looked over at the witness and began lecturing him. "When you say it's a happy look you are characterizing her state of mind. If she smiled you could say she smiled."

Parco neither understood nor cared about the legal nuances. "She smiled," he shot back, as the jurors laughed and the judge shook his head.

McCarty jumped in before Carey could chastise his witness any further. "Now, Mr. Parco, can you describe your relationship with Miss Warmus in the fall of 1988?"

"I was seeing more and more of Miss Warmus," he said. "She would stop by the office and we'd meet more regularly as far as having a cup of coffee or dinner or having a drink. Sometimes it was once or twice a week, maybe three times. Our relationship was basically social."

Directing the testimony back to Warmus and guns, McCarty asked, "Can you tell us whether during fall of 1988 you again had conversations with her about firearms?"

Parco smoothly followed the lead. "Almost every time that I saw her she became fairly persistent as far as asking me to acquire a firearm for her. She kept stating that she was afraid that there were many burglaries and she was afraid that this particular person who might have sabotaged her father's plane and who might have been involved with the hit-and-run accident with her sister might be after her, and she wanted a gun for protection. She kept asking me to get her something similar to the gun I had shown her in my office, the .25-caliber Beretta."

"Did you tell her you'd help get her a gun?"

With every eye in the courtroom focused on him, Parco slowly sipped water from the white plastic cup in front of him, took a deep breath, and said, "In the beginning, I first said no to her and then after a while I said yes, just to placate her. I really didn't look for one for her, nor did I speak to anyone about getting one, so she became persistent in possibly acquiring the one that I had. That conversation was probably about the middle of November of 1988."

McCarty moved to bring out another point, which the jury would find even more significant as the case unfolded. "Mr. Parco, recalling the conversations you had with Miss Warmus about getting a gun for her, at any point in time did you discuss with her the need for identification?"

"We did have a conversation that in some states you could use identification and purchase a firearm such as in Florida and Georgia."

"What was her response to that?"

"She said she didn't have any identification, but at one point in time she showed me an identification that wasn't hers. My best recollection was that this occurred around December of 1988, before I gave Carolyn the silencer-equipped Beretta. She told me one of the employees or teachers in her school had left a pocketbook or wallet in the locker room and that she had picked up some identification that she might use in the future. I looked at it briefly and it looked like a school or identification card for someone's employment."

McCarty knew Lewis would be jumping out of his seat with his next question, but it had to be asked for the jury's benefit. "Could it have been a driver's license?"

"Objection," shouted Lewis.

"Sustained," the judge said, fixing his glare on the prosecutor. "Mr. McCarty, that is not permissible. You know that!"

Parco sat back in his chair and clasped his hands around his large belly while looking out at his captive audience.

When Carey finished his admonishment of McCarty, the witness continued.

"There were other conversations with Carolyn about the gun," he said. "One or two times I mentioned that even if she had the gun that she was not familiar with firearms and wouldn't be able to practice with it at a pistol range because they require a gun permit. And somewhere in the conversation the subject of a silencer came up."

McCarty leaned on the lectern, carefully balancing his weight. "How did it come up?" he asked innocently. Parco's testimony had obviously captured the attention of everyone in the room, even the judge.

"I mentioned to her that if you're going to practice with a gun and you're not at a range, it makes a lot of noise. And somehow, either myself or she brought up the fact that a silencer suppresses the noise and that if a silencer was used you could practice in relative obscurity and no one would know about it. And from that time on she became persistent about getting a silencer for the firearm."

"And what did you tell Carolyn Warmus you would do?"

"I told her that I had a friend that was a master mechanic, that he could make anything. I told her that I had discussions with my friend— his name is George Peters—over a number of years about his ability to make a silencer. At some point I told her that an arbitrary price probably would be about $2,500 for the gun and silencer. She agreed to pay any price."

McCarty spent the next several hours taking Parco through his contact with Peters. Parco told of giving the gun to Peters so the machinist could manufacture a silencer for it. He then told of getting the weapon back from Peters, testing the finished weapon in his courtyard, and conversations he'd had with one of his employees, Rocco Lovetere, and Peters about how the silencer was made and attached to the gun.

"Did you eventually give the gun to Miss Warmus?"

Parco looked at his well-polished shoes, apparently trying to recall the moment when he had given her the weapon. "I believe it was in the first week of January 1989, on a Thursday, I recall. I called her up and told her I was bringing something over for her. I went up to her apartment at about 7:30 P.M., and I brought the same cigar box that Mr. Peters had delivered the gun and silencer to me in, along with what appeared to be ten or twelve .25-caliber bullets in a small plastic bag.

"I put the box and the gun on the floor next to the door, and when I rang the bell she answered. I said, 'Oh, there's a box on the floor.' And she picked it up and we went back in the house. I took out the gun and showed it to her. I put two bullets in the magazine and showed her how to chamber a round and how to put the safety on. I then took the bullets out of the gun and I showed her how to screw the silencer on. She then took the gun and cigar box upstairs to her bedroom. I think I had a soda and then left."

Taking him through his January 14, 1989, movie date with Warmus to see *Tequila Sunrise,* and her mistaken belief that he had given her his gun to hold, McCarty brought out Parco's own alibi for the following day, January 15, and for the time Betty Jeanne Solomon was gunned down.

The private detective appeared to become more nervous at that moment, his voice catching several times as he described taking his twin ten-year-old sons to the Pancake House in Douglaston, Queens, as was his habit every Sunday. Later, about 5:30 P.M., Parco said, he drove them to visit his father, Carmine Parco, who was recovering from surgery at the Albert Einstein Hospital in the Bronx, and did not arrive back home until about nine that night.

The moment had now come for the guillotine to be dropped on Warmus's soft, murderous neck. Before McCarty asked his next question, he let his gaze travel around the courtroom, noticing the rapt spectators crowded together on the hard benches. The bulk of his case rested on whether or not the jury would believe what Parco was about to tell them. Lewis would no doubt spend several days trying to rip the witness apart, much as he had done with Jimmy Russo, but for this moment Parco's next words would be all-important.

He began simply. "Mr. Parco, the next day, January 16, 1989, did you speak with Carolyn Warmus?"

On this next bit of testimony hung Parco's partial immunity for sell-ing the gun and silencer. His lawyer, John Jacobs, and the assistant district attorneys had made that abundantly clear. He licked his lips and answered.

"Yes, we were supposed to meet Monday, January 16. I think that was Martin Luther King's birthday, and she had mentioned something about maybe we could get together or something and I said fine. But she called me at the office that day and told me she couldn't see me that night. I said why, and she described to me an incident that occurred the night before. She said she was at a bowling affair with a bunch of teach-ers from her school and that when she got home some police officers from Westchester had questioned her about someone being killed.

"And the first thing I asked her was how did this person die. And she said the person was stabbed or bludgeoned about eight or nine times. And I said, 'Are you sure the person wasn't shot?' And she says, 'No.' "

Taking another sip of water, Parco wiped his hands on his pant legs and continued. "Then I had asked her about the gun. I said, 'What did you do with that particular gun?' She said, 'Oh, I want you to pick it up tomorrow night.' And I said, 'Why do you want me to pick it up?' She said, 'Well, when these police officers came to my house I had the gun hidden in the bedpost.' I think she had had a large brass poster bed with large round brass posts, and I think she said because it's small she had placed it in there.

"I asked her, 'Why were you nervous?' She said, 'Well, I'm not sup-posed to have a gun and I think you should take it back. I don't need it and I don't want it,' something to that effect. I said, 'Fine, I'll pick it up tomorrow night.' "

McCarty interrupted. "Did she tell you who had been killed?"

"She said the wife of a teacher in her school."

"Did she tell you anything about that teacher?"

"No. I asked her who was this person and she says, 'It's a casual acquaintance,' something like that, someone she knew from the school."

"When was the next time that you saw or spoke to her?"

Wiping his hand across his brow, Parco squinted several times before responding. He kept his eyes locked on McCarty, never looking to see whether Warmus was watching him or not. "I believe I told her I was going to see her the next night," he continued, "which would be a Tuesday night, to pick this gun up and get rid of it, take it back. I didn't know what I was going to do with it, just take it back. And I think I called her before going up to her apartment and she said, 'You don't have to come and pick it up.' I said, 'Why not?' She said, 'I don't have it anymore. I threw it away.' This conversation took place on January 17, 1989."

"Did you have any other discussions about that weapon?"

"Well, I was a little concerned because I said to her, 'Where would you throw it? Where would you get rid of it?' And she said something to the effect, 'I threw it away on a parkway, off a parkway.' And I didn't want to talk too much on the phone, so I said, 'I'll talk to you tomorrow.'

"My best recollection, I think the following night I stopped by to see her because I was a little concerned. And she just told me she threw it away and I didn't have nothing to worry about. She said, 'I didn't use it. I didn't give it to anybody. I threw it away.' I wasn't crazy about the fact that she threw it away, but what was done was done, and that was the last conversation I had for a while about the gun."

"Now, did there come a time, Mr. Parco, when the Greenburgh police spoke to you?"

"Yes. The first time was the beginning of July 1989."

"Did you tell them everything that you knew?"

Parco squirmed slightly. "No. I was afraid. I realized that I had done something illegal and stupid by giving her, by selling her a firearm, and I decided not to mention it to anyone."

McCarty moved to bring out another important piece of the puzzle. "Did there come a time that she made a request of you to do certain investigative steps such as a license check?"

Parco nodded. "In August 1989 she had asked me to check a telephone number in the 914 area code and a Michigan license plate. We were able to access through public records the license plate number to a man in Michigan named Ballor. The phone number that she had given us belonged to a Barbara Ballor in Yonkers."

Hoping the jurors remembered Ballor's name and her relationship with Paul Solomon from his questioning of Solomon, McCarty decided to wrap up his questioning of Parco by getting him to reveal how Warmus had repeatedly lied about her affair with the married teacher.

"Mr. Parco, prior to summer 1989 had Miss Warmus ever mentioned the name of Paul Solomon to you?"

"No."

"After you spoke to the Greenburgh police in summer 1989 did you discuss Paul Solomon with her?"

"Yes. I had a conversation with her asking her if she knew a Paul

Solomon. And she said he was a teacher in her school. And I said that some police are looking into a matter in which she might have been involved in Westchester County. She told me that Paul Solomon was just a friend from the school and that she didn't have any affair or anything like that with him. I asked her about it six to eight times after that and her response was always the same."

The murmurs from the back of the courtroom grew louder, soon drowning out the whispers of the jurors, who were looking back and forth between Parco and Warmus.

A court officer called for silence and Judge Carey leaned toward his microphone. "I think we'll stop here and resume this testimony next Monday," he said, smiling at the sixteen-member panel. "Everyone have a good weekend."

The angry look on Warmus's face as she slammed her ball-point pen down on the table told reporters watching the scene that there was at least one person in the room who wouldn't be enjoying the time off.

Lewis was in court early on Tuesday, February 26. The previous day had been totally wasted. A bomb threat had been phoned in to the courthouse only minutes after he had begun his cross-examination of Parco, and the judge had sent everyone home. The caller hadn't said why he had planted what turned out to be an imaginary bomb, but a major organized crime murder case was being tried two floors above, and one of the defendants had probably wanted the day off. The same thing had happened the week before, but luckily it had come at the end of the day.

Today he would be hitting the witness with rapid one-two punches, bringing up one bad act after another and letting the jury know just what kind of a guy Parco really was.

An hour later when the judge and jury arrived, Parco strutted up to the witness chair in a dapper, charcoal-gray Armani suit, and Lewis began what would turn out to be a two-week marathon of questioning.

"What's the name of the course you teach at the Learning Annex in Manhattan?" he began.

" 'How to Be Your Own Private Detective,' " Parco responded, wondering what that had to do with the murder case.

"You sure?"

Parco hesitated. "It was changed to 'How to Get Anything on Anybody.' "

"There were various ads put out for that course, including one where the course was advertised in part as 'Spying on Someone,' do you remember that?"

"Vaguely."

"Do you remember also that the course was advertised as being able to teach someone to alter their physical appearance in seconds?"

"I recall that."

"And learning how to gain information or evidence through your target's garbage?"

"Yes."

"In fact, in your course, sir, one of the things you tell your students is that if you want to find information out about someone, what you do is you go to their house on the night before the garbage is to be collected and you scoop up and collect the garbage, right?"

It couldn't have taken Parco long to figure out what Lewis was up to with this line of questioning.

"Mr. Parco, one of the other things that you taught as part of this course was something called 'voice distorters,' that someone can make a call on a telephone, for example, using a voice distorter and disguise their voice, right?"

"Sometimes."

"You'll agree with me that deception is an important part of some of the work you do?"

Parco nodded.

"When you teach your course at the Learning Annex, you tell your classes 'I'll do anything, lie, cheat, or steal, to get information, right?"

"I might have said that."

Lewis might have wanted to add "and murder for money," but, if so, he held his tongue. He needed to convince at least one member of the jury that Parco was quite capable of killing someone if the price was right, and to do that Lewis needed to keep pounding on him with the private eye's own unsavory past.

To show that Parco would probably rat on his own mother to save his skin, Lewis asked about certain statements the private detective had made to the authorities about his alleged friends. "Do you remember going to the Greenburgh Police Department on April 26, 1990, and mentioning that Ray Melucci did an electronic sweep for members of organized crime to determine if there were any bugging devices that were in place? Do you remember that, yes or no?"

"Yes."

"Was it true?"

"I don't know," Parco finally admitted.

"Why did you do that?"

"Because I felt it was pertinent to this case."

Lewis pressed further.

"Do you remember also telling the Greenburgh police that Melucci and Rocco Lovetere and George Peters got together and made illegal silencers for guns?"

"Yes."

"For organized crime figures?"

"Yes."

"Was it true?"

"I don't know. I told them what I heard on the street."

Lewis moved on to new territory. "The story you've told us about the gun in the cigar box being given to Carolyn, there wasn't a single soul there, according to your story, except for you and her?"

"Yes, there was no one there."

"Now, you're married, is that right, Mr. Parco?"

"That's true."

"It's fair to say that you dated Carolyn, isn't it?"

Parco hesitated.

"Having trouble with the word *dating*, Mr. Parco?"

"I'd call them social meetings. As I testified earlier, we went out for coffee a few times, a drink, a light dinner. You want to characterize it as a date, then I guess you could say it's a date. Well, it's a little more than social. I guess you could say social bordering on dating."

If Lewis wanted the jurors to consider an alternative to Carolyn Warmus as the killer, a love-struck Vinnie Parco jealous over her sexual rendezvous with Paul Solomon, might be one possibility.

"Was there an infatuation on your part with her?"

"I believe so, yes."

"An attraction?"

"Yes, an attraction," Parco admitted.

"In fact, you wanted at some point to sleep with her, right?"

Parco leaned back and thought for a moment. The jurors' attention was riveted on the witness. Reporters sat with their pens poised. This was better than any soap opera on television.

"Yes," came his reply.

"She wouldn't sleep with you, would she?"

Parco said nothing.

"Would she?" the defense lawyer repeated.

"She invited me."

"And you, being the gracious and wonderful gentleman, you declined, right?"

"Yes," came the response.

"And you declined because you're a married man, you don't do that, right?"

"No."

"Because we know that's not true, don't we?"

McCarty tried to object, but was stopped by Carey.

Parco apparently forgot the question. "What's not true?" he asked.

"It's not true that you are monogamous?" Lewis shot back, his words dripping with genuine distaste.

"That, I'm not," Parco almost bragged.

Lewis couldn't let the issue go. "So why is it, sir, you declined this infatuation opportunity with Miss Warmus?"

"Because of the circumstances," he said, almost matter-of-factly.

"And the circumstances were such that it wasn't convenient for you, right? Is that what you're telling us?"

"Yes. On the night in question we were at Windows on the World, a restaurant in the World Trade Center. We both had a few drinks, we ate, we enjoyed the party. Eventually Carolyn left, took a taxi home.

"Later on I went back to my office. I had facilities there to sleep over, which I did every so often. After I had taken a shower and I was ready to go to sleep, I received a phone call from Carolyn and she invited me to come over. She said, 'I'm in black, sexy lingerie,' she says. 'I'd like you to come over.' I was very tired so I said, 'Why don't we save this for another night, like a Saturday night when we have more time?' She said, 'Okay.' And that was it."

The incredulous look on Lewis's face told everyone how much he believed of that story. "So it's kind of like you were tired and had a headache so it didn't happen, right?" he asked, clearly enjoying the laughter from the crowd behind him.

"I didn't have a headache," Parco volleyed, receiving his own smattering of appreciative snickers. He then launched into the next sexual request from Warmus.

"The second time she called me we had a Christmas party at my office and she was invited, as were a lot of clients and employees. My wife was present. Carolyn called me toward the end of the party and she sounded a little tipsy and I think she even said she had had a few drinks. She told me, 'I'm feeling good, why don't you come over. I'm really horny.' I told her, 'I really can't make it, I'm here with my wife.' Again we left it for another time."

Lewis later moved to another topic, sure to turn the stomachs of every woman juror and maybe a few of the men.

"As part of your job, one of the investigative techniques that you developed is something called 'panty analysis jobs,' right?"

"Excuse me?"

"Panty analysis jobs, do you remember those? Do you remember that there was a discussion about your ability to confirm a woman's fidelity to her man by having the men bring in soiled panties and a semen sample that you were to have tested to confirm fidelity? And that it ended up with a procession of men coming through the door carrying these items to get you to do these tests. Do you remember that?"

For the first time since he took the stand, Parco seemed to be blushing.

"A few years ago one of our investigators, Jimmy Russo, had gone to analysis school and he had all kinds of electronic and forensic equipment and he claimed that he could do sort of an analysis."

"And he would be able to do this and he would be able to tell people whether their partner was faithful or not?" Lewis asked.

"He would be able to tell them, due to the chemical reactions, if there was protein in the particular subject material."

Lewis smiled at Parco's attempt at semantic niceties. "And this particular subject material"—he drew out the words—"was semen, right?"

"Yes, allegedly semen or supposedly semen."

Lewis, scoring more points against his hapless target, moved on. "Mr. Parco, you also go about making a determination whether somebody is homosexual, don't you?"

"We don't make determinations," the tired witness countered. "We follow their lifestyles and we report to the client. We've had occasion to investigate people who have frequented establishments where known homosexuals hang out."

"And because people frequent establishments where known homosexuals hang out, you write a report that indicates they well may be homosexuals, right?" Anger had crept into Lewis's voice.

"I just write a report indicating they go to this place," Parco said, ignoring his inquisitor's obvious emotional bias.

"Do you do the same type of investigations on people with AIDS?" Lewis continued.

"On one occasion a few years ago we had an individual who was a client that asked us about that, and the client knew that this person went to a particular hospital a few times a week and they asked us to find out if this individual was being treated for AIDS. One of our investigators was able to call up the patient information and utilizing a suitable pre-text was able to get the information."

Lewis stood at the lectern shaking his head. "Is it fair to say that your position on doing these things is that you don't make the moral judgments?"

"Correct," Parco answered, apparently indifferent to whether Lewis, the jurors, or anyone else looked down their hypocritical noses at him from their lofty moral thrones.

As the days dragged by, Lewis found no lack of slimy capers or repulsive tricks with which to degrade Parco in the eyes of the jurors.

Everything in the private detective's past was fair game. His problems with the IRS; his lying to the Immigration and Naturalization Service in an effort to deport a young Irish woman because she had brought a rape charge against one of his clients; his bribing people with expensive dinners, concert and sporting-event tickets to gain information; even having his men come on to women who worked at companies from which he needed information.

When the questions turned to why a renowned private eye with a million-dollar business would risk throwing it all away by illegally selling Warmus a silencer-equipped gun, Parco dropped his voice.

"I blame a series of personal problems for my stupidity," he said. "At the time I gave her the gun, I wasn't thinking straight. My daughter had just been in a traffic accident, my father was hospitalized, my father-in-law had died, my mother-in-law had had a coronary, the IRS was auditing me, and I was excited while waiting for a book about me to be released."

During further questioning and while anticipating McCarty's and FitzMorris's introduction of Ray's Sport Shop of North Plainfield, New Jersey, into the trial, Lewis pulled out a surprise of his own. "Mr. Parco," he began, "can you tell us why it is that you made a phone call from your Manhattan office on January 15, 1989, the day of Betty Jeanne Solomon's murder, to North Plainfield, New Jersey?"

Lewis had found the number on Parco's office phone bills while investigating, and although the call was to a residential number, not the gun shop, the jury didn't have to know that. Perhaps they would find the call more than just a coincidence and start looking anew at the private eye's possible motive for murder.

Asking to see the copy of the phone bill that Lewis was reading from, Parco studied the document for several long minutes before answering. "I don't know why that call was made," he said, shaking his head. "I know I didn't make it. That was a Sunday and I have people working in my office on Sundays. I assume one of them made the call, but I don't know anything about it."

Not all of Parco's two weeks of testimony dealt with angry, heated exchanges between him and Lewis. There were a few light moments, as well.

Deciding to finish up his long cross-examination on March 6, the defense lawyer saved the most ludicrous story for last. "Mr. Parco, have you ever been involved in supplying guns to anybody at all?"

"No," Parco replied, looking surprised.

Lewis pounced again. "In 1984 were you hired by a client named Parodi?"

"Doesn't ring a bell," came the response.

"How about with respect to an island off the coast of Ecuador?"

Parco flinched as the memory came back. "I recall 1984 and the family name I think was Villar. She might have been related to Parodi."

"The woman who hired you was Olga Eljuri de Villar. Does that help?"

It all came flowing back to him. "Olga was the mother of one of our investigators. She had a parcel of land, I believe it was an island that they raised shrimp on in Ecuador. Apparently they lost the island to what they term were bandits or thieves, and they asked us to supply a security force to secure the island. Mrs. Villar was going to show us certain documents proving they were the rightful owners of this particular property."

"They asked you to supply about thirty men, right?"

"I'm not finished," Parco snapped, wanting to tell the story in his own way. "Approximately thirty to fifty men. And at the time she was going to pay us to outfit the men and all the expenses of the assignment. Subsequently she did not give me the necessary documentation and we did not take the assignment."

Lewis smiled at the witness. "Well, you dealt with a company to order arms, didn't you?"

Parco nodded, knowing what Lewis had up his sleeve. He sat back to listen.

"In fact, you dealt with a company to order, for example, thirty

Rugers, thirty round magazines, scopes, ring sets, grenade launchers, jungle hats, ponchos, uniforms, jungle knives, cases of ammunition, .38 special ammunition, .9-millimeter, buckshot, ten cases of hand grenades, ten cases of fragmentation grenades, four cases of smoke grenades, and two hundred rounds of grenade launching cartridges. Isn't that right, Mr. Parco?"

The private eye blinked quickly. "Yes, it's true. The individual we were dealing with was a registered firearms dealer and he had an export license which covered that sale to be legal. I was going to outfit the security force with those supplies if needed."

"And the security force was designed to establish a six-month perimeter guard duty around an island in Ecuador, right?"

"Yes."

Lewis was hoping the jurors were finding this story as fascinating and frightening as he did. He also hoped they saw that Parco was a man who would do virtually anything for the almighty buck.

"Mr. Parco, did you also try and buy Cobras? You know what a Cobra is?"

"Cobra is a snake."

"Not a snake," Lewis said, eyeing the man. "Cobra is an armament. Do you know what it is?"

"I believe it's a helicopter."

"Now, Mr. Parco, you said that operation never came off, is that right?"

"I said that the operation was not conducted by my firm," he said quickly, seeing where the questions were heading.

"I believe others took the assignment, went down to Ecuador, and it was an aborted mission from what I understand. I believe that they left the country with several hunting rifles and you're only allowed by federal law to leave with three. They went to Ecuador to secure the island.

"I understand that when they got there the police arrested them and they spent about five days in jail. They suffered, besides the indignity, they suffered quite an economic loss."

For the next forty-five minutes, Lewis prompted Parco to testify about his involvement in international arms sales, or more precisely, his attempts at buying AK-47 assault rifles and Uzi submachine guns to sell on the world market. When he finally turned his questions back to the hostage shrimp farm, McCarty couldn't bear it any longer.

He slowly rose to his feet and held his arms up in despair. "Your honor, I object, I object, I object," he said, his voice filled with a tired resignation. "What on God's green earth has any of this to do with the murder of Betty Jeanne Solomon? An Ecuadoran shrimp farm with bandits and soldiers of fortune? How far are we going to go with all this?"

The judge called the lawyers to side-bar.

"Mr. Lewis, I can't see what all this is accomplishing. It's late in the day and I wish it would move forward. If there's nothing else we're going to hear about this, why don't you just stop cross-examining him? There's no relevancy to any of this that I can see."

After that, Lewis concluded his questioning quickly and McCarty completed his redirect in record time.

At 4:45 P.M., Carey looked at Parco and uttered the words the private detective had been waiting two weeks to hear. "That'll be all, sir."

Buttoning his jacket as he stepped down, Parco walked past Warmus and, when she looked up and caught his eye, gave her a sneer she would probably long remember.

23

BY MARCH 12 the end of the trial still seemed nowhere in sight. The double-tiered metal cart that carried the scores of files and boxes of evidence the prosecutors used each day was rolled next to the prosecution table, allowing McCarty to reach in and grab his witness list.

Among the long list of those already called were Thomas Alvarez, who had delivered Warmus's message in Puerto Rico; Alturo Alcover, one of the security agents at the Condado Plaza; Madlyn Newman (now Madlyn Inserra) and Tammy Rogers, who recounted their strange phone calls from Warmus while she was trying to locate Solomon and Barbara Ballor; Julianne Lombardi, another Pleasantville teacher who had worked with Warmus and who had told the jury of Warmus's repeated pledges of love for Solomon and his daughter; Walter Sekinski and Hope Rosenthal, Solomon's bowling friends who, he hoped, had established Paul's alibi for the time of the murder; the sickly George Peters, who readily admitted his silencer-making role in the bizarre case; and then Rita and Carmine Parco, Vinnie's daughter and father, both of whom tried to back up Parco's alibis. But McCarty wondered, however, just how much they had helped. Rita was a classic Brooklyn spitfire, complete with teased hair and funky nail polish, while Carmine was so old he couldn't remember where he was, let alone whether Vinnie had visited him in the hospital on January 15, 1989.

McCarty tossed the list down, and for the first time since the trial began, felt this was the day the case would turn for the good guys.

An hour later, he stood facing the judge. "Your honor, the government next calls Patricia January to the stand."

Lewis continued writing on his legal pad. He had already gone over the statement she had given police almost a year earlier, and the school nurse didn't know anything that could hurt Carolyn. He seemed barely to be listening as McCarty began his questioning.

January was a slightly built woman with dull brown hair and plain features. She had a quiet, slow way of speaking and looked distinctly out of place in the courtroom. She looked worried and frightened.

After gently going through the preliminaries, McCarty bore into the heart of her testimony. "Can you tell us when you first met Carolyn Warmus, Mrs. January?" he asked.

"I met Carolyn when she first came to the Pleasantville School District and was a fifth-grade teacher."

"Where was Carolyn Warmus teaching at the time? Where was her classroom, and where would you meet?"

"She was teaching diagonally across from me, from the nurse's office where I worked. I would talk to her in the faculty lounge right next door to my office. We would have coffee, gathering the morning before school, and have conversations. It was a small room with a round table, a telephone, and a bathroom."

"Can you tell us or approximate how often Miss Warmus would use that phone in the fall of 1988?"

January looked down, thinking back in time. "She would be on the phone a lot."

McCarty directed the questioning to a workshop January and Warmus attended together in the fall of 1988, hoping she would help the jury to see that the doe-eyed, blond-haired defendant wasn't such an innocent as she was now pretending, but a woman obsessed with her married lover.

"It was a workshop on 'A World of Difference' and we had speakers come in and speak about prejudice, and then we broke down into small groups of about ten people in each group. Carolyn and I were in the same group."

McCarty peered down at his notes. "Mrs. January, at one point in time did Miss Warmus speak about Paul Solomon?"

Warmus finally glanced up from her doodling and peered through her brown, horn-rimmed glasses at the witness, careful not to turn her head enough to let the media cameras in the back of the courtroom get a clear shot of her.

"We were asked to draw a crest of meaningful things in our life, and Carolyn said that she drew, or said that Paul Solomon and his daughter, Kristan, were very meaningful to her."

Taking a deep breath, McCarty began what might well have been the most important direct examination in the case so far. FitzMorris put down his pen, folded his hands, and gave all his attention to the witness. Lewis continued to review his own notes.

"Now, can you tell us whether there was a break at school during Christmastime 1988?"

"Yes, and then we came back to school after the new year."

"Mrs. January, can you tell us whether or not after the new year you saw Carolyn Warmus in the faculty room?"

Staring at her thin, bony hands, the nurse took a moment to compose herself before beginning the story that was her real reason for being there.

"I came into the faculty room to make a cup of coffee, and Carolyn was on the telephone talking to someone who had—his television had gone on during the night and it woke her up, and she was calling him to tell him not to let that happen again.

"After she got off the phone she said that she was tired because she couldn't get back to sleep. And I said to her, 'Are you afraid to live alone?' And she said, 'I'm terrified.' And I said, 'I would be, too. How does someone like you handle it?' And she said, 'I had to buy a gun.' And I said, 'A gun?' And she said, 'But of course I would never kill anybody, and I don't have any ammunition or anything like that.' And I said, 'I know. My husband has Civil War guns, and I guess it's nice to know that if they are under the bed, if you ever need one you could use it as a prop.' And she said, 'Exactly.' "

By this time Lewis put aside the notes he had been trying to read and sat back in his chair. His mouth was open in surprise. He turned to look at his client, who just as quickly turned away as January's testimony continued to echo throughout the room.

"I then asked her, 'How do you get a gun? How do you buy a gun?' And she said, 'I had to order it. I had to have it specially made, and it's taken a long time to get it.' And I said, 'Who does that?' And she said, 'A private detective.' And I said, 'Who would put you in contact with a detective?' And she said, 'My father.' And then she went on to say, 'It would take another whole day to describe the events of my family and the things that have happened to them.' After that I left, and we ended the conversation."

Lewis's head slumped forward in despair. This testimony—especially coming from a woman who looked and sounded like Mother Teresa—was about as damaging to his case as all the rest of the evidence so far presented.

McCarty pressed ahead, clearly delighted with the smoothness with which his surprise witness was able to describe the conversation and the aura of believability she put forth.

"In connection with this conversation, did she tell you the make of the gun, if you recall?"

"She told me the make, but I don't remember. I remember her describing it, but I don't remember what it was. She said it was a lot of money. I cannot remember the figure, but it was a lot of money."

With the smile of a Cheshire cat, McCarty told the judge, "No further questions."

Requesting a side-bar conference, Lewis wasted no time explaining his predicament to the judge.

"There is not a single piece of material that reflects this. I'm curious as to when the prosecution learned of this, how they learned about it. There is nothing anywhere in the files or anything that we can view that reflects this."

McCarty piped in, "Judge, it's not documented in the files. I don't believe I have to tell him anymore."

FitzMorris added, "He can pursue it on cross-examination."

Carey looked at Lewis. "I guess that's your answer."

The man who walked to the lectern to cross-examine Patricia January was not the David Lewis everyone had come to expect. Working off the prepared notes that he and his staff had so meticulously put together, Lewis was second to none in his unrelenting and searing crosses. But this time, totally unprepared for what he had just heard, he didn't know which way to turn.

"Mrs. January, did the police interview you in this case back in February 1990?"

"Yes."

"Did you tell them the story you've told us today?"

"No, I did not. They didn't ask me."

Lewis was puzzled. "They didn't ask you about a gun or anything like that?"

"No. I have told my husband about this, and I have told my friends."

"And the reason you didn't tell the police was because they hadn't asked you about it?"

"They did not ask me specifically if I knew she had a gun. Mr. Lewis, I did not volunteer it to the police at that time. I was clearly under the impression that everyone knew that there was a gun involved here and that the gun belonged to Carolyn Warmus. I thought that was common knowledge."

Lewis stepped back, reluctant to continue questioning the witness until he could be sure what her answers would be.

He walked back to the defense table and the obviously shaken Warmus. Looking up at the judge, he slapped a sheepish smile on his face and said, "Your honor, I think it's apparent to everyone that this witness came as a complete surprise to me. I'd like to request an adjournment to prepare for this."

Carey didn't need much prodding. "I think that's only fair."

McCarty and FitzMorris exchanged disbelieving looks. Surprise witnesses were part of the game, and neither could remember the last time a judge had allowed a lawyer a day off from trial to prepare for one sprung on him.

Lewis told the judge he would be preparing a subpoena for January's personnel records. Privately, he told DiSalvatore and Ruggiero to get their asses out on the street and dig up anything he might be able to use to discredit her testimony.

As the two private detectives virtually flew out of the courtroom, Lewis sat down, refusing to look at his client.

Enraged at the damaging testimony, Warmus once again stormed out into the hallway, beckoning to Carol Agus, the New York *Newsday* columnist who had been cultivating her since the trial began in hopes of getting an exclusive interview when it was over.

"She's lying," Warmus said, putting on her mask of sincerity. "Why would that woman make all those things up? Did you see how strange she looked?"

It seemed to Agus that the defendant was trying to convince herself more than anyone else that January had indeed lied about their conversation. But forgetting her true feelings, and hoping all these brownie points would earn her that exclusive, the reporter commiserated with Warmus and dutifully pulled out her notebook to record the interview.

The next day, armed with little more information than when he had started, Lewis spent two hours at the delicate task of trying to chip away at the credibility of a witness who looked more like a candidate for sainthood than the bored, insecure, and deceitful woman he was trying to make her out to be.

Unable to make her change her story, Lewis finally gave up. January had now bolstered Parco's claim that he had sold Warmus a gun, but perhaps the private eye's credibility had been so well demolished that the jury's disbelief of him would somehow carry over to the nurse.

The prosecution's case seemed to take on new life after January testified. McCarty and FitzMorris began sailing through witnesses, each one bringing to the table one more nail that they hoped the jury would use to seal the coffin of guilt around Carolyn Marie Warmus.

Richard Dwight Shamp of Warren County, New Jersey, the law enforcement sales manager at Ray's Sport Shop, who also just happened to be the owner's son-in-law, had been a little shaky and unsure of himself at first. But Shamp had done what he had to do, namely testify that someone had come into the gun shop on the afternoon of January 15, 1989, and used a driver's license belonging to a L. S. Kattai to purchase one box containing fifty rounds of Winchester Western .25-caliber automatic cartridges with an expanded point.

Gary Noble, a New York Telephone senior systems analyst for billing, had done his job by producing copies of Warmus's phone bills, which showed not only the fifty-six-minute call she had made to Paul Solomon just hours before the slaying, but also the series of calls she had made to Solomon's and Barbara Ballor's homes on August 15, 1989.

Noble had also been able to retrieve the January 15, 1989, phone calls from the Solomon and Tilden homes, thus supporting their version of events.

The last witness had been Peter De Forest, the renowned crime-scene expert, who more than lived up to his reputation during his short time on the stand. The professor of criminalistics had talked about working with his assistant, Francis Sheehan, and Detective Constantino at the crime scene the day after the murder and finding bullet fragments under the carpet.

He had also succeeded in defending the work of the Greenburgh Police Department when Lewis, on cross-examination, attempted to persuade him to indict their shoddy techniques. He said, "Mr. Lewis, I've seen crime-scene analyses around the country and none of them are all that great. This one done by Greenburgh was one of the better ones I've seen," he had testified.

The next of the prosecutors' scheduled witnesses, Laura Sestito, a supervisor of the accounts support department for the MCI long-distance telephone company, was intended to provide another bombshell for the jury, Warmus's MCI home phone bill showing the call to the New Jersey gun shop at 3:02 P.M. on the day of the murder.

"Mrs. Sestito," FitzMorris began, "can you tell the jury how a call record is made when someone uses their telephone?"

The shaggy-haired witness nervously played with her pearl necklace and thought for a moment. "As much as I know is that when you pick up your phone to place a call, the local phone company, in this case being New York Telephone, receives a signal that it's your phone now placing a call. When you dial the actual digits, a record is kept of the digits and that information is passed electronically to MCI's network, and it is recorded at each point it passes into MCI's network."

FitzMorris spent the next forty-five minutes having Sestito explain to the jurors how MCI stores all its records on computer tapes and microfiche so that they can later be retrieved should a question or problem arise with a customer's account.

Handing her a piece of paper taken from his files, the prosecutor asked the witness to describe it.

"This is a microfiche print," she answered, checking the information on the form. "It's the data set we used to create Miss Warmus's phone bill. This information comes from what we call a 'data set,' which is used to create the microfiche and the microfiche created this copy. It's a magnetic tape that looks like a reel-to-reel tape."

"What is the name and phone number of the subscriber on that sheet and can you circle it?" FitzMorris asked, handing her a red felt-tip pen.

"The subscriber is C. Warmus," the witness replied, and repeated Warmus's phone number.

Warmus looked up when she heard her phone number being read aloud, perhaps wondering how many crank calls she would now get once it was made public.

"Now, on that invoice you have there for C. Warmus, what was the total amount due MCI for that bill on January 22, 1989?"

"Thirty-two dollars and forty-seven cents. The records also show there were twenty-eight calls for a total of 204 minutes made from that number during the billing period."

FitzMorris began zeroing in. "Could you focus your attention, please, to the telephone calls made by the subscriber—Miss Warmus—on January 15, 1989. How many do you see that day?"

"Two."

"Do you see a call made on January 15, to Plainfield, New Jersey, and can you tell us what time that call was made?"

Sestito ran her eyes down the document. "Yes, here it is. The call was made at 3:02 P.M. . . ."

"Mrs. Sestito, you indicated there was another long-distance call made that day from Miss Warmus's home? Where was that to?"

"That call went to Traverse City, Michigan, at 10:32 A.M."

Warmus looked up again, probably hoping the woman would not be asked to recite publicly her mother's home phone number.

The document having already been accepted into evidence, FitzMorris sat down.

Lewis tapped his fingers on his ample stomach before getting up. After tossing out several softball questions concerning the information contained on the form given her by FitzMorris, Lewis sharpened his sword and prepared to send the prosecution reeling.

"You'll agree that the customer gets the same material that we've got on the microfiche copy there, right?"

Sestito nodded. "Yes."

"And there would be no reason to get something different, right?"

"It's the same information, yes," she replied.

In a grand gesture, Lewis reached into the back pocket of his trousers and pulled out a copy of an MCI phone bill. Handing the three-page document to the prosecutors, Lewis stepped back and folded his arms, watching as they discovered the discrepancies between his version of Warmus's MCI records and theirs.

While the 10:32 A.M. call to Traverse City, Michigan, appeared on both documents, the gun shop call—the call that tied her to the store that sold the bullets used in the murder—was conspicuously absent from Warmus's version.

"Jesus Christ, look at this," FitzMorris whispered, pointing out to his partner a brand-new call that never appeared on MCI's records, "another call to her mother's house made at 6:44 P.M. on the night of the murder."

During a short side-bar conference, McCarty pointed out the problem to the judge, but if he was hoping that Carey would be outraged enough by the apparent fraud to declare Warmus's version of the bill inadmissible, he was to be disappointed. Carey, after looking over the documents, allowed Lewis to continue questioning Sestito in an effort to convince him that the defense version of the phone bill should be accepted as evidence.

"You've seen original bills that have gone out to MCI customers?" Lewis asked Sestito, who by now must have been totally confused.

"Yes, sir."

"You know what they look like?"

"Yes, sir."

"Would you be able to recognize one?"

Sestito nodded. "I believe so, yes, sir."

Handing the witness the defense exhibit marked DDDDD, Lewis asked her to look it over and compare it to the microfiche copy of Warmus's bill that the prosecution had already shown her.

Lewis began by asking several more questions intended to show the jury that the information on the two documents was almost identical, including the total amounts due MCI, $32.47.

"Who's the subscriber?" he asked.

Sestito looked for the front page of the alleged phone bill and found it missing. She knew that that was the page that contained not only the customer's name and address, but also computerized bar codes that would have been nearly impossible to forge.

"The name and address is not indicated here, but the account number is that of C. Warmus as compared to our records," she finally answered.

Lewis looked pleased. "Your honor, at this point I offer defendant's DDDDD as evidence."

FitzMorris interjected.

"I have a few questions, if I could, your honor. Miss Sestito, have you ever seen that document before?"

"No, sir."

"Do you have any idea where that document was before it was in court today?"

"No, sir."

"Do you have any idea where it came from?"

"From MCI possibly."

"How do you know that?"

"It has an MCI logo on it."

"Other than the fact that it has an MCI logo on it, can you verify the information that's contained on that particular invoice?"

"No, sir."

Concluding his questions, FitzMorris objected to Lewis's being allowed to introduce his bill as evidence and thus confuse the jury.

"Judge, Mr. Lewis has not been able to authenticate his version of the phone bill at all, and without that authentication, the law does not permit this type of material to be admitted in as evidence."

Carey pondered the dilemma for several minutes. "I'm going to think about this overnight, gentlemen," he said, shortly before sending the jurors home for the evening.

The next morning the sun shone through the large, plate-glass windows lining the eastern wall of the courtroom, but it wasn't enough to pierce the dark, gloomy cloud hanging over the prosecution table.

While Carey had publicly admitted that only one version of the MCI bill could be authentic, he had decided to allow the jurors to review Lewis's version and compare it to the prosecutor's MCI records. The decision had resulted in a very happy defendant.

With a grin as big as all outdoors, Warmus several times looked over at the two men trying to put her behind bars and shot them a confident, defiant look.

The prosecutors' course was clear. While McCarty would continue to present their case, FitzMorris would be busy meeting with MCI security officials, the FBI, officials of the company that manufactured the paper MCI used, and anyone else who might help them prove Warmus had forged her phone bill on a home computer. If they could show she had forged that document, the jury would have to believe she was capable of anything, including murder.

Through the next several witnesses McCarty stalled for time. While some of the testimony was important, his main job now was to give FitzMorris as much of an opportunity as possible to ferret out whatever information on the forgery he could.

Liisa Kattai told the jury about her friendly relationship with Warmus and stated that Carolyn would have had access to her purse when her driver's license was stolen in August 1988.

But Lewis, true to form, had successfully diffused some of the impact of her testimony. "Miss Kattai," he said, "isn't it true that you don't really know whether your license was stolen or not? Isn't it true that you could simply have lost it?"

The uncertain look on Kattai's face before she spoke told the jurors the answer before she gave it. "Well, yes, I suppose that could have happened," she responded. "All I know is that it was missing and I had to have it replaced."

Lewis then passed around to the jurors a copy of Kattai's 1988 driver's license picture. The point he had clearly gotten across was that Kattai did not really resemble Warmus all that closely. In his inimitable fashion, Lewis softly suggested through his questions that Warmus would have had to be very stupid to think she could pass—under close inspection by a bullet salesman—as the woman whose face appeared on the missing driver's license.

McCarty had managed to salvage what he could.

"Miss Kattai, you now have darker brown hair, has it always been that color?"

Subconsciously running her fingers through her hair, the witness replied, "No. At one time my hair was frosted from 1988 to May of 1990. It was frosted blond."

The next witness, Diane Santabara, wasn't much help to the prosecution, either.

Santabara had been the sales clerk at Ray's Sport Shop on January 15, 1989. And while the records showed she was the one who sold the box of .25-caliber bullets to a woman using the identification of L. S. Kattai, she couldn't for the life of her remember what the woman looked like. "There are so many people who come into the store that I waited on and this was such a long time ago, I really can't recall who it was that bought those bullets," she said, adding that the police had first spoken to her about the incident more than a year after it happened.

Still playing for time, McCarty then called one of his office's own investigators, Joseph Knapp, who regaled the courtroom with a detailed story of how he had helped search Parco's office on November 15, 1989, after the private eye had been slapped with a search warrant, and found what appeared to be part of an oxidized bullet in a courtyard flower box.

Christopher Chany, a specialist with the county's forensic science laboratory, was next, and he took his moment in the sun to detail the examination he had made of Paul Solomon's clothing and bowling bag, looking for the elusive nitrites that would prove they had been in contact with a fired weapon.

"I found no trace of nitrites to indicate a recently discharged weapon had been in the pockets of his overcoat or his pants pockets," Chany said.

A test was also done on the clothes Betty Jeanne Solomon was wearing the night she was slain, he added.

"There were nitrites found on the back of Mrs. Solomon's T-shirt," he said. "The gunshot residue around the shoulder was more tightly packed around the bullet hole than the others. The gunshot holes in the back of the shirt indicated nitrites, but I found none around the holes in the front and back of the left leg on the victim's sweat pants."

"Wait a minute," Lewis said when it came his turn to ask questions. "You said you found no residue in his overcoat and pants pockets. Did you test the sweatshirt he was wearing that night?"

Chany shook his head. "There was no need to. It didn't have any pockets in it. We only analyzed the pockets."

"So if he had had the gun tucked up under his sweatshirt or in his waistband, we wouldn't know that because you never tested them, correct?"

Looking a bit dismayed at the question, Chany responded, "Well, I, um—no, I guess not. We only tested where we were asked to by the police."

The string of less-than-dynamic witnesses continued when a very nervous FBI special agent, Robert C. Halberstam, took the stand, having arrived on a hurriedly scheduled flight from Washington, D.C.

Looking at his watch every few minutes, Halberstam quickly explained that he was the forensic expert who had analyzed the gunshot-residue test performed on Paul Solomon's hands the night of the killing. "I found an insignificant amount of nitrite residue, the element found in gunpowder, on the test swabs of Mr. Solomon," the agent told the court. "It would be comparable to the same amount that might be found on any person's hands, regardless of whether a firearm had been handled," he added, noting that a certain amount of nitrites are a natural part of the environment, thus accounting for its presence on human skin.

Lewis countered this testimony, which seemed to indicate Paul Solomon hadn't fired a gun that night, by bringing up an incident already testified to by Greenburgh Patrolman Michael Cotter.

"Agent Halberstam, would the gunshot-residue test be an accurate method of determining whether someone fired a gun if that person had washed their hands before being tested?"

McCarty flinched. Lewis clearly had not forgotten about Solomon's being allowed to wash the blood off his hands before the detectives had a chance to give him the test that night.

"If I knew that that had happened, I would decline to analyze that test," the agent responded. "It would make the test unreliable, since it was possible that most of the residue could have been washed away."

Before he was allowed to leave, McCarty thanked Halberstam publicly, telling the judge and jury that his nervousness was not so much due to his testimony as it was to the fact his wife was waiting to give birth at any moment.

Several of the jurors broke out in quiet applause, bringing a smile and a thank you from the beaming man as he hurried out of the courtroom.

Westchester County Detective Joseph Reich, the crusty ballistics expert McCarty next called to the stand, was a twenty-two-year county veteran, and he wasn't about to let David Lewis or any lawyer bend his words to suit their purposes.

Under direct questioning, Reich testified that on January 18, 1989, the Greenburgh police delivered to him "a pellet; two whole bullets with pellets still in the nose; a whole bullet badly flattened; another badly flattened bullet with no pellet in the nose; a bullet split in two; and six shell casings.

"I examined them and found they were .25-caliber Winchester expanding bullets and casings," Reich said in a gravelly, weathered voice.

"Detective Reich, were you able to determine anything else about the bullets or shell casings recovered from the murder scene?" McCarty probed, knowing full well what he wanted the ballistics expert to bring out.

Reich knew as well. "I found there were markings on the nose and base of the bullets that told me a silencer was used in the shooting."

Asked to describe the mechanics of a .25-caliber Beretta Jetfire, the gun Parco had testified he'd sold to Warmus, Reich detailed the workings of the popular and well-made firearm. "The barrel of the Beretta Jetfire flips up on a hinge for loading or unloading," he said. "It also has a magazine that fits into the gun that you can put up to eight bullets in. Another bullet can be chambered, giving you a nine-shot capability."

Handed the board that Constantino and Lind had found at George Peters's workplace, Reich cast an experienced eye over the piece of lumber.

"All I can tell you about this is that it contained three .25-caliber slugs, but I can't say whether the markings on them matched those at the crime scene because they were so badly damaged after being fired into this here hard wood."

Given a plastic evidence bag containing the brass shell casing Constantino had found under the drill press at the J. B. Slattery Company, Reich checked the evidence tag.

"Can you tell us what your ballistic tests revealed about that?" Mc-Carty asked.

"Yes, sir. I can tell you that in my opinion I found this here shell casing matched those other six shell casings found at the Solomon murder scene."

Then, during Lewis's confrontational cross-examination, Reich really came into his own. For the first time, a prosecution witness seemed to find the defense attorney's third degree more amusing than anything else.

"Detective, can you tell us your tests proved conclusively that those shell casings and bullets found at the murder scene and at J. B. Slattery's all were fired from the very same gun?" Lewis challenged.

"Well, sir," Reich began slowly, pondering the wording of the question carefully, "I would need the barrel of the murder weapon to make a better and more perfect comparison, but I'm confident they were."

Pushing hard to get the man to say what he wanted to hear, Lewis asked, "Are you telling us that with three missing shell casings from the murder scene you can scientifically say that only one gun was used in the killing?"

"Sir," Reich chortled, as if speaking to a very stupid child, "while it cannot be scientifically proven, I'm certain only one weapon, a silencer-equipped .25-caliber Beretta Jetfire, was the only gun used to kill that Greenburgh mother."

If Lewis didn't take kindly to the witness's condescending tone of voice, Reich didn't give a damn. He'd been around and had seen too much to give much mind to what any of these silver-tongued ambulance chasers thought of him.

McCarty sat back and enjoyed the verbal sparring, content for the moment to see someone giving Lewis a dose of his own medicine.

He also knew that FitzMorris was at last ready with their new batch of witnesses concerning Warmus's version of her phone bill. When the court reconvened after the weekend, they would proceed with this now-critical aspect of their case.

24

FITZMORRIS stood at the lectern, a confident glow shining through his boyish good looks as the packed courtroom waited silently for him to continue.

He had spent the past several days locked behind closed doors with a telephone suctioned to one ear while picking through the remains of half-eaten deli specials. On his cluttered desk the overflowing files and notes continually battled for space with the creamy-brown-stained Styrofoam cups that held his liquid energy.

The hard work had paid off. He turned to his witness.

Rita Polera, with her intelligent, compelling presence and her deep, soft Italian beauty, commanded the attention of everyone in the crowded courtroom. An assistant district attorney herself, she had come forward when she heard her co-workers were looking for anyone who still possessed a copy of his or her January 1989 MCI phone bill.

"Mrs. Polera, please take a look at the document I have just handed you and tell us if that is the customer bill MCI sent you at your home in January 1989."

"Yes, it is."

"And this, please tell us if this is your MCI home phone bill for February 1989," he said, handing the witness a small stack of paper.

"These are the bills that MCI sent me, yes."

"Can you tell us, Mrs. Polera, is there some kind of logo or saying printed across the face of each page of your bills?"

Stepping back and folding his arms while she leafed through the several sheets, FitzMorris took a moment to look at the faces of each of the sixteen men and women in the jury box, silently praying the brains behind those unsmiling looks were working today.

"Yes, there is," she finally said. "They all have printed on them the saying 'Communications for the Next 100 Years.' "

"Now let me show you what's been marked as defense exhibit DDDDD, which is the document the defendant claims is her January 1989 MCI home phone bill. Do you see that saying, 'Communications for the Next 100 Years,' on any of her pages, Mrs. Polera?"

"No. It's not here."

FitzMorris took the documents back from the witness. "Your honor, I would now ask that Mrs. Polera's MCI bills and the defendant's version be shown to the jury for comparison."

Once again he folded his arms as the jurors studied the paperwork. How could Warmus have made such a stupid mistake?

With a quick call to MCI the prosecution had learned this slogan had appeared on all the company's bills up until February 1989.

Lewis had few questions for the witness. He had paid an outside expert to examine the bill after Warmus had handed it to him months ago, and had been told it appeared to be a real MCI document. The burly barrister now cast a heavy-lidded look at his client, who again ignored him as she continued to take notes.

"I would say this is not an MCI invoice," Thomas D. Sabol, senior manager for East Coast billing, said with authority after spending several minutes looking at defense exhibit DDDDD.

For the next few hours, the assistant district attorney led Sabol through a detailed discussion of how MCI prepares their customers' bills. When the witness had finished, FitzMorris flashed Lewis an icy smile.

"Your witness, Mr. Lewis," he said, gesturing with a little flourish toward the witness box.

For the next two hours Lewis tried to make Sabol recant his earlier statement about Warmus's phone bill, and for the same two hours the MCI official refused to budge.

Trying to steer attention away from the damaging company slogan, Lewis continually hammered, pressed, and cajoled the stubborn billing manager. "Putting the slogan aside for the moment," Lewis began almost pleadingly, "what else about the bill makes you believe it is not a genuine MCI document?"

"Mr. Lewis, it is precisely because of that missing slogan that I believe this bill"—he held up Warmus's version and shook it in the air—"is not an MCI invoice. Also, since the front page is missing from your document here, we have no way of checking the bar codes to determine whether this was actually printed from MCI billing computers."

Lewis continued his assault, but found the going tough. Finally, he decided to end his fruitless attack and save his ammunition for the next expert he was sure his opponents would call.

Since it was late in the day, Carey dismissed the jurors and once again warned them about newspaper and television reports.

As Lewis began scooping up the mass of files, notes, and diagrams spread out before him, Warmus raised her arms above her head and let out a loud yawn. Both turned their heads in surprise when McCarty began addressing the judge.

"Your honor, we have another matter here we'd like to bring up."

Handing both Carey and Lewis a seven-page typewritten document, McCarty began to explain its significance. "Judge, these papers contain a list of Carolyn Warmus's prior bad acts that we are seeking to have brought before the jury."

Her face clouding over in anger, Warmus tried to snatch the material from Lewis's hand, but a sharp look from the attorney stopped her. She began reading over his shoulder.

McCarty continued. "Included in this document, judge, is proof that Carolyn Warmus forged a letter in 1989 in an effort to convince a lawyer that she was not the person involved in a June 14, 1987, car accident where a woman was injured.

"On that date, Miss Warmus drove her car into one being driven by a Dorothy Fazekas, a sixty-two-year-old woman from Keansburg, New Jersey. Mrs. Fazekas's lawyer, a Ron Konray, filed a personal injury lawsuit in New Jersey against Miss Warmus. When Mr. Konray contacted the defendant to get her side of the story, she denied being involved, claiming that on the day of the accident she was on a field trip in Washington, D.C., as a teacher with the Scarsdale schools where she then worked."

McCarty paused to see if everyone was following his story and noted they all were, especially the scores of print and TV reporters busily scribbling down his every word. "When Miss Warmus sent a letter to the lawyer denying she was involved, she attached a letter allegedly written by the principal of her school, a Dr. Richard Sprague, which said she was indeed on a school field trip in Washington, D.C., on the day of the accident.

"Your honor, after Mr. Konray saw Warmus on TV on trial for murder, he became suspicious and wrote a letter in February to Dr. Sprague. On March 4, Dr. Sprague responded saying that he had not written the letter Warmus had sent to him; that Carolyn Warmus wasn't on any school trip, and, in fact, that that trip wasn't even on the day of the accident. Mr. Konray has now refiled the lawsuit."

Seeing he had the rapt attention of both Lewis and the judge, McCarty continued. "This new evidence should be shown to the jury, your honor, so they can see that Miss Warmus has a history of committing forgery in an effort to extricate herself from whatever legal trouble she happens to be in. We are offering this to show that if she is capable of committing forgery to get out of trouble for a traffic accident, then she would certainly be willing to forge her home telephone records to try and escape punishment for committing a murder."

Warmus sat back in her chair, her face now a pasty white. She dug her fingernails into the arms of her chair and locked her gaze on the far corner of the courtroom.

Lewis stared at his client for a moment and then turned back to the judge. "Judge, I object to this being introduced," he finally said. "First of all, these are only allegations, and secondly, the prejudicial effect of this information far outweighs its probative value and should not be allowed in."

Carey, who had also been looking at the defendant, turned to McCarty, "Do you agree that this material is prejudicial?"

"Absolutely. That's why we're offering it."

Carey reread a couple pages of the offering. "Gentlemen, once again I'm going to have to consider this before rendering a decision. I'll get back to you."

A tug on his coat sleeve brought Lewis's attention back to his client. After listening to her whispered message for more than a minute, the weary lawyer addressed the court. "Your honor, my client informs me that she hasn't been feeling very well today and that she thinks she may be sick tomorrow and have to miss the trial."

McCarty leaped in. By now he had come to know Warmus's little tricks. Every time something happened in court that she didn't like, or when it appeared things weren't going her way, she came down with some alleged illness and wanted some time off. "Judge," he said, "if Miss Warmus is really sick, then all we would ask is that you order her to see her doctor for an examination and have him produce a letter stating she is too ill to be here."

"I think that would be appropriate," the judge told Lewis. "If she is ill, I will expect a written or verbal verification from her doctor."

Warmus once again tugged on Lewis's arm.

"My client is concerned what will happen to the doctor's note if one is sent. She's concerned that you may make it public if someone from the media requests it."

Looking down at the defendant, Carey said, "I'll make that decision if and when there is a need to."

FitzMorris leaned over and whispered to McCarty. "You better believe she'll sure as hell be here tomorrow. I'm betting she's too worried that the press is going to find out that her doctor is really a psychiatrist and she's being treated as a head case."

The next day, Judge Carey ruled against allowing Warmus's previous forgery attempt into evidence. But even that not-surprising decision didn't do much to help the defendant.

John Guarente, a sales rep for the Walter Computer Paper Company, the sole supplier of the paper MCI Telecommunications used for its customer billing, had flown up from Galesburg, Maryland, to testify that his company had not shipped MCI any paper without the incriminating slogan until February 10, 1989, too late to have been used for their January billing.

Under scathing cross, the perplexed defense lawyer tried desperately to goad Guarente into admitting that it was somehow possible that a batch of the new invoices without the slogan could have mistakenly been mixed in with the old ones and shipped to MCI, resulting in them being mailed out to some of MCI's customers in January 1989.

"Nah, our inventory control is pretty tight and MCI would have notified me if that had happened," he said.

Lewis continued to press, but was met with the same assuredness over and over. Guarente was a man who lived by whatever the company records showed, the lawyer soon realized, and since his forms showed no mixing of the old and new forms, that was the answer to which he was going to stick.

Guarente was followed by Bruce Wells, whose stunning testimony could not have been better designed to punch the hole that would finally sink Warmus's already foundering story.

"Mr. Wells," McCarty began, "can you tell us what you discovered

after you were asked by me last week to see if there were any computerized records other than what we have already presented as evidence, in
regards to Carolyn Warmus's home telephone calls on January 15,
1989?"

"Yes, sir. The MCI company computers have a security system and
storage data-bank capability known as VOLSER. After a customer
makes a telephone call, the information as to where the call was dialed
from, what number was called, whether it was answered and if so, how
long the conversation lasted, all that data makes its way through the
regular computer channels so it can be processed, and we can then bill
them for the actual time they talked.

"The VOLSER stores the same information within days after a customer makes a call and the data is then transferred onto what we call
VOLSER tapes," he said, pausing to see if the jurors looked like they
were following his layman's explanation of the highly technical system.

They did.

"The VOLSER tapes are then placed in a secured library in Rockville,
Maryland. Usually those tapes aren't kept permanently, because we can
reuse them. I would say on the average the VOLSER tapes are reused
every six months to a year. However, at your request last week, I authorized a search of the VOLSER library and we found the tape of January
15, 1989. Apparently it had never been reused and was safe and
sound."

After several more questions and a long, drawn-out lesson on how the
VOLSER system works, FitzMorris got to the main point. "Mr. Wells,
did you bring us a printout of what that VOLSER tape showed?"

Lifting a long sheet of computer paper in his left hand, the witness
nodded.

"Judge, I ask that the new information be shown to the jury," the
excited prosecutor said, anxious for the panel to see that the data on
another, secured MCI computer showed that their version of Warmus's
phone records was accurate.

It was a startling revelation, but Lewis wasn't conceding a thing.

His two-day cross of Wells bordered on legal assault, as he continually
tried to force the computer security expert to admit that someone—
anyone—could have tampered with the VOLSER tapes after they had
been made.

"Isn't it true, Mr. Wells, that with the number of people in MCI who
have access to those tapes that one of them could have bypassed the

security system, gained access to the VOLSER library, and changed the data on them, if they were so inclined?"

Wells wasn't buying any of it. "Sir, to begin with, there are several levels of actual physical security systems that someone would have to go through to even get to those tapes. That includes having a high-level security clearance and a computer-coded passkey to open doors.

"But let's say someone was able to penetrate that far," Wells suggested. "Those tapes are in binary language, and I don't even know a handful of people at MCI who would even know how to read binary language, let alone be able write it to add to one of the tapes like you're suggesting."

Lewis was getting frustrated. He had to make the jury believe that someone like Parco, or someone paid by Parco, could have gotten through to those tapes and manipulated the data as part of the grand conspiracy to frame Carolyn Warmus for the murder of her lover's wife.

"Mr. Wells, isn't it theoretically possible for the scenario I am suggesting to have occurred?"

"I'm sorry, Mr. Lewis. I just can't see that happening."

In a louder voice, the defense lawyer pushed his point. "I said theoretically, Mr. Wells. Theoretically!"

Wells laughed and shook his head. "I guess anything in this world is theoretically possible, Mr. Lewis, if you want to put it that way."

If McCarty and FitzMorris had had their druthers, Michael Yeager would not have been the last prosecution witness called in the murder case against Carolyn Warmus.

Everything that Wells had been, Yeager was not.

It wasn't so much that the young MCI computer expert was frightened of testifying—he was—or that he had forgotten part of his assignment, to make a printout from MCI's security computers of all Warmus's calls from her home on the day of the murder—he had. It was mainly that his generally confused demeanor undermined his believability.

The sweating, stammering witness tried his best to explain the significance of the sheets of paper he had brought with him from Washington, D.C. He began telling the jury, "I was asked to run a check of the computer storage unit that takes in calls from all of New York City on any given day. I was given Miss Warmus's home telephone number, and I then ran this specific computer program that can identify any calls that were made from that particular phone. The day I was asked to check was January 15, 1989."

Yeager held up the long computer sheet that contained only a fraction of the calls placed by New Yorkers on that day. He pointed to a particular line that he had earlier circled with a red felt-tip pen. "This was the number dialed from Miss Warmus's home telephone on January 15, 1989," he said, proud of the program he had personally designed. His next words sent many of the jurors' heads nodding.

"The number that was dialed belongs to a North Plainfield, New Jersey, business."

"Mr. Yeager, can you tell us if your records show another call at 6:44 P.M. that same day from Miss Warmus's phone to a Traverse City, Michigan, number?"

FitzMorris already knew the answer, but wanted the jury to hear it for themselves.

"No, sir. None at all."

Lewis skimmed his copy of the sheet from which Yeager was reading. He noticed something the prosecutors had apparently failed to detect, and minutes after beginning his cross-examination, he brought the blunder to light.

"Mr. Yeager, on your printout of all the calls you say were made that day from Miss Warmus's home phone in New York City, is there any call from that number at 10:32 A.M. to Traverse City, Michigan?"

As the man spent the next five minutes carefully perusing his sheet, Lewis leaned on the rail of the jury box and cast a knowing look along the two rows of jurors. Meanwhile, the prosecutors were frantically scanning a copy of the same sheet.

"No, sir, I don't see any such call on here," the confused witness finally responded. Nobody in Washington, D.C., had mentioned to him anything about a 10:32 A.M. call.

"And you've told us that the computer program you ran would have pulled up every call made from Miss Warmus's home phone number that day, isn't that correct?"

Yeager began stammering, searching for the right words. "Well, you see, I, well—yes it's supposed to do that. I don't know why that call never showed up when I did my search. There are a couple of other computer programs I could have run and maybe it would have showed up on them, but no one told me to look for that specific call."

Handing the witness a copy of the MCI documents the prosecution had entered as evidence, along with defense exhibit DDDDD, Lewis asked him whether the 10:32 A.M. Michigan call showed up on both.

"Well yes, it does," Yeager said, looking nervously at McCarty.

"So it's fair to say that at least on that point, there is no disagreement between the defense and prosecution that a call was definitely made from Miss Warmus's home that morning?"

"Yes, sir, according to both of these records."

"Then how do you explain, sir, why your MCI computer records don't show the call?"

All eyes in the courtroom were on the now totally confused young man, who looked first at this questioner and then back at the sheets of paper in front of him.

"If those records are wrong, then isn't it fair to say that it's possible all of the records produced by MCI for the prosecution relating to Miss Warmus's January 15, 1989, phone records could be in error?"

"That just can't be," Yeager argued valiantly, but with little certainty in his voice. "If those records are wrong, then all of MCI would be a pretty screwed-up place!"

Lewis let the man's own words hang in the air for several long seconds. "That's all, your honor."

McCarty and FitzMorris looked at each other and nodded. Slowly McCarty rose from his chair, looking first at Carey and then the jury.

"The prosecution rests," was all he said.

Once the jurors had been taken out of the room, Lewis didn't waste a second making his motion.

"Your honor, I would now ask that you dismiss the charge of second-degree murder against my client as the prosecution has produced insufficient evidence to support the accusation. I'd also ask that you dismiss the felony weapon possession charge on the grounds that the prosecution failed to prove its case."

Carey allowed McCarty to provide a quick overview of his evidence against Warmus.

"Mr. McCarty, do you believe it is legally permissible to build your case on circumstantial evidence that heaps inference on top of inference against Miss Warmus?"

"Yes, your honor, I do," he answered. "But please also remember that our case consisted not only of circumstantial evidence, but also of direct evidence linking Carolyn Warmus to the cold-blooded execution of Betty Jeanne Solomon."

Carey listened patiently for more than ten minutes as the feisty lawyer outlined the testimony that he felt backed up the charges.

Tapping his pen against his forehead, the judge finally spoke. "As all of us know," he began, "I now have to look at all the evidence presented in the light most favorable to the government as I determine whether it has been sufficient to sustain the charges brought forth here. This is not a decision that I have to make now. I will ask both lawyers to furnish me with memoranda of law citing pertinent cases, and I will then rule."

Looking toward Lewis, he said, "We will now break for the day, and I will expect you to begin your case two days from now, on Thursday, April 4."

25

WHEN ANTONIO CARLO GAMBINO lumbered into the tenth-floor courtroom wearing a silver sharkskin suit that had seen better days and a black turtleneck sweater that matched the color of his thick, tousled hair, he could have been chosen by central casting for a role in the hit movie *Goodfellas*.

Ignoring Gambino's arrival, Carolyn Warmus appeared to be more concerned with her wardrobe than with her first witness. Reaching under the defense table she tugged hard at her tight, mint-green skirt, which had started to rise up her thighs. That accomplished, she buttoned the skin-tight matching jacket that showcased her large breasts so well, completing the job by adjusting the collar of her pink silk blouse. Lewis had already started questioning his witness when she brought her attention back to the stand.

"Mr. Gambino, have you been known by any other names?"

The defense lawyer wanted to bring out the man's use of an alias and his criminal record so the jury wouldn't think he was trying to hide anything when the prosecution attacked Gambino later on.

"Timothy Fitzgerald. That's it," came the response.

"And what are the circumstances surrounding the use of that other name?"

"Well, my mother wanted to protect us," he answered, choosing not to elaborate. "My mother was married to that gentleman, Fitzgerald, and she just picked up the name for us and we used it."

"Have you ever been convicted of any crimes?"

Gambino paused as if giving the question serious thought.

"Assault and theft. I believe that's it. I never served no jail time."

Lewis then cut to the heart of the unlikely-looking witness's testimony. "Did there come a time when you contacted my office?"

"Yeah, I believe it was about a month and a half ago."

"At the end of the summer of 1988, were you approached by an individual at some point?"

Gambino's glance darted about the room. He cleared his throat and began his story. FitzMorris and McCarty sat with their eyes narrowed, their mouths opening wider at each new, incredible tale.

"Well, I'm a truck driver, see? I pick up at a certain stop every day in Brooklyn. It's on Third Avenue where they make Christmas-tree lights, okay? And there's all kinds of individuals that come up to my truck, they try to sell me things, everything. Ask me if I want this, I want that. And I was approached by an individual that asked me to do a murder."

The spectators in the gallery, along with the jurors and judge, appeared fascinated by the testimony.

"Who was the individual and what did he look like?"

"I didn't . . . I couldn't identify the individual until I had seen him on TV. He looked short, fat, no hair. I think he might have had a mustache at the time. I was busy working at the time, okay? It was so hot that day, okay? It was so hot I just told him to get lost, and it was the individual I would never have seen if I wouldn't have seen him on TV that night."

"You saw him on this very same night, the night he approached you?"

"No, it was right before I called you. I usually go to bed about nine o'clock every night because I have to get up early the next morning. I stayed up a little late that night and I got a little glimpse of him on TV and that's when I contacted your office."

"Who was it you saw on TV, what's his name?"

Gambino rubbed his chin as if deep in thought. "I guess this Mr. Parco. Is that his name?"

McCarty tossed his pen on the table and slumped back in his chair. There wasn't a word out of the guy's mouth he believed.

"Now, did you see anybody else with him?" Lewis continued.

"I seen an individual with him, yes."

"Can you describe that person?"

Again rubbing his chin, Gambino seemed to be trying to recall the scene.

"The individual had a beard, but he was laying back up against the wall. But he was at a clear view. He had a beard with black hair, that's about it, that's all I can remember."

Reaching into one of his dozen open folders, Lewis pulled out four photographs. One was a shot of Parco mugging for the camera, the other a head-and-shoulder shot of a bearded Paul Solomon. The other two were simply add-ins.

Handing the photos to his witness, Lewis asked, "Can you pick out the two individuals you say you saw on that day?"

A second later Gambino held up the picture of Parco for everyone to see. "That's the man I seen that day and on television."

Two seconds later he picked out and displayed the photo of Solomon. "I said possibly it could be this individual that was there that day also."

After pulling out a map of Brooklyn and having his witness point out for the jury where the murder request was made, Lewis walked closer to the stand. "Mr. Gambino, when is the first time you met me?"

"Today. On the twelfth floor. We rode down on the elevator together."

Pointing toward Warmus, Lewis asked, "You know her?"

Gambino craned his neck to get a good look at the stunning blonde. "I never seen her before."

Lewis pointed again to his two private investigators, sitting several feet behind the defense table. "You know either of these two fellows?"

Again Gambino looked across the room. "What is their names?"

"Ruggiero and DiSalvatore."

The stocky truck driver shook his head. "No, I never seen them."

"Have you ever met or talked to them?"

"Absolutely not," came the reply.

Turning toward Carey, Lewis ended his direct. "No further questions, your honor."

McCarty remained sitting in his chair, staring at the top of the worn, scratched table that had served as his courtroom office for the past two months. The hard part for the prosecutor would be choosing which area of the man's testimony and life to discredit first.

"Mr. Gambino, you said that you recognize Mr. Parco from TV and that you saw him on TV?"

"That's correct. That night, yes."

"Are you telling us that you followed this case?"

"Absolutely not."

"And you're telling us you have never seen Carolyn Warmus's picture on TV or in a magazine or in a newspaper?"

"Absolutely not."

"You read the newspapers, Mr. Gambino?"

"Not until I had . . . I didn't follow the case until I had seen his picture on TV."

McCarty moved into the man's criminal past, trying to so completely discredit the witness that the jurors would laugh him and his patently ridiculous story right out of court.

"You still tell us you've only been convicted for assault and theft and that's about it?"

"That's correct."

"Now you indicated that you changed your name to protect yourself, is that right?"

"My mother did."

"And what was she interested in protecting you from, what did she tell you?"

"Well, that's what she said," he answered in a short, clipped voice. "She wanted to protect us kids."

"And did you ask her from what so that when you walked the streets you could be aware of what you needed to be protected from?"

The man was a consummate liar, and McCarty intended to use that to his advantage. He asked, "Do you remember living in the Phoenix Apartments in New Jersey on January 14, 1978, and do you remember the maintenance man there?"

"Yes, I do very clearly."

"You remember pointing a gun at the maintenance man and remember being arrested and convicted for possession of that gun?"

Gambino was incensed. He had been told the prosecutors had no idea who he was and that his testimony would be a breeze. It was turning into anything but that.

"Would you like to hear the story behind it? It was a starting pistol. I might have pleaded guilty, but I didn't do no jail time."

"Did you also plead guilty to trespassing in the Phoenix Apartments?"

"Yes, that's a good possibility. I can't remember too clearly. I believe I was sleeping in my bed, okay? And the maintenance man had come in. I heard someone come in the front door without identifying himself or anything, and I went into the closet where the guy was, okay, to see who the person was. And he was sifting through my drawers, and I pointed a starter pistol at him."

McCarty stood shaking his head. "And for this, Mr. Gambino, you were arrested and pled guilty?"

"I don't think I had a case, to tell you the truth," he responded. "Because they were a little crooked in that township."

McCarty lost his cool at that point. "I'm not surprised that somebody by the name of Gambino would say that or suggest that."

The reference to the historic mobster wasn't lost on anyone.

Lewis jumped from his seat. "Objection. Objection!"

An angry Carey almost shouted at the prosecutor, "Mr. McCarty, that was highly unprofessional of you and I'm very much surprised, and I want you to apologize right now."

Looking at the steamed jurist, McCarty didn't hesitate. "I apologize, judge."

Carey turned to the jury. "Ladies and gentlemen, as I made clear to you many times, lawyers are not allowed to make comments and only allowed to ask questions. That kind of thing, what you just saw, is what you sometimes see on television in courtroom dramas. I am really disgusted to have seen it happen in a courtroom over which I was presiding. We will take a five-minute recess."

He needed the time to cool off.

When the trial resumed, McCarty refused to let up. For the next hour he tried to slam Gambino's credibility with every criminal act and sordid detail he had been able to find out about the witness since Lewis had been forced to give him the names of his witnesses only days before.

"Do you know a girl by the name of Donna Bertino?" he asked. "Do you remember being with her in September 1978 around 3 A.M. in Beverly and being approached by a police officer? Do you remember telling him that you were a narcotics detective and then you showed him an investigator's shield?"

"Absolutely not." It was Gambino's turn to start getting mad.

"Do you remember that officer finding a gun, an automatic pistol, in your Lincoln Continental on September 15, 1978?"

"No. I don't recall that."

McCarty then showed the forgetful, red-faced witness a copy of a police report of the incident. "Now, Mr. Gambino, at some point in time you also lived and were arrested in the state of Illinois. Isn't that correct?"

"Yes, I was."

"You were arrested April 8, 1982, for battery and criminal damage to property, right?"

Apparently figuring that the abrasive prosecutor had his entire rap sheet in front of him, Gambino decided to tell the story his own way. "I had a problem with a girl friend and some other people," he began. "I was in business with some people out there, okay, and I guess they were a little bit more smarter than I was at the time, okay?"

"How did that lead to the problems that resulted in the assault and battery?"

"It was over money. I think a lot of these charges that you have there were a result all over money, people owing me money. I tried to be a nice guy, and it seems like I always get hurt in one way or another. At that time I was in the vending business, you know, arcade games. My partners reneged on the lease agreement we had."

McCarty knew he was coming to the good part. "You hit somebody, didn't you?"

"I hit my girl friend because she was seeing the guy that was with the video machines."

"How big are you?" McCarty asked.

"About six-six. I didn't really hit her, it was just like a slap. She might have had to go to the hospital, I'm not really sure what happened."

McCarty brought the hulking witness back to the time when, he claimed, he was approached by Parco to commit a murder. "Had you ever seen the individual who approached you before then?"

"Absolutely not."

"How about the man who was standing back aways, you ever see him before?"

"Absolutely not."

"Mr. Gambino, you want us to believe that this individual who you never saw before just approaches you and asks you to commit a murder in the middle of the day on a street corner in Brooklyn?"

The snickers from the back of the courtroom made him visibly angry.

"Well, I have a lot of people who come up to my truck and they try to sell me drugs, hot tires, you name it. I don't know if you're too familiar with the Red Hook section in Brooklyn, but it's a very rough neighborhood."

McCarty couldn't be put off that easy.

"But this person, on this occasion, out of the blue, came up to you and asked you to commit a murder for him?"

Gambino paused, and then began changing his story. Lewis's sharp glance apparently went unnoticed.

"Well, I don't think it was quite phrased like that. I think maybe it was phrased as, 'Would you like to take care of a job for me?' You know? I told him I wasn't interested."

"You told him you weren't interested before you even asked him what the job was?"

Gambino started losing his composure, the sweat starting to stain through his sharkskin suit.

"Well, I was so busy that day, okay? I get so many people come up to my truck that I just shine them on."

"So you said no to him?"

"I told him I wasn't interested, and I would say he then mingled off. He was stuttering to himself like, you know, he was shaking his head and walked off."

FitzMorris let out a chuckle. This was like something out of an old B movie. Lewis must have been desperate to try and float this character.

McCarty pressed on. "Now, you didn't tell anybody about what happened on that day, like the police or the District Attorney's office, now did you?"

"Nah, all I said to myself was 'there goes another idiot,' you know?"

"So the first people you talk to are from Mr. Lewis's law firm, a Mr. Fiore was it?"

Gambino nodded.

"Yeah. I called him on the telephone. Later on I met him at the Freehold Race Track and spoke to him for two, maybe three hours. He was there with some old guy he said was his father."

At that point, McCarty threw out another of Gambino's criminal problems. "Do you remember pleading guilty to the crime of assault in Trenton Criminal Court in December 1981?"

Shifting his considerable weight, Gambino stared at the skinny lawyer who was causing him so much trouble.

"It involved my brother-in-law, okay? I loaned him $10,000 and he refused to pay it. I finally see him about three or four months later driving in Trenton and pulled him over, and I said, 'Pete, when am I going to get my money?' And he threw a vulgar name at me and he sped off, and I chased him to the police station. He told them I had pulled a gun on him, which I did not."

Jumping back to Gambino's problems in Illinois, McCarty asked the now-perturbed witness about stealing $13,000 worth of arcade games.

"No, I didn't steal anything," he began.

McCarty cut him off. "Let's cut to the chase, did you not plead guilty on October 27, 1982, in the circuit court of Winnebago County, Illinois?"

Gambino knew he'd been caught. "Well, that was by the advice of my attorney I did that," he admitted sheepishly.

"And didn't you also have to pay $2,987 to the Rockford Memorial Hospital in Illinois for the medical bills for the injuries your girl friend Maureen suffered after you just slapped her a little?"

Gambino nodded. "Yeah, yeah."

McCarty ended his questioning, satisfied he'd proven what type of person Lewis's big witness really was.

The defense lawyer stood up to begin redirect, trying to salvage what he could from the wreckage of Gambino's testimony. "When you first told us what was said by Mr. Parco to you, you used the word *murder*, right?"

Gambino pulled the rug out from under him.

"No, I said job."

Visibly upset, Lewis tried to recover from the flip-flop testimony of his first witness.

"Did Mr. Parco describe the job at any point?"

"Well, if somebody asks you to do a job, okay, on somebody, and I guess in street lingo that would be to commit a murder."

"And from that you assumed he meant murder?"

"I would think so, yes, that's what it is."

Before getting the man off the stand and out of his life, Lewis asked one more question.

"Why did you come forward?"

Pausing to think out his answer, Gambino finally sputtered, "Why? I felt that maybe there was an injustice here some way. You know, to the defendant."

Lewis kept New York City Detectives Michael Bachety and Bryan Mc-Cabe on the stand for only five minutes each.

Their testimony was the defense lawyer's quick one-two shot to damage the credibility of Jimmy Russo, should any member of the jury give any credence to his story that Carolyn had come to him to buy a silencer-equipped machine pistol.

The detectives were the two people Russo said he had probably called to notify when Warmus first made her illegal request.

"No, I don't remember ever getting a call from James Russo about that," Bachety said. "Oh, I know Russo, all right, but I think I would have remembered if he'd called me with that info."

McCabe seconded his colleague's testimony. "No, I checked my files and there's nothing about any call from Russo," he said. "And I don't personally remember him ever mentioning anything like that at all."

The Thursday ended with Carey wishing the jurors a pleasant weekend.

On Monday Lewis began what he intended to be the last day of his case.

Joseph Lisella, the first witness, looked as if he'd just stumbled off the red-eye from Los Angeles. He wore a pair of cheap, plastic sunglasses, an open-necked white shirt with stains splattered down the front, and a rumpled sports coat and slacks.

"I apologize for the sunglasses, your honor," he said to Carey with a grin. "But I got this eye problem. They're sensitive to the light."

To prove his point, he pulled off the eye wear and began blinking rapidly.

Court clerk Dennis Murphy took in the scene, and when the protective lenses were back in place, he asked the witness to give his name and address for the record. Lisella said he was from East Hartland, Connecticut.

Lewis then rose, appearing uncertain whether he wanted anyone to know this was his own witness. "Mr. Lisella, did there come a time when you were contacted by any member of the defense team in this case?"

"Yes, I believe it was the first of June, 1990. I met Michael DiSalvatore. He's right over there." The witness pointed to the silver-haired private detective.

"Can you tell us what you heard and saw and when it was that you heard and saw it?"

Lisella looked puzzled. "You're referring to the incidents in the bowling alley?"

"If that's what you heard and saw, yes," Lewis responded.

McCarty and FitzMorris settled back in their chairs.

Lisella sat back in the witness chair and crossed his legs, as if preparing to tell his grandchildren a bedtime story. "I was coming back from Atlantic City on January 15, 1989. I turned off the highway to get some gas. I had my Ford Tempo, license plate on it is L-I-S-E-L-A. I stopped, to be honest with you, I got a little lost. I ended up stopping for gas. I then stopped at the Brunswick bowling lanes on Route 100."

"Not for gas at the bowling lanes?" Lewis interrupted.

"No. I stopped there to go to the bathroom and to get something to eat. I bought a hamburger and then I went to the bathroom. While I was in the bathroom I overheard a conversation by two men."

Lewis leaned against the podium, speaking up only to move the witness's story along. "Can you tell us what you heard?"

"I wrote it down on a letter. Can I read the letter?"

Lewis shook his head. "Just tell us in your own words what you heard."

Lisella thought hard for a moment and then spoke. "The first man had asked the second man, 'Did you bring the money?' I think he said 20 K. The other man said 'Yes.' Then the other man said, 'Count it if you don't believe me.' "

Lewis broke in again. "At that time did you see the two men?"

"No," came the answer. "I was in a bathroom stall with the door closed." He continued retelling the men's conversation. "Then the other gentleman said to the first gentleman, 'Where's the gun?' He said, 'Don't worry about the gun, it's in the deepest part of the river.' Then he said, 'You're going to see the girl?' And I believe the other guy said, 'Yes, I'm going to meet her in a few minutes at the Holiday.' "

"Anything else said?"

Lisella started to reach into his pocket, but then stopped. "If I could refresh my memory with this letter it would be a very helpful thing. I wrote it back in February of '89, a couple weeks after this incident."

Carey allowed the letter to be marked as a defense exhibit.

"I wrote it to my attorney if something should have happened to me," Lisella continued. "I signed it, 'Love, Joe.' "

After being allowed to reread his own letter, Lisella said he was ready to continue telling his story.

"The one gentleman called the other one Vinny. The other man's name was Paul. I did not know who was talking at the time. When I wrote this letter I put the men as 1 and 2, but one man I assumed was Vinny said to the other guy, 'There's only two people that can catch us and get us in trouble. One is you and one is me. It's not going to be me. If it's you you'll join your wife.' Then the other guy says, 'Don't worry, Vinny. I'm not stupid.' Then the first man said, 'Hold it, don't talk.' "

"What happened then?" Lewis probed.

"I come out of the bathroom and got out of there very quickly. I faced both of the men. I didn't know what I was in the middle of. One man was five foot six, beard, brownish hair. The other was five foot three, a little shorter than the first, stocky gentleman, bald head and a mustache.

The shorter guy followed me out to the parking lot and watched me drive off."

Pulling out his never-ending supply of photographs, Lewis handed the witness a picture of Solomon.

"Yeah, I believe this is the one called Paul."

Shown a photo of Parco, Lisella nodded immediately. "That looks like the second guy."

McCarty received permission to conduct a short voir dire of the witness. A voir dire would allow the prosecutor to ask questions of Lisella about what he had just testified to, even though he was still under direct examination by Lewis.

"Mr. Lisella, when you came down to New York in June 1990, did you meet with anybody?"

"I met with Michael DiSalvatore and the other investigator, Vic."

"And did you show them anything?"

"They took me to several different bowling lanes for, I think, for me to pick out the bowling lane that I was at."

"And which one did you pick out?"

"The one that I was at."

"Mr. Lisella, have you ever been to that bowling alley prior to January 15, 1989?"

"Never in my life, sir."

McCarty sat down, making notes he would use later on cross. Lewis returned to the lectern.

"Mr. Lisella, why did you write the letter to your attorney dated February 10, 1989?"

"A couple of weeks after this incident, I almost completely put it out of my mind. Then I got a threatening phone call. I got a call from, I don't know who it was, and the guy told me, 'You better'—he said a nasty word—'forget what you saw in New York or heard in New York.' "

"Were there any other threats?"

"About a week and a half later I got another one—another phone call. Then I believe it was in July 1989 on a Sunday morning I found a dead raccoon on my mail tubes, you know, the place where they put newspapers. Then I got another call. During that one the guy said, 'If you don't forget about New York, this is what's going to happen to your family.' "

As ludicrous as Lisella's story sounded, Lewis wanted the jurors to know that the defense had had to virtually drag him into the courtroom to get him to testify that day. "Now, Mr. Lisella. Do you want to be here?"

"No."

"How did you come to be here?"

"I had to fight your lawyers in court in Connecticut. I'm here because a judge ordered me to. I don't need the involvement and I don't need the grief for my family."

Lewis took a long pause, apparently reluctant to broach the next topic with Lisella. "Did there come a time, Mr. Lisella, you discussed some arrangements or agreement with the defendant's father, Tom Warmus?"

"Yes."

"And, in fact, did you finally sign an agreement with respect to those arrangements?"

"I have signed an agreement. I don't have any per se agreement with him."

"When did you sign that document, Mr. Lisella?"

"About thirty-five minutes ago in the hallway. I signed it to maintain protection for my family."

Carey agreed to a request to show the Lisella contract to the jurors. The agreement called for Warmus's multimillionaire father to pay him for six months of housing, food, moving expenses, and lost wages so he could relocate his family.

"Hey, it's a great deal if old man Warmus is stupid enough to pay the guy for that pile of bullshit testimony," a reporter whispered to his crony. "For the same deal, hell, I'll get up there and testify I saw Parco pull the trigger."

The court officers shot dirty looks at the two laughing journalists.

Lewis sat down to let the prosecution take over.

"Mr. Lisella, how frequently had you gone down to Atlantic City prior to January 15, 1989?" McCarty asked.

"My wife and I usually go down twice a year, three times a year."

"And based upon what you're saying, this would be the only time that you went down there by yourself to Atlantic City?"

"No, sir. I have gone before by myself."

"Now, Mr. Lisella, did you eat in a restaurant or a coffee shop on that trip, and do you recall whether or not you sat at a table or counter with other people?"

Removing his sunglasses and wiping the lenses with the untucked tail of his shirt, Lisella thought about the question.

"There was several people at the table, none that I knew. One gentleman had a—he was from France, he had a sweatsuit on. I believe it was maroon in color and some sneakers. He was losing fairly heavily at the tables, he had said. There were a couple of ladies, I think, in their fifties. There was another elderly gentleman there."

"Now you indicated that this person from France had on sneakers. What type of shoes did the individual you identified as Vinny have on on January 15, 1989?"

Lisella looked at McCarty with a strange look. "I believe they were regular shoes, sir."

"Can you identify them any better than that?"

"No, sir, I can't," the witness responded a little testily.

McCarty moved on. "Now what route did you take to get to Atlantic City on January 15, 1989?"

"The route I take all the time. I come from 319 in Connecticut to Route 8, Route 8 to 84, 84 to 287, and 287 to the Garden State Parkway in New Jersey. I'd then go back the same way."

"This is the route that you travel, based upon what you told us, on many occasions prior to January 15, 1989?"

"If you consider three or four times a year many occasions, that's correct, sir."

"And what you're telling us and you want this jury to believe, is that on January 15, 1989, you just happened to get lost in the Scarsdale area?"

"I didn't happen to get lost, sir, I did get lost," Lisella shot back.

The tired prosecutor then began to bring out the witness's propensity for shady deals, con games, and lies.

"You went to Hawaii on July 19, 1984, with your wife Bernice, isn't that true?"

"Yes, sir."

"And you brought a certain amount of baggage with you to Hawaii, did you not?"

Lisella looked toward Lewis and Warmus. "What has this got to do with . . ." He stopped. "Yes, sir, we did."

"Tell us what you maintain happened to that baggage."

"It was lost, and it was returned to me when I got home."

"Now, you filed a claim with the airline for that baggage, for eight items of luggage, did you not?"

"Yes, sir, I did."

"And it was your estimate that the total value of those items was in excess of $8,000?"

"That's true."

"And in that claim for lost baggage you told the airline that every item that was contained in those bags was bought by you with cash?"

"Probably, sir."

"When the postal service and police began investigating your report, didn't you tell their investigators that you never filed any claim with American Airlines at all?"

"I, uh, I don't remember that," Lisella choked out.

McCarty jumped to another area intended to enlighten the jury as to why Joseph Lisella was a man in need of money, money he hoped to get from Tom Warmus by testifying in the murder trial of his daughter.

"What do you do for a living, Mr. Lisella?"

"Right now I'm opening a restaurant, La Familia, in Southfield, Massachusetts."

"And since August of 1990 you have been unable to open that restaurant, isn't that true?"

"No, not true."

"Well," McCarty said, grateful for the opening, "has it been opened?"

"No, sir."

"Have customers gone in there and eaten food?"

"Not one person, sir."

"Now, sir, do you have any documentary evidence to show that you were in Atlantic City on January 15, 1989?"

"None that I can recall," the witness replied.

"Mr. Lisella, you told us you love Italian food, eat it whenever you can, is that correct?"

"Yes, sir, it is. Love Italian food."

"Then, sir, when you say you got lost and ended up in Yonkers and were looking for a place to eat, why didn't you stop at Luigi's right next to the Brunswick bowling lanes?"

Lisella saw what the clever lawyer was doing. "Never saw the place and, first of all, I don't eat any sauce but my own, sir."

"Why didn't you stop at Ricky's Clam House which is also right next to the bowling alley?"

"Never saw it, sir."

"Did you see the McDonald's that is right there as well?"

Lisella made a face. "I don't eat at McDonald's."

It was McCarty's turn to look surprised. "But you had a hamburger at the bowling alley, isn't that right?"

"Yes, sir."

"Bowling-alley food is food that you do eat?"

The jurors and spectators laughed, earning a sharp look from the judge.

"Yes, sir, that is correct."

"You eat hamburgers at bowling alleys?"

"That's exactly what I had, sir."

McCarty moved the questions back to the bowling-alley bathroom scene the witness had so vividly described. "After you entered the rest room and while you were in that stall you, needless to say, closed the door to that stall while you were going to the bathroom?"

"Yes, sir, that's exactly correct," Lisella responded.

"Needless to say, you couldn't see out, could you?"

"No, sir. I could not."

"Now the stall that you're sitting in, the door doesn't go all the way down to the floor, does it?"

"No, sir, it did not."

"So if one were to walk into that bathroom one could see feet or shoes of someone who is seated on the toilet?"

"I would have to say so, yes."

McCarty went for the kill. "One would see feet, unless, of course, the person on the toilet was holding up their feet as they went to the bathroom?"

Lisella blushed. "I don't usually go to the bathroom in that fashion, sir!"

"And you certainly were not holding up your feet on January 15, 1989, as you went to the bathroom?"

Lisella's answer sparked a new round of laughter. "I'm sorry, you're wrong. After I heard the conversation I was holding up my feet."

"Don't laugh, Mr. Lisella, but had you made any noise before you heard the conversation?"

Looking serious, the witness asked, "Well, you talking about natural noise?"

"Natural or unnatural, Mr. Lisella."

"I don't remember. I don't think I made any unnatural noise or natural noise."

"So while you're sitting there, not making any natural or unnatural noise, suddenly you hear a conversation?"

"That's correct, sir."

The repartee drew howls of laughter, forcing the judge—with a smile on his own face—to call for order.

"Mr. Lisella, at some point you say you burst out of that stall and ran by these people? Ran by them as quickly as you could?"

"I come out with a little penknife in my hand," he answered, demonstrating with his right hand held out in front of him. "I figured if I was going to die I was going to hurt somebody else. I opened that door and it swung to the right, and my face was face to face with these two gentlemen."

McCarty could barely maintain his composure. "How long did it take you to get out of that bathroom?"

"Ten seconds."

"Let me get this straight, Mr. Lisella. It took you ten seconds to go what, fourteen, fifteen feet?"

Lisella wasn't done with his story. "I stared them in the eyes for about three or four seconds, then I left."

"When you got home you told the local police?"

"I didn't tell anybody, sir. I wrote out that letter to my attorney, and the letter was placed in an envelope that says to be opened if something unusual happened to me."

"And you gave that letter, signed 'I love you, Joe,' to your attorney, right? 'I love you, Joe.' That was for your attorney's benefit?"

Lisella became angry, seeing the implication McCarty was trying to paint.

"Excuse me, please. I'm married. Are you implying I'm a homosexual or something, sir?"

"I'm not implying anything, Mr. Lisella," McCarty replied curtly. "I'm just asking."

Deciding to move on to Lisella's numerous, documented insurance scams, McCarty dug through his files to pull out the Connecticut police record of the man before him.

"Mr. Lisella, you've been to police stations before many times to report your cars being stolen, isn't that true? How many claims have you made to insurance companies through the years for thefts of your vehicles?"

Lisella squirmed. "I can't truthfully answer because I don't remember."

McCarty helped him out. "Would it be fair to say that it's in excess of five?"

"Probably. I have a lot of vehicles."

After listing several cars Lisella had reported stolen along with thousands of dollars in items for which he had also filed insurance claims, alleging those items had been in the cars when they were taken, McCarty brought up the "pièce de résistance" of his cross-examination.

"Prior to going into the restaurant business, Mr. Lisella, can you tell us what it is you did for a living?"

"I worked for Lisco Builders and then J & D Builders, both were construction companies that specialized in renovation work."

"And one of your specialties was renovating or rehabilitating houses that had sustained fire damage?"

"That's correct, sir."

McCarty began his long, slow presentation of Lisella's rather unfortunate, if not incredible, history of fire insurance claims.

"How many fires have you had in your home in the last fifteen years, Mr. Lisella?"

"Two."

"Wasn't there another fire on your property?"

"My parents' home, correct."

"And on each occasion claims were put in for proceeds from your insurance company, right?"

"That's correct, sir."

"You know a woman named Barbara Huntington?"

"Yes, sir."

"And while you were staying on her property in a trailer her house burned down and you coincidentally got the contract to fix the home?"

"That's correct."

"And isn't it a fact that you had a conversation with Barbara Huntington, offering to torch her house for $100?"

Lisella put on his most outraged face. "Oh my God. No I did not, sir."

"You know a man named William Dunn who hired you to fix the roof of his business?"

"Yes, I do."

"And in September 1987, while you were working there, that building suffered a fire?"

"You're correct there."

Once again Lisella looked toward Lewis for help, but the defense lawyer was busy with his own problems. Carolyn was bending his ear once again about the damnable cameras in the courtroom.

McCarty didn't let up. "Do you have a sister named Mary Black-burn?"

"Yes, I do."

"How many fires has she had at her home?"

"I think she may have had two."

"And was your company contracted to do the renovation after those fires?"

"For my sister? Yes."

"Mr. Lisella, do you have a friend named Robert Trufer?"

The witness was getting steamed over the continuing onslaught. "Yes, I do."

"And this friend of yours, he had two fires in his house, didn't he? And you fixed the house on both occasions, did you not?"

"Yes, sir, I did," sighed Lisella.

"Isn't it true, Mr. Lisella, that people know you by the name 'Toaster Joe'?"

The nickname struck a chord with the spectators, and Carey had to pound his gavel to quiet the laughter.

"I never heard anybody call me that, sir."

McCarty once again moved on to other areas. "Mr. Lisella, isn't it true that you once reported your son kidnapped? That there was a ransom for $75,000?"

"That's correct."

"And didn't you borrow $5,000 from your father-in-law to pay that ransom?"

"No, sir. I borrowed it from my brother-in-law."

"What happened?"

"I went and got my son," Lisella said matter-of-factly. ,

"And that $5,000, what was done with it?"

"It was kept by myself and my wife."

"And when the FBI spoke to you about all this and wanted to question you about it, you refused, isn't that right?"

"Yes."

"And when you were asked to testify before a grand jury on what had happened, you told them you didn't want to waive your right against self-incrimination, did you not?"

Looking beaten, Lisella replied, "Yes, sir."

McCarty wasn't done. "Now, Mr. Lisella, let me bring your attention to an incident you claim happened on February 12, 1991, in Granby, Connecticut. Can you tell the jury what happened to you that day?"

"I left my grandson and my wife home," he began. "I was going to the Granby Drugstore to get some medicine for myself. I left my home and I was about half a mile from St. Theresa's Church and the post office when this older Thunderbird passed me, a gentleman hung out the window and fired two shots at my windshield, either two pellets or BBs or small-caliber bullets. All I saw was this big thing pointed at me. It was a big, long gun. That's all I can tell you."

After explaining that he had filed a police report about the incident and told the Granby police chief he believed the shooting had something to do with a murder in New York State, Lisella sat back, waiting for the next barrage of questions.

"Mr. Lisella, do you recall talking with Mr. Lewis on March 17, 1991, and telling him that one of his own investigators, who was with Mr. DiSalvatore when he came to talk with you, was one of the individuals who shot at you on February 12, 1991?"

"That's correct."

Lewis didn't flinch.

"Now, Mr. Lisella, until your restaurant opens you're not presently employed, are you?"

"No, sir, I'm not."

After several more questions designed to make Lisella look more and more like a man who would sell his mother, family, and dog for a quick buck, McCarty sat down.

When the judge permitted the witness to leave, Lisella tucked his written agreement with Tom Warmus back into his coat pocket and strutted out of the courtroom.

"He'll have as much luck collecting on that agreement as you and I will of being invited to Carolyn's next dinner party," FitzMorris whispered to his smiling colleague.

Everyone's eyes turned to watch Tom Warmus walk into the courtroom when Lewis called him as the next witness. The curious thing about his behavior during his entire short testimony was that he never looked at his daughter.

Pathetically, Carolyn strained her neck and waved her hand several times in an effort to catch her father's eye, but he did nothing more than turn his chair toward the jury box, away from his child.

Lewis had asked the multimillionaire to leave his Florida estate to testify about a strange phone call he'd received during the summer of 1989.

"I was at my home in Franklin Hills, Michigan, when I received a call from a man who identified himself as Vincent Parco," Warmus said, in a smooth, soft voice.

"The man said, 'Your daughter is a friend of mine and she's been running around with some shady people and may be in some trouble.' He then offered to help me, but said that it was going to cost big bucks. He said, 'I'm talking about big, six-figure money.' I gave him the name of my lawyer and told him to call him. That he handles all of that kind of thing."

"Mr. Warmus, did you ever hear that voice again?" Lewis asked.

"Yes, I did. It was this past Sunday after I arrived here. You played a tape for me of some news broadcast that had that Mr. Parco on it."

"Was that the first time you connected a face to the voice that called you?"

"Yes, it was. I knew right away it was the same voice, because there was something unique and different about it, almost like a Looney Tunes or cartoon character."

Lewis stepped back from the podium, having made his last possible point.

If the jurors believed Tom Warmus's testimony, they would have to believe that Vinnie Parco had tried to shake him down for a lot of money to help protect his daughter. From what, he hadn't really said, but the fact that he had made what boiled down to an extortion call could be enough to convince at least one member of the jury that the whole Betty Jeanne Solomon murder was nothing more than an elaborate setup by Parco to blackmail Carolyn's wealthy father.

A short time later, Warmus stepped down from the witness box, still avoiding his daughter's eye.

For the next several minutes, Lewis worked to roll a large television set in front of the jury box. He intended to show a ten-second segment of videotape that Judge Carey had already approved.

"Ladies and gentlemen, what you are about to see is a videotape of Vincent Parco being interviewed by a reporter from WNYW-TV immediately after one of our witnesses, Antonio Carlo Gambino, finished testifying," Lewis said.

Carey's law clerk bent down and flipped the switch. The jurors saw a female reporter interviewing the loquacious private eye on a busy Manhattan street corner.

After acknowledging that he had heard about the New Jersey truck driver's testimony identifying him as the man who was looking for a hired killer, Parco snorted.

Sticking her microphone in his chubby face, the reporter asked, "What would you say to him?"

"Not what I would say," Parco responded.

"What would you do?" she pressed.

"I can't say."

With that, the court clerk hurriedly clicked off the set so the jurors could not see the rest of the broadcast.

Lewis looked pleased. He had fought to get the clip before the jurors in the hope that they would see that Parco was a man not above threatening violence against someone who had angered him. While no direct threat had been made, the implication might be enough to convince one or two members of the panel.

Looking at the jury, but speaking to the judge, Lewis announced with a flourish, "And with that, your honor, the defense rests. At this time I would like to renew my motion for dismissal of the case based on insufficient evidence."

Carey gave a silent sigh of relief. Almost three months after they had begun—outlasting a war, he had joked with the jurors—one of the most celebrated cases in Westchester, if not the United States, was winding down.

He dismissed the jury with the usual cautions and turned to the lawyers. "Gentlemen, please have your closing arguments prepared for next Monday, April 15. That's all."

26

CAROLYN WARMUS and her bodyguard Vic Ruggiero, had grown quite close during the trial. Now they were about to enter the courtroom together to hear closing arguments. Ruggiero put his hand on the small of Carolyn's back and pulled her close. With a glance over his shoulder to see if anyone was watching, he gave her a quick kiss.

On one side of the room sat Lewis, already busy rehearsing his closing arguments.

Across the aisle, the prosecutors poured over their notes. McCarty would give the closing. He had on his lucky gray pinstripe suit and had privately told his partner that he felt they were going to pull it off.

Judge Carey blew into the courtroom in a swirl of black, adjusting his robe as he motioned for the court officer to bring in the jury.

The jurors looked tired as they inched into their now-familiar seats and sat stone-faced while Lewis rose from his chair to begin what would be a four-hour summation.

"Our system of justice in this country comes from the English rules and the English had a tradition that was called the 'Scot's verdict.' The Scot's verdict consisted of one of three verdicts: guilty, not guilty, or not proven.

"This, ladies and gentlemen of the jury, is a case that has come before you all these many weeks and at the very end of what we have is a case that has not been proven."

The theme set, the passionate defense lawyer went about explaining his case and the law that bound them all together.

"Judge Carey, at the end of the closing arguments, will tell you what the law is and how you must apply it in your deliberations," Lewis said. "He will define for you the terms 'reasonable doubt' and 'circumstantial evidence.'

"There's another expression the judge will talk to you about, something called a 'presumption of innocence.' A defendant in these courts is presumed innocent, presumed with all the weight and force and majesty of a law as important as our flag, as the Bible, as all the symbols around you.

"Now the judge will tell you that you can't use the fact that Carolyn hasn't testified in any way in this trial. You can't. But the presumption of innocence says that when she pleads to the indictment 'not guilty,' she is saying to you by that presumption and by the plea of not guilty, 'I did not kill Betty Jeanne Solomon. I did not possess a gun. I did not do it.' "

Along with describing reasonable doubt, circumstantial evidence, and the changing system of laws in America, Lewis once again touched on the Salem witch trials of 1692.

"They took those women, they had trials because there was no 'presumption of innocence' and there was no 'beyond a reasonable doubt' and there was no 'moral certainty issues' about circumstantial evidence. They took them and they tied them to stakes and burned them alive before there were these principles.

"And years later, when the people who made this country sat down to write a constitution and to write a declaration of independence, the smell of the burning witches still hung over the country and they decided that there would be rules to make this country different from Europe and from Salem, Massachusetts, in 1692."

Taking the prosecution's case apart one brick at a time, Lewis began pointing out every inaccuracy, every razor-thin fallacy of which he could think, in order to pump into the jurors' heads some scintilla of doubt that would allow them to acquit his client. "What about the forensic evidence?" he asked, pacing in front of the jury box, focusing in on the jurors' eyes. "What about the science technology they went in to collect? There is no hair connected to Carolyn. No fibers. There's no cosmetics. No other prints. They didn't bother to look for tire tracks of the car or cars that went in and out of the area. They didn't bother to look for footprints. They stopped looking for a gun in November of '89. They never dragged the rivers like they were told in the anonymous call. They did a gunshot residue test on a man who washed his hands and didn't bother to tell the technician who did the test who still found some presence of chemical on his hands."

He continued to hammer on the lack of evidence tying Warmus to the murder scene.

"No one saw anything. No one saw a blond girl go up two flights of stairs and take a gun and silencer, screw it on, get into the house, fire the shots, and walk away. Nobody saw that!

"We know no one saw the killer because no one stepped forward," he continued. "But because no one saw it, it doesn't mean that it's Carolyn. And there's no evidence that it's Carolyn, and it's Carolyn who is on trial before you."

Lewis brought up one of his favorite anecdotes from the police investigation.

"Do you remember Constantino told you about getting help from the New York City Police Department? That Lieutenant Sullivan asked Constantino to ask for the New York City Police Department's help. What he wanted was the name of psychics. Remember that? They were going to talk to people who can see the future or see the past. Because that's what they were up to in this case. Never mind footprints. Never mind fingerprints. Never mind doing the things that cops do."

He began pointing the finger of guilt at Solomon while taking another jab at the cops.

"There's something else floating around with this case that's got to give you tremendous pause and reasonable doubt. It's called a black glove. Paul Solomon tells you that he saw that black glove. He described it interestingly enough as a leather glove. And he told the cops about it."

He paused for effect.

"Not a single police officer came here and told that story. No one backed up that story. More importantly, Dr. De Forest said he saw a glove too. He saw a black knit glove. You know something? No police officer thought that a glove under the body of the dead person was important enough to pick up. And then, after the police gave the apartment back to Paul Solomon, we never see that glove again. Well, if it was that important that he knew it didn't belong there, that glove should have been turned over to the police by him, but it wasn't."

Knowing he had to at least address Toaster Joe's testimony, Lewis put his own spin on the man's tale.

"Did Vincent Parco and Paul Solomon conspire and combine together to kill Paul's wife, to pay $20,000 for murder? What did Joe

Lisella get other than an agreement that he signed alone? What did Lisella get to come in and tell what he heard?

"Okay, you want to believe Joe Lisella sets fires? Believe it! Does it make him deaf in the bathroom? Does it mean he couldn't hear what he heard? We're sorry that we couldn't get a priest, a rabbi, that we couldn't get some prominent person to be there to hear it."

He also attacked the one person whose testimony did the most damage.

"How is it that Pat January can come in and recite, verbatim, word for word, that script 'she said and I said'? Do we talk like that? I'm not telling you that Pat January came in to lie. I'm telling you something else. You got to have a doubt about whether that conversation that she related ever existed.

"What's the story with Pat January? In the years to come, however you vote, you'll always be known as someone who was on the Warmus jury. You'll go through the years and find that suddenly, the people who say they were on the Warmus jury can fill Yankee Stadium. Because a lot of people want to be there as part of something that happened. People claim to be part of things because they are part of nothing else in their lives. Because human frailty and human weakness makes you want to be more important.

"The reality is that Pat January basically never had anything to say and nobody wanted to talk to her. Nobody wanted to come back and talk to her until she came up with the story."

Parco, Russo, Sekinski, Rosenthal, and Peters. Lewis left none unscathed in his colorful diatribe against their testimonies, memories, alibis, and motives.

He spent the lunch hour working on the remaining two hours of his speech. At 2:39, he began his conclusion.

"There's a criminal court in London called 'Old Bailey,' and carved around the outer building, the outer edge of the building, are the words 'The Crown Never Loses.'

"The reason is because if through this process you go into the jury room and come out and vote not guilty, the Crown, or our country, gets one of its citizens back, freed from the docket, freed from accusation. And when one of the citizens is passed through this refiner's fire and comes out with you doing your job by saying they have not proven guilt beyond a reasonable doubt, then the triumph is not one side over the other. The triumph is of the law and your oath as jurors and the people. That's why the Crown never loses.

"I'm reluctant to let go, because once I sit down I can't talk to you again, there's no more questions, there's nothing. Now you might be happy that once I sit down you can't hear from me again. But I'm afraid I left something out, that there is some question, something I haven't given you, something in my own preparation that I missed or over-looked, something that protects Carolyn."

He looked beseechingly at each one of the men and women staring back at him. In a low, dramatic voice, he added:

"There is a reason for us to come together and come here. People have struggled to get to these shores from all over the world. People have fought in the streets and in the legislatures for dreams. One im-portant, singular dream. The dream not of wealth, the dream not of power, and the dream not at all of privilege. But a dream of justice.

"Carolyn and I do not flinch from whatever it is you do, one way or another, and neither should the prosecutors or anybody else. You will have done the highest calling of a citizen. You will do the most impor-tant and difficult job of judging another human being.

"I don't envy your task. I'm glad it's not one that's mine, but in getting ready to do it and in sending you away from me and away from Carolyn, all I can wish you is God speed."

With that, the lawyer slowly turned away and walked back to his wide-eyed client.

Judge Carey looked at the courtroom clock.

"As it's so late in the afternoon, Mr. McCarty will present his closing statement tomorrow at 9:30 A.M."

The bright, chipper look on McCarty's face masked the bone-tired wea-riness he felt. It wasn't only because he hadn't been able to sleep, tossing and turning with the specter of Carolyn Warmus invading his night, it was because, deep in his soul, he believed she was a cold, calculating killer who deserved to hear heavy iron bars clanking shut behind her forever.

With a slap on the back from FitzMorris, he began his closing argu-ments.

"We all recognize that jury service is a substantial interruption in people's lives and that this particular case, because of the length of time it has taken, is even more than the usual sacrifice that we ask individuals like yourself to make, to come into this courtroom and ensure that justice is done.

"Ladies and gentlemen, we ask that you do that because you represent the very cornerstone of our system. We ask that you come in here to decide the truth, to listen to the evidence, to weigh the evidence. Decide what is true and from the truth give us justice.

"How do you do that? You do that by utilizing your God-given common sense. There's no magic formula. There are no extraordinary talents that are necessary to perform the task that we ask you to do."

McCarty stood tall before the jury box, his down-to-earth, friendly personality inviting the jurors to relate to him. He wasn't showy. He wasn't dramatic. With him you got what you saw.

"The defendant has asked you to look at her as the victim of a frame-up, an innocent young person who has been framed by venal and malicious people. Now, ladies and gentlemen, we have been here for upward of three months. Does that have the ring of truth to you? Does that make sense to you, given all of the evidence that you have heard?

"On the other hand, I have indicated to you during the opening remarks that we would present to you a body of evidence, bits and pieces of evidence, that would come together and create a picture much like a puzzle, and demonstrate to you that the person who killed Betty Jeanne Solomon on January 15, 1989, is seated in this courtroom and is Carolyn Warmus."

All eyes turned to the young woman sitting several feet away, who was ignoring the prosecutor's words and once again staring into the far corner of the courtroom, apparently lost in her own thoughts.

McCarty moved to destroy the image of the poor, misunderstood heiress Lewis had fought so hard to present.

"We have shown to you that the defendant is not just your average elementary-school teacher. On the contrary, she's an elementary-school teacher who is an erstwhile private detective, a buff, if you will, a person who befriended and hung out with people involved in the private-detective business. Is that an average elementary-school teacher?

"More than that, we have shown you through evidence of her actions that she's intelligent, she's beyond intelligent. She's cunning, she's opportunistic. She's even manipulative in her dealings with other people.

"We have also shown to you, ladies and gentlemen, that based upon all of the evidence and looking at all the individuals who could have been involved in this case, that she alone had the motive, the means, the opportunity to kill Betty Jeanne Solomon on January 15, 1989."

He did not try to sidestep the fact that theirs was not a direct-evidence offering.

"Now, I told you at the outset that ours is a circumstantial case. We made no bones about it. But look at the evidence. It is far too inter-twined to argue that it's not connected. There's too much of it to say that these are just a string of coincidences. It's too convincing to say that the defendant hasn't been proven guilty beyond a reasonable doubt. It is so convincing that the defense themselves have paid it the ultimate compliment. They have said they will come into this courtroom and show that she has been framed."

He looked from person to person, trying to will his thoughts and his beliefs into their souls.

"Use your common sense. How many people would have to conspire together in this case to frame Carolyn Warmus? Ryan Attenson, a friend of hers from Michigan? Liisa Kattai, a woman with whom she worked for a short period of time in the summer of 1988? It's not just Paul Solomon and Vinnie Parco, ladies and gentlemen. This case rests upon many witnesses.

"Lisa Lang, Julianne Lombardi, are they involved in this conspiracy? Is MCI involved in this conspiracy? Did they come into this courtroom to frame Carolyn Warmus? Or did they come into this courtroom to present evidence to you in the best way that they can so that you can piece it together?

"And Pat January, perhaps the most important witness in this case. Is she part of this frame-up? Where is her connection to Paul Solomon? Where is her connection with Vincent Parco? It simply isn't there, ladies and gentlemen."

He tried to reinforce for them the power of a circumstantial case.

"We use circumstantial evidence every day in our daily lives. We use it to make determinations in everything that we do, and the same can be said here. You don't need a videotape of this crime to know who com-mitted it. You don't need a signed confession to prove this defendant guilty beyond a reasonable doubt.

"Use your common sense. This is a premeditated, plotted-out crime. Any individual who sets about to commit this crime is going to attempt to avoid from the get-go getting caught. There will be attempts to mini-mize the evidence that could demonstrate the path that the person takes, and there will be attempts to cover up what was done thereafter. That's what we see here.

"Use your common sense. When people go about to commit a crime, they don't go in announcing their presence. They sneak in. And after-ward they sneak out, and they attempt to hide where they were."

FitzMorris sat listening to his colleague, admiring his dedication to a case that some—including people in their own office—had said couldn't be won.

Warmus poked her head over Lewis's massive shoulders to watch McCarty through slitted eyes.

For several hours the prosecutor took the jurors back through the case, through each witness's story, through each piece of evidence. He led them to her forged phone bill, to the incredible tale told by Gambino, and the uproarious bathroom scene related by Lisella. He pointed out Parco's detailed description of how he had delivered a silencer-equipped, .25-caliber killing tool to the vivacious teacher and how Pat January backed it all up.

And when he felt he had covered each and every story, had pulled back the curtain of smoke that Lewis had worked so hard to put before their eyes, McCarty wrapped up his evidence, tied it with a bow, and placed the package before the men and women he prayed would accept his gift.

"The defendant is entitled to the presumption of innocence," he concluded, "and that I'm sure you will accord. She's entitled to a fair trial and that you can see she sure has gotten. She is entitled to the effective representation of an attorney and Mr. Lewis has provided that throughout these proceedings."

Stopping for a moment to give his final words more impact, McCarty looked over at the defendant and then back to his audience.

"But the people of the state of New York are entitled to something too. Betty Jeanne Solomon is entitled to something, too, entitled to a just verdict. We're entitled to a verdict based upon the credible evidence and the logical conclusion that can be drawn therefrom. And the only logical conclusion that can be drawn from the credible evidence in this case, ladies and gentlemen, is that Carolyn Warmus killed Betty Jeanne Solomon on January 15, 1989.

"I ask you, therefore, in the interest of justice, on behalf of the people of the state of New York, to return a verdict of guilty."

When the jurors marched off to the large, quiet room behind the plastered wall that had served as a backdrop for Judge Carey, Ruggiero hustled Warmus to another floor to await her fate.

Lewis yanked the *New York Times* from his briefcase, took off his dark blue suit coat, and settled in for what he expected would be a long deliberation.

McCarty and FitzMorris chose to spend the first few hours hanging out in the courtroom, chatting with fellow prosecutors and friends. They then made their way to McCarty's office. As they plopped into the soft chairs, they noticed the several bottles of champagne dotting the room. Their compatriots hadn't forgotten the tradition of celebrating a big victory, and should Carolyn Warmus go down in flames, they knew it would be a big victory indeed. FitzMorris picked up one of the bottles and held it in his lap, rolling it softly between his hands as if anxiously awaiting the moment he could pop its cork at the planned victory party.

Meanwhile, the judge remained on the bench, opening up what looked like a small suitcase containing one of his favorite toys, a laptop computer, and immediately began typing out the draft decisions for other backlogged cases.

The herd of reporters began swapping their opinions on the verdict and entering one of the several pools as to the exact day and hour the jury would return with a verdict.

Not long after the twelve jurors had begun their talks (Carey had ordered the four alternates to be sequestered in another room), they sent out their first request for a written copy of the judge's legal instructions, which had followed McCarty's closing.

When the first day's deliberation ended, the jurors were surrounded by court officers and taken by elevator to the basement parking lot, where two large vans awaited to take them to the secret hotel where, on the judge's orders, they would be sequestered until they reached a verdict.

Day one. Day two. Day three. The time passed slowly—9:30 A.M. to 7 P.M.

The defendant appeared every morning, shepherded by one or two bodyguards, to run the gamut of flashing cameras and elongated microphones dangled over her by reporters hoping for that one word or comment to go along with the increasingly repetitive pictures.

On day four, they got their wish.

Carey, on directions from his boss, Administrative Judge Angelo Ingrassia, had been told that Warmus was to get no more special treatment than any other defendant, so VIP rides on security elevators to bypass the media were no longer an option. She had to walk through the lobby to get to the bank of elevators that would take her to whatever floor she chose to wait on that particular day.

On this morning, Warmus failed to notice that Ruggiero had fallen behind her, delayed at the door by a troublesome umbrella. Wearing a long black cape with an attached hood that extended past her face, blocking her peripheral vision, Warmus didn't see the cameraman with a sound microphone sprinting toward her.

In his rush to get a shot, the man thrust the microphone too close to his target's face. When Warmus caught sight of man and microphone only inches from her nose, she let out a bloodcurdling scream. "YeeeeeeeeeeeeAhhhhhhhhh. Leave me alone!"

Covering her face with her hands as if to ward off a blow, she ran toward the safety of the security checkpoints.

When she finally got to the tenth floor, Warmus stormed into the courtroom and grabbed a chair next to her attorney, who was unaware of what had just taken place. "I can't take this anymore. I just can't take this," she yelled loudly at Lewis, who watched his client's finger waving in his face. "You have to do something. Now!"

Lewis calmed her down, then took a moment to talk with Ruggiero, who was still breathing heavily from his struggle to catch up with his client. When Carey entered the room, the lawyer asked for a side-bar conference and informed the judge of what had happened.

Warmus, accompanying her lawyer, began crying loudly. Shoulders heaving with each sob, she told Carey in a loud, tear-filled rage, "No—nobody loves me. Nobody cares what happens to me."

When she was finished, she turned away from the judge, and the sobbing immediately ceased. As she grabbed her purse and strode through the court, she even flashed a smile at a female spectator.

"Did you see that?" asked *New York Daily News* reporter Sherri Cremona. "That two-faced whore wasn't up there five seconds ago putting on her little crying jag for the judge's benefit and then, whammo, no tears and the manipulative bitch is smiling as she walks out!"

That night, every television station in New York ran its tape of the defendant's scream. The long, anxiety-filled wait was taking its toll on everyone.

Frazzled reporters, forced to camp out at the courthouse, became short with one another and with Warmus's two private eyes who tried every method of intimidation they could think of to keep the media away from their client.

As calm as he appeared on the outside, Lewis was having his problems as well.

On the morning of the eighth day of deliberations—April 23—Lewis left his Hastings-on-Hudson home at 8:35 A.M. in his favored red Jeep. Making his way to the courthouse, the preoccupied lawyer drove east on Mount Hope Boulevard, rounded a curve, and plowed into a woman trying to maneuver her 1988 Eagle into a tight parking space. When the pair got out to exchange insurance information, Lewis discovered that the woman was none other than Hastings-on-Hudson Mayor Frances MacEachron.

Two days later, on April 25, Carey received a note from the jurors, saying they were deadlocked. "Jurors are unable to reach unanimous agreement," the note read. Carey had his law clerk call the lawyers back inside.

Once he had informed the lawyers of the problem, Carey called the panel into the courtroom to give them an "Allen Charge," the first of an increasingly stringent set of directives designed to push them into reaching a verdict.

A lot of time, energy, and taxpayers' money had been spent on the internationally publicized trial, and no one—not even Carolyn Warmus —wanted to face a repeat performance.

The judge put on his sober face while addressing the men and women of the jury. When he finished reading his prepared text, he added a short comment.

"During the course of your deliberations, do not hesitate to reexamine your own views and change your opinion if otherwise convinced by the evidence. But do not surrender your honest convictions."

With that, he sent the group back to the jury room.

Intermittent notes from jury foreman Patrick McGowan requesting drinks with their hotel dinner, copies of *Sports Illustrated,* and an outside picnic lunch, drew chuckles from seasoned court watchers and the judge himself.

Carey happily provided the magazines and allowed those so inclined to have a drink with dinner, at their own expense, but he was forced to turn down the luncheon venture after the court's administrative judge, Angelo Ingrassia, cited security concerns.

The judge was touched by the group's apparently determined effort to come to some kind of decision, and he was bothered that he could not even allow them the simple pleasure of an hour outside for a meal in the bright sunshine.

Voicing his displeasure in open court, Carey said, "Even prisoners sentenced to a lifetime in prison get an hour a day outside. I don't see why jurors should not be treated at least as well as lifers."

The requests had added meaning for Lewis, McCarty, and FitzMorris. The lawyers' experience told them that at least some of the jurors had turned their attention away from the task at hand and toward other, more personal concerns. If that were true, it didn't bode well for either side.

Day nine. Day ten.

Day eleven brought only a note from a female juror whose mother had taken ill two weeks before. She asked permission to call her sister to make sure Mom was okay. Carey granted the request.

The twelfth day of deliberations, April 27, marked a record for a Westchester County murder case. It was unusually hot and muggy, and reporters—now sick and tired of the long wait, Carolyn Warmus, and the whole case—read their newspapers, sprawled out on the lobby benches, or played penny-ante poker.

The boredom was broken at 4 P.M. when word filtered down to the lobby that Carey had received an important note from the jurors. The stampede of reporters for the slow-moving elevators resembled a Texas cattle drive.

When the pushing, shoving journalists burst through the courtroom door, they spotted Warmus standing next to the judge's bench with Lewis, McCarty, and FitzMorris looking on.

Once again, true to form, the defendant was crying as if she had been beaten with a steel chain. "I"—sniff—"I can't take this. I—" Despite everyone's best efforts, Warmus's next words were spoken too softly to hear.

When they had finished, Warmus and the lawyers returned to their seats, and the judge took out a piece of paper to pen a note back to the waiting jurors.

Five minutes later, a court officer handed Carey an envelope. He tore it open and, his face expressionless, stared at the words before him. He then handed the note to his court clerk to show Lewis and McCarty.

Looking out at the expectant throng perched on the edge of their seats, Carey cleared his throat. "I'm sorry to have to report that it looks like we now have a hung jury."

A year-long murder investigation, another year spent preparing for the case, a three-month-long trial, and a record deliberation, all for nothing.

"It's like kissing your sister," FitzMorris was able to spit out through his disappointment. "All that work and we have to settle for a tie."

McCarty looked over at Warmus, who was busy dabbing her eyes with Kleenex. Quietly the word was passed to him and Lewis that the stalemated vote had been 8 to 4 to convict. Holding his thumb and forefinger only an inch apart, McCarty looked at his depressed colleague. "This close, pal. This damn close."

Carey barked out an order for silence.

"The defendant will remain free on her $250,000 bond, pending a decision by the District Attorney's office on how they wish to proceed."

Looking at the three tired, disappointed men before him, Carey felt a rush of sympathy.

"Gentlemen, I still have Mr. Lewis's two requests for dismissal of the case based on his claim the prosecution presented insufficient evidence to warrant the charges. I'll expect memoranda of law from both sides, and I'll set May 29 as the hearing date."

McCarty slowly began throwing his numerous files and scraps of paper into the boxes resting on the metal cart beside him, while the reporters jockeyed for position in ragged rows outside the courtroom door—as if forming a gauntlet for the exhausted lawyers to pass through.

Lewis sat back in his chair, for one brief moment closing his eyes and enjoying the serenity he found in the darkness.

Warmus was still sniffling loudly. Ruggiero stood by, trying to comfort her, while DiSalvatore watched, a puzzled, disappointed expression on his face.

A frail, wrinkled old woman in the back row of the spectator's gallery stood up, grabbing the back of the next bench for balance. She looked down at the old man sitting next to her.

"So much for that," she said quietly. "Are there any other good trials starting up today?"

27

THE ECHO of his footsteps resounding through the empty, cavernous courtroom brought back for McCarty the memory of the countless days he had strode to the prosecution table in the firm belief that he was serving justice by trying to put Carolyn Warmus behind bars.

That belief hadn't wavered during the many months that had passed since four jurors allowed her to remain free.

He made a silent vow to himself that this day, January 22, 1992, would mark the beginning of the end for the doe-eyed, devious schoolteacher who, he was convinced, had not only savagely murdered her perceived rival, but was now laughing at him and the legal system from behind her veil of feigned innocence.

Today would mark not only the start of Warmus's second murder trial, it would be the beginning of a judicial show filled with a couple of new—and hopefully devastating—surprises.

After unpacking his briefcase and fingering through the scores of exhibits he would again use, the prosecutor sat back in his chair to wait.

It hadn't taken long after Judge Carey's denial, on July 9, 1991, of his final request to dismiss the case against her, for David Lewis to remove himself as Carolyn Warmus's attorney.

Lewis's quick departure came as no surprise to the legion of reporters and court watchers who had, numerous times during the trial, stared in stunned disbelief as the sweet-smiling defendant turned into a sharp-tongued viper outside the courtroom doors, often snapping venomously at her lawyer over some perceived wrong.

Quickly stepping in to fill Lewis's large legal shoes was William I. Aronwald, a White Plains lawyer and former federal prosecutor, whose limited experience in handling state criminal cases appeared to hold no problems for his client. White-haired and bearded, Aronwald had been a fixture on the fringes of Warmus's close-knit group ever since he had struck up a hallway conversation with Ruggiero during the late stages of the trial.

Even though he was not her attorney at the time, Aronwald had responded to Warmus's request for some routine legal research with speed and pleasantness.

"If Carolyn Warmus is not acquitted and wants to retain another lawyer, that is her prerogative," Lewis had said earlier to a group of reporters who were curious about Aronwald's repeated appearances at the defendant's side.

Some in the media wondered why any lawyer would want to entangle himself with Warmus or her legal problems.

Lewis had repeatedly evaded reporters' questions about his legal fees during the trial. But that information became public knowledge on October 29, 1991, when he was forced to hire a Michigan law firm to file a civil lawsuit against Tom Warmus to collect his unpaid legal bill.

The lawsuit, which was filed in Oakland County Circuit Court in Pontiac, Michigan, revealed that Tom Warmus had agreed to pay Lewis $2,000 per day for each full day of trial and $1,000 per day for any trial day when court was in session for only the morning or afternoon period, with those fees covering both trial preparation and work during the proceedings.

Lewis had billed the multimillionaire $251,826 for legal services plus $126,976.89 in expenses, and $154,683.19 for investigative services. Tom Warmus had managed to cough up all but $172,316 of the total due, but often times late and not without several angry calls from the hard-pressed lawyer.

It was that $172,316 that Lewis was now suing to collect. Part of those expenses still owed belonged to Ruggiero. To top it off, Warmus had given up her New York apartment and moved in with the swarthy private eye shortly after the first trial.

Newspaper and television reporters had a field day for months after the hung jury, staking out Ruggiero's Ardsley home in Westchester County and watching the comings and goings of their favorite tabloid queen.

Once the new addition to their block had been spotted, Ruggiero's irate neighbors wasted no time telephoning the police and the media to alert them to Warmus's almost daily ritual of donning a slinky bikini and sunning herself in the open backyard. Often she would be seen playing with her two cats, Sherman and McCoy, named after the lead character in one of her favorite books, Thomas Wolfe's *Bonfire of the Vanities*.

"Can you believe the audacity of this woman?" screamed one next-door neighbor to a bemused newspaper reporter. "She snags another married man while she's awaiting trial for killing her other lover's wife, and she's walking around out here half-naked like she owns the place! We want her the hell out of here!"

A short time later, the manager of a drugstore in nearby Hartsdale called the Greenburgh police to report that Warmus had just come in and purchased a shopping bag full of prescription drugs: uppers, downers, and anything else you could think of. Since she produced signed prescription slips from her doctor, he had filled the order. But recognizing her immediately as the *Fatal Attraction* femme fatale, he felt it was his duty to report the incident to the police.

When Constantino checked the story out, he discovered that Warmus had first tried to have her rather large drug order filled at another nearby pharmacy, but the pharmacist there had flatly refused to help her.

Ruggiero appeared to take everything in stride. Having devoted himself almost full-time to working with Lewis on Warmus's case, he counted heavily on being paid for his efforts.

But refusing to pay his debts was a Tom Warmus trademark, evidenced by the string of lawsuits and investigations launched against him in Michigan by angry insurance customers who claimed their policies had been suddenly dropped when it came time for them to collect. The state's attorney general, Frank Kelley, had initiated several investigations against Warmus and his American Way companies for allegedly illegal and unethical business dealings.

For her part, Carolyn continued to defend her father to everyone.

In a development that had tongues wagging in the corridors of the Westchester courthouse, the *New York Daily News* reported one day that Warmus—bedecked as usual in one of her sexy ensembles—had spent the previous evening at an off-Broadway play. It wasn't her desire for some entertainment that sparked the knowing winks among lawyers and judges familiar with her case. It was the name of the production she had chosen to see: *Perfect Crime*.

More than anything, McCarty wished he could have been a fly on the wall on December 4, 1991, when Warmus got the news that a grand jury indictment had just been unsealed, charging her with four new criminal counts stemming from her presentation of the phony phone bill during the first trial: second-degree forgery; second-degree criminal possession of a forged instrument; tampering with physical evidence for creating an allegedly false document; and tampering with physical evidence for presenting the allegedly false document to a public servant or office. If convicted on the four counts, Carolyn would be facing a prison sentence of two and a half to seven years.

Judge Carey, however, had issued a ruling on December 18, 1991, prohibiting the prosecution from using her phony phone bill as evidence during the retrial. In the same decision, the judge had also decided that he would let them tell the jury about Warmus's following Solomon and his then-girlfriend, Barbara Ballor, to Puerto Rico. Aronwald, realizing their importance to the circumstantial case that had been built against her, had sought to keep both pieces of evidence from the new jury.

"He's just throwing us a bone so that he looks like he's doing us a big favor," said FitzMorris, noting that the judge had already ruled during the first trial that the Puerto Rico episode could be presented. "What was he going to do? Overrule his own decision from the first time? I take that back. With him, anything's possible!"

McCarty took the decision about the forged phone bill in stride, believing that they'd have enough evidence without it.

Aronwald had also tried, unsuccessfully, to persuade Carey to dismiss the murder and weapon charges, claiming the prosecution had failed to inform him that the police had seized computer disks and files from Parco's and Russo's offices back in 1989. McCarty had, in fact, given his new opponent a list of all the files and disks already seized. It was Aronwald's one last shot, and nobody could blame him for trying.

January 2, 1992, had marked the start of the long and arduous jury selection process for the retrial. McCarty and FitzMorris were pleased with the results, though they both knew the usual doubts would slowly begin to surface as the trial wore on.

McCarty also knew that no retrial of Carolyn Warmus would be complete without some bizarre new twist to get it off on the right foot.

It had come on Tuesday, January 14, 1992.

As McCarty and FitzMorris prepared for another day of jury selection, Aronwald cleared his throat to get the judge's attention. "Your honor," he said, "something very important has come up. May we have a side-bar conference?"

Carey waved the men forward, FitzMorris shooting his partner a quizzical look as they sidled up to the raised bench.

"Judge, my client advises me that she apparently has a growth in her reproductive organs which has been growing substantially. And from what she understands it may necessitate a biopsy be taken to determine whether or not there is a malignancy.

"Your honor, what I propose is to have jury selection postponed tomorrow so Carolyn can visit her Manhattan gynecologist for a tissue biopsy. We're asking for tomorrow off, judge, because her doctor won't see her on Friday, which we know is the only day of the week we don't meet."

Both prosecutors grimaced at the request. While they had no way of knowing whether Carolyn's latest medical malady was fact or fiction, they suspected it was but another attempt on her part to buy herself some time, or, at the very least, to work on Carey's sympathy. They waited for the judge's expected decision to postpone.

But this time, Carey surprised them.

Asking a perplexed Aronwald the reasons why Warmus's doctor wouldn't see her on an emergency basis that Friday, Carey made it very clear he was not in favor of delaying jury selection or the trial for any reason short of a life-or-death emergency. After several "I don't know" responses from the defense lawyer, Carey sent the men back to their respective tables and denied the request. His last statement about the matter was a terse suggestion that Warmus find another doctor if she felt an immediate need for medical help.

Later that same afternoon, when Gannett Suburban Newspaper reporter Cam McWhirter telephoned Aronwald to ask about Warmus's problem, the lawyer blew up. "This is a highly personal matter . . . and publishing a story on Carolyn's condition would be irresponsible journalism," he shouted. "We're not talking about an in-grown toenail here!"

An hour later, the reporter sent the story to his editor for the next day's editions. Neither Aronwald nor Warmus raised the issue again.

Now, FitzMorris joined his colleague at the prosecutor's table and handed McCarty a folder full of papers.

It was only the day before that McCarty had called Paul Solomon and, in a last-ditch effort, asked him to go through his house one more time to look for the missing black glove that Lewis had so successfully used to make them look like chumps.

It didn't take any genius to figure out that Aronwald would probably take the same tack. But what no one save the prosecutors knew at that moment was that Solomon had found two gloves neither he nor Kristan recognized, both located in a cardboard box in the bottom of a cluttered bedroom closet.

More importantly, one of them was a woman's black cashmere, left-handed glove with short fingers and long wristlets that matched perfectly the one shown in the crime scene photographs. Solomon had said he found it clinging to a Velcro strip inside an old leather motorcycle glove he hadn't worn in years.

"When I hired those cleaning people to come in after the murder and straighten things up, they must have thrown the glove into the box in that closet," Solomon had told them when he delivered it to the prosecutors' office.

"The only thing I can think of why I didn't notice it before was that for some reason I always thought the glove I saw that night next to Betty Jeanne's body was a black leather one. Don't ask me why. Even during the first trial when you asked me to look for it, I told Kristan to look for a leather one. With everything going on that night, I guess I really didn't pay that much attention to the glove."

McCarty was glad Solomon had paid attention to his request to search again. The glove was now in the hands of nationally renowned forensic specialist Dr. Peter De Forest, and Robert Adamo, the senior forensic scientist in charge of serology and trace evidence at the county's Department of Laboratories and Research. They had said it might take a few weeks, even a couple months, to complete a microscopic review.

With luck, the scientists' findings would give the prosecutors the direct evidence they needed to solidify their otherwise circumstantial case.

Moments later, William Aronwald walked confidently into the room, followed by Carolyn Warmus, who was wrapped in a white plastic raincoat and a multicolored scarf that covered most of her face. Once again she was attempting to frustrate the television and still cameramen camped out in the courthouse lobby. A puffing Victor Ruggiero came in like her shadow, his face flushed from carrying the lawyer's thick and heavy briefcases.

The prosecutors looked up from their table in time to see Warmus's glassy-eyed look as she carefully unpacked her own small brown briefcase and placed her now-famous pillow on the defense table in front of her. Several reporters had also noted her vacant stare and decided she must have been tranquilized to deal with the stress of another murder trial.

Once both sides were settled in, Carey emerged from his chambers and politely welcomed the combatants back to his arena. Noting that everyone was in place, the judge asked one of his court officers to bring in the new jury.

Six men and six women nervously filed in and took their assigned places. The four alternates filled the seats on each end of the jury box. When they were settled, Carey wasted no time in beginning the second *Fatal Attraction* trial.

"Mr. McCarty, your opening statement, please."

It hadn't taken the prosecutor long to prepare for this moment. His words would be almost identical to those he used during his first opening almost one year ago. His voice rising and falling for optimum effect, McCarty smoothly took the jurors through the sordid story, noted the incredible defense witnesses and the tales they would tell, and wrapped up by pointing the finger of guilt directly at the young woman who was busily scribbling a new set of notes.

Walking behind Warmus's chair, McCarty told the jurors, "She couldn't let go, and Paul Solomon was too weak to tell her to get out of his life.

"Ladies and gentlemen, Carolyn Warmus had the motive, the means, and the opportunity to kill Betty Jeanne Solomon. She developed an obsession for Solomon. She had the means to kill his wife with a silencer-equipped gun she had purchased from Vincent Parco, a private investigator, and knew from a telephone conversation the day of the killing that Mrs. Solomon was going to be home alone."

When he got to his description of Parco, McCarty didn't try to whitewash his witness's character. He acknowledged that Parco was a key witness, who would testify under an agreement of immunity.

"He is not an Eagle Scout," he warned the panel. "But the beauty of this case is that it doesn't have to depend on Vincent Parco. A school nurse and another private investigator, James Russo, will back up Parco's testimony."

Conceding that no single piece of evidence or witness would tell the whole story, he assured the jurors, "that if you use common sense, it will come together like pieces of a puzzle."

Two hours later when McCarty ended his remarks, the judge nodded at Aronwald, signaling him to take the podium and begin his efforts to prove his client's innocence.

As he began, everyone in the courtroom realized that Aronwald's plan was not to repeat Lewis's strategy of claiming a grand conspiracy against Warmus, but to try and convince the jurors that Paul Solomon was the actual killer of his own wife.

Unlike Lewis, he did not have the luxury of showing the panel Warmus's own version of her phone bills. Now that she had been indicted on forgery charges for that ploy, he could not mention them at all without opening the door for the prosecution to tell the jury she had been charged with illegally concocting her own evidence.

During his opening, Aronwald pounded out what he hoped would be a believable scenario.

"You will see from the testimony that Paul Solomon was as much the pursuer as the pursued," he said, pausing a moment to stroke his beard.

"He was not a babe in the woods. It is entirely possible Paul Solomon was at home and was the one who, in fact, murdered his wife. He routinely, regularly and frequently, as a matter of course, lied to his wife Betty Jeanne Solomon."

He paused to let the jurors digest his words. Then his voice became forceful, almost adamant, as he tried to pound his point home. "Our job is not to convince you of that," he bellowed, "but that there is insufficient evidence to convict Carolyn Warmus."

He glanced over at his client, who during his opening statements had turned around in her seat and was now staring at the people who would decide her fate. Often during her lawyer's stirring speech, she would smile brightly as if trying to convince them that a happy woman was an innocent one.

When Aronwald began trying to tear down the credibility of Vincent Parco, Warmus nodded her head in agreement.

"The prosecution's case depends on Parco's testimony, and he simply cannot be believed," her lawyer argued. "He makes his living by lying, deceiving, and conning complete strangers."

Switching again to the lack of evidence linking Warmus to the slaying, he said, "There is no physical evidence or eye witness to tie her to the murder scene. When she met Solomon that very night for dinner she was not in an excited or agitated state."

Noting that Betty Jeanne Solomon's killer, based on what he called the "expert marksmanship" displayed at the time of the murder, would have to be someone knowledgeable about firearms, Aronwald said Warmus "was not at all adept or familiar with weapons."

Three hours after he began, Aronwald wrapped up his presentation. Scooping up his notes and returning to his seat, he gave Warmus a small grin. She stared back expressionlessly.

Carey waited until the defense attorney was comfortably seated before he, too, sat back in his large, cushioned chair. If the first case was any indication, this second trial would last for months. As if the thought of another lengthy trial suddenly tired him, Carey weakly waved his hand at McCarty. "Please call your first witness."

And with that, it all began again.

In what seemed like the rerun of a favorite old movie, the next three months were filled with the same sinful, sick, and saintly witnesses, each with their own incredible tale.

Marshall and Josette Tilden. Kristan Solomon. Paul Solomon. Parco. Constantino. January. Attenson. Rogers. Kattai. Peters.

On and on, more than forty in all, marching up to and away from the witness box, leaving behind their memories sometimes clouded by the passage of time, sometimes as detailed as if the events had occurred only the day before.

The prosecution's evidence remained the same. Warmus's lack of an alibi. Her MCI records showing a call to the New Jersey gun shop on the day of the murder. Her friend Liisa Kattai's stolen driver's license, which was used to buy the bullets. The obsessive love for Solomon that had driven her to Puerto Rico.

Through it all, the jurors listened intently but gave no outward sign as to their thoughts.

McCarty untiringly reasked his questions of the now-experienced witnesses, drawing from them the information, and sometimes subtle nuances, the new jury might pick up on.

The only real surprise for the two prosecutors was their inability to locate Jimmy Russo. Although McCarty hadn't any reason to suspect the Brooklyn-born private eye would make himself scarce for the second trial, that was what had apparently happened. The lack of Russo's testimony wasn't a death blow by any means. Whatever Russo's reasons for not showing, the prosecutors could live with it.

In his five days of testimony, Paul Solomon again kept the courtroom riveted with his recountings of a troubled marriage, extramarital affairs, his passionate affair with Warmus, and the string of lies he had told his wife to maintain that lifestyle.

Although he had told these stories before, a new air of resignation now accompanied his words. He appeared to be a man beaten down by forces beyond his control. He left the witness stand as he had arrived: bitter, sorrowful, and with little fight left.

On March 30, 1992, more than two months after the trial began, McCarty dropped his bombshell. Out of the jury's presence, he offered into evidence the mysterious black glove that Solomon had found and given him the day before the trial started.

The forensic evaluation of the glove had been completed a few days earlier and the written report had finally been turned over to the prosecutors.

Despite the evidence of the forensic field test conducted on the glove by Linda Duffy at the crime scene, the new analysis, which had been made with the help of a high-powered electron microscope, revealed minute particles of blood imbedded in the fibers. They were too small to make a DNA match, but by using special chemicals, De Forest and Adamo had been able to photograph the stains.

When McCarty first saw the photographs, he had stared in stunned amazement. The bloodstains clearly resembled fingerprints, as if someone with a bloody hand had grabbed the glove. Perhaps Betty Jeanne had grabbed Carolyn's gloved hand and pulled the glove off in the struggle.

The report also indicated that fibers on the glove matched the fibers found underneath Betty Jeanne's fingernails. Even though the chain of evidence had been broken, the fibers established the fact that this was indeed the same glove that had been found at the scene of the crime.

And last but not least, there had been a blond hair on the glove. Although Warmus would certainly not provide the prosecutors with a sample of her hair to use for comparison, and Carey would certainly not allow it into evidence, for McCarty and FitzMorris it banished any lingering possibility of doubt.

Now in court, trying to persuade Carey to permit the jury to hear about their devastating findings, McCarty realized that he faced another uphill battle. The judge appeared to be agreeing with Aronwald's arguments against its admission.

"Your honor, not only do we not know where this glove has been for the past three years, there is no credible evidence to show that this is the same glove that is seen in the crime-scene photographs," Aronwald said. "There are many other inferences that can be drawn from this glove and the bloodstains. One such inference is that Paul Solomon, in an effort to frame Carolyn Warmus, has put blood on the glove."

McCarty and FitzMorris both looked up in disbelief. They knew their counterpart had to make the argument, but the suggestion that somehow Solomon had tampered with the glove flew in the face not only of common sense, but of the forensic evidence as well.

Earlier in the trial, McCarty had opened the door to the new evidence ever so slightly by showing the glove to Constantino and having him testify that it appeared to be the same one he had seen the night of the murder. Now it was time for the coup de grace, if only Carey would cooperate.

After hearing both McCarty's and Aronwald's arguments, the judge decided he wanted to know more. Calling for an evidentiary hearing—outside the presence of the jury—Carey spent the next several days listening to De Forest and Adamo. To bolster their case, the prosecution also called Solomon and his daughter back to court.

During the hearing, Solomon testified that Betty Jeanne did not own a pair of gloves like the one being shown him. He also retold the story of how McCarty had asked him to look for the glove and of its discovery.

Kristan's testimony was even more damaging. "Carolyn and I were on that ski trip back in February 1988 and I had forgotten my gloves. She let me borrow a pair of hers, and this is exactly like the gloves she lent me," the now-eighteen-year-old testified, holding up the glove that McCarty had handed her.

During his cross-examination, Aronwald repeatedly tried to break down the teen-age girl's testimony, but his only success was in getting her to say that the glove she now held in her hands "is almost exactly like the pair she lent me." The defense lawyer then tried to make the most of this subtle difference in testimony in his arguments to Carey. "Your honor, there is just not enough evidence here to prove that this is the glove that was at the crime scene," he finally concluded.

McCarty argued strenuously, but the judge gave him little reason to doubt what the final outcome would be.

Several days later, on April 1, 1992, Carey released an eleven-page decision saying the glove could not be used as evidence unless the prosecutors were able to produce stronger legal arguments by the following Monday morning.

On the fateful day, a smiling McCarty pushed his evidence cart into the courtroom. "Your honor," he began, "last Friday the District Attorney's office subpoenaed the American Express credit card records of Carolyn Warmus and have discovered that on November 9, 1987, this defendant purchased a pair of gloves at Filene's Basement in Scarsdale on Central Avenue matching the glove found in the Solomon residence."

McCarty's words sparked a mad scramble as reporters sprinted from the room to report the new evidence against Warmus.

While Carey agreed to the prosecution's request for a few days' time to produce the new evidence, including obtaining the actual receipts and computer records from Filene's, Aronwald sat in his chair getting angrier with each passing second.

"This is trial by ambush," he finally exploded at Carey. "This comes as a complete surprise to us. The prosecution should have told me about all this over the weekend."

Carey shook his head. Even he could not fault the prosecutors for that slight oversight, since it was he who had put their feet to the fire in the first place.

Warmus, looking haggard and angry, said nothing.

During the next few days, Aronwald and Ruggiero conducted their own investigation into the glove, quickly discovering that the type in question had been mass-produced beginning in 1981 and that Filene's sold them for $10.

Checking both Warmus's American Express and Filene's store records, they discovered the prosecution could prove that the type, style, material, and manufacturer of the gloves she had purchased matched those of the glove they were trying to introduce as evidence, but one thing they could not determine was color. Filene's sold the same make of glove in nine different colors—including black—a minor but perhaps important point that Aronwald would have to hang his hat on.

After another hearing, during which Aronwald continually reminded the court that the prosecutors couldn't determine the color of the gloves Warmus had purchased, Carey issued a new written decision that nearly frazzled the frenzied prosecutors.

The judge this time ruled that the glove would be admitted if the prosecution could show that Warmus's gloves had "similar intrinsic characteristics," including color, size, material, and style. The judge also barred them from mentioning in the presence of the jury the minuscule bloodstains they had found on their glove.

McCarty again refused to give up. Five days later, he and FitzMorris saw their hard work pay off when, after more lengthy debate and scores of legal briefs, Carey made his ruling.

Saying he had taken into consideration Paul and Kristan Solomon's testimony, along with that of the forensic experts, and had reviewed Warmus's credit card records and Filene's purchase receipts, the judge decided to permit the admission of the glove into evidence.

But in his inimitable style, Carey couldn't give the prosecution a total victory. He also ruled that they would not be allowed to mention to the jury the blood or blond hair found on the glove unless the defense brought it up first.

But the theatrics were far from over as the jury was once again allowed into the courtroom. In what McCarty and FitzMorris and many experienced trial watchers all agreed was a puzzling—if not foolish—decision, Aronwald chose to question a witness about the blood found on the glove, thus opening the door for the prosecution to bring forth all their charts, pictures, and lab reports tying that glove to the crime scene. McCarty, through the testimony of De Forest and Adamo, was now able to provide the jury with its first piece of hard evidence linking Warmus to the actual murder scene.

Another very important piece of the puzzle was now in place. Soon the prosecution would bring Solomon and Kristan back to the stand—this time in front of the jury—to solidify the link between Warmus and her glove. Her American Express records would follow.

In a hallway interview, Aronwald tried to explain his reasoning: "While Judge Carey had excluded the recent blood-test findings as prejudicial, he was going to allow a scientist to explain that white marks on the glove resulted from chemicals he put there during tests.

"That decision forced us to put before the jury the issue of the blood specks. Otherwise the jury was going to be forced to speculate about why there were tests done on that glove. I had no choice."

Trying to salvage something from the day, Aronwald attempted to persuade the reporters that the blood evidence actually helped Warmus. "I'm really bothered by the fact that there certainly is a suggestion of tampering here," he said, noting his earlier statements in court about the possibility Solomon had planted the blood specks to frame Warmus. "If there is a conviction," the tired lawyer added, "an appellate court would have little difficulty reversing the verdict based on the judge's erroneous decision to admit the glove."

With that, Aronwald walked away.

Warmus's legal problems multiplied when, on April 15, 1992, a stranger walked up to her as she waited out a break on the sixteenth floor. "Excuse me. Are you Carolyn Warmus?" the man asked politely.

Warmus only nodded.

Ruggiero, several feet away, overheard the exchange and started moving toward the unknown man, not quite sure what his intentions were. Throughout the first trial and now this one, he had tried to keep the well-wishers and glad-handers away from Carolyn. This time, he was too late.

"Miss Warmus, my name is Ronald Marsico and this is for you."

With that he pulled out a folded piece of paper and put it in her hands. All too quickly Ruggiero realized that Carolyn had just been subpoenaed once again, but for what he wasn't sure. He began screaming at Marsico, who just smiled and walked away.

Opening up the paperwork, Warmus saw she was being sued by the B & L Management Company, the Manhattan-based landlord of what was once her apartment on First Avenue.

The legal documents noted she had vacated the apartment on August 4, 1991, and hadn't paid her back rent, which now amounted to $4,233.68. With a look of disgust, she tossed the subpoena to Ruggiero. She was at that moment being sued by the woman in New Jersey whose car she had hit in a traffic accident [the case involving the forged letter brought out in the first trial]; she had only a few months before been indicted on four felony forgery counts stemming from the MCI phone bill she introduced at the first trial; she was in the middle of her second murder trial . . . and now this.

"When is all of this going to end?" she wondered aloud.

On Monday, May 4, 1992, the prosecution, with little fanfare, rested its case. The following day, Aronwald tried to gear up for what he knew was going to be a short but, with hope, spirited defense.

Calling to the stand Irene Powers, a secretary at the Bedford Road Elementary School where Warmus taught at the time of the murder, he quickly brought out a pink message slip.

Trying to prove that Solomon had lied on the witness stand when he said that he had not tried to contact Warmus in the months preceding his wife's murder, Aronwald asked that the jury be allowed to read what was written on the piece of paper.

In pencil on the type of message slip used by the school was the message that "Mr. Solomon" had called "C. Warmus" at 12:24 P.M. on January 6, 1989—nine days before the slaying.

But Powers's testimony was less than helpful to the defense. "I'm sorry, but I don't remember writing that note," she testified. As a result of Aronwald's continual prodding, she finally admitted the handwriting resembled her own.

On cross-examination, FitzMorris quickly got to the point. "Do you have any idea where this exhibit has been for the last three years?"

Powers shook her head. "No."

Unlike Lewis's colorful witnesses from the year before, the new defense offerings appeared dull and, worse yet, left many in the courtroom wondering why they had been called at all.

Aronwald brought Kristan Solomon to the stand in an effort to point out some minor inconsistencies in her earlier testimony. With her, the pressing defense lawyer violated the cardinal rule of the courtroom: Don't attack old women or young kids with tough questioning.

Ripping into her testimony that Warmus had shown up at one of her basketball games about a year after her mother's slaying, Aronwald brought her to tears. From the back of the courtroom, one could almost feel the jurors' growing animosity toward the man who was now making this poor, motherless child endure such abuse.

Warmus, however, was smiling broadly as Kristan sobbed.

Next came retired schoolteacher Charles Cundari, who testified that he was the coach of a junior varsity team that often played Kristan's squad and that he did not recall seeing Warmus—who was teaching at his school at that time—at the game Kristan said she had attended.

In a further effort to discredit Kristan, Aronwald called Jonathan Hale, the brother of a woman Kristan had supposedly misidentified in a picture with Warmus.

Confused about the reasons for Hale's testimony, several reporters asked Aronwald during a break what he was trying to prove.

"Kristan had identified Hale's sister as someone else, even though they all had had dinner together in late 1987," he responded with a knowing wink.

The reporters scratched their heads in confusion and asked why he was focusing on such minor points.

"These aren't minor points," the lawyer said in exasperation. "Kristan Solomon's credibility is critical to this case."

He next called Pat January to the stand to try and break her story that Warmus, only days before the murder, had told her she had purchased a gun with a special attachment, for protection, from a private detective.

January, unmoved by Aronwald's obvious attempts to unnerve her, ignored his occasional jabs at her veracity and remained steadfast in her testimony.

Constantino; his fellow Greenburgh detective, Ronald Elsasser; and Assistant District Attorney Kevin Kennedy, were all paraded to the stand to testify to some previous misstatement or apparently wrong decision in the Betty Jeanne Solomon murder investigation. While Aronwald was able to get them to admit to minor problems in their investigations or preparations, none of these appeared to exonerate his client.

In an apparent last-ditch effort to provide the jurors some reasonable doubt about Warmus's phone records showing a call to the New Jersey gun shop on the day of the murder, the defense attorney called John Holder, a former New York City police detective who had worked as a repairman for the New York Telephone Company.

Holder told the jury that just before he came to testify, he had visited the building where Warmus lived at the time of the murder and examined the terminal box in the basement where all the phone lines from all the apartments converge. He explained that by attaching the clips of an apparatus known as a telephone handset to the wires of a telephone line at the terminal box, it was possible to make a call without using the actual phone on that particular line.

While Aronwald beamed, many of the jurors slowly shook their heads.

Tom Warmus once again made his grand entrance, but unlike the first time, he made a point of acknowledging his eldest daughter, if somewhat perfunctorily with a smile and a little wave.

It was obvious by his brief testimony about Parco's phone call that he would rather have been anywhere else but in that courtroom. When he had finished, he again graced Carolyn with an empty little smile, a gesture she appeared to delight in.

For those reporters in the courtroom who had investigated her past, the sight of Carolyn's stepmother, Nancy Dailey, strolling into the courtroom brought expressions of disbelief. If Warmus had made one thing clear to her few friends and family, it was her complete and utter hatred for the woman now coming to testify on her behalf.

After establishing Dailey's background for the jury, Aronwald quickly directed her attention to a duffel bag full of clothes that he picked up from the defense table. "Ms. Dailey, have you ever seen these before?" he asked, removing the clothing from the bag.

"Yes. That's the gold ski jacket, black ski pants, black circular scarf, black fur headband, and matching black gloves that I purchased for Carolyn at a Michigan store in December 1986 or January 1987."

Bringing the gloves to the witness stand, Aronwald asked his witness to examine them carefully. "Is there anything special about those gloves that convinces you they are the same gloves you bought for your step-daughter more than five years ago?"

Aronwald believed that if he could establish for the jurors that Warmus had just received a new pair of black gloves, they would see there was no reason for her to buy another pair in New York only a few months later, on November 9, 1987.

Running her fingers over them, Dailey responded, "Yes, they are ribbed at the wrist."

"Is there any doubt in your mind that those were the items you purchased for Carolyn in December 1986?"

She hesitated only a second. "No doubt."

FitzMorris, in his cross-examination, wasted little time getting to the heart of the matter. "Ms. Dailey, you wouldn't know if your daughter purchased another pair of black gloves at Filene's Basement?"

"No, no I wouldn't," she answered.

"Ms. Dailey, do you recognize this?" FitzMorris asked, handing her the prosecution's bloodstained black cashmere glove.

"I've never seen it before," came the reply.

FitzMorris thanked her and took his seat. She could have bought Warmus a million articles of clothing during the past few years, but there was no way she could ever testify that Carolyn hadn't bought another pair of gloves in New York before the murder.

Aronwald's last witness was Jerold Steinberg, an employee of International Testing Laboratories in Newark, New Jersey. Steinberg had been hired by the defense to try and make a silencer in exactly the same way George Peters had described making and attaching one to Parco's .25-caliber automatic.

"The device which has been so described would not work," Steinberg said confidently, as he was led along carefully by Aronwald. The technician bolstered his testimony by holding up tools, testing devices, metal parts, and a two-foot-high diagram of a gun while demonstrating his conclusion.

Although his explanation had sounded authoritative enough, it didn't survive the first few seconds of FitzMorris's questioning.

"Mr. Steinberg, what are you basing all your conclusions on? Have

you read the transcript of Mr. Peters's testimony about how he manufactured a silencer?"

The witness looked surprised. "No. My conclusions are based solely
on what the defense team has told me."

FitzMorris saw his opening. "Would you have preferred to have a
transcript of this testimony?"

"Yes," came his reply.

A hastily called recess and some quick coaching by the defense lawyer
did little to repair the damage.

The pressure had gotten to Warmus as well. As Steinberg continued
his testimony, the defendant suddenly yelled out loud: "Shhhh! I'm
having difficulty hearing with these two talking." Her reference to Mc-
Carty and FitzMorris drew muffled laughter from the spectators.

Clearly frustrated by the way things were going, Aronwald bowed his
head and rested his case.

But McCarty wasn't about to let the case end on that note. Clearly
annoyed by Aronwald's last witness, he decided to recall Peters to the
stand to explain, step by step, how he had made the silencer.

Peters, however, was mortally ill, dying of emphysema and colon
cancer. He appeared, coughing, stooped and grasping a cane, the following day, but told McCarty he was too sick to testify. The prosecutor
asked Carey to postpone Peters's testimony until the following Monday,
but the judge ordered him to the courtroom so he could see for himself
just how sick Peters was.

When a court officer opened the door to allow him to enter, Ruggiero
was standing just inside the doorway, arms folded, glaring. To the shock
and horror of everyone seated in the wooden pews, Ruggiero virtually
shouted in Peters's ears, "He looks okay to me. Yes sir. Looks real
healthy to me. I can't see what his problem is. He looks damn healthy."

The frightened witness, overcome by a bout of coughing, barely made
it to the stand.

McCarty, who had looked on in stunned disbelief as Ruggiero ver-
bally assaulted his witness, held his boiling temper until Judge Carey—
who had been in his chambers when the incident occurred—entered
the courtroom. Furious, he then explained what had just happened and
demanded that Ruggiero be barred from the courtroom.

Aronwald stood to respond. "Your honor, if Mr. Ruggiero did what
Mr. McCarty claims—"

Before Aronwald could utter another word, McCarty jumped to his feet. "What do you mean, 'if,' Mr. Aronwald? Everyone in this court-room heard what Ruggiero said, including you. There's no 'if.' "

Looking sheepish, the defense lawyer could only apologize for the outburst. "He's right, your honor. I did hear it. All I can say is that Mr. Ruggiero was wrong to do that and I apologize to the court for him. I will also speak to Mr. Ruggiero after we're through today and inform him that if anything like that occurs again he will be dismissed. That's as much as I can do. I'm sorry."

Ruggiero stared at his boss with disdain, while Warmus, watching her attorney embarrass her lover so publicly, became enraged. With a warn-ing to the unrepentant private eye that if another such outburst should occur, expulsion from the courtroom would be the least of his worries, Carey agreed to postpone Peters's testimony until the following Mon-day.

After the judge had left the room, Warmus angrily grabbed her be-longings and stormed out into the hallway, where she waited, tapping her foot, until Aronwald stepped through the doorway.

"Just what in the hell did you think you were doing in there, embar-rassing Vic in front of all those people?" she raged in front of reporters and spectators alike. "He didn't do anything wrong."

Unsure of how to quiet his belligerent client, Aronwald just stood there, red-faced. "And another thing," she screamed, "why does he always have to carry your bags into court? He's not your private errand boy."

With that she stomped off to join her lover. Aronwald said nothing as he continued his walk to the elevators.

The following Monday, Peters took the stand. Guided by McCarty's well-planned questions, he slowly and carefully explained to the jury every step he had taken in making the silencer for Parco's .25-caliber Beretta automatic.

When the machinist's jargon became a little too technical, McCarty pulled out charts and diagrams drawn by Peters himself to help the panel understand the procedures.

For seven minutes the courtroom was silent as the jurors, leaning attentively forward in their seats, watched Peters carefully diagram the silencer. He illustrated how he used a piece of gas pipe one-eighth of an inch wide, a piece of tubing into which the gas pipe could be inserted, couplings, washers, and silver to construct his silencer.

"It worked good, to my satisfaction," he boasted to the jurors, bringing a smile to the faces of many. And when he was finished, everyone in court that day must have felt they could go home and make a silencer with no problem at all.

Quite pleased with himself and more than content with Peters's performance, McCarty told the judge, "The prosecution rests again."

Epilogue

THE TWO DAYS of final summations contained no surprises. Both sides had exhausted their respective bag of tricks during the hard-fought trial. Now, in their last chance to persuade the jury, both McCarty and Aronwald continued to stick to their game plans.

Aronwald led off by minimizing and ridiculing the prosecution's mostly circumstantial evidence, telling the jurors it was much too little and suspect for them to reach a conclusion of guilt. "Reasonable doubt," he repeated over and over. "Reasonable doubt." He wanted each member of the jury to grab hold of that phrase and carry it into their deliberations.

McCarty countered Aronwald's oft-repeated "reasonable doubt" with a phrase of his own: "common sense." At times during his closing, he almost pleaded with the jurors to use their God-given abilities to discern between what their hearts told them was fact and what was fiction. "It's a powerful, compelling body of evidence for you to work with, for you to mold together and follow to the truth," he said. "And the truth is that on January 15, 1989, Carolyn Warmus shot and killed Betty Jeanne Solomon in her own home."

On Thursday, May 21, Carey gave his instructions to the jury. But in one final, strange twist to an already bizarre case, the judge directed the panel to go to the jury room, but not to begin deliberations.

Calling the lawyers into his chambers, Carey listened to Aronwald's application to have juror number 8, a quiet, middle-aged black woman, removed from the panel because he had noticed her doze off during the judge's speech. She was called in and, when asked by Carey, admitted she had, indeed, fallen asleep. Going to work each day at 5 A.M., before coming to court, and again at the end of the day, had taken its toll.

Under questioning by both attorneys, she also conceded having slept through some of the testimony of Paul Solomon and Patricia January. Carey thanked her profusely for her efforts, but agreed to her removal. The first alternate was officially added to the panel, making the composition seven men and five women.

Calling the jurors back into court, Carey quickly explained what had happened and then, at 12:20 P.M., they began their deliberations.

Warmus received her first bad omen that night, when Judge Kenneth Lange released an eight-page decision upholding the forgery indictment against her.

Questioned the next day by reporters, she merely shrugged it off. "First things first," she said coyly. "My acquittal on this murder charge and then I'll deal with that."

As Thursday turned into Friday and Friday into Saturday and Saturday into Sunday, the prosecutors' hopes increased while Aronwald and his group grew more unsettled. During this time, the jurors had made numerous requests to have key testimony read back to them and to be provided certain evidence in the jury room.

As they asked for and received Warmus's MCI phone bills, the black glove, and other apparently pro-prosecution evidence, including readbacks of several damaging portions of testimony against Warmus, McCarty and FitzMorris found it almost impossible to hide their glee.

Speculation among the reporters and court watchers also seemed to favor the prosecution, and for a while during that fourth day of deliberations, everyone seemed to agree that Warmus was going down.

But Sunday ended with no verdict, and by mid-Monday, the euphoric feeling among the prosecution supporters had disappeared. Once again the jurors were asking for testimony to be read back, and this time it appeared to be testimony that favored Warmus.

While no one could know for sure what was going on inside the deliberation room, experience told the prosecutorial pair that something was wrong. Seriously wrong.

By Tuesday, Aronwald's confidence appeared to have grown by leaps and bounds. The initial days of deliberation had found him testy and snappish with the media and anyone else who dared disturb his thoughts. He had interpreted the jurors' initial requests the same way as McCarty and FitzMorris: definitely pro-prosecution. He had steeled himself for the inevitable, but now the tides appeared to be turning and it was his opponents' turn to sweat.

Feeling more assured with each passing moment that they would all soon be hearing about another hung jury, Aronwald decided to share his joy with the press. "Every day that goes by, from the defendant's standpoint, is a cause for optimism," he said.

Wednesday, May 27, 1992, broke clear and sunny. While Warmus and her entourage began the day by once again trying to dodge the ever-present cameramen in the courthouse lobby, the prosecutors arrived with diminishing hope that she would ever see the inside of a jail cell again.

The morning passed slowly with no new requests from the jurors.

It was 11:15 A.M., and Aronwald was sitting on one of the padded benches outside the courtroom, picking lint off his stylish gray pinstripe suit, when Carey's law clerk walked up and informed him that the jury had sent in another note and the judge would like to see him and McCarty immediately.

"Gentlemen," Carey said, as soon as all were assembled, "the jury has sent me a note saying they have reached a verdict. Mr. Aronwald, will you please get your client so we can see what they've decided?"

Aronwald nodded and nervously stroked his well-groomed beard. Carolyn, he knew, was with Ruggiero on the eighteenth floor, the place where she always went to get away from the nosy newshounds and the staring, finger-pointing spectators.

As the elevator doors opened, she looked up to see her lawyer walking toward her. His next words sounded hollow and distant: "The jury has a decision."

As she stood to better search his face for some small sign of hope, the impact of the message slowly began to take hold.

"I'm frightened," she said with such emotion that those around her could almost feel the anxiety coursing through her body. "I'm nervous. I'm scared," she almost screamed.

Aronwald lightly touched her arm, as if to steady her. "Let's go downstairs and see what the decision is."

The clearly anguished defendant composed herself with several deep breaths and then gathered up her legal papers and ever-present note pad. With Aronwald leading the way and Ruggiero following behind, she boarded the elevator.

On the sixteenth floor, an adrenaline-induced buzz had already whipped through the crowd.

A mad rush by reporters to secure the only two pay telephones on the floor resulted in some not-so-good-natured jostling, but by the time Warmus and her group emerged from the elevator almost everyone had already reclaimed their courtroom seats.

In the deathly silent courtroom, Carey walked in with a flourish, the rustling of his long, black robe the only sound to be heard. Nodding to a court officer, he quietly said, "Will you please bring in the jury?"

Every eye was riveted to the faces of the twelve jurors as they slowly entered the room. Reporters, spectators, lawyers, and the defendant studied each one in the hope of detecting something to indicate what their decision might be.

Trying to read a jury is as much a part of courtroom tradition as the banging gavel or the flowing robes, and while it is a favorite pastime during a trial and at the time of a verdict, most laymen and legal scholars would readily agree that the practice is as worthless as a plugged nickel.

When the group had finally been seated, Carey glanced toward jury forewoman Anne Marie Heanue. "Have you reached a verdict?"

Heanue stood, and in a quivering voice responded, "We have, your honor."

Once again the judge looked at his court officer and gave him a slight nod. In a booming voice that reverberated off the four walls of the large room, the officer bellowed, "As to the first count, how say you?"

Her voice stronger now, and with no hesitation, Heanue replied, "Guilty."

At the very second she became a convicted murderer, Warmus stared straight ahead and made only a small, whimpering sound, which was almost drowned out by a yelp and a spattering of applause from several spectators. A stern look from Carey quieted the gallery.

Again the court officer almost shouted, "As to the second count, how say you?"

"Guilty," Heanue said, and a moment later slumped back into her seat. The bodies of the jurors appeared to sag almost in unison. Two women in the front row began wiping away tears. The strain of the almost four-month-long trial and the week of deliberations was evident in all of them.

Warmus remained staring straight ahead, as if in a deep trance. She looked neither to her left nor right and her unblinking eyes remained as large as saucers. Aronwald sat back in his chair, apparently stunned at how suddenly the end had come. Ruggiero, seated at a table behind his now-lost love, slowly shook his head.

After a few words of thanks to the jurors for their patience and perseverance, Carey bade them good-bye and watched as they slowly shuffled from the room.

Turning his gaze back to Warmus, Carey said, "I am setting a sentencing date of June 26. Miss Warmus, as required by law, you are remanded into custody pending your sentencing."

Aronwald watched the sunken face of his client, who had no family member or friend in the courtroom that day to show her support or love.

She turned to him and quietly asked, "What about bail?"

"There is no bail on a Class A felony," he responded gently.

"Oh, yes, you told me that."

As she turned her gaze back to the front of the courtroom, Aronwald added, "I'll visit you at the jail and call your folks."

With that, three court officers who had silently moved behind the convicted woman reached out and grabbed her arms. In passive acquiescence, Warmus placed her hands behind her back and only bowed her head when she felt the cold, steel hoops snap around her wrists.

Without a word, she was led through a door behind the judge's bench, still wearing the shiny white raincoat she had favored throughout the long deliberations. Within the hour she would be stripped searched, given jailhouse clothing, and spirited away to the Westchester County Jail, where she would be placed alone in a twelve-by-six-foot cell and put on a seventy-two-hour suicide watch.

While McCarty and FitzMorris sat in their seats and shook hands, Aronwald grabbed his briefcase and made his way to one of the hallway pay phones, ignoring the loud, shouted questions of the reporters, who had begun to swarm around him.

Ruggiero followed him out. "You have her mother's number?" the lawyer asked his private eye.

"Yeah, I got it."

Reaching a phone, he quickly dialed a number and waited. "Hello, I need to speak to Tom Warmus. This is Bill Aronwald."

Minutes passed as he was put on hold, impatience and anger beginning to show on his face. After a few more seconds, he slammed the receiver down and then redialed the same number.

"Hello, yes, I need to speak to Tom Warmus, Senior. This is Bill Aronwald."

Another few seconds passed. "Yes, Tom Warmus. Can you get him on the phone?" Again he waited.

Speaking out loud to no one in particular, the perturbed lawyer snarled, "They put me on hold for five minutes. Do they have any idea what this is all about?"

Finally, the father of his client came on the line.

"This is Bill Aronwald. They found her guilty on both counts at 11:30 A.M. this morning . . . the glove . . . very damaging piece of evidence . . . My sense was the prospect of an acquittal was not terribly good. . . . We thought . . . might be a hung jury . . . Transcript . . . We're going to need it now. . . . Costly. . . . No, there's no bail on a Class A felony."

Within a minute, a suddenly worn-out-looking Aronwald hung up the phone and turned around to face the reporters.

"How'd her father take it?" one reporter yelled.

"He was stunned," the lawyer answered.

"Why did Carolyn show no emotion when the verdict was read?" yelled another journalist. "She just stood there. She didn't say or do anything. It was like she was a zombie!"

Aronwald decided to tell the truth. "Carolyn has been under heavy medication for her nerves and stress. She's been under medication for the entire trial. It was something she needed to get through it."

Several reporters shared knowing looks. Many believed that Warmus had been doped up ever since she flipped out in the courtroom during the first trial. Now that her own lawyer had admitted it, they wondered how the blond-haired bombshell would fare in prison without her mood-altering drugs.

Back inside the courtroom, McCarty and FitzMorris ignored another group of reporters and accepted congratulations from the stream of assistant D.A.s who came up to shake their hands.

When the back-patting and smiles had ceased, they both remained in their seats, each appearing lost in his own thoughts. Downstairs, in the courthouse lobby, awaited a press conference and their boss, Carl Vergari.

Paul Solomon received the news in the District Attorney's office on the third floor, where he had been waiting patiently. A breathless secretary shouted the verdict to him as she whisked by, making her rounds to alert everyone to the exciting news that would spread throughout the courthouse like wildfire.

For a moment, he felt his legs start to buckle. He groped for a nearby chair and fell into it. Burying his head in his hands, he began to cry. After several long minutes, Solomon gathered himself together and stood up, brushing the wrinkles from his black suit. He was disheveled and his eyes were circled with red, but as he made his way to the courthouse lobby, he felt at peace, something he hadn't felt in a long, long time.

The television cameramen were the first to spot the haggard-looking widower as he emerged from a hallway. Their lights clicked on in unison and a stream of reporters fought their way to his side.

Friends who had kept a steady vigil throughout both trials, got to him first, hugging the man who had been vilified for what they perceived to be his one and only mistake.

As he turned toward the shouting reporters, he held up his hand to speak. "What has been lost in this trial," he said, "is that someone took Betty Jeanne's life. The right person was punished, but that does not bring Betty Jeanne back."

When he was finished, he walked alone toward the front doors of the courthouse.

Several hours later, William Aronwald sat with Vic Ruggiero and a reporter in the safe and familiar confines of his well-furnished office. He asked Ruggiero about his call to Carolyn's mother.

"I didn't get ahold of her. I reached her stepfather. He told me, 'It's going to be a tough night for her mother.'

"You know, she already spent one night in that jail. The night she was arrested. They put chains on your legs, chains on your wrists, and you have just twelve inches to move. You almost just shuffle. Carolyn said it was barbaric, chained like an animal."

At about 3 P.M., the office phone rang. Aronwald picked up the receiver and accepted the collect call. For several minutes he sat listening, saying nothing, and only occasionally rubbing his bloodshot eyes, as, between sobs and choked gasps, Carolyn poured out her heart to her lawyer, railing at her accusers and the unfairness of life.

Aronwald had tried to send her stress medication to the jail, but the authorities had reminded him that she would have to be drug-free for the next month while the Probation Department conducted their presentence interviews.

A minute later, Aronwald held out the receiver to Ruggiero. "She wants to talk to you," he said. "The reality of the situation is sinking in. She never expected this. She's stunned, shocked. It came as a complete surprise."

His own voice shaky, Ruggiero said hello to his former housemate.

Her response would remain indelibly etched in his mind, and would continue to fuel his remaining, lingering belief that maybe, just maybe, she was indeed innocent. Others who heard about her remark would chalk it up to arrogance and her delusions that she was so much more clever than everyone else.

"Oh, Vic," she said when she heard his deep and reassuring voice. "I can't believe the jury convicted me."

On June 26, 1992, at 4:45 P.M., Judge John Carey asked Carolyn Warmus if she had any statement to make before she was sentenced.

Disheveled, wearing a University of Michigan sweatshirt, blue jeans, and a pair of blue prison slippers, she stood up unsteadily. In a quavering voice and through loud sobs, she said: "I never made a phone call to Ray's gun shop and I never went to Ray's gun shop with a stolen license. I never bought a gun or ever received a gun from Vincent Parco, and I never bought a black pair of gloves from Filene's Basement.

"The most important thing of all," she cried, "I did not kill Betty Jeanne Solomon. I had absolutely nothing to do with it. I had no knowledge of it. I was not a participant."

Carey looked scornfully at the woman before him, straining to catch her words through the almost hysterical ramblings. "I can't hear you," he told the convicted killer.

Warmus tried again. "I had no knowledge of it, and I was not a participant, and I was no where near the apartment on that day. I am standing here before you, Judge Carey, devastated about being sentenced for a crime that I did not commit, and I can only ask you for leniency because I am innocent. If I am guilty of anything at all, it was simply being foolish enough to believe the lies and promises that Paul Solomon made to me and allow myself to be manipulated by him. That's all. Thank you."

With that, Warmus sat down to await her fate. And it was as bad as it could get.

Carey sentenced her to twenty-five years to life in prison for her conviction on the charge of second-degree murder. She was also ordered to serve a concurrent five to fifteen years for her criminal possession of a weapon. Under New York State law, Warmus must serve a minimum of twenty-five years before becoming eligible for parole. At that time, she will be fifty-three years old.

She was sent to the Bedford Hills Correctional Facilities in Bedford

Hills, New York, where Jean Harris had served her sentence for the killing of "Scarsdale Diet" Dr. Herman Tarnower.

At the time of this writing, no appeal has been filed with the New York Supreme Court's Appellate Division. In yet another strange twist, Tom Warmus refused to pay the $50,000 fee for the trial transcripts that would allow Aronwald to prepare an appeal. He said he would no longer be responsible for his daughter's legal bills. Carolyn Warmus then filed for indigency, which, if granted by the state's appellate court, would force the state of New York to pay for her appeal. At this time, after several hearings before Judge Carey to determine Carolyn's financial status, no decision has yet been rendered by the appellate court.

On February 5, 1993, Carolyn Warmus avoided trial on felony criminal forgery charges by accepting a plea bargain agreement with the Westchester County District Attorney's Office. In exchange for her pleading guilty to attempted criminal possession of a forged instrument, Warmus was sentenced to serve one to three years, the sentence to run concurrently with the twenty-five-years-to-life term she is serving for the murder.